ALL MY YESTERDAYS

AN AUTOBIOGRAPHY

EDWARD G. ROBINSON

WITH

LEONARD SPIGELGASS

ALL MY YESTERDAYS

AN AUTOBIOGRAPHY

HAWTHORN BOOKS, INC.

Publishers/New York

Grateful acknowledgment is made to George Sidney for his help in preparing the photographs reproduced here.

ALL MY YESTERDAYS: AN AUTOBIOGRAPHY

DESIGN BY S. S. DRATE

1   2   3   4   5   6   7   8   9   10

To Jane

ALL MY YESTERDAYS

AN AUTOBIOGRAPHY

1

If you think that what you are about to read is an autobiography of Edward G. Robinson, I'm afraid you're in for something of a disappointment. What begins here and will go on for as long as my patience and memory hold out is the life and times not of Edward G. Robinson but of Emanuel Goldenberg.

When I was a young student at the American Academy of Dramatic Arts, it was suggested to me, ever so tactfully, that Emanuel Goldenberg was not a name for an actor. Too long, too foreign, and, I suspect, though no hint was made of it, too Jewish.

I also suspect it was already assumed I was not exactly an ideal leading man. I was short, swarthy, and stocky, hardly significant competition for a theater that worshiped tall and handsome actors like John Barrymore and Lew Tellegan. The few parts I would play—and they would be few indeed, it was subliminally predicted—would not be Anglo-Saxon. The predictions were wrong. I played an Anglo-Saxon—*once*.

Back to the name. The thought of changing it was unpleasant, somehow a denial of my beginning, somehow unfaithful to my mother and father and five brothers. Disloyal. How could I tell them? And, more important, *what* would I tell them?

The obvious ploy was translation, except Emanuel Goldenhill didn't work, and Goldenmount was too pretentious. I played with all the permutations and combinations, including the French *"dormont"* and the Italian *"montedore,"* but they sounded foreign, and God knows they were contrived.*

Well, I continued to debate lists of names in the phone book, catalogs, and encyclopedias I picked up in the Astor Place Library (now converted into three playhouses in which Joe Papp is breathing new life into the theater that refuses to die), and none would satisfy me. Then one night I went to see a play, a highly urbane English drawing room comedy, and from my perch in the rear of the second balcony I heard a butler on stage announce to a lady (could it have been Mrs. Fiske?), "Madame, a gentleman to see you—a Mr. Robinson."

Mr. Robinson!

I liked the ring and strength of it. And, furthermore, it was a common change. I knew many Rosenbergs, Rabinowitzes, and Roths who'd switched to Robinson. Yes, that was it. From this time forward I would be Robinson—Emanuel Robinson.

That decision was greeted at the Academy with something less than enthusiasm. Emanuel and Robinson were an odd coupling. What other names began with *E?* Edgar? Egbert? Ellery? Ethan? Edward? Why not Edward, then King of England? Good enough for a king. Good enough for an Emanuel.

Edward Robinson. But I could not desert the Goldenberg entirely. That became the *G,* my private treaty with my past.

But that wasn't enough. Some managers didn't like the *G,* and quite arbitrarily one of them translated it to Gould. And so, if you ever look at the early programs, you will see me billed as Edward Gould Robinson, a King of England, a Wall Street tycoon, and a visitor announced by a butler to Mrs. Fiske.

Edward G. or Edward Gould, let me confess right off the bat that deep down in my deepest heart, I am, and have always been, Emanuel Goldenberg.

Still, there was a day when I came to accept it—a day when all my family referred to me as Manny but a day when I knew that the alias, now legally changed by a humdrum ceremony in a courthouse, was irrevocable.

I had made a picture called *Little Caesar,* and, for reasons I leave to social scientists who deal with matters of public taste, it was a hit.

---

* To give you an idea of how important nonforeign names were: When Stella Adler starred for Paramount, they put an *r* in her name, making her Stella Ardler. In my day it was inconceivable for an actor to be named George Segal, Barbra Streisand, or Steve McQueen. I think today Tony Curtis might still be Bernie Schwartz, and Cary Grant, Archie Leach.

Jack Warner, Hal Wallis, and *Variety* told me it was a hit, and I had some small intimations of it in fan mail and rather deep bows from headwaiters at Victor Hugo's Restaurant in downtown Los Angeles. But I was not actually aware that it was a watershed in my life.

Immediately following, Warner's pushed me into the part of Nick Venizelos (in *Smart Money*), a barber with two weaknesses: gambling and blonds. (For the record, I am the most penny ante of gamblers and I prefer brunettes.)

I had never seen the film, not even the "rushes." For those of you who are not involved with the manufacture of movies, rushes are "dailies," and whichever word you use, they are the bits and pieces of scenes on celluloid that were shot the previous day. They are, by nature, repetitive, since they include all angles of a scene. There is a long view of the set with all the actors, and we say the words. There's a more limited view of, say, two of us, and we say the words. There's a closeup of each of us, and we say the words. And there are as few as one, or, in some cases, as many as twenty angles of each of the shots. To look at these as a member of the cast is to see yourself in so many guises, so bad once, so good once, so boring most of the time, that in the end you leave this chore to the director, producer, and cutter. Rushes and dailies can drive you crazy.

In the first one or two films I made I looked and cringed and sweated and suffered. But sweating in *Little Caesar* was so intense that I decided never to see the rushes again. I refused to dwell on one small aspect of the character, shot usually out of sequence; I preferred to see the character emerge as a whole man—even though the man on the screen and the man watching him, presumably identical, were worlds apart.

In any case, I had never seen *Smart Money*. It was playing at the Winter Garden, a legitimate house taken over by Warner Brothers, and while that theater had known major successes, never had there been anything like the lines of waiting patrons that stretched up and down Broadway. Mounted police were called out to control them.

Warner's insisted I come in from the Coast to attend the premiere. My plan was to present myself at the Winter Garden, buy a ticket, and have a look. But from my arrival at Grand Central Station I knew that something incredible and cataclysmic had happened to my life. After forty plays and a couple of movies I had always been able to walk into an A&P or Macy's or stroll the art galleries on Fifty-seventh Street with no one bothering me, no one looking at me, no one having the faintest notion who I was. But today was different. I was surrounded by autograph hunters, redcaps, crowds, people shoving me, pushing me, stealing my handkerchief, and tearing off my shirt buttons. I'd never known anything like it; I was frightened, and, deep inside, a little excited.

Warner's had a sleek black limousine waiting and security guards and publicity people to guide me to it. I was ensconced in the largest suite in the largest hotel and fawned on by bellboys, maids, and valets. I felt as if I were in a lunatic asylum.

The lunacy continued. In order to get into the Winter Garden, I hid on the floor of the car. I was escorted in the back way, saw somebody up there on the screen who bore an occasional resemblance to me (the voice was totally unfamiliar), and then the publicity people sneaked me out again. During these episodes I was able to get a glimpse of the sign above the Winter Garden, even though the best I could make of it was an enormous *E* and an enormous *D*.

And so, later that night, in dark glasses, my overcoat collar turned up to hide my face, a fedora deep on my head, I got into a cab and, hunched down, went to see what that sign really said.

It said "EDWARD G. ROBINSON" in letters twelve feet tall stretching the entire block from Fiftieth to Fifty-first Street. I didn't know whether to laugh or cry, and when I can't make that decision, it's always made for me. I cried.

And I said to myself: "Face it, Manny. You're a movie star!"

What is it like to be a movie star?

Or, now, in my case, what *was* it like to be a movie star?

If you like adulation, deference, the best tables, autograph hunters, and lots of money, it is absolutely wonderful. If you like it so much that tomorrow you feel it will be taken from you, it is terrifying.

Impermanent it is, and shaky; and if you become obsessed with retaining it, you acquire some of the basest qualities in man. Greed, for one. Greed for better parts, larger billing, more publicity. And greed for money, too, not only for its own sake but because your status depends on your being right up there with the others—better still, to *exceed* the others. If you're not, you are plagued with jealousy and envy, self-destructive vices that eat you up. And you develop extravagance, joined with miserliness.

Surround yourself with agents, lawyers, accountants, tax experts, form corporations, buy tax shelters, drive yourself into furies to keep the money, and, at the same time, buy a bigger house or give a more sumptuous party.

Hate being plagued by your adoring public—and terrified when you pass through a Chicago hotel lobby and nobody asks you for an autograph. Smile smugly when told by the fan mail department that you're getting more letters than Cagney or Bogart. Be terrified when you get two letters threatening your life because you're a "dirty, filthy, Communist, Jew gangster." (Certainly a self-contradictory accusation.)

Read yards of print about your private life discussing divorce before you even thought of it yourself, romantic entanglements with ladies you've never even met; accusations that you're a flaming radical when you've lent your name to help the victims of the Spanish Civil War; reviews of your work by critics who've sharpened their pencils into daggers the night before they've seen that work.

Need an inlay in a tooth? Be prepared for the receptionist to a) fawn over you; b) insult you to prove she couldn't care less about your celebrity.

Be prepared, too, for a dentist bill three times higher than anybody else's—and that goes for butchers, grocers, and chiropodists, too.

Have a barber come to your house—an insane extravagance, because if you appear in a barbershop, you cause a small riot.

Do I make it all sound awful? Well, a lot of it is. Most of it is lovely and ego-caressing. Pity it is so short-lived.

Still, it happens to only a few immigrants from Rumania.

2

Rumania is a lovely country, and after many years of refusing to return to it, I did a few years ago. And I was right. It *was* a lovely country. Paris of the East, Bucharest is called, and while I think that an exaggeration, it still has grace and style—but it is Communist now, and that makes you a little wary.

Not much change from almost eighty years ago when my parents were very wary indeed. They were involved in a series of repressive measures that were epidemic in Eastern Europe. At the time I was unaware of these, except peripherally, but through the years I've dug into them, and a bit of history will do no harm; it might perhaps illuminate the chronic plight of a minority.

Despite the treaty that ended the Russo-Turkish War, which stipulated that the Jews of Rumania should receive full citizenship, the government began a systematic persecution of the Jews. Various laws were passed until the pursuit of all vocations followed by the Jews was made dependent on the possession of political rights, which only Rumanians might exercise. Even against the Jewish workingmen laws were enacted that forced more than 40 percent of them into idleness.

Similar laws were passed in regard to the liberal professions, affecting Jewish lawyers, physicians, pharmacists, veterinarians, etc. The most malicious law was one enacted in 1893 (the year in which I was born) which deprived Jewish children of the right to be educated in the public schools. (Though our family had lived in Rumania for two hundred years, *we* were considered foreigners.) This law provided that the children of foreigners might be received only after those of citizens had been accepted, and that they should, moreover, pay exorbitant tuition fees. In 1898 another law was passed excluding the Jews from the secondary schools and the universities.

We lived at 671 Strada Cantemier in Bucharest—one of a series of attached buildings surrounding a court, where the outhouses were, where we washed and dried our clothes, and the children played. There were nine of us—mama, papa, my five brothers, my maternal grandmother, and myself. It was a warm time, I well remember, and I do not think we were disadvantaged; we had plenty to eat, and mama was a beautiful cook. Grandma was even better, and I must admit there were occasional tensions between mama and grandma.

As for grandma, I am not certain I can reevoke her, but it seems important to me that I do because, in a very real sense, she shaped me. By inductive reasoning, I've determined that she was born in Rumania in the late 1830s and that her parents and grandparents before her had been native Rumanians as well. Thus, it was all the more desecrating that she should have been officially known as "foreigner."

At the age of twenty-eight she was widowed and the mother of ten children. It was an article of faith that a widow would remarry, but she refused, fearing that a new husband might exploit the children. (Children, in a sense, were an economic asset; they could be sent out to work in the fields or the light industries; they could, in a Yiddish phrase almost impossible to translate, "bring in.")

But the various plagues that swept Mittel Europa finally brought her tragedy. Most of her children died; in her fifties, she came at last to live with her daughter, my mother.

Nothing very extraordinary about her? Oh, yes, something very extraordinary. She could read and write.

My mother couldn't. Few of my grandmother's contemporaries could. But by a process unknown to me, she had learned, and decades later, when the nonreading women would go to religious services, they would gather about her to have her read to them.

I remember her as a slight figure, her head draped always in a kerchief, reading or telling stories—grandmother stories, they were called—stories out of the Bible. And while she was religious and God-fearing, she had a certain tone in her voice as she recounted the biblical fables, as if to say: "They're not literally true. Take them with a little smile. Put on them a little salt."

When, together with the rest of us, she was uprooted and taken to America, she took that experience, too, with a little salt, a little humor, a kind of resignation. On the Lower East Side and in the Bronx she would spend her days looking out of the window, never ceasing to assess and analyze and think about a strange world passing in front of her eyes. Subsequently, when I went into the theater, she would read the Yiddish papers, concentrating almost entirely on the theatrical page.

When I was on the road, in later years, I would write to her, and she would read and reread my letters and keep them under her pillow.

Outside of my bar mitzvah speech, she never saw me perform, never even entered a theater as far as I can recall. But she knew who was in what play and what the critics said.

And forever she cooked.

Bucharest was famous for its gourmet food because it combined the culinary arts of both East and West—and mama and grandma, while they kept a kosher house, were influenced by the ingredients and recipes of their neighbors. But to each dish they added their own special touch. I learned then that cooking is among the more skilled of the arts, and certainly one of the most creative.

We had, among other delicacies, my favorite: Greek eggplant chopped with onion and olive oil accompanied by black radish sweated with salt. With it we had *mamaligah*, a corn flour that served a variety of purposes. It was a cereal, and peasants actually used it as bread, much as the Mexicans use tortillas. We had *pitcha*, which is calf's-foot jelly, and fish baked with tomatoes, curiously Oriental with a subtle taste I've never been able to savor since.

The wonder of it was that mama, pushing grandma out of the kitchen, made all these splendid things herself. For instance, *vishnik*, a kind of cherry brandy, was prepared at home—as indeed was all the Friday bread. I recall no bread to match it. Nor comparable coffee. When I listen to all the coffee ads on television today (and I've even perpetrated one), I'm very tempted to suggest that the secret of a good cup of coffee is that it be freshly ground. My mother took the freshly roasted beans (she might even have roasted them herself, though I do not remember) and placed them in a hand grinder. The resulting grains were rich and full-bodied, and the flavor was distilled sunlight. (I have, among the few of her possessions still around, the very coffee grinder she used in Bucharest. It is a wondrous object.)

I think my mother's coffee and cooking made me anti-restaurant. To this day I much prefer to eat at home. Mama never used to tell us what we were going to have in advance, and so each course was a new wonder. In a restaurant you have to order, and so the zest is gone. Part of the joy of eating is surprise.

Besides being a cook, mama was a no-nonsense housekeeper. You may remember a play called *Craig's Wife* in which Mrs. Craig made a fetish of neatness and cleanliness and drove everybody crazy. Well, mama made a fetish of neatness and cleanliness, but drove nobody crazy—because she never imposed; she merely suggested. And she always smiled, though, I suppose, there were times when there was little enough to smile at.

But troubles or not, we always had immaculate linen and floors you could eat off. We boys tried to help her with the housework—but it never was good enough for her. When we were certain there was no longer any dust, she could still find dust.

Remember, too, that we were living in a city. If you have had too long a diet of Sholom Aleichem and *Fiddler on the Roof*, you think of most Jews as living in *shtetls*, rural villages. Untrue. We lived an urban life in an urban environment, and I am still city oriented.

The city of Bucharest, on the few occasions when I dared venture from the Jewish compound (though it was not, in the strict sense, a ghetto), was lovely and filled with sophisticated amenities. It seemed to me that every other day there was a parade, with the soldiers in glittering uniforms and military bands and all the pomp of the horse guards. There were verdant *Bois*-like parks and Greco-Roman museums (though their treasures tended to be severely conventional) and expansive garden cafés.

My father, who insisted on sharing the life of the city about him, took me on many occasions to one of those cafés, and we would have little cakes and coffee, though the coffee could not, of course, compare with my mother's. And I can't swear the cakes were kosher, but my father never asked. Anyway, how unkosher could they be? Papa was observant, but pragmatic.

Once, even, we went to see a movie. Yes, a movie. It was silent and it lasted all of five minutes. The wooden benches where we were allowed to sit were hard and inhospitable, and what erupted before us was a terrifying scene of a train under attack by cowboys and Indians. It was the first movie I ever saw in my life, and neither papa nor I considered it very impressive. We decided we didn't like the movies and that they were a passing fad. I never did get to like the movies for a very long time.

Another time we went to a café and saw a play—a Rumanian miniversion of Jules Verne's *Around the World in Eighty Days*. I loved that, and I thought the actors were making up the words. It was many years before I learned that wasn't true.

Of course during this period I was going to school, unaware that it was a parochial institution, combining dogma with arithmetic, theology with geography, God with history, a *cheder* (the two-year study

of the Torah), with a four-year curriculum, the first two years devoted to the study of Hebrew, the latter years embracing lay subjects,
including, at the age of eight, the study of German. And, at the end of
four years, what?

My brother Zach, the oldest of us, provided the answer to that.
Four years and then apprenticeship to a trade—upholstery, in his
case. That did not mean stuffing tacks in your mouth and applying
fabric to settees; at the outset, it meant doing the most menial of
chores—cleaning toilets, sweeping floors, being beaten for real or
fancied infractions of duty. I have no doubt that London and Bucharest were widely different, yet there are passages in Dickens that
graphically describe the fate of an apprentice in Bucharest. While he
may be out of fashion now, I always thought Dickens wrote with a
universal pen.

Certainly, because of the restrictive laws, Jewish youth was denied
a position in the professions, and that was not easy for Zach to accept.
But, accept it he did; for each penny he earned, he saved. He was
dreaming what must have appeared then as hopeless fantasies of
America. We—all of us—were, through letters, rumors, and covert
conversations with friends whose relatives had already migrated,
aware that far across the land mass of Europe and the great Atlantic
Ocean, there was a nation based on freedom, opportunity, and tolerance for all people.

I have deliberately used the most cliché of expressions, for, in
theory, that was what far-off, inaccessible America meant to us. It
sounded like Paradise—but Paradise Lost, because reaching it involved scrimping, saving, and incredible sacrifice. One had to have a
schiffscarte, a ship's card, which meant that you had to obtain money
for passage. It was not money easy to come by. (The Zionist movement was weakly flourishing under the urging of Theodor Herzl and
Nordau, and their organizations were able to provide a pittance for
those who wished to walk their way to Palestine. We did not so wish.)

Still, we would somehow accumulate money for America. My father, a builder and tinsmith, worked relentlessly from dawn to dusk to
give hope to his six sons. He called us by the numbers.

Zach, Number One son, continued his career (*sic*) as an upholsterer. Jack, Number Two son, was apprenticed to a metal-worker.
After the usual toilet swabbing and floor scrubbing, he discovered an
innate talent for taking raw copper and molding it into candlesticks
and tableware. He had a sure hand and an excellent eye, and today
it might have been considered artistic talent. In those days it was
drudgery.

Oscar, Number Three son, toilet swabbing and floor scrubbing behind him, was apprenticed to a cabinet-maker, and he, too, exhibited carving skills that brought in a few more pennies.

Willie, Number Four son, and my younger brother Max, Number Six son and I, Number Five son, contributed nothing, for we were all too young to work, though in other families in Rumania there was no such thing as being too young. Child labor was common, especially on the farms and in the factories. But it was not acceptable to my mother and father who put school above all things.

Without really understanding what their hopes and aspirations were, I knew they existed. I knew because there was our secret *knippel*. A *knippel* is literally a knot and means that you save money in a handkerchief, tightly knotted and zealously guarded. My father, Zach, Jack, and Oscar were adding to it penny by penny, and my mother was its custodian. To my eternal shame, when I was barely five, I brought their plans to nothing.

It was Friday night, the loveliest time for the family, and my mother had laid the table with the first course, that fish with tomatoes, I think, and, to preserve its freshness, she had covered each portion with paper, against the time we would sit at supper. At sunset, of course, as it was laid down for centuries, as the lady of the house, she had *bensched licht*, that is, thanked the Lord, our God, King of the Universe, Who has sanctified us with Thy Commandments, and has instructed us to light the Sabbath Lights. Amen.

Then she lit the Sabbath candles and went into the kitchen to see to the soup, confident that all was well. It was *not* well. It was not well because I found myself alone in the dining room, fascinated by the flickering candles. For reasons known only to a five-year-old, I wondered what would happen if I took a piece of paper that covered the fish and held it to the candles.

I soon found out. The paper burst into flame. It seared me, and I dropped it. The table immediately began to burn, the fire reached the curtains, and there it was: ruin and tragedy. Nobody was hurt, but the need to refurnish took all the money that was in the *knippel*, and the American dream was postponed, it seemed, forever.

But did that stop the Goldenbergs? No. It merely delayed them.

The working and the saving and scrimping started again, and one golden day there were enough pennies for *one* ship's card. *One*. Who should go—or should we wait until there was enough money for all of us, father, mother, six boys, and grandma? I'm instinctively sure that it was grandma's pragmatic voice that suggested that the father must remain but that Number One son, Zach, should go to prepare the way and somehow secure an economic base for the rest of us.

Thus, one dread day, with feelings of fear and faint hope, Zach left Bucharest, and the family endured its first fragmentation. How we suffered and worried as we heard of his wanderings, first to Berlin, then to Paris, on to London, until finally we had his first letter from New York. It was wonderful, marvelous, beyond any of our dreams, and he had found work! Imagine it, work right away—work that paid, work as an upholsterer.

What had we dreamed? Could we have been so naive that we really believed Zach would get off the boat and in a matter of months be a doctor with a frock coat and a silk hat? I believe that's what *I* thought.

But upholstery couldn't have been so bad in America, for Zach sent money, and together with our own *knippel* now, not bulging but barely ample, there was money for two *schiffscarten*. Again, the dilemma. And again the pragmatic answer. The next two brothers, Jack and Oscar, would go.

There was a question about Jack. Not long before, in what had been a rough-and-tumble fight with an anti-Semitic mob, he had been hit on the forehead by a sharp stone, and because there were no X rays then or other diagnostic procedures, the wound was sewed up and the possibility of fracture or brain damage was not even hinted at. That there was more than laceration was indicated by periods of blackout and forgetfulness, and eventually, in America, institutionalization, but that was not considered at this point. So Jack and Oscar went off.

Papa, mama, grandma, Willie, Max, and I remained. Can you conceive the torment of the good-byes? Or the waiting for the new letters—the announcement that Jack was already a lawyer, that Oscar was a dentist? The letters came, and they contained no surprises: Jack was a metal-worker; Oscar was a cabinet-maker. But those three Goldenberg young men were full of praise for America.

When more letters arrived, we read and treasured every word. How wonderful and marvelous America was. Oh, they never said the streets were paved with gold, which was the conventional knowledge of the immigrant, but they told of miracles. Small miracles to an American; incredible miracles to us. No anti-Semitism. No restrictive school laws. The air was free and the streets were free. That the streets were grimy and crowded and beastly cold in winter and Equator hot in summer, they did not tell us. They did not lie. They simply did not tell us.

And the letters certainly contained ample evidence that if our brothers were not prospering beyond dreams of avarice, they were certainly making a living—enough of a living to send money for one more ship's card.

The obvious choice this time was my father—a wrenching, heart-searing choice but inevitable. He did not want to go. Bucharest was his home; to tear himself away to go to a new land was almost unbearable for him. But he realized there was no future for his sons in Rumania. And so for us, he did it.

Calmly and without betraying his deep fears he announced that *he* would go to verify the stories of his first three sons. If they checked out, he would prepare the way for his wife, his elderly mother-in-law, and his three very young sons. In the meantime they would be left alone in Bucharest without the protection of a strong father or three strong brothers.

How can you assess such a decision, except perhaps to equate it with the American pioneers moving west? I have read no real accounts of these emotional breakups of families. Perhaps it's just not possible to sort out the elements of courage, terror, dedication, and heartbreak that were the elements of these traumas.

I have lived through these shattering moments, and I have no way to convey them to you. Or, indeed, to convey the inestimable glory of that day, a few years later, when five *schiffscarten* arrived. *Five!* All of us would go now—mama and grandma, Willie, Max, and me.

It was God's will, at last, and we set out for America, *goldeneh* America, a blessing on Columbus!

The five terrified travelers were not without some help. The Hebrew Immigration Aid Society, an organization established by immigrants already settled in America and financed to some extent by the Rothschild family and the Baron de Hirsch Foundation, had developed a more legitimate version of the Underground Railroad. We were sent from Bucharest to Budapest by wagon and train, then to Vienna, then to Paris—where I ached to see some of its glories and saw none of them—and then tortuously to Le Havre, where we boarded *La Touraine*, a ship of the Compagnie Générale Transatlantique.

Try to picture us. In our arms and hands were bundles and bales of everything we owned and loved in the world: pots, pans, clothes, knives, forks, an occasional bit of silver, sheets, pillows, feather beds, candlesticks, rolling pins, and, certainly, mama's coffee grinder.

When you read the inscription on Bartholdi's Statue of Liberty and its reference to "huddled masses," think not of us. We were certainly huddled in steerage—a thousand of us or more—but we were not masses. We were people, individuals, forced to share this monstrous hold, but our reactions were not group; they were individual.

What was common to all of us—Poles, Italians, Lithuanians, Bulgarians, French, and even Scotch and Irish—was simply a capacity to endure . . . endure the stink and the vomitous food (eked out by provisions my mother had brought along), the lack of privacy, the foul and dank air. Where we differed was in our capacity to withstand the rolling and pitching of *La Touraine*. Grandma managed it well. So did Willie and Max. Mama tried her best. I did not even try. I had never been so sick in my life.

So sick I longed to die. The trip took twenty-three horrendous days. I do not even remember arriving at Castle Garden, and what surely must have been a dramatic and joyous reunion with papa, Zach, Jack, and Oscar. I recall not an instant. Willie reminds me that we arrived on Lincoln's birthday and were unable to leave Castle Garden until the holiday was over. We slept on the floor, and America seemed inhospitable.

I was nine years old. I was in the United States, North America, all of which translated into a walk-up flat on Broome Street, cramped and ugly, though once my mother had gotten her hands on it, it became scrupulously clean. When I was able to see the streets, I discovered tenements and pushcarts and filth and no open court as there had been in Bucharest and, God knows, no trees. Could this be the wonderful, glorious America of which I'd been told? Bucharest seemed fresh and airy by comparison, and I experienced a fleeting moment in which I wished a *klug* ("curse") on Columbus.

The year was 1902. McKinley had been assassinated, and Teddy Roosevelt was President. People, other than those who lived in the slums, were going to see *Floradora*, and in the saloons there were infinite choruses of "Bill Bailey, Won't You Please Come Home?" Others were reading Owen Wister's *The Virginian*, and in the theater Clyde Fitch had a big hit, *The Girl with the Green Eyes*.

To me it meant nothing. I could speak no English. Only the repulsive Lower East Side was real—and, if you want to know how it looked to me, I commend you to a painting of Robert Henri's *New York Street in Winter* in which evening falls over a snow-covered street lined by tenements. The mood is that of sadness and nostalgia. And, when years later I saw the Henri painting, it seemed to me he had caught all my sadness, loneliness, and fear.*

* My hackles still rise, too, when I look at the 1905 Steichen photograph of the Flatiron Building—and Childe Hassam's painting of Union Square, New York (1890).

I am tempted, for a moment, to speak of the painter as the man who captures a moment that is all moments; who sets down a city block that is all cities; who re-creates the face of a woman who is all women.

I think there is no Paris like Pissarro's Paris, no water lilies as bursting with life as Monet's, no sadness comparable to Picasso's blue clowns, no birds as heavy with flight as Braque's, no marble to rival the agony of the *Pietà*. But, no talk of art now. The art then was to live.

When I talk now in the garden these autumn afternoons to my granddaughter, Francesca, and tell her of that long-ago time on Broome Street, I feel an empathy in her. She speaks of the blacks in Watts and the dispossessed Indian tribes and the Chicanos because, besides being quite beautiful (a grandfather's assessment), she is intelligent, with a very real feeling for what she calls the underprivileged and I call the poor.

I dispute the word "underprivileged" with her—and I cite from the Pantheon the names of those who came with nothing and died with celebrity and eminence in science, music, art, mathematics, and the humanities. I have suggested that she read Zangwill's *Melting Pot* and Jacob Riis' *Making of an American*, two works of which she has never heard.

Actually, she disputes the whole melting pot theory, pointing out, with some justice, I must admit, that assimilation, the effort to turn all aliens into one standard American image, has been a dismal failure. People tend to be what their fathers and grandfathers were; their palates insist on the same spices and herbs (or lack of them); they persist in remembering their ancestral language, if only through an occasional untranslatable phrase. And she adds that this *dis*similarity is the strength of the nation.

It did not seem to be so in 1902. It did not seem so even though Manhattan, merged only five years before with Brooklyn, the Bronx, Queens, and Staten Island to become the unwieldy and, I think, even then, ungovernable, City of New York, was a jigsaw of ethnic neighborhoods. There was the Jewish section, of course, on the Lower East Side, home to me, and close-by compounds of Italians, Syrians, Greeks, Poles, and Irish. Further to the south there was Chinatown, to which I never dared go, and in the north there was Harlem, which was not yet Negro.

There had been neither Negro nor Chinese in Bucharest. In New York I saw them for the first time. I even went to school with them.

I matriculated—though that seems far too grand a word for it—at P.S. 137 on Grand Street between Eldredge and Ludlow. I think it was my brother Zach who took me, but the prospect was so frightening that I cannot actually recall the process by which I entered the school basement and finally the principal's office.

I was left alone with her, and, if I cannot remember her name, I recall vividly that I thought she looked like George Washington. She was prim and businesslike, dressed in a starched white blouse and a navy blue skirt that scarcely revealed her high button shoes. She realized I spoke no more than a few English words, but she pantomimed that she would like me to answer some questions on a test paper.

I had an infinite sense of relief. The questions were in arithmetic and were concerned mainly with fractions, a branch of mathematics in which I was singularly adept. (But the skill has left me; today the process of balancing a checkbook strikes terror in my heart.) In any case, I solved the problems. Mrs. Washington (as forever I think of her) peered at my replies and after a moment smiled. Then she took me to my home room and introduced me to Miss Clark, my teacher, who was a younger version of the principal, wearing almost the identical waist and skirt.

It was recess time, and Miss Clark pointed to her watch, which she wore pinned to her bosom. Then she went to the blackboard and drew a huge clock, indicating I was to return at one o'clock.

I didn't want to go. I wanted to recite the alphabet for her, because by then I knew it and the numbers in English, but I had no opportunity to show off my erudition.

Realize I speak Rumanian, Yiddish, German, and read Hebrew—but English was strange and different until, through the ensuing months and years, I found that both English and Rumanian had words with the same Latin roots. (Yes, Rumanian is based on Latin and is not Slavic, as everybody seems to think. And since we're on the matter, Rumania is named Rumania because it was one of the first of the Roman provinces.)

Just as I was one of the first of the immigrant children not to be segregated into a class for the foreign born. Whether because of Mrs. Washington's delight with my fractions or because the other classes were filled, I was assigned to a classroom with American born students. Even from the beginning I was not treated as a greenhorn.

It was a great piece of luck, though at the time I do not think I so regarded it.

Can that random decision be the reason I speak without accent? Do you realize how difficult it is for a Rumanian—or a Japanese, for that matter—to say the word "the"? *Th* as in "they" or in "thing" are the two letters that are the Mount Everest to those who would speak

English. And there are others. *Ough*, for instance, as in "enough" or "though"; *i* as in "fine" or "hit"; *o* as in "bore" or "role."

Let us say *o* as in "role." I imitated my classmates, and I suppose that was the first role I ever played.

3

By 1904, halfway through the first four-year course at P.S. 137, I was no longer terrified by English.* I could speak, and I could write, but mostly I could read, and I devoured the newspapers.

There were perhaps eight or nine or ten of them in those days in New York, unlike today, when there are only three. Among all of them my favorite was the New York *Evening Journal*, published by one of my first American heroes—you're not going to believe this— William Randolph Hearst. His paper, I suppose, was sensational. Could even, in retrospect, be accused of yellow journalism, but to me he said all the things that were important to say about America and the world. He attacked the "trusts" and the "interests," and generally made himself a nuisance to anyone in power. To a young immigrant a journalist who had the courage to speak frankly and fearlessly about the rulers of a nation seemed courageous beyond belief.

His chief columnist was a man named Arthur Brisbane who wrote, under the heading "TODAY" on the front page, praise for democracy and freedom and denounced graft and corruption.

I was, you may be sure, a Hearst–Brisbane nut. In the years that followed, Hearst, of course, went into the movie business, chiefly to star Marion Davies, and the two of them hosted brilliant and unbelievable weekend parties at the castle he built at San Simeon, California. Every shining moving picture star was a guest—the Shearers, Crawfords, Gables, Menjous, Astaires, Dunnes, Grants, the full

* In those days public education consisted of two four-year required courses. Thus, I attended P.S. 137 for the first sequence and P.S. 20 for the second.

panoply—and they would dine in medieval splendor among the glorious and inglorious treasures Hearst bought by the carload. Carload? Shipload!

I cannot describe them to you. I was never invited to San Simeon. In all my life I never met William Randolph Hearst. There may be many reasons for that, though I've never been told them, but I like to think the chief one was that Hearst was at M.G.M. and I was at Warner Brothers and each studio was a tight social cocoon.

At eleven, of course, it never occurred to me that I would ever be in a position where I was likely to meet him—much less in a position where he would choose not to invite me.

But Hearst's *Journal* was not my only reading. I discovered *The Saturday Evening Post* and Jack London's tale of the sea, *The Sea Wolf*. I had no idea at the time that the domineering Captain Wolf Larsen was to be characterized by critics as a Nietzsche superman; I just considered him to be a wonderful character. And that's how I played him, decades later, with John Garfield (who had changed *his* name from Julie Garfinkel) playing George Leach.

Certainly, then, barely twelve, it never entered my mind that I would be a player, but I read the drama page and saw the great names—Henry Dixey, Mrs. Leslie Carter, Ethel Barrymore—stars of the first magnitude.

Some day I would see them. Some day I would even play with them. But never *with* Nazimova, never *with* George M. Cohan, though eventually I did work *for* him. Nor for Oscar Hammerstein, who opened his Manhattan Opera Company in competition with the Metropolitan. I mention this only because my resemblance to Oscar Hammerstein got me a part in my first and only silent movie.

When it came to the opera the price was, of course, far too high for the Goldenbergs. The music to which we listened (we had no gramophone) was the popular junk of the period, and I recall vividly that one of the most widely sung pieces of 1906 was *Everybody Works But Father*.

That you couldn't say about the Goldenbergs. Even before we'd arrived in America, papa had gotten a job with the New York Eveready Battery Company, and he didn't like it very much. A new facet of his nature, long submerged, was beginning to surface. Here and there, from pushcarts and junkmen (does anybody remember how they would patrol the streets of the city in their wagons, pulled by sorry nags, shouting, "I CASH CLOTHES"?) he would buy an occasional piece of porcelain, a figurine, a picture frame, a commemorative ashtray, a jardiniere, a pewter mug. He had an inborn sense of proportion, design, and craftsmanship. Call it taste. I have

never been able to define "taste"; perhaps there really is no definition.
(Take a look at photographs of San Simeon if you ever have the
chance.)

In any case, it was not long before he had a little store. Those fancy
biographies the movie companies would prepare of me later would
say that it was an antique shop. It wasn't. Jumble shop, perhaps—
with an occasional treasure gleaming through the merchandise. Believe me, he knew which were treasure and which were dross. (And
he taught me.)

Perhaps his major motivation in putting the business together was
that he wanted to be his own boss. That was a very popular motivation among all us Goldenbergs. Zach eventually set up his own upholstery business. Jack studied hard, took Regents Examinations (rather
like college entrance boards) and became a manufacturer's representative, on commission. He, too, was his own boss and remained so
until one day when the stone that hit him in Bucharest took its final
toll and, in Toledo, Ohio, he lost all rationality. He was, it breaks my
heart even now to report, "sent away."

Still, Life Had To Go On—one of those dreadfully banal sentences
that is all the more despised because it happens to be a pretty good
summing up of truth. Oscar unflinchingly went his own way. Even
though he had been an excellent wood-carver in Bucharest, he was
plagued with the family disease to be his own boss, and he got a job
with the Zesse Wilkinson Company as a photo engraver and etcher.
The company did lithography and color reproductions for magazines,
and one summer Oscar got me a job as an errand boy. There I
saw reproductions of the work of Remington and Metcalf, and Oscar
even brought some of the not quite perfect ones home. They were my
first pictures, and to this day I cannot tell you whether I adored them
because they were wild West or because they were beautifully painted.
(Whether one likes a work of art for its subject matter or its execution is certainly one's own decision. It's wonderful when you
like them for both reasons.) Anyway, Oscar went to Cooper Union
and soon had his own business.

Willie, a little bored with school, got a job with a luggage company
and finally opened his own shop on Sixth Avenue.

Of all of us my youngest brother Max brought, I think, the most joy
to my parents' hearts. He became a dentist.

I think I gave them more than a few moments of pain.

I became an actor.

I hope you don't mind if I demythologize the process. No understudy I, who went on in place of the star. No lounger, surely, in

Schwab's Drug Store, discovered by a talent scout. No burst of talent that suddenly appeared from on high.

No, I went to school. I learned acting as Max learned to be a dentist. I learned by studying it and doing it. But why did I do it? Ah, that's the heart of the matter. And let me answer it in a way that may seem at best irrelevant, at worst silly.

Where I live in California, almost every garden has a swimming pool. Not mine. There are those who think it snobbery—*not* having a pool is an inverse status symbol. Not true in my case. I give you my case: I cannot swim!

Nor play golf, or tennis, or polo, or row, or high jump, or chin, or run the hundred-yard dash. I am, in short, the most unathletic of men—and, while I'm an avid fan of the Dodgers and the Rams and spend hours looking at almost any kind of game on television, I can play none of them.

And not to play games at P.S. 20 (the school to which I went after P.S. 137) was like having two heads. P.S. 20 was on Rivington Street between Eldredge and Forsythe, with hardly an open space for athletics. But whatever open space existed was in continual use because all the kids were determined to win the Oscar, the Emmy, the Tony, the Nobel Prize of the New York Elementary School District—the Public School Athletic League silver or bronze medal. It was not long before I realized that it was forever out of my grasp. Coming in last became monotonous.

I recall no instant decision to turn to other more reachable goals, but I was beginning to be able to concentrate. Thus I was skipped, did 4A and 4B together, 5A and 5B together, 6A and 6B together, and was finally graduated at thirteen and a half, an age below the average at that time.

But being a good student wasn't enough; I longed for recognition —call it deference, distinction. I'm sure then I hadn't the faintest idea I was seeking my potential, but in retrospect that's what it was all about. How do you get to be recognized for yourself? How do you not be part of the mass? How do you win an equivalent of the P.S.A.L. medal?

Well, weekly there was a gathering of all the classes of P.S. 20, and by an architectural miracle, the partitions that separated the classroom units were rolled back, and we were all one huge class. Week after week I would watch as one or another of the students would get up and read a composition, with rhetorical flourish, to applause and high commendation.

Dared I?

I dared.

Summing up all my courage, I wrote and read a paper on "Keeping Our Streets Clean," thus, in one fell stroke, making my debut as an elocutionist and simultaneously predicting the current passion for ecology.

Heady with this success, I also made my debut at the University Settlement House, and with the aid of a book of recitations I bought for a nickel at a bookstore on the Bowery, I was soon thundering publicly such gems as Spartacus' speech to the gladiators, *Gunga Din*, *Tommy Atkins, The Betrothed*, and such deathless lines as "A woman is only a woman but a good cigar is a smoke!"

I even engaged in debate, taking either side of the question: Is the pen mightier than the sword? I must say I did better when I defended the pen.

To be sure, I won no P.S.A.L. medal, but I did capture other prizes—paltry little ones, but to me the equivalent of the Congressional Medal. And, of course, I gained instant entree to the literary and dramatic clubs, both at P.S. 20 and the Settlement House.

You would think that all this would be enough for a twelve-year-old, but it wasn't. Like all other Jewish boys at that age, I was preparing for my bar mitzvah, going to a New York *cheder*, or Hebrew school, in the women's section of our new American temple. The rabbi who taught me was a wizened refugee from Rumania, thin and dyspeptic, who had a gas burner on the floor next to him where he cooked his meals. He was a hard taskmaster and rough with all of us if our lessons were less than perfect, but his eyes shone with belief in the Lord and the Talmud, and he was one of those rare beings, an inspiration.

Then, one day I discovered that the inspiration had left, had resigned for reasons never explained to me. His replacement had neither his zeal nor his capacity to teach, and I was heartsick. I longed for him to return, and when he did not, I chose to do something about it.

I found out he was now living in Williamsburg, and I walked across that bridge, one bristling cold November day, and searched the maze of streets in that section of Brooklyn until I came upon his address. He was now the proprietor of a grocery store—oh, how meager a grocery store.

He presided over sparse shelves of Hecker's flour, Cream of Wheat, Runkel's cocoa, Quaker Oats, Pechter's bread, Sheffield milk, Domino sugar, Bon Ami, Dutch Cleanser, Fairy soap, Fletcher's Castoria (which all the children did *not* cry for), and almost empty barrels of pickles and herring. His chief preoccupation seemed to be swatting the cockroaches that were everywhere.

He was glad to see me and listened gravely as I pleaded with him to return or, at least, to teach me himself. I was prepared to undertake the walk across the Williamsburg Bridge daily. But he would have no part of it. He was now in the retail business, and teaching was behind him. But I think he was infinitely touched by my devotion to him, and he encouraged me. Perhaps it was the bar mitzvah speech I was to make in less than a month that bothered me the most.

"Have faith in the Lord, *mensheleh*," he said to me in Yiddish, "and faith in yourself, and God will show you the way. As for the bar mitzvah speech, buy a book of speeches and select one you like." He hesitated and curled his forelock, musing, "And if you don't like all of it, change it!"

To the authors, playwrights, and screenwriters who have had some minor troubles with me later, you can put the blame on the little grocer in Williamsburg who suggested that it was possible for a performer to alter the text. Blame him, too, for my passion to emulate him and become a rabbi. I told papa, I think it was that very night, that I was determined to be a rabbi, and I pleaded with him to take me to the yeshiva on East Broadway where such matters could be decided. For weeks I begged until papa wearily gave in, and down we went to East Broadway, where the bearded and somber professors tried not to smile as they were told I was only twelve years old and not yet confirmed. With great gentleness they suggested they would be delighted to receive me when I was graduated from high school.

But their questions deflated me and forced me to look into myself. Did I really have the call, the vocation? Was I prepared to·make all the necessary sacrifices? And my conscience told me I had to indulge in painful introspection. I came to the conclusion that it was not possible for me to occupy the pulpit because I was not an ascetic.

My bewilderment and doubts seemed to be personal, private, and solitary. I did not know that they were shared by all other sensitive children who were trying to find an answer to the future. The answer is best not found when so young because it can be wrong.

But I did not know that then, and in my dreams (egged on by the *Journal*, which was forever pleading the case of the innocent or deprived) I would visualize myself as a lawyer, never prosecuting but always defending, serving the causes of justice and the downtrodden. I played that lawyer part superbly every night before I went to sleep. Oh, the speeches to the jury I made up!

But the real speech lay ahead of me—the bar mitzvah speech—and it was to be a bilingual exercise, first in Yiddish and then in English.

On a rainy Saturday morning in December, trembling and shaking at the prospect of the ordeal, my family and I entered the *schul.* I went through the blessing and the reading of the portion of the law with glassy-eyed terror, and then I was on.

In my kneepants, black stockings, white shirt, and blue serge, I stood up for the first time in my life to address a congregation of adults, the men in front of me, the women segregated at the back. There was utter silence, and I began, my voice faltering at first and then growing stronger as I felt the curious power of being able to control the audience. Of course, I had stage fright.

I still do. The first moments are always agony, and nothing will ever change the terror. But when the juices flow, a kind of confidence surges through you. Perhaps it's actually adrenaline, but I've never been able to interpret the art of acting in physiological terms. Confidence or adrenaline, how many times has it happened to me!

You start hesitantly, using all your strength and concentration just to remember the words, and then (and it is a miracle at which I never cease to marvel) the words become part of you; it is no longer necessary to strain to recall them. With a rising inflection here, a pause there, an emphasis accompanied by a compatible gesture, you are in charge, and the audience gazes at you, rapt and controlled.

I loved it then, and I love it now.

But when I finished that first performance, there was no applause, no "Bravos!"—no standing ovation. It is not permitted to applaud in a synagogue.

But I had my first notice, if something less than a rave review. At the required reception later at a hall on Rivington and Allen Streets, an elderly parishioner said to papa in my hearing, "Perhaps, with that voice, he'll be the savior of our people!"

I never played that role, believe me, but at P.S. 20 I became the savior (with a small *s*) of the graduating class. The commencement arrangements were in disrepair, and Mr. Ryan, my home room teacher, put me in charge. I rehearsed the kids on the roof of the school (one of my first assignments both as producer and director), and we marched up and down to the strains of Elgar's *Pomp and Circumstance.* I was a martinet at these rehearsals, but it was worth it.

We presented a fine picture as we went through the commencement exercises, and being producer and director, I assured myself the starring role. Before we were handed our diplomas, I read the declamation speech, taken in large part from Teddy Roosevelt's second inaugural address.

This time there was applause, and I think that's when I was hooked.

4

Now I was at Townsend Harris High School. It was located, in my first year, on Twenty-third Street. I would walk and cross the Bowery to the Spring Street station of the subway, passing, as I did, inhospitable neighborhoods, becoming aware of the poverty and frustrations of the people of the streets. Occasionally they took their frustrations out on me, but I ignored them because, even as I walked, I studied.

I was bound to complete the four-year course in three years. That was not easy, though I made a wise choice when I decided against Latin and Greek. My elective language would be French. German I already knew. And Spanish did not come hard. I did not know it then, but I had an ear for tongues, and having a good ear is not talent; it is something acquired in the genes.

In my second year Townsend Harris moved from Twenty-third Street to 137th Street and Convent Avenue (already the old urban patterns were breaking up), and at the dedication exercises of the new building, far in the distance, I saw Mark Twain and heard him deliver the principal address.

He was the first celebrity I ever saw in my life, and I was stricken with wonder that I could actually see and hear the creator of *Tom Sawyer*. It is a wonder that has never left me. I am still in awe of great authors, painters, and actors, and if it doesn't show as much as it did that windy afternoon in the Bronx, it is there all the same.

The move of Townsend Harris to the Bronx* must have inspired

* Note from L.S.: 137th Street and Convent Avenue is actually Manhattan and not the Bronx, but at his age, Eddie did not know the difference between Upper Manhattan and the Bronx. He was convinced that Townsend Harris (and C.C.N.Y.) was in the Bronx.

mama and papa, because we all moved to the Bronx too. It was better because there were trees on the Grand Concourse and Bronx Park and the zoo, and going to school was much easier.

But school was a hotbed of politics. It was 1909, and my hero, Hearst, was running for mayor of New York against McClelland, a creature of Tammany Hall. A man named Murphy was boss of the Hall, a worthy successor to Boss Tweed, and, impressed by the Brisbane editorials, I was a wild opponent of machine politics in general and Tammany in particular.

Looking back now, I cannot report with total candor that it was solely passion over the issues that led me to stump for Hearst; additionally, there must have been mixed up in it my delight at standing on a soap box and addressing an audience. Still, there was some degree of moral indignation as I described how in previous elections Tammany had thrown ballot boxes into the river and had indulged in every kind of swindle and chicanery to achieve dominance by the machine.

The Committee to Elect William Randolph Hearst must have heard of this lunatic child in the Bronx swaying audiences, because I was invited to campaign headquarters in the Hermitage Hotel and sent out in an automobile to harangue a crowd on Eighth Avenue in the Fifties.

Involved here were two remarkable firsts for me. First first: It was the first time I'd ever ridden in an automobile. Second first: It was the first time I'd seen Broadway.

And what did I see on my way to Eighth Avenue? Posters: "David Belasco presents Emma Dunn and Frances Starr in *The Easiest Way* by Eugene Walter"; "Harrison Grey Fiske presents Mrs. Fiske and Henry Dixon in *Mrs. Bumpstead Leigh*"; "Liebler & Company present Mr. George Arliss in *Disraeli* by Louis N. Parker"; "Doris Keane in *Romance* by Edward Sheldon"; "Cohan & Harris present Wallace Eddinger in *Seven Keys to Baldpate* by George M. Cohan from the novel by Earl Derr Biggers"; and "*On Trial* by Elmer Rice"; "*The Unchastened Woman* by Louis K. Anspacher"; "*Good Gracious Annabelle* by Clare Kummer," and, on this last one, because the poster was close at hand, I read the small print, "produced and staged by Arthur Hopkins."

I barely noticed his name. I was too busy arguing politics to think about the theater—and, looking back on it, I suspect I was using argument to sublimate my aggressions.

Perhaps an analyst can explain why, if people were shoved on the subway, I involved myself in the fight and sought out the conductor to help the weak against the bully. Maybe he can even figure out how it was that at P.S. 20, when Benjamin Stein was given a gold medal because he was the teacher's favorite, I led the contingent that complained in class, and later in the principal's office, that the award was unjust and unfair and unmerited and that it should go to Abraham Usdansky, the logical winner in the opinion of his classmates.

Additionally, perhaps he would even reason why I was so bitterly angry with a boy named Foss on the subject of the World Court that we both wrote searing papers, he attacking, I defending. Could it have been that it was a competition that led us both to read these passionate documents on the stage of Carnegie Hall?

Finally, perhaps he could illuminate the reason why, in later life, I was a patron and supporter of causes that sought to help the Okies, the blacks, the migrant workers, the victims of the Nazis—causes that landed me in *Red Channels*, an odious and slanderous catalog of those with presumed and unsubstantiated Communist sympathies— and why, at my own request, I testified voluntarily three times before the House Committee on Un-American Activities. I think his answer would be that I was seeking to be separated from the huddled masses and, at the same time, to identify with them. A show-biz character might say I was beginning to show evidence of being a ham. I doubt now that I would disagree with either of their diagnoses.

There certainly was some slight degree of ham in me. When I was nominated to be class president at Townsend Harris High School, I was overjoyed, and the speeches I made were filled with the longest words I could find about civic responsibility and the glory of the Townsend Harris tradition, plus quite a few words about Townsend Harris himself (whom I longed to play in a picture, but John Wayne was far more Anglo-Saxon and got the role).

My opponent in the election was James W. Donahue, a tall and articulate young man of impeccable Irish stock and equally impeccable campaign manners. But our supporters would have none of fair campaigning. The underground supporters of each of us began filling the school with comments like "You want a mick for president?" "You want a kike for president?" Mick. Kike. Kike. Mick. It was sickening.

And Jim Donahue was as sick about it as I was. We got together, agreed this must stop, and by walking arm in arm in front of the student body, proved we harbored no such racial madness.

Jim Donahue was elected and was magnanimous to me in his acceptance speech. It was the beginning of one of the closest friendships I ever had.

Jim studied law, became District Attorney of the Bronx, and married Gertrude Callahan, who wrote lovely verse. When he died, Jim left me his most precious possession, a figurine bestowed on him by the Salmagundi Club in New York, whose lawyer he was.

That figure stands on top of a bookcase in my bedroom, and whenever I look at it, I think of Jim and I have no way not to miss him.

I think his grandchildren might like to know.

I imagine there is some peculiar mystique that binds together those who are classmates at a New York high school. Through the years people have come up to me with delight to say, "Hey, Eddie, me, I went to Townsend Harris, too." And even though I antedated them by years and years, we still have a special bond. It happened to me once in Kenya when I was making a picture called *A Boy Ten Feet Tall*. And in Haifa in 1971. And it's practically an everyday occurrence in London.

The City College of New York alumni have the same curious fraternal tie. Oh, I'm sure it happens to those who've been to other schools in other cities, but it's perhaps the latent chauvinist in me that makes me think it happens more often and longer with those who went to Townsend Harris and C.C.N.Y.

And I went to C.C.N.Y. more than sixty years ago. I was a precocious seventeen-year-old, outwardly composed, but inwardly insecure. I matriculated with no clear idea of what I wanted my future to be. Accordingly, I took a course that would lead to a bachelor of arts degree, and I thoroughly enjoyed the classes in English, sociology, philosophy, history, and literature, and my grades were good.

But—and it's a big "but"—I, who had been so good with Mrs. Washington's fractions and was a whiz at arithmetic, had to fake my way through algebra. I detested geometry, spherical geometry, and calculus. And when it came to biology and physics, Einstein you could not call me. My grades were appalling.

I would cut those classes and go instead to the great hall, with its Gothic chairs, where I loved to listen to the sublime organist Samuel Baldwin rehearse Palestrina and Bach; I began to find that music was very important to me; it would continue to be for the rest of my life. (Later on in this chronicle, remind me to tell you about my piano.)

As I sat and listened to the organ, I engaged in an internal debate: What was I going to do with my life? I'd passed through the preadolescent rabbinical and legal phases, and my proven lack of ability in the hard sciences certainly ruled out medicine. What else could C.C.N.Y. offer me?

Well, chiefly, there was the Elizabethan Society, to be a member of which was a signal honor. And in order to achieve it, it was necessary to have an audition. After deep soul-searching, I came up with a reading of Antony's soliloquy in *Julius Caesar*, and was duly admitted.

At last I was beginning to see the shape of the future. That shape spelled "theater," and "theater" spelled "actor." Not that I really knew what it was like to be an actor. I had to find out. So I haunted the Astor Library, reading the lives of the great actors: Edwin Booth, Robert Mansfield, David Garrick, Henry Irving, for instance, and the great plays of Aeschylus to Ibsen, and the dramatic criticism of George Bernard Shaw.

And with every penny I saved, I'd get second balcony seats for any play that was running in the Bronx. In addition, I secretly traveled to Broadway and peered from the highest point of the Empire and the Lyceum theaters at the great actors and great plays, and some lousy actors and lousy plays, and God gave me the sense to know the difference.

Parenthetically, I might add that on my excursions to the Astor Library I would pass bookstores on Fourth Avenue, and there I would find postcard reproductions of Rembrandt, Vermeer, El Greco, Rubens, and Goya, ranging in price from a penny to a nickel—the great pictures of the world. Sometimes I had to decide between a play and a picture (not moving). And together with Oscar's flawed Remingtons and Metcalfs, you might say that was the beginning of my art collection.

Willy-nilly, the twisted path of my young life was beginning to straighten out, and the direction it was taking was terrifying. How could I tell mama and papa that I wanted to go on the stage? I knew they would not try to stop me; I also knew that their hearts were set on one of the professions. Still, there were deep wells of understanding in them. But I could not test them until I was certain myself. Introspection gave me no answers.

I needed external advice, and I needed it badly. There was at C.C.N.Y. a Professor Adolph Werner, an aged and wise man with enormous empathy for young people. I gathered all my courage and went to see him. He was preoccupied and busy but gracious and, I suspected, skeptical.

I find this attitude in myself sometimes now when young people ask me how to become an actor. As Professor Werner, at first, tried to discourage me, I try to discourage them. You cannot be, in Lady Macbeth's words, "infirm of purpose." It requires firm purpose, indeed, to interpret man, which is what acting amounts to, and it takes persistence and a great capacity to deal with disappointment.

Professor Werner wanted to be sure I had those essential ingredients. I must have persuaded him, because he gave me a letter to

Benjamin F. Roeder, General Manager for David Belasco, and a member of the Board of the American Academy of Dramatic Arts, which together with Rada, the Royal Academy in London, are two of the best acting schools in the world.

Roeder, however, could make no final decision about admission to the American Academy; he was on the board, but ultimate admission rested with Franklin H. Sargent, the academy's chief executive.

All this occurred during the summer—the longest and bleakest summer I've ever known. Roeder was in Europe, and it was weeks before I could reach him. Then he gave me a letter of introduction to Mr. Sargent.

Jubilantly and instantly I went to see Mr. Sargent, only to find that he, too, was in Europe and was not expected to return until autumn.

By autumn I had to make the decision whether to return to C.C.N.Y. for my junior year, and I had to tell my parents—were I accepted at the Academy—that I would be a college dropout, something I feared telling, something I feared *not* telling.

When finally I did get to Mr. Sargent, he required an audition. I blanched, but one of those miracles occurred. The previous April, 1911, some of us had put on a reunion program for the college. I still have the program. It read:

Program

1. Nathan Lifshitz
   Monologue

2. Hernando Caicedo
   Violin Solo

3. Emanuel Goldenberg
   Recitation

4. Alfred C. Bennet
   Piano Solo

5. Morris Gluck & Co.
   Impersonations

6. William P. Sullivan
   Popular Selection

7. Joseph Saltman
   Ragtime

REFRESHMENTS!

Standing in front of Mr. Sargent, I recalled nothing of the violin solo or the impersonations or the popular selection or the ragtime, but

I *did* recall Emanuel Goldenberg's recitation, which I had given to gain admission to the Elizabethan Society: Antony's soliloquy from *Caesar*.

In the years that have passed, I have seen hundreds, thousands of actors reading for authors and directors on stage, and even more young people making tests for movies. The most important element involved is the choice of material. It should be familiar but not *too* familiar; it should start low and end high; it should be an excerpt that has a beginning, a middle, and end, and is self-contained.

Antony's soliloquy had all these elements—and thank God (this was certainly no time for agnosticism) I was awarded a scholarship to the American Academy.

My mother and father were not overjoyed; they reluctantly accepted the will of God and their son, Manny, alias Edward G. And, when even after agreeing, they still began to raise doubts, they were faced with the counterarguments of Zach, Oscar, Max, and Willie.

The Brothers Goldenberg stood together.

And so drama school began. Reading. Movement. Fencing. Interpretation. Articulation. Voice placement. History of the theater. And scenes played with one fledgling actor against another. *My* alter fledgling turned out to be a tall, handsome, graceful young man named Joseph Schildkraut, known affectionately to us as Pepe. Even then he had an air, because his father, perhaps the most celebrated of Yiddish actors, was the venerable Rudolph Schildkraut whose name was known all over Europe, South America, and the United States.

Pepe Schildkraut had learned well from his father the large gesture, the mumbling when an audience was inattentive, followed by the sharply shouted line, even though the line was innocuous in itself. These were means of expression that worked well on the Jewish stage; I was to learn (as did Pepe) that they were not entirely acceptable in English.

Not that I had ever really played in front of an audience. And it was time. The Academy was loosely affiliated with Charles Frohman, and I had visions of appearing at special matinees at the Empire.

Instead, I played Consul Bernick in Ibsen's *Pillars of Society* in the twenty-ninth year of the Academy at the Carnegie Lyceum on Fifty-seventh Street. It was performed by members of the school, and (this is the only time I'll say it) I was pretty good.

Unfortunately, I was short, and a nameless member of the faculty, insisting that Bernick must dominate the other members of the cast physically as well as spiritually, forced me to wear shoes that were practically stilts. That made me miserable.

I am indeed short, but never again have I resorted to built-up shoes—Adler elevators. A short actor has to *think* tall. I learned it then, and I've never forgotten it.

I thought Consul Bernick would immediately get me a professional job. It did not.

And then came the summer—that strange hiatus in life which affects every student. What to do? Well, Pepe Schildkraut and I read in the *Journal* that there were to be professional tryouts in various Loew's theaters. They were not, I hasten to tell you, amateur nights, which were populated by mimics, jugglers, off-key sopranos, and Irish tenors, mostly whisked off the stage by a hook. No, these were to be skits or sketches or short one-act plays.

I had long been fascinated by Henry James' *The Bells*, a story of a burgomaster of more than middle age, who many years before, as an innkeeper, had murdered and stolen and had kept his secret for years. This was the time of Mesmer, the great hypnotist, and James wrote how, under hypnosis, the burgomaster revealed his horrendous crime.

I sat up all night with a friend (I don't think it was Pepe, but it might have been) and dramatized the James story, giving myself, of course, the juicy part of the burgomaster.

I tried it out at Loew's, and they booked me. Two of the other actors in the cast were professionals. The others were fellow students, and the Loew's circuit booked us for four split weeks, opening at the Plaza Theater on Lexington Avenue.

It was at this juncture that I changed my name, and the program read:

EDWARD G. ROBINSON
in
BELLS OF CONSCIENCE

It was the first time my name appeared on any professional program. It certainly, by definition, was the first time my name appeared above the title.

It did not happen again for fifteen years.

During my senior year Pepe Schildkraut came to me with a very strange and complimentary request. His father, Rudolph, needed a replacement for an actor in the cast of *Number 37*, a play in which he was appearing at the West End Theatre. It was the part of the district attorney, occurred in the second act, and was mostly a dualogue between Schildkraut, the accused, and the D.A. The D.A. was supposed to be a man in his fifties, and I was barely nineteen, but that did not

bother the senior Mr. Schildkraut. In the Yiddish theater it was nothing for a child of fifteen to play a man of seventy, though I doubt the
reverse ever occurred.

In any case, I was delighted and thrilled—until I discovered that
the play was in Yiddish. Now there have been rumors, through the
years, that I had my start as a Yiddish actor. It is sadly not true. The
truth of it is that the only role I ever played in Yiddish was in that one
play with Rudolph Schildkraut, and I appeared under the name of
Edward Golden.

Let me make some deeply felt observations about the Yiddish theater at this point. It was a great classic theater, and companies would
travel from Poland and Eastern Europe to South America, South
Africa, and the United States, playing Chekhov, Sudermann, and
Shakespeare. These were superb repertory companies, most of them,
and they specialized in tragedy. What else?

Of course, from time to time, there were also comedies, usually
with bitter and satiric undertones, with lovely actresses like Molly
Picon and Bessie Thomashefsky. But tragic or comic, they played to
enormous audiences. The Yiddish theater is all but gone due to the
restrictive Johnson Immigration Act of 1920 that cut off the flow of
Yiddish-speaking immigrants, and thus, at the same time, cut off
the new audiences. Many of the great Yiddish actors made the
wrenching and difficult transition from Yiddish to English. Among
them are Jacob Ben-Ami, Maurice Moscovich, Bertha Kalich, Muni
Wiesenfreund (who changed *his* name to Paul Muni), Molly Picon
(who in her seventies can still do handsprings), and even Rudolph
Schildkraut himself. I am certain he demanded from his American
actors the same rigorous rehearsing he demanded from me.

I remember him as a painstaking director, but I was a quick study
and pretty optimistic about my chances to cut the mustard. Unfortunately, I mingled with members of the audience on the sidewalk before the curtain rose on the first performance, and a gentleman, an
actor, came up to me and said, "Congratulations. You're playing with
Schildkraut. What will happen to you if you forget your lines?"

Such a prospect had never occurred to me. But from the moment
he said it, it never left my mind. While I was on stage, his words kept
interfering with the text of the play. And I dried up. I fluffed. I could
not recall one more line of the play. Mr. Schildkraut politely gave me
the cue again, and exactly nothing happened. I was catatonic. I managed to ad lib something and looked beseechingly around for the
prompter—but he was nowhere in sight.

Desperately, I burbled something to the effect that I would have to
go into my office (off stage) to check on some law books relevant to

the case. I left Mr. Schildkraut to the mercies of the audience and fled backstage, looked for the prompter, and found him eventually. As he gave me the line, *mirabile dictu*, I also remembered the rest of the play.

And so I walked back on stage to find that Mr. Schildkraut had been ad libbing with bits and pieces of previous plays he had been in, and it was perfectly evident that the audience had no idea anything was wrong.

We finished our scene; Mr. Schildkraut took all his bows and actually motioned me forward to take one of my own, and then the curtain rang down.

"So what was it, young man?" asked Mr. Schildkraut.

"I'm terribly sorry," I said, "I forgot my lines."

"So what was such a problem?" asked Mr. Schildkraut. "All you had to do was ask me and I would have told you."

5

What is it like to be nineteen, a graduate of the American Academy (with Mr. George Arliss, in person, having delivered the commencement address) and ready for all the great roles ever written? I'll tell you what it's like: It's sheer frustration. You are ready for every challenge, and there are none. Which brings me to Matisse, by not so roundabout a fashion as you may think. He told me something years later that seemed somehow to illustrate my feelings at nineteen.

His son took me to see the master in his atelier in Paris. Because of the scarcity of my French vocabulary or my awe at being with one of the greatest of the then living painters, I'm afraid I mouthed a great number of vapidities.*

"I can't believe you're seventy," I said.

"It is not a question of believing. It is a fact."

"Your eyes have the sparkle of youth."

"I do not see as well as before."

"But your hands are steady and your work better than ever."

"Debatable."

"What keeps you so young?"

He looked at me sternly. The question clearly was often asked of him. (It is one often asked of me now, and I have a stock answer.) Matisse did not have a stock answer.

"Every day," he said, "I've got to get hold of something by the throat and strangle it. And that keeps me young."

* I do not vouch for the exact accuracy of this dialogue between us. It is filtered through translation and memory, but it is a reasonable facsimile.

35

Well, at nineteen, I was looking for a throat to strangle. I am not given to paranoia, but it seemed then that everybody was out to strangle me. There just seemed to be no jobs. I toyed with the idea of going into vaudeville with a singing act. Maybe I could be a stand-up comic. Maybe I could deliver dramatic readings. Was it too late to learn to sing, to juggle, to play the violin, to dance?

What was getting my goat was not only that I couldn't get a job but that I wasn't even able to afford the wonderful "red ink" restaurants like Guffanti's or the vaguely swell ones like Lorber's, lately moved from Grand Street to Broadway across from the Met. I could barely manage the Café Royale on Second Avenue which was the early Sardi's of the Jewish theatrical world in which the Adler family* and the Kesslers and the Thomashefskys reigned like the monarchs they really were. And certainly Rector's, Shanley's, Reisenweber's, Mouquin's, the Brevoort, and the Lafayette were outside the reach of my wallet. No, like other struggling actors who used Broadway from Thirty-eighth Street to Forty-eighth Street as a club, I found myself eating in Thompson's, where the table was the side of your chair, or, later, the Automat. I have not been in an Automat recently, but I remember with undiluted joy their raisin pie and pork and beans.

You heard me. *Pork* and beans. And from time to time, other forbidden unkosher food. My first clam took an act of courage, but I soon grew to love them—and oysters, too—and I'm not at all sure there wasn't an economic reason. They used to be sold from pushcarts on beds of ice, and they were cheap and filling—and, somehow, even more exciting because they contained the cheap thrill of sin.

I was still living at home in the Bronx, and I confessed my perfidy to my mother (taking care to assure her that I still preferred home to restaurants). She did not look in the least surprised or shocked, and I tried to persuade her to join me.

"Mama, you know," I said, "you're missing out on an awful lot."

And she smiled that all-knowing smile and said, "For me, Manny, it's too late to change."

Now I know what she meant.

As I reflect on the events of those years, I realize that I had an enormous preoccupation with what we used to call the opposite sex and we now simply call sex. It was a wondrous, tempting mystery to me, mostly because the knowledge of it came from the street, and I had some highly exotic sexual theories thrown at me. I had had a

---

* Speaking of Jacob Adler, I'm told that once he played Shylock in Yiddish while the rest of the cast played it in English. I would have given anything to see that performance.

highly erotic adventure in Bucharest once trying to find out what mysteries lay beneath the skirts of a little girl; let me tell you now about my love affair with Sadie Bodner at the University Settlement House. We were both thirteen, and I played her elderly father in a play called *One Touch of Nature*. Let me tell you that one touch of Sadie and I was guilty of theoretical incest.

Later, when it came to what is now quite frankly, even in *The New York Times*, called masturbation, known to me as self-abuse, I remember my younger brother giving me a piece of advice that froze me into inhibition. "If you masturbate," he said sagely, "you're liable to have a baby, and they'll find out!"

Was it any wonder that later on, when my fellow actors took me to a brothel, I would accompany them and, at the last moment, decide to sit it out in the waiting room?

And that's almost the last of sex you'll get in this book. Except to say that it has tortured me and elated me and I have to tell you (whether it please or disturb you) it is like money; having it is not important—*not* having it is appalling.

But at that time sex was at the bottom of my agenda; my whole being was centered on getting a job. Today it's easier; there are many talent agencies that service all the arms of the entertainment industry. In those days, there were very few, chiefly those in vaudeville, circus, variety, burlesque, and cabaret. Few, indeed, in the legitimate Broadway theater.

The one that was loosely connected with the Academy was the Wales Winter Agency, and I went to it. Though the people there were coolly polite, I could sense that they thought I was a ridiculous jerk. I tried my last card, using a vocabulary I'd picked up at the Academy. "I know," I said, "I'm not much on face value, but when it comes to stage value, I'll deliver."

That did little to perk up their interest; fundamentally, they were comparing me with the tall blond actors with gorgeous profiles who were waiting in the outside office—some of whom they might go to bed with. Oh, yes, that was pretty popular in those days, though I got mighty few passes. I'd have kicked them in the genitalia.

In my first days at the Academy, I'd written George Arliss asking for advice, and he'd written me a letter in his own hand suggesting that I work hard, ignore failure, and *plan!**

I conceived a plan: First, I'd get basic training by pulling the curtain up and down in any theater, anywhere. Next, if necessary, I

---

* I, following Mr. Arliss' personal response, answer all such letters.

would become an actor in a stock company, because I knew that it was invaluable experience—so many plays in a season, so many parts. You become a new person every week, and that gives you a sound theatrical education.

But I had no intention of remaining in that league. I would graduate to the position of road actor, which is to say, a player appearing in a road company of a New York hit. But that, too, would only be an intermediate step. What I wanted finally was to be a Broadway actor.

The problem, of course, was that these categories appeared to be frozen. Stock actors remained in stock; road actors spent their lives touring what in England is called the provinces and here is called the sticks and rarely reached Shaftsbury Avenue or Times Square; the Broadway actor, even though not a star, was an established figure.

It was a utopian ambition, and it was not one to be revealed to the Wales Winter Agency. I would take anything they could dish up.

For weeks they could dish up nothing. Then, when I was almost in despair, a few weeks later, a letter came from them suggesting a time and place of meeting.* I wrote back, confirming the appointment, having visions of appearing with George Arliss. Instead, it turned out that there was a place with the S. M. Stainach Stock Company in Albany, New York.

There is today a word for what I was offered (obviously, the bottom of the barrel)—a "gofer"—a young man who goes for coffee, cigarettes, smelling salts for the leading lady, and incidentally is assistant, assistant stage manager, and, from time to time, appears in a tiny part, not carrying a spear but its equivalent. It was the lowest rung on the professional theatrical ladder, and I hesitated before I gave my answer.

I hesitated for about an eighth of a second.

Recently, while discussing the dilemma of the new actor today, one of my close friends, George Burns, who combines cogent comment with fabulous wit, said: "The trouble is there's no place left to be lousy!"

---

* Note from L.S.: In E.G.R.'s files I find many of these letters:

"Will you please call upon me Friday next at ten? Sincerely, Brock Pemberton."

"Would Tuesday at four be convenient? Professionally, David Belasco."

"I suggest, if it be convenient, Wednesday at half-past three. With best wishes, Arthur Hopkins."

Apparently, until the late twenties, appointments were made by letter. The telephone was ignored. And there are, too, letters of regret from playwrights like Channing Pollock, sad that E.G.R. turned down a part. And other letters from producers regretting they, for one reason or another, had to turn down E.G.R.

His extremely trenchant point was that once the young actor could try his talents he would begin to perfect them even before audiences that did not expect perfection. Today, even a small bit in the movies or television can knock off a career almost immediately; it is seen by so many people and reviewed by so many critics. The obverse is equally true, of course; a small bit, either well played or because of the startling nature of the part, can bring an unknown to notice, to stardom even. But he can be destroyed by the next part, because one accidental piece of casting hardly prepares him for the ability or the right to carry a play or a show.*

I could name names, but I won't, of those who shone once and were subsequently forgotten. To prove my point, I'll do the reverse: name one of the very few who appeared once brilliantly and continued brilliantly until his tragic death: James Dean.

Just a few more comments on this: Nobody expects a new doctor to be Paul Dudley White; nobody expects a new lawyer to be Clarence Darrow; no one expects a new physicist to be Einstein; no one expects a high school pitcher to be Sandy Koufax. They all learn and work at their jobs, honing their skills, adding experience to their gifts.

They all, to mix a metaphor, open in Albany.

The Stainach Stock Company consisted of a small repertory group.

I did all chores, including ringing the curtain up and down, but what I remember most is the night I went on as Sato in *Paid in Full*, and the leading man, secure in his frock coat, pomaded mustachios, and malacca cane, sneered at me on stage.** I expect no thanks for it, but from that moment on, I have always tried to treat every actor on the stage or on the set with consideration. I may not have succeeded, and there may be those who hold a minority view, but that mustachioed snob is always with me.

(As is the fact that, in Binghamton, New York, I met a lady at a restaurant—and today I am a man. It was my first sexual experience, and it was so fast and sickening and clinical that it almost turned me off forever.)

When the Albany engagement was over (and calling it an engagement is a euphemism), back to New York to Wales-Winter I went, and things were a little different. I now had credentials, and if I

---

* As for athletes or notorious figures, who become television actors, and perform without training or experience, I have not contempt, but pity.

** I also doubled in *The Gambler* as Thomas, the butler of the Emersons (Emanuel Golden) and Hicks, a plainclothesman (Edward G. Robinson).

exaggerated the importance of the parts I'd played, it was, I think, more imagination than deliberate falsehood.

At home mama and papa were praying this would be the end of it. I'd sowed my wild oat; I was thinner than when I'd left. Maybe now I'd be willing to go back to C.C.N.Y. and emerge with a diploma, and then on to medical school. Or why not even a C.P.A.? What they wanted for me was security; what I wanted for myself was to play Othello. Note I do not say Romeo; I was reconciled to the miserable fact that I was a character man—a character man at twenty. Not exactly a gilt-edged security.

But you had to have relentless push, and when I discovered there was an opening with a stock company, The Orpheum Players in Cincinnati, I got myself an appointment. Again I was viewed with disdain, and again I used the sentence that was becoming part of my arsenal: "Not much on face value, but when it comes to stage value, I'll deliver."

It worked. Out I went to Cincinnati, and I stayed there for twenty-two weeks. We had a varied repertory. I played in *Alias Jimmy Valentine* (the character of Dick the Rat, a sneak thief) as E. Gould Robinson, and in the same play, the character of "Williams, a bank clerk," billed as Edward Gould Robinson. My notices were minimal.*

I was becoming adept at doubling—that is, playing two parts in one play, in suitable disguises. I did it all season.

I played many varied non-Anglo-Saxon parts during those twenty-two weeks, and never have I been directed with such rigidity. You enter. You walk to this exact point. You say your words. You wait. You walk there. You stand. You say your words. You exit. The discipline was total. You might as well have been a robot. No responding to the audience. No shift in position that made the character more believable or you more comfortable. No reciting the lines as if you were saying them for the first time and reading speeches as if they were actual conversation.

Now, I well knew how important it was to be firmly grounded in technique so that I could not be shaken off my feet, but to be so cut and dried, to use the identical gesture night after night without giving the part a chance to breathe and grow—well, that was like being in a chorus line: "One, two, three, kick!"

But that was theater fashion in those days. Our Cincinnati matinees were on Wednesday, and the other legitimate house had its mati-

---

* I try not to pay attention to notices, reviews. I try not to read them. But I have no discipline. I try to be cool about the good ones; the bad ones kill me.

nees on Thursday, so I was able to see the touring companies that played there. One week Robert Mantell was starred; the next week it was Sothern and Marlowe. As I sat in the balcony and watched these famous stars, I realized they, too, were having this same kind of discipline inflicted on them—or choosing it themselves.

Many years later, when Jean Jacques Copeau, the most distinguished of French directors, was engaged to do *The Brothers Karamazov*, he tried to impose this rigidity on the Theatre Guild Acting Company of which I was a member (together with those glories of the American theater, Alfred Lunt, Lynn Fontanne, Claire Eames, Margalo Gillmore, Dudley Digges, Henry Travers, Helen Westley, and Earl Larrimore). Because we respected his international reputation, we tried to do as he asked, but in rehearsal our performances were wooden and stilted. On opening night we rid ourselves of his restraints, breathed free, and were a company of artists, not automatons.

Twenty-three weeks later I was back in New York, having amassed some additional credentials but no new job. I thought—seriously this time—that, were I to succeed in the theater, I would have to do a solo act where I could direct myself. Maybe there was a place for me in burlesque or the circus, where an actor could—to use a phrase that has already become as old-fashioned as "cut the mustard"—"do my thing."

Mama and papa were still hopeful that my thing was C.C.N.Y., and I'm not at all sure I didn't have moments when I agreed with them. In having them and their home in the Bronx, *my* home, I was lucky, indeed. Most actors returned to New York and took up residence in those flea-bitten theatrical boardinghouses, cooking their illegal meals over a gas jet. I, at least, had a warm home and generous portions of eggplant chopped with onion and olive oil accompanied by black radish, sweated with salt. And coffee. Mama's freshly ground coffee.

Coffee on the road was undrinkable swill.

As I was soon to find out again.

6

Otis Skinner for many years had achieved great success with a play called *Kismet*. If you never saw it as a play, surely you saw it as a musical or as one of M.G.M.'s super movies. Well, a man named Charles Dalton was going to take it out on the road again—a debatable decision. Once a play is identified with an actor, it's tough for a road actor to follow him in the part.

But Harrison Grey Fiske (and his partners, Klaw and Erlanger) looked up the routing sheets played by Mr. Skinner and discovered he had never set foot in northern New York State or Canada. (Mr. Fiske had an enormously prominent name, and you can figure it out if you replace the "Mr." with "Mrs.")

The part of the guide Nasir was open, and I auditioned for it. Because it was a character part and required an older man, I auditioned, not as twenty, but as fifty, and I got it.

It was a real part with perhaps ten sides* and some wonderful, if secondhand costumes. The setting was Baghdad ("The Hall of the Caliph's Palace"), and I got a real salary, maybe twenty-five bucks a

* I've been wracking my brain trying to explain "sides." Here's a stab at it: In those days actors, of course, read the whole play, but then their parts were excised from it, with only the lines of the other players that constituted cues being included; these parts were then bound into small booklets, and they were called "sides." Thus you learned your own part but not the others. The practice has virtually disappeared in this country, but in England and on the Continent, it is still occasionally used.

week.* We toured successfully in Ottawa and Montreal, and then, one day in 1914, the papers announcéd that some Austrian duke or other was assassinated in Sarajevo.

Canada joined England in the war, and that put the whole kibosh on the tour. We closed in November.

If I appear to be frivolous about the start of World War I, you are entitled to an explanation.

I was—I do not know how to say it now without appearing idiotic —pro-German. I set down the reasons for my attitude in no special pecking order; they were all equally compelling.

In the first place, as all of us who had come to America from Middle Europe, we had taken the history of the United States seriously. While the bulk of the population had long since forgiven England for the Revolutionary War and the War of 1812, we had not. So we were not disposed to be friendly to the British.

And if we were not, our Irish friends were doubly anti-Albion. It was the time of the Troubles, and most of the Irish I knew prayed for Britain's defeat.

Add to this the fact that both Rumania and Russia were fighting Germany—and name two countries that had been more villainous in their relationship with the Jews. Any nation *against* Rumania and Russia, I was automatically *for!*

What you had then was layer upon layer of ancient animosity and enmity and, in some cases, complete hatred. When I look back upon it now, I cannot conceive myself as pro-German. But that's the truth of it.

I was not as pro-German as I was antiwar. To close a play in Canada in November and make your way back to New York to try to find a job in the middle of the season, when all the plays were cast, was enough to make *anybody* antiwar.

There were no jobs. I made the rounds. New agencies had opened. The answer was always the same—a phrase that became part of the actor's agony: "Nothing today. Try us next week."

Well, there were just too many next weeks. Then I thought there was a sudden light. I found a sketch called *Electrocution* and auditioned it for a vaudeville agent. He booked me into the Hammerstein Victoria for the first part of a split week. I was also billed as the director, and I swelled with pride. Management didn't even wait until

* There was a beautiful young dancer in the cast named Leah Salisbury. Years later she became a literary agent and sent me a book by Bill Burnett called *Little Caesar*. "Eddie," she said. "Read it. It's for you!" The actors in those days were serious, dedicated youngsters . . . for Christmas Leah gave Eddie a copy of *Marcus Aurelius*, and Eddie gave her a copy of *Plutarch's Lives*.

Wednesday to cancel me. Too downbeat in the middle of a war.
That damned war!

I went from manager's office to manager's office, from agent to
agent, day after day, hat in hand. Nothing.

Meanwhile, there were conferences at home. If I didn't want to be
a doctor or a lawyer, why not become a teacher? Teaching was acting, wasn't it? Standing up in front of a class? Look, a year or two at
C.C.N.Y. taking some courses in The Theory and Practice of Education, and I would no longer have to make the dreary rounds of managers' offices.

But the arguments around the dining room table about my career
were often crowded out by arguments on the war. Whether because of
George Creel's propaganda machine and the stories of Belgian
women bayonetted to walls by the Germans, whether because of the
stories of war orphans and the Hun and the rising American interest
on the side of the Allies, the balance was shifting. Even my own.

In the *Journal* I would read President Wilson's speeches, and they
made sense, and I thought him the greatest man in the world. He was
keeping us out of war, and I agreed with him.*

And then came the *Lusitania*, the sinking of an unarmed passenger
vessel at sea with thousands drowned. Last year I read in the late *Life*
magazine that the *Lusitania* was exactly what the Germans charged—
that she was armed and carried munitions. But I didn't know it then,
and I'm not at all sure I believe it now. Even though I try to be a
realist, I prefer to keep my illusions unshattered.

In any case, the *Lusitania* did me in. I was no longer pro-German.
I was, together with the vast population of this country, now a bitter
enemy of the Kaiser.

Thank God I was able to tell Mr. Klauber that. As an ethnic German, he was doubly pro-Ally. It was a time when sauerkraut became
liberty cabbage, and to play Beethoven and Bach was to be accused
of treason. As for Heine and Goethe, they were banned. Mr. Klauber
disdained even Dutch comics like Weber and Fields.

Why all this concern about Mr. Klauber?

Well, Adolph Klauber was general manager and casting director for
the Selwyn Company. Arch and Edgar Selwyn were brothers and
highly distinguished producers.** They had considerable success with

---

* He was my first presidential vote; there have been thirteen more—all Democratic—though, once or twice, I had to force myself.

** When the Selwyns joined forces with Sam Goldfish to make films, the name of
the corporation they selected was Goldwyn. Mr. Goldfish liked that name so
much he took it for his own—and covered it, in the years that followed, with
glory. I give you *The Best Years of Our Lives*.

an author named Roi Cooper Megrue, and now he had a new work, *Under Fire*, "a play of yesterday, today and tomorrow in three acts." As the author of *It Pays to Advertise*, Mr. Megrue was accustomed to success, and he had great hopes for *Under Fire*. Even then, however, costs were a consideration, and Megrue had written a play with four sets and over thirty-one speaking parts.

Thus, Mr. Klauber had to have an actor who could double.

Me—I was the greatest doubling actor ever seen in Cincinnati.

Mr. Klauber had to have someone who could do a French dialect and speak French.

Me—I could do a French dialect and speak French.

Mr. Klauber had to have someone who could do a German dialect and speak German.

Me—I could do a German dialect and speak German.

Mr. Klauber had to have somebody do all those things, and also play a Cockney.

Me, I hadn't the faintest idea how to play a Cockney, but by the time I read for Mr. Klauber, I did a pretty fair imitation of one, courtesy of an ex-fellow student at the Academy.

Have I forgotten to say that the play was highly pro-Ally and distinctly anti-German, so that my newly found dislike of the Boche was not only sincere but well-timed? (To repeat: Klauber was of German descent and thus had to be more patriotic than anybody else.)

So, there it was. I got the part. I mean I got the *parts*, four of them: a Belgian spy, complete with cutaway, goatee, and a dictaphone he had sneakily hidden in a Belgian inn. He exited and one script page later reentered (I mean *I* reentered) as a hysterical Belgian peasant in smock and sabots, crying, "The Germans are coming! The Germans are coming!" I then had five minutes to change into a German officer, complete with monocle and uniform, and when he exited, I came back as a Cockney soldier from the trenches. For that I got thirty dollars a week, but when Klauber and the Selwyns saw how dandy I was with quick change and instant dialect, I also replaced some other players (oh, those poor guys), and for twenty bucks more a week I managed to be a soldier of the British Army, a member of the English Red Cross, and off and on, various soldiers in the German Army.

In case I've forgotten to mention it, William Courtenay starred as Captain Redmond of the Irish Guards; Frank Craven, of whom you may have heard, played Charlie Brown of New York; and Violet Heming, that loveliest of ladies, played Ethel Willoughby, Georgy's governess. Georgy never appeared.

I was in a top-drawer, first-class company! We toured the sticks and then finally opened at the Hudson Theatre in New York. And I was, at last, a New York actor. The notices: "In minor roles, exceedingly good work is done by E. G. Robinson and Henry Stephenson." "G. Robinson was excellent as Andre." "E. Robinson contributes to the success." "The most versatile actor is E. C. Robinson."

Well, you play three parts (one was cut before we opened in New York), and you get different notices for each one of them. It appeared, however, that almost nobody was able to get my name straight.

It was a hit, but it took rewriting and restaging to make it so. I remember one Saturday morning out of town when we were herded on stage and given a whole new scene to play for that afternoon matinee. Megrue read us the new lines.

The curtain went up. The Messrs. Selwyn and Megrue were out front watching. We stumbled through part of the scene, then all of us went blank, and Megrue, ready to be ill, left the theater hurriedly. When he returned, nothing whatever had changed on stage, for nobody had a copy of the changes—certainly not the stage manager. Megrue had the only one, and he'd left the scene at his hotel. We got out of it somehow.

Actors always get out of it somehow.

So we were a hit—a big, fourteen-carat-gold New York hit, and I was in it, and I got a raise, and you know what I bought with it? Do you expect to hear that it was a reproduction of a Raphael?

The answer is spats.

It seems to me that I should take a breath here to remind myself (and you) that I was not quite twenty-four years old, and in that span I'd made the journey from Bucharest to the Hudson Theatre. Certainly it required zeal, dedication, ambition, and resolve. Does all that add up to *chutzpa* and/or monomania?

I make no judgment upon myself; I think that had I not enjoyed the advantage of the migration, I would have ended up, in the thirties and forties, in an oven in Dachau. I think that what moved me was a fierce need for recognition—deference—an unbearable hatred for inferiority. But the achievement and upward mobility, to use a phrase made prominent by my friend Harry Golden, could really have happened *Only in America*.

It is the fashion, in some circles these days, to put America down; certainly the old Horatio Alger newsboy-to-governor aspect of this culture is viewed with disdain. But how can I view it with disdain when I am a living attestation to it?

It is equally the fashion these days to believe that America is the property of the venerable and aged and that only recently has youth gotten a piece of the action. Well, I repeat, I was playing at the Hudson Theatre at twenty-three. And that's pretty youthful.

I think part of me was very grown up and adult; another part of me was still childlike. I loved being an actor in an important Broadway play; I loved being interviewed. (But in my heart I knew it was absurd. To myself I said—and frequently still do—like now—"What the hell have I got to say that is of interest to the world?")

I loved the girls who liked me and went out with me because I was an actor (even though there were very few of them. I never felt I was attractive to women. Certainly they scared the hell out of me, and approaching them to Go All The Way left me sweating and stuttering); I loved the cane I carried; I loved the excitement of taking an occasional taxi instead of the subway (I have had a long and consistent loathing of subways); I loved giving the even more occasional autograph that was asked of me (*that* disease was not as prevalent as it is today); I loved the new suits of clothes I bought at Moe Levy's (Walk a Flight and Save Ten); I think I loved every single thing about 1916.

When *Under Fire* was a hundred performances old, the Brothers Selwyn sent out the following invitation:

SELWYN & COMPANY

REGRET
THAT A SENSE OF DUTY
COMPELS THEM TO GIVE
A PARTY
AT THE

HUDSON THEATRE

SUNDAY DECEMBER NINETEENTH
AT TEN P.M.
REGARDLESS OF THEIR
PERSONAL INCLINATIONS
THEY RELUCTANTLY URGE
YOU TO BE PRESENT
LET US KNOW IF YOU'RE COMING†

† *Modernist for R.S.V.P.*

The bar was set up near the box office. The tables were installed in the lobby and lounges. Three bands worked the stage, where anybody who wanted to did the one-step or the maxixe. Sherry catered, and the theater was filled with diamonds, orchids, satins, pearls, mink, sable, and white and black tie.

Me, black tie. Rented.

Every cast of every play then running on Broadway was invited, and the great tables, heavy with champagne bottles and fantastic food, were populated by such incredible stars as Mitzi Hajos, Lina Abarbanel, Cyril Maude, Elsie Ferguson, Lewis Stone, Mable Taliaferro, Guy Bates Post, Lew Tellegan, Lucille Laverne, Chauncey Olcott, Blanche Ring, William Faversham, Olga Petrova, and Margaret Anglin.* I have never been at so star-studded an occasion (and God knows I've been to a thousand since), or maybe it only seemed that way because I was part of it.

William Courtenay, Frank Craven, Violet Heming, and other members of our cast were distributed by the Selwyns among the different tables—and so was I. There must have been a misshuffle of the place cards because I was seated with John and Ethel Barrymore.

The incomparable Barrymores, no strangers to champagne, offered a considerable number of exaggerated toasts to the cast in which I enthusiastically joined—after which they toasted *me*—and if the alcohol made me heady, being toasted by the Barrymores made me even headier.

I drank numberless glasses of wine. I got drunk. I didn't feel well. Our stage manager, seeing that I was pifflicated, steered me to a hotel to spend the night; there was no question of my attempting to reach the Bronx and even less question that I could show myself to mama and papa in this condition.

I was so drunk and so sick that I felt almost as I did in the hold of *La Touraine*, crossing the Atlantic.

Talk about being young. . . .

Under Fire ran for six months, and in October of 1916 the Selwyns (may their names forever be inscribed in the Book of Life, as my father used to say) again engaged me for a new play by Roi Cooper Megrue, written this time in collaboration with Irvin S. Cobb.

When we tried it out in Stamford, it was called *John W. Blake*; by

---

* Forgive the encrustation of long lists of actors. I can't help it. In some ways, it's homage to the greats I knew and saw and admired. I'm going to try to avoid the lists from now on, but I can't guarantee my success. How can I? I love actors.

the time we got it to the Harris Theatre on Forty-second Street, it was called *Under Sentence* (Mr. Megrue apparently had a passion for titles that started with "under"), and it was a melodrama concerned with frenzied finance and prison reform.* I played a convict called Fagan, and if I could not bring to the part any personal knowledge of the brutality of prison life, I certainly was an advocate of prison reform. Arthur Brisbane and William Randolph Hearst had taught me well.

My notices? Well, from here on in, I'll try to avoid them, except when bad. Anyway, the best notice an actor can get is the next job. The worst notice he can get is from the draft board.

Since the *Lusitania*, America was running a collision course with the Central Powers. I knew—and everyone else knew—that war was inevitable, only I tried not to think about it. At heart I was what was rapidly becoming a dirty word—a pacifist. I hoped and prayed I wouldn't have to go, but I would have been less than human if I weren't considering in what way I could best serve.

The answer was obvious. In intelligence. I did not look like an Anglo-Saxon; I could speak languages other than English; I was an actor; I could play a German or an Austrian or a Russian. If it came to it, clearly the best thing for the United States was for me to involve myself in espionage.

The United States did not think so. But it did not yet have to make up its mind.

When *Under Sentence* closed, I got a role with Frank Keenan in *The Pawn*. It was a turkey and lasted two weeks.

On April 6, 1917, President Wilson declared war on the Central Powers.

Even though I'd duly registered with the draft board (writing on the form: "I conscientiously object to all wars, but I will serve if my country needs me") and mama was observing meatless days and we were all collecting peach pits for gas masks and buying Liberty stamps and I was ready at a moment's bidding to lead the nation's intelligence division, I heard nothing from the draft people.

I did hear from the Messrs. Shubert, who gave me a part as a Japanese with Walker Whiteside in *The Pawn*. The climax came when I read the shocking line: "Me no Japanese. Me Filipino." It didn't help. We bombed.

---

* Fifty-five years later the subject still makes headlines. Roi Cooper Megrue had some good ideas in that play. Maybe the reformers ought to read it. *Under Sentence* could well have taken place at Attica.

I did not hear from the draft board.

So I followed my September bomb with an October turkey. *Drafted*, it was called, of all things, and I played a German soldier, Lieutenant Haenkel. In the cast was Pauline Lord, for whom I conceived what was then known as a crush.

Drafted closed. It never got to New York.

I did not hear from the draft board.

But this time I heard from Arthur Hopkins (whose name I'd first seen on a Broadway billboard when I was stumping for Hearst). Mr. Hopkins, plump and large-boned, was one of the most revered of Broadway producers, a man of intellect, wit, and substance. He had optioned a new play by a Swedish dramatist, Henning Berger, called *The Deluge*. It was perhaps the first of the plays in which a group of people are forced to remain together because of external calamity, a plot much admired and much imitated by subsequent playwrights, screen and television writers. It is, indeed, a staple of all the media.

I was excited when Mr. Hopkins asked me to read for the part of Nordling, an engineer. I was nervous because not only was Mr. Hopkins present but Pauline Lord as well.

In the pantheon of actresses who've graced the American theater Miss Lord is somewhere up among the first ten or the first five. Her special manner of speech, her ability to grasp a role and *be* it, were marvels to behold—and have you not beheld them, you are the poorer for it.

I not only beheld them, I played with them (and I saw her gravitate from folly to compassion, from being languidly beguiling to being tragically desirable), and it is hardly a confession now to say that I was by this time desperately in love with Miss Lord, and, you know, I think I still am.

She was the first woman I ever proposed to. "Oh, Eddie," she said, "you could knock me over with a feather." Which I had to assume meant "No!" It did little for my self-esteem. Since we opened in August and closed in September, I had only a month to heal my bruised ego.

How to describe your feelings when a play, in which you've had faith, to which you've given your guts, is a flop? You treat it all with gallows humor, but you know that basically it is a denial not only of your own judgment but of the intelligence of people like Arthur Hopkins. But he had not been certain of it himself. I remember him saying on the first rehearsal day, "I love this play. I don't know if it's box office. Probably isn't. I do know if we do any acting in it, the author will show us up. Just say the words, and *be* the character!"

He meant we were not to put ourselves, as actors, above the play. It was superb advice. We followed it, but we closed anyway. However, I was swinging as an actor, and in some small demand.

In December I was trying out in *The Little Teacher*, starring Mary Ryan, produced by George M. Cohan and Sam Harris. We opened in New York in February, and I played Batiste, a French Canadian.

It was a success. Early in the run S. Jay Kaufman interviewed me and asked me how I liked being a success. He reported in his column "Round the Town" that I said,

> Don't like it. I like my part and the play and I am glad to get salary regularly, but there's a lot of fun in playing different parts. And the parts that I have had this season, in spite of the other three plays being failures, were wonderful advertisements for me. Oh, yes, being in failures is the only way an actor can advertise—the managers see him oftener.

I have no recollection of ever making that dumb comment or certainly ever thinking it. Let's put it down to a press agent. They've made up lots of things for me to say without my knowledge or consent, and I don't blame them. Getting your name in the paper is their job.

My job was to get on with *The Little Teacher*. But not for long. In the middle of the run the draft board began to make funny noises, and so I left Miss Ryan and Batiste and sought a role for which I was totally miscast.

I enlisted as a sailor in the United States Navy. But I was confident I would not simply be a gob. George M. Cohan had become a friend, and he took steps to insure my naval career. He wrote the following letter:

New York, July 3rd, 1918

Mr. Mason Peters,
c/o Intelligence Bureau,
Washington, D.C.

Dear Mason:—

This letter will introduce to you Mr. Edward G. Robinson, a young gentleman who was in our *Little Teacher* cast last season. Mr. Robin-

son states he is very desirous of entering the Intelligence Bureau
Service, and he thinks he can qualify for same. Any courtesy you
can consistently show him will be appreciated by

Yours truly,
Geo. M. Cohan

GMC/BG

I put all my faith in Mr. Mason Peters.

7

If you listened to my family the night before I went to war, you would have had to believe that Josephus Daniels, Secretary of the Navy, having consulted with Mason Peters, was devoting his entire time to plans for me to take over naval intelligence. Against the day I would go behind the enemy lines, I was deluged with hand-knit scarves, gloves, and socks. There were tears and hugs as I left to make the world safe for democracy.*

It was not a very long trip because Pelham Bay Naval Station, where I was to report, was slightly less than eight miles from my home in the Bronx.

I can best sum up my hitch in the navy by admitting that I learned more about ships and navigation and the fleet from a picture I made years later—*Destroyer*, with Glenn Ford—than I ever learned at Pelham Bay. I also learned to make a knot.

I did all kinds of clerical and K.P. chores, worked on the coal pile doing what was widely known as shovel arms, even once got to get on the water (in a rowboat), earned three stripes as a first class seaman (though by no stretch of the imagination could I agree with the rating), and waited endlessly to be informed that I was to be sent to Washington to enter naval intelligence.

---

* I never cease to regret how glorious coinage, by sheer repetition, becomes meaningless and cliché. When President Wilson first used that phrase, it had the ring not of oratory but of incandescent truth. And would you believe "Lafayette, we are here!"?

It did not happen, but I was assured that it was being considered. And, mentally, I was already wearing that fabulous naval cape, the kind that President Roosevelt wore at Yalta.

Meanwhile, Philip Dunning, who later wrote the fabulous hit, *Broadway*, asked me to join an entertainment unit he had formed to tour military establishments and hospitals.

I turned him down because I hadn't joined the navy to be an actor. James Crane, my navy buddy (son of Dr. Frank Crane and later husband to Alice Brady), agreed with that position. We both felt that it was disgusting to put us in uniform under discipline and then ask us to perform our craft under conditions a great deal less than professional. If they wanted actors, they should have let us remain actors. There is a kind of insolence about asking you to double as a sailor and a performer. And anyway, naval intelligence was the goal.

After the armistice (I cried at the false one on November 9 and was dry-eyed at the real one on November 11) I was called into the commandant's office and told that my application for intelligence had been accepted. It seemed a little silly, what with the Kaiser at Doorn and Wilson pressing for his fourteen points at Versailles; the world was already almost safe for democracy, and I saw no need to continue in the navy. I was ready to be demobed.

I was not.

Those were miserable days, and I spent a lot of time at the movies. I disliked them, and except for an occasional Chaplin or Keaton or Fatty Arbuckle film, I thought them badly acted, insipid, and scarcely an art form. It seemed to me then that the only people who went into the movies and succumbed to their lure of gold were writers, directors, and performers—failures who couldn't make it on Broadway. To me, the living theater was the only theater and all the rest was nonsense.* I could not then see how the media would explode, how opportunities would extend beyond the silent movies to the talkies, to radio, to television, to God knows what.

But the movies could not completely fill the aching boredom of my peacetime navy life, and out of sheer desperation Jim Crane and I agreed to join with Philip Dunning to entertain in camps and hospitals.

There, for the first time, I saw what war was. In the hospitals, that is. Among the patients at some of the hospitals were casualties who had suffered "flash burns," the result of explosions of shell or gun emplacements or ammunition storage quarters aboard ship, sending

---

* Do you know, after over a hundred films, I still think so? I wish I could have arranged my life like Laurence Olivier. But I guess I got greedy.

sheets of flame through all open compartments and burning the ex-
posed flesh of men on duty there.

These men had lost ears, noses, mouths, eyelids, and fingers and
were so pitiable to look at that when their next of kin came to visit
them, they were advised to wait before seeing them until some recovery had been made through skin grafts or plastic surgery.

The ward in which these men were isolated was considered hard-
ship duty, for the smell of burned and decaying flesh was apparent
long before we approached the closed doors that led to the ward.

We went in and "entertained" them. Christ, what a word to use!
What I saw and smelled made me hate war with every fiber of my
being.

It seems to me now that the maturing process had begun to take
hold, though, God knows, I cannot attribute it entirely to the war.
After all, Pelham Bay was not Château-Thierry, but I did learn what
it was to live under involuntary restraint, and that takes the child out
of you—but not sufficiently for me to have the guts to hurt my parents by telling them that I would no longer live with them in their flat
in the Bronx.

By this time most of my brothers were married and procreating;
only Oscar, my Number Three brother, stayed at home with them.
For the record, he never married, never left them. I was caught in the
identical web, though now I realize it was a web of my own making.

My mother and father and Oscar had come from another tradition;
it bewildered them when I feebly suggested that I might like a place of
my own. I was struggling to find a way to be a bohemian and a
bourgeois at the same time. I was a coward. The bourgeois won. Why
not? Living with them made life easier: the washing, the ironing, the
mending, the eating—all of these were not a problem. Mama took
care of everything—and so, out of the navy at the age of twenty-six, I
continued to live with them.

It was not an easy thing to come to terms with; I wasn't with them
on a full-time basis. As much as I disliked touring, tour I did. And
in fact, right after my navy hitch, I signed with the Garrick Players
in Washington, D.C. I think I was rationalizing when I told myself I
would play a little stock and get back on my feet as an actor; the
truth may be closer to the fact that I wanted a transition between
the navy and the Bronx. I'm not certain now, but I've discovered
that no motive stands by itself; decisions are made seemingly on one
level, even though the deeper levels are invisible. Anyway, I played
such roles as "A Stranger" in *Polly with a Past*, and I think that was
type casting because I was a stranger to myself.

I was not alone. The atmosphere, after the joys of the armistice, was strange and foreboding for those of us who sought a world of peace and international comity. Woodrow Wilson had, as Martin Luther King had decades later, a dream, and I shared that dream—all fourteen points of it—and watched it come to nothing.* What a splendid vision the League of Nations was; how sickening to watch it scuttled.

And to watch freedom of choice scuttled as well in the guise of the Eighteenth Amendment and the Volstead Act was a further disappointment. As I listen now to the arguments about the legalization or decriminalization of marijuana, I remember Prohibition, and while I am sickened by those who need alcohol or pot to shut out the world, I know that it is impossible to impose morality by legislation.

I have seen in my personal life, with sadness and despair, the effects of alcohol in many people; show business seems to spawn alcoholism in many players and their children. But I know that no law will prevent an alcoholic from getting his booze, as no law will prevent a junkie from getting his fix. The impulse to quit must come from within. If determination and self-decision are not there, no law, no psychiatrist, no parent can cast out the sick craving.

My own craving was for work that would combine my trade with my social attitudes, but that was hard to come by then and is equally hard to come by now. The social play, except in the hands of a few masters, is difficult beyond measure to write. In lesser talents its good intentions are matched only by its dullness. It takes a genius to be significant without being boring.

Well, *Dark Horses*, in which I was rehearsing for William Harris, Jr., in 1919, was certainly not significant—and certainly it was not boring. But it wasn't really much of a play—a passable bit of entertainment, memorable to me only because I did not play a Japanese (who was really a Filipino) or an Italian or a Mexican or a Frenchman or a German or a Cockney, but an Anglo-Saxon. That was the first and only time.

It was also the only time I ever went on strike. And I'll tell you why: Up to the formation of Actors Equity, no actor was paid for unlimited rehearsal. (And I mean unlimited: Twenty-hour days were not exceptional.) In performance he could be hired for as little as fifteen dollars a week. No actor was paid subsistence for going on the road. No actor could be certain, if a play closed out of town, that his

---

* I was in the press gallery of the House of Representatives when President Woodrow Wilson returned from Europe and addressed Congress. I saw Senator Henry Cabot Lodge avoiding him. I heard Wilson's muted passion, and I cried.

fare would be paid back to New York. Or indeed that he'd get his salary. Few actors were paid more for doubling or tripling. The dressing rooms stank; lots of times we dressed in public toilets. Conditions were intolerable.

But the managers refused to recognize Equity, and large meetings were held. To their eternal glory, the stars then appearing on Broadway (notably Ethel Barrymore) joined with the lesser fry to strike until Equity with its minimum (oh, so minimum) demands would be recognized.

We marched. We picketed. We almost closed down Broadway. But not entirely. George M. Cohan, an actor himself and hero to most of us, stood adamant and almost singly against the strike. He tried to form The Fidelity League, a company union, if you like, but the rest of us would have no part of it.

I considered George M. a friend. Had he not, indeed, written to Mr. Mason Peters for me? I thought it time to write to him, and I did. Here's the best I can make of my first draft in my own handwriting. Half a century later, I find it somewhat illegible. The stationery was that of the Green Room Club:

George M.

In spite of the fact that this fight has taken on such profound dimensions my deep affection for you insists on keeping you a very central figure. Only the fact that I am deeply moved will excuse me for this note which I am writing with great respect.

At the Equity meeting yesterday afternoon the thought occurred to me often, notwithstanding the thrill and fine feeling of the occasion itself, that it was not perfect without you, that I couldn't get the idea out of my mind that you would be happier if you were there. This occurs to me as so possible a course for you that from my modest position I am going to suggest it: that you do now, with the situation locked, forgive some things that have offended you and acknowledge— with the humility which will exalt the high position that *your people*, the actors, have so generously given you—that you yourself did temporarily lose your way.

As I said in the beginning of this note, my deep affection for you will surely absolve me from an attempt to instruct you impertinently. I am honestly trying to serve you.

Very hopefully yours,
Eddie

He did not answer me.

Marching and picketing one day, we passed the George M. Cohan

Theatre on Forty-third Street and Broadway, and there in the lobby was Mr. Cohan, watching us, his face grim and set and angry. He turned from us as if we were offering him a personal affront.

But, after agony, Equity won, and we went back to work. Mr. Cohan never engaged me again, nor did he talk to me or acknowledge my existence.

Once the strike was settled, *Dark Horses* opened, only its title was changed to *First Is Last*, and the most memorable thing about it was that it made a star of Richard Dix. I think I experienced some envy.

I have from time to time.

In April of 1920 I was back in stride, and back, too, with Arthur Hopkins, playing "Satin" in Maksim Gorki's. *Night Lodging.*

I think I've already discussed the fact that I tried to pay no attention to critics, but I have to tell you that Alexander Woollcott, in reviewing the Gorki, stood me on my ear. He said of Edward G. Robinson (I use the third person because it hurts less):

> Here is a young actor seemingly without an atom of what is feebly called "personal distinction." His speech . . . is what dear Mrs. Sanders used to call "barbarous." He takes the keynote of the play where Satin cried out "What is truth? Human beings—that's the truth," and devastates it by saying "youman beans."*

Woollcott devastated me, and I don't think I've ever said "youman beans" since, and if there were such a thing as tape recordings in 1920, I might be able to prove that I hadn't said it then. But who am I to dispute Alec Woollcott? He was a brilliant critic (if, occasionally, sacrificing the exact truth to the felicitous phrase) and certainly one of the most urbane and civilized men I ever met in my life. When I look back upon the decade of 1920 to 1930, I recall it, too, was urbane and civilized.

Everybody else (well, not everybody else, but certainly a great many pseudo-historians) seems to recall it only as the Jazz Age. Let me assure you that there were complete half-hours in that time that I did not sip from a hip flask or do the Charleston. I never met Al Capone (or any other gangster); I had little truck with Joe College or

---

* Note from L.S.: Eddie wanted to use the Woollcott quote up to here. Here's the of it:

"Yet he might befoul a hundred speeches and still be worth his weight in gold. For the meaning of the role is in his mind, and the glow and the spirit of it comes forth from him. It is just such playing as his that answers best all the pishposh written in the critiques of the puppet-school."

Betty Co-ed or any other of John Held Jr.'s flock of long-legged, flat-chested flappers. I did go to speakeasies and Blind Pigs, but they seemed to be perfectly normal restaurants, and if there were any members of Flaming Youth around, I don't recall meeting them.

It was, indeed, the era of Warren Harding, Calvin Coolidge, and Herbert Hoover; certainly the stock market was climbing, and everybody toward the end of the decade, including shoeshine boys and men's room attendants, was accumulating shares of Cities Service and Yale and Towne on 10 percent margin. Most people were hardly aware that the Versailles Treaty would inevitably spawn a Hitler and that the Soviet Union, unrecognized by us, would eventually become a superpower. It was, in the view of the young and middle-aged who reflect upon it now, a mindless time.

On the contrary, it was the Golden Age of the novel and the the ater and of America's intellectual coming of age. Now I recognize that a Golden Age is always the one that preceded you. You never seem to be living in it; you've always just missed it by a hair—and thus, the 1920s did not seem all that golden to me, but they were. Believe me, they were.

Who was writing then? Well, forgive me another list, but when have we had novelists and poets comparable to Sinclair Lewis, Upton Sinclair, Amy Lowell, Edith Wharton, Ellen Glasgow, Edna St. Vincent Millay, Theodore Dreiser, James Branch Cabell, Sherwood Anderson, Edgar Lee Masters, F. Scott Fitzgerald, Zona Gale, Edward Arlington Robinson, Willa Cather, E. E. Cummings—need I go on?

And if we were singing "Yes, We Have No Bananas," and "Barney Google," in the theater, we were looking at the plays of Eugene O'Neill, Elmer Rice, Philip Barry, Bob Sherwood, Max Anderson, Hatcher Hughes, Lawrence Stallings, Sidney Howard, George Kaufman, Marc Connelly, George Kelly, and Paul Green. In music we had Rodgers and Hart, and Irving Berlin, Cole Porter, Jerry Kern, and shining above all, our first authentic American musical genius, George Gershwin. And don't let me leave out Ira.

Only in painting were we without extraordinary gifts. I would, during that decade, haunt the museums and the galleries, and while I had respect and admiration for Winslow Homer, Joseph Pennell, the Soyer brothers, George Bellows, and Reginald Marsh, my own emotional tastes ran, of course, to the Rembrandts and Goyas and Raphaels and Giottos, but even more emotionally and more securely to the French Impressionists, hardly yet in vogue. And, making an odious comparison, you could say that about me.

You could also say about me—and I'll say it about myself—that I was attaining some reputation as being more than a utility actor. Versatile is the word.

Booth Tarkington and George Arliss thought so, because later that year I was cast in the new Tarkington play, *Poldekin*, in which Mr. Arliss starred. No, he did not remember that I'd written him so long ago for advice, nor did I remind him. He was a remote figure, and the play, an anti-Bolshevik comedy, did not work very well. We opened in September, and guess when we closed. September.

By November I was at the Greenwich Village Theatre, courtesy of my great and by now good friend, Arthur Hopkins, playing in *Samson and Delilah*, staring Ben-Ami and featuring my one-sided romance, Pauline Lord. And there was another superb actor in the cast. His name was and is Sam Jaffe (unchanged, I hope you note), and today and for years and years before today, he is the closest friend I have in the world. He is a classical actor of mammoth proportion. I love him—and you'll hear more about him later. He was—and is— an enormous influence on my life.

At rehearsals Sam and I used to watch Ben-Ami, rapier slender, profile like a Greek god's, a matinee idol in the great tradition, and we would look at ourselves and each other and wonder. Well, we had one thing in common. We were all Jewish.

In many ways Ben-Ami was Jewisher than either of us. I remembered Rudolph Schildkraut's enlarged gestures and booming delivery. And that's what Ben-Ami was doing in this almost first off-Broadway theater.

It was Arthur Hopkins' technique as a director to have a first reading of a play and then disappear for a week while the actors got the play on its feet by themselves. Explanation: Without direction the cast takes the stage and finds its own movements. For instance, an actor (actress) walks stage left when he is comfortable or sits down when it seems suitable or rises when it seems even more suitable. These matters are usually supervised, indeed *ordered*, by a director. But in Mr. Hopkins' case he preferred to allot the cast one week to sort it out for themselves.

In many cases it worked, particularly if the actors saw themselves secondary to the play—the best interpretation of the text being the whole point. The actor's job is to plead the case of the play. The roles must be properly balanced—and, of course, if the play is a success, there is triumph enough for everyone. When the actors see themselves as *more* important than the play, anarchy!

I'm afraid Jacob Ben-Ami didn't agree. He was pig-headed, arrogant, and, I think, stupid.

He had theories about the profession, chiefly, his belief, I think, that he never had to freeze a part—that is, play it substantially the same. Now I know this may appear contradictory to something I said earlier. I do not believe in rigid performance, but when it comes to cuing another actor or being in position to confront or be confronted, I believe you have to say certain words and be in a certain place on stage.

Well, in that first week it was clear that Ben-Ami was very mannered and that, short of an accident, you could not count on his being where he was supposed to be.

Hopkins came in after the first week and did what he could. None of us was very happy, but we opened, and you never read such notices in your life—for Jacob Ben-Ami. He was called soul-shocking, thrilling, triumphant, convincing, wonderful, remarkable, the creator of a fourth dimension as an actor. Maybe he was the first of the method actors—or the last of the hams—but the audience worshiped him. I cannot say the same for the cast.

One night, when he was supposed to be facing me so that I could deliver a telling line, he turned away so that (I think) the audience could have a better view of his profile. I did the unforgivable. With one hand I grabbed him and turned him to me, and with the other I threw my prop cane.

You can bet the audience was now paying attention to me. It was a good trick. I learned it from him.

All this happened half a century ago (we ran a year), and Ben-Ami went on to become a truly distinguished actor. In the audience I've admired much of what he's done and possibly that works the other way around. But we've never discussed it, even when by miscalculation we played together again; our relationship has always been correct but cool.

My one scene in *Samson and Delilah* was hardly enough challenge for me, and I was delighted to do special matinees at the same theater of *Elvind of the Hills*. Playing with Margaret Wycherly was a joy, but I still wasn't content.

Arthur Hopkins came to me one afternoon and made a suggestion: The Selwyns and Sam Goldfish and their Goldwyn Company were making a movie at Fort Lee, New Jersey. Irvin Cobb had written it, and it was called *Fields of Glory*. Mr. Hopkins, interested in how films were made, was observing. There was a part exactly right for me. Would I take it?

Well, why not?

I'll tell you why not. I hated it. I tried. God knows, I tried, but there was no way to create or sustain a character, and how could you communicate nonverbally? I had to have words, speeches, scenes, confrontations, dilemmas. Above all, I had to begin slowly with a character and follow him through to a climax. (Acting is rather like sex that way.)

Well, in *Fields of Glory* the first scene I shot was the last scene in the movie, and when I went to look at the rushes, I couldn't believe that little gargoyle on the screen. I hated him. I hated me. I hated all movies. They were beneath me. Dorothy Gish, a glorious veteran of the movies, tried to comfort me and explain how it would all come out all right once it was cut and titles added—but I was unconvinced.

I didn't fit in, and I asked to be let out. I was refused.

Then one day Sam Goldfish (not yet Goldwyn) saw some of the cut stuff and sent a message that he heartily agreed with my request.

In a funny way, I was relieved—but hurt.

It was coming on to summer now, and in those days before air-conditioning or climate control, Broadway shut up tighter than a drum. And so I accepted an engagement at Elitch's Gardens in Denver, where we did a summer season of five plays. (I spare you the list.) Why?

Well, it was what President Nixon calls a "working vacation." I have rarely, if ever, had a vacation per se. I am no sportsman. I am not really comfortable away from paved streets. The most satisfactory nonwork interludes for me are those that occur while I'm working. That couple of days off from a film in Israel. Or that weekend in London. Those are my best times.

And that summer Denver got me away from the heat of New York (and the confinements of that flat in the Bronx) and the company was fun and talented and the girls of Denver were beautiful and willing and the schedule was not so tight and demanding that I did not have time to read.

No longer *The Saturday Evening Post*. And not novels. (I read those only when I'm told one of them will make a film.) No, nonfiction and magazines. I gorged on *The New Republic, Atlantic Monthly, The Nation,* and *Harper's;* I read books on politics, social problems, and comment. I was concerned then not only with a war that had apparently accomplished nothing but with a society that seemed to find no compromise between squalor and affluence and a nation in which the Ku Klux Klan was suddenly and appallingly revived.

If you add it all up, Rumania, the immigration to the Lower East Side, and the New York schooling, the Hearst editorials, C.C.N.Y., my considerable view of America as a traveling actor, the war, the disillusion with the election of Harding (I didn't vote for Cox; I voted for Norman Thomas), the consuming ideals that still motivated me, you have the makings of a textbook liberal.

The word "liberal" today really defies definition. So much of what plagued and tormented me then has already been obliterated. To my impatient granddaughter I try to explain the incredible advancements I've seen; she points out what there is left to be done. And I can only suggest that perfection in society is impossible to obtain. Which does not mean that it should not be sought.

All my life I have been on the side of those who try for it. I have, for years, deluded myself into thinking that I was an independent voter—that I didn't vote for a party, but for a man. (And I might add that it is my religion to vote—the most measly election with only one candidate on the ballot sees me at the polling place.) But I am not an independent, I am a Democrat.

I may be prejudiced and bigoted, smallish in my outlook, but I have rarely voted anything but the Democratic ticket. I may be naive to characterize the Republican party as being exclusively interested in the perpetuation of a hierarchy of privilege—and equally naive to believe that the Democratic party nationally believes in and cares for the people. That is not to suggest that the Democrats have not from time to time fielded some extremely unattractive candidates and that I have not been disappointed and disgusted by their performance, but, in sum, I prefer the Democrats to the Republicans, and that may be a faulty evaluation, but it is my evaluation.

On the whole subject of actors involving themselves in politics and causes—well, that certainly did not bother me that summer in Denver. This summer, in Beverly Hills, I think the answer lies in the fact that two actors with whom I've played had no qualms about entering the political arena when the opportunity presented itself. George Murphy recently became an ex-senator, and Ronald Reagan became governor of California, and God knows neither of them is a Democrat.

But, then, Jane Fonda is not a Republican.

During the summer Arthur Hopkins (how much I owe him!) sent me the script of a new play called *The Idle Inn*, and I liked the part of Mendel so much that I agreed to do it. What I did not know was that the starring part of Eisik was to be played by Jacob Ben-Ami.

Well, a job's a job, and I played the part for a few months at the Plymouth Theatre. We were not a howling success, and pretty soon we were (without Ben-Ami) rehearsing *The Deluge* again. Yes, *The*

Deluge. Mr. Hopkins loved that play and was determined that it would be a success.* We struggled with it; Arthur Hopkins kept it open until spring—but it never really made it.

Another summer was soon upon us, and again I did a season at Eltich's. They liked me in Denver. I had my picture on the cover of the program. When I look at it now, I cannot believe I was ever that young. I wasn't quite twenty-nine, and while I had now totted up a significant number of theatrical miles, that potential I'd always sought had not yet been found. I wasn't sure it ever would be. Looking back, I'm not sure it ever was.

Still, the important thing was to work, and that summer William Harris, Jr., sent me a script of a French play by Alfred Savoir adapted by Clare Kummer. It was called *Banco*. The part of Count Alexandre de Lussac (nicknamed Banco) was to be played by an actor named Alfred Lunt, who had recently married a young lady named Lynn Fontanne.

It was great fun when we all met again recently at a celebration of their fiftieth wedding anniversary.**

---

* This is not altogether unusual in the theater. Take the case of Tennessee Williams and *The Milk Train Doesn't Stop Here*. It was a flop in New York; but he did it twice more—and it was a flop all three times—but he loved it.

** Note from L.S.: I was there, and when Eddie was introduced, Mr. Lunt said, not entirely in jest, "Before he speaks, let me say he is the one actor in the world better than I." And Miss Fontanne said, "Nonsense. What we both know about Eddie is that he is an aristocrat!"

8

In due course I shall talk about the Lunts and the Theatre Guild, because my association with them led to one of my most fulfilling—and difficult—periods on the stage. But playing *Banco* with Alfred, I did not know that would happen. I was impressed with his total professionalism, but he was not easy to know.

Banco did not fare too well, and it looked as though I were about to have an unaccustomed period of unemployment when I received a visit from John Robertson, a movie director. He was to make for Inspiration Pictures a film called *The Bright Shawl* by Joseph Hergesheimer, and in it there was the part of Domingo Escobar. It was not the starring role; that was to be played by Richard Barthelmess, and Dorothy Gish, Mary Astor, and William Powell were also slated to be in the cast.

"Escobar," said Robertson, "should look like Oscar Hammerstein, and you look like Oscar Hammerstein. At least you looked like him in *Samson and Delilah*, and it's yours if you want it."

I didn't want it. I hated the movies, but I was unemployed, and there was no unemployment insurance then, and the money Robertson offered me was equivalent to twenty weeks' salary in a play. To top everything, the film was to be shot in Havana.

Now there you have the two elements that made the movies very appetizing: money and travel. And I have been motivated the same way a number of times since, not the money as much as the travel. In my later years I frequently accepted roles that would take me to a part of the earth where I'd never been before, all expenses paid.

(Where had the idealist gone? Well, all I can say is I was not really an idealist on a full-time basis. Sometimes, materialism was bound to take over.)

In any case, *The Bright Shawl* was not nearly as heartrending an experience as *Fields of Glory*. Still, the manufacture of a movie seemed silly and unrewarding to me. The only joy was the paycheck and being in Cuba.

That land's been so Castroized that you can't possibly imagine how gay and glorious it was then. No Prohibition, of course, and gambling to boot, blue movies, and a perpetual New Year's Eve–cum–Mardi Gras; I shamelessly confess that I never once looked at the ghastly conditions of the Cuban peasant. I was a tourist.

The film was finished in short order and opened at the Strand in New York. If you have forgotten what you got in the movie palaces of the twenties for less than a dollar, I think you might be interested in the program of the Strand Theatre when I went to see my horrible self in *The Bright Shawl*. Here it is:

PROGRAM

WEEK COMMENCING SUNDAY, APRIL 22nd, 1923

1. OVERTURE
    Selections from "TANNHAUSER" . . . . Wagner
    with Kitty McLaughlin, Soprano

    MARK STRAND SYMPHONY ORCHESTRA
    Carl Edouarde, Conductor

2. MARK STRAND TOPICAL REVIEW
    Pictorial News of the World, presented as fast
    as modern equipment can deliver

3. Prologue to "THE BRIGHT SHAWL"
    a) "In Old Madrid"
       Strand Male Quartet
    b) "Malaguenas"
       Maria Palay
       Amata Grassi
    c) Spanish Dance
       Maria Montero and
       Anatole Bourmann
    d) "Juanita"
       Strand Male Quartet

4. Inspiration Pictures, Inc.
    Chas. H. Duell, Pres., Presents

RICHARD BARTHELMESS
with Dorothy Gish
in
"THE BRIGHT SHAWL"
by Joseph Hergesheimer

5. Hal Roach presents
The Dippy Do Dads
in
"DON'T FLIRT"
Released by Pathe Exchange

6. ORGAN SOLO

Percy J. Starnes, Mus. Doc.⎫
⎬ Organists
Ralph S. Brainard   ⎭

Is it any wonder the movies were beginning to whittle away at the theater's audiences? The legitimate playhouses in New York and on the road were old, uncomfortable, drafty, cold in winter, and beastly hot in summer. The seats were narrow, and the space between the rows even narrower. On the other hand, the movie houses that were being built were marble and gold and red velvet and lit by enormous crystal chandeliers. I give you the New York Paramount or Capitol or Strand or the Roxy. I give you all those Balaban and Katz castles in Chicago.

Where the difference lay was, of course, in content. Rarely, then, did a picture say anything or deal with reality. It was pretty much all escape, but that's what the mass audience wanted—and the first significant slippage in theater attendance began to be noticed.

Not that anybody in the theater was aware of it—including me. What could compare to the theater, we asked, looking through imaginary lorgnettes? The silent movies—don't make me laugh! Radio? Well, really, good to listen to a Dempsey-Firpo fight, perhaps, but the A. and P. Gypsies and the Happiness Boys? Are you suggesting *they* could wean an audience away from Broadway? Nonsense!

As for talking pictures—if they were ever invented—just a fad! And in the big studios in Hollywood, the identical words, years later, were used about television.

When I went to the Strand to see myself in *The Bright Shawl*, it had to be a matinee, because the rest of the time I was appearing in Ibsen's *Peer Gynt*, which starred my classmate and friend, Joseph (Pepe) Schildkraut. It was the fourth production of the fifth subscription season of the Theatre Guild. I played the Button Moulder, a role that has some magnificent passages. While the Ibsen play is, in fact, a gruelling four-hour mixture of ballet, melodrama, and occasional profundity, it is curiously both classic and commercial. For Pepe, it was, of course, a field day.

For the Theatre Guild, it was the middle point of a dream that had started with the Washington Square Players. Lawrence Langner, Theresa Helburn, Philip Moeller, Maurice Wertheim, Lee Simonson, and Helen Westley, all authentic theater buffs, had nursed a dream for years. Beginning with the Washington Square Players, they'd planned a new era in the theater: repertory.

After all, every major nation except the United States had a national theater. The system of having a nucleus of an acting company that would play great plays, exchange roles, grow together as a unit, had been historically investigated and found sound in such great repertory companies as the Comédie Française, the Moscow Art Theatre, the Habima, the National Theatre in Britain. It had never been permitted life in the United States.

I have no clear idea why. I know some of the elements, if I cannot put them together as a viable whole. I think chiefly the arts were, until after the Second World War, considered effete, unsuitable in a pioneer nation. What would a red-blooded American male say if his son were to come to him and suggest that he wanted to be a ballet dancer?

What would a congressman say if the national treasury were to be used (even in some minuscule part) to fund an opera company or a symphony orchestra or an acting company in which the players wore doublet and hose and wrote letters with feathers?

We were a nation, I think, obsessed with the Judeo-Christian ethic and the supermale frontier tradition. It was all right to have museums, if they were housed in pseudo-Greek temples and hung the old masters. Government would help with that, all right, but it took private groups to permit modern art (contemporary art, twentieth-century art) in public view. It was perfectly all right to do the Greek plays or Gogol as long as no public money was involved and there was no obscenity.*

It was in this period, you must remember, that a patrol wagon

---

* A recent statistic might be of interest. It appeared in *Variety*:

"A combination of the old Puritan bias against entertainment and a habit of limiting the Washington pork barrel to the building of new post offices and such has kept the U.S. relatively backward on a per capita basis as to arts subsidy. We average 15¢ a head, whereas Western Germany spends $2.42 and little Austria and Sweden manage $2 a head to the arts. Our northern neighbor, Canada, appropriates $1.40 per head per year."

drove up to the stage door and carted Mae West off to the Tombs for appearing in a play called *Sex*, the subject of which was clearly sex—and for another patrol wagon to cart Helen Mencken off for appearing in *The Captive*, which gingerly dealt with the most subtle emanation of lesbianism.

Well, why not? Books were being banned in Boston. You were arrested if you brought a copy of James Joyce's *Ulysses* into the country; the United States had had its moral lines drawn by that fanatic antipornographer Anthony Comstock. The painting of *September Morn*, a badly executed female nude, was considered outrageous and detrimental to public morals.

Today, when anything goes (and most things should), we look back upon that time as absurdly regressive. I wonder how we'll look back upon these times. As absurdly vulgar? Could be, you know.

In any case, the Guild, in the best tradition of private enterprise, was doing its damnedest to bring the great playwrights and the great plays to America under circumstances that would also provide the very best performance, direction, and design. And to a very large extent, they succeeded.

They were hell to work for.

Not the least of the agonies was the way all of the guild board members would appear on a Sunday afternoon during rehearsals while we ran through the play. There they were—each member making notes, each having his separate and individual opinion. Art by committee is, by definition, impossible. That the Guild people made it work says something for their zeal and their dedication. Reflecting on the matter over the years, I think the theater owes them all a great deal. I could only have wished they had been less authoritarian and more generous. Still, I suppose I was doing well enough. You could say I was doing what comes naturally—living beyond my means.

By this time I was a member of the Green Room Club and the Lambs. The great restaurant, denied me earlier, now became commonplace. I took, like a duck to water, to custom-made suits and those great and glamorous black-tie-and-tails (I now had both) parties at the Ritz Carlton, now sadly replaced by a stupid office building. My favorite restaurants were on lower Fifth Avenue—the Brevoort and the Lafayette—now replaced by stupid office buildings. Going to them, I'd always sneak a look at Mark Twain's house, now sadly replaced by a stupid apartment house. I would go to those wonderful Sunday night concerts at the Metropolitan Opera House, now sadly replaced by a stupid office building. And I went to Carnegie Hall (unstupidly not replaced by anything) and heard Heifetz,

Elman, and Geraldine Farrar and listened to Toscanini scale ecstatic heights.* And I heard Gigli and Caruso and saw Pavlova and Nijinsky.

For me, New York was the center of the world—glamorous, filled with gorgeous women, paradise for a young bachelor with a featured part in a successful play.

A young bachelor who continued to live in the Bronx with his mother and father. Well, at least, he now took cabs instead of the subway, watching the clicking meter with fearful concentration.

During the run of *Peer Gynt* I remember that Rudolph Schildkraut came to see his son, Pepe, and I talked with him backstage afterward.

"Aren't you proud of your son?" I asked him.

He nodded, and then added sadly, "So after *Liliom* and *Peer Gynt*, what is there left for him to do?"

I was not unaccustomed to that kind of particularly Jewish attitude. Success was all very well, of course, but current success made future success all the more difficult. My own father, who would come to see me, was always very guarded in his criticism. "That was very nice, my boy," he would say, "but it could have been maybe a little nicer."

I found that kind of unwillingness to go all out in praise difficult to take then; I find it is precisely what I myself do now. Maybe it comes with years; maybe we learn that success and fame are transitory, that a sweet today is almost certainly to be followed by a bitter tomorrow. Who knows that better than I? Thank God, I didn't know it in 1923.

If He has given us one marvelous gift, it is that He does not permit us to know the future. It would be unbearable.

During the run of *Peer Gynt* Terry Helburn came to me and offered me, on behalf of the Theatre Guild, the role of Shrdlu in Elmer Rice's *The Adding Machine*. I read it with fascination. It was an extraordinary work, far ahead of its time, symbolic, avant-garde, and marked by a deft use of stream of consciousness. To somebody like myself, accustomed to the well-made play, depending on cause and effect, it seemed that one scene didn't go with another. And yet it cast a spell. It was expressionism in the theater, and I hastened to agree to do it.

Philip Moeller directed, and he was a man bursting with ideas,

* I have a review of him. "Not a single failing; impeccable virtuosity in every section; admirable sonorities, rounded, full, warm and brilliant . . . passages of ethereal sweetness and an inexorable precision of rhythm."

completely uninhibited. Sometimes they were odd and ridiculous, but if you sifted them, some of them turned out to be significant and marvelous. He illuminated the play for the actor—and, I think, for the playwright as well.

Ludwig Lewisohn, reviewing it for *The Nation*, summed it up well:

> Mr. Rice's vision of the world may infuriate you. There were people behind me at the Garrick who first grumbled and then cursed politely. You cannot miss it; you cannot withdraw yourself from its coherence and completeness. Examine his play scene by scene, symbol by symbol. The structure stands. There are no holes in its roof. It gives you the pleasure of both poetry and science, the warm beauty of life and love, the icy delight of mathematics.
>
> I am aware of the fact—critics should make this confession oftener—that my profound sympathy with Mr. Rice's substance necessarily colored my reaction to his play. Not, however, to its form, not to the heartening fact that here is an American drama with no loose ends or ragged edges or silly last-act compromises, retractions, reconciliations. The work, on its own ground, in its own mood, is honest, finished, sound. . . . The play constitutes one of the major achievements in the entire field of the American arts.

Alec Woollcott, on the other hand, said: "It's another stage version of 'Gee whiz, what's the use?' " Still, he urged the people to see it. They ignored him. We ran for nine weeks, seventy-two performances. But the play did not die. It has been revived a thousand times since, because its comments on an automated society now seem more relevant than ever.

The durability of a play, its performance, its ability to speak across the years, indeed, across the centuries, is the peculiar miracle of drama as it is of music—great music—art. And literature.

What "great" means I cannot presume to know; it is, in the end, a cumulative decision of the literate—not necessarily the individual decision of the critic. Critics today, it seems to me, are tougher, harder, and equipped with lesser credentials. They tend to treat fad as art, symbolism as pervasive, experiment as genius. Just read some art criticism, for instance (I find it gobbledegook), or drama reviews in the more advanced little magazines or movie reviews in your local paper. I think the new breed of critic puts himself above the work, and what I find unforgivable is not that he has never done the work but that he is ignorant of the process by which it comes to be created.

The critics in Chicago who reviewed *The Voice*, in which I worked again with William Courtenay in Chicago in the late spring of 1923, murdered us. In absolute contradiction to everything I've said a moment ago, they were right. The play was terrible. Mr. Courtenay was terrible, and so was I. And, let us face this clear fact: We knew it, but as you rehearse and the play begins to come to some kind of life, you tell yourself little lies that you *have* to believe if you're to go on, and the play doesn't seem so bad after a while. Actually, it begins to feel pretty good. Then you open—and *wham*!

What the critics are telling you, you knew all along.

Take the next job—*Launzi*, written by Ferenc Molnar and adapted by Edna St. Vincent Millay. Miss Millay certainly knew her figs from thistles; Molnar had been hailed for *Liliom*. Pauline Lord was the great star, and Arthur Hopkins, a man of whose taste you must be tired of my telling you, was the producer and director. None of us had the slightest doubt about this play; we were nuts.

The reviews were mixed, which is simply another way of saying that some critics loathed it and some could barely tolerate it. We closed forthwith.

That was October 1923, and, believe it, in a few weeks I was rehearsing with Ethel Barrymore in *A Royal Fandango*. Hey, what about the kid from Bucharest even *walking* on the same stage with Ethel Barrymore!

Well, I've got news for you; it wasn't much fun. Arthur Hopkins pulled his usual stunt of leaving the actors alone for a week to find their own places and get the play on its feet. I soon discovered that Miss Barrymore—and why not?—did what came naturally to her: took the stage, filled it, and left the rest of us to stage rear.

Among the rest of us was an intense young man playing Holt, whose name was Spencer Tracy. I have no way of checking this, but I think it was his first appearance on the stage. I saw nothing remarkable in him.

And I saw no chance for me in *The Royal Fandango*, which we referred to (not facetiously) as *The Royal Fiasco*. Looking back on it now, I have unconsciously, now and again, been guilty of Miss Barrymore's position. When the play is written for you and you are a star, you automatically take stage center—not intending to humiliate or upstage the rest of the cast, but doing it nonetheless. After all, the audience would pay to see Miss Barrymore, not Spencer Tracy or me. And she was, as I have been, instinctively aware of that.

Nevertheless, I found it distressing, and when Mr. Hopkins appeared to take over, I gathered all my courage and said to him, "I'd like to be let out."

He did not seem in the least astonished. He merely asked why. I told him, "I know I'm a supporting actor and Miss Barrymore's a great star, but the way the play is staged, all the values are distorted."

"Okay," said Mr. Hopkins, and with the skills and subtleties I envied him, he made no great point of what I'd said but maneuvered and restaged the scenes—with Miss Barrymore fighting every position change. Actually, she finally gave in. Hopkins' direction gave the play more vitality and reality—but not enough.

We ran twenty-four performances. Miss Barrymore *was* indignant. Even for her, the theater was a crap game. Throw the dice and come up hit or flop.

I thought there had to be a better way. I still think there has to be a better way.

In 1923, however, there were almost a hundred playhouses in New York; the road was flourishing; stock companies were still viable in almost every city, and few paid any attention to the theater as art, as a mirror of society, as a cultural resource. But then few people were really paying much attention to what later we could see as an inevitable race to depression and eventual war.

Warren Harding died in San Francisco, and Calvin Coolidge was sworn in as President by his father. I guess we were keeping cool with Coolidge (curious that "cool," a Republican word, became so fashionable in the sixties as a thoroughly non-Republican word), and we paid little or no attention to Senator Walsh's investigation of Tea Pot Dome or the inflation surfacing in Germany or the fact that Dr. Lee de Forest unveiled a process for producing sound motion pictures called Phonofilm. That last was a small item in *The New York Times*. I read it when we were rehearsing *Royal Fandango*, and I sniffed. But I kept the clipping.

I didn't carry it with me when I went dancing at the Biltmore Cascades and the orchestra played "I Want to Be Happy" from *No, No, Nanette*. I think that was what 1923 was about. Everybody wanted to be happy. What we didn't take into consideration was that Vincent Youmans, who wrote it, made it quite clear that we couldn't be happy unless you were happy too.

That's Christian and political, and pretty symbolic of what all the minority agony is today. None of us can be happy unless all of us are, and maybe that's why *No, No, Nanette*, in revival, is a hit again.

I just thought I'd mention it.

9

In the winter of 1924 Harry Wagstaff Gribble and Gertrude Purcell completed their dramatization of Olive Higgins Prouty's *Stella Dallas*, a novel that had had major celebrity. (It's all about how Nobody Came to the Party.) The Selwyns, chiefly Arch, loved the script and cast about for an actress of some eminence to play Stella. Somebody came up with the name of Mrs. Leslie Carter whose eminence could not be in doubt but whose age was somewhat older than Stella's.

Mrs. Carter was not only a name in the theater; she was by way of being a legend. Her talents were undisputed, her reputation for attracting audiences phenomenal. So what if she were a bit long in the tooth? She could play *anything*.

I was offered the role of Ed Munn, Stella's sometime lover and later husband. It was too good to turn down, and the prospect of playing with Mrs. Carter was tempting. I had seen her in those early forays I made to Broadway in my C.C.N.Y. days when I was sixteen and she was a mature woman. But, as frequently happens in the fantasies you have about actresses, it had never occurred to me that she had aged. She had.

We rehearsed. I was skeptical. When we opened, I had even more reason to be. Mrs. Carter wore the same dress on stage, in performance, as she had in rehearsal. As far as I knew, it was the only one she owned. Her dressing room was locked shut so that we could not see her making up or become privy to the fact that her hair was a wig.

Today wigs are in fashion. Back then a wig on a modern character was unmentionable.

That was not the only unmentionable. First, she thought I might marry her;* secondly, on stage Mrs. Carter would doze, waking just in time to step on my line. I mentioned it to her courteously, then a little more firmly, and finally even angrily. But nothing would change her. Who could blame her? The critics, blinded by their adoration and memory of her, threw bouquets and words like "imperishable" and "thrilling." I got a "commendable."

I'm surprised I reached even that height, because playing with her was so difficult. In order to achieve some balance in our ages (I was thirty and she was God knows what) I put a ton of cornstarch in my hair to try to look as white and old as possible. She said to me: "Aren't you putting too much gray in your hair, Eddie?" Then she went to sleep again, waking up just in time to kill my laugh. Nothing I could say to her would stop this deplorable habit, which I suspected was deliberate. Finally, I stopped talking to her.

It was the custom in those days to take your bows at the end of each act, thus firmly destroying any illusion. During one of those, when she (of course, first) stepped back from the apron, I bowed to the audience and then to Mrs. Carter, and then the curtain rang down. I started off. She held my arm.

Coyly she said to me, "When are you going to start talking to me again, Eddie, darling?"

I replied, "When you learn to behave yourself, Mrs. Carter, darling."

Mrs. Carter darling kissed me and promised to behave, but she never did. The stage manager understood my plight and did his best and would report to me in my dressing room, and we'd chat—and I was astonished at his knowledge of the theater. I shouldn't have been. His name was George Cukor.

I am sorry I did not understand Mrs. Leslie Carter then; I understand her now. She had been playing all her life; she was determined to go on with it. As *I* am now.

What I learned from her and from other actors who grow older is that you must play only those parts that are suitable to your age and your remaining range (though sometimes that range is far less limited than you tell yourself). It seems to me that a gifted actor of experience can do almost anything on the stage or screen; the one thing he

* Note from L.S.: Eddie was so conservative in his speech that he didn't really mean "marry." The twinkle in his eye meant that Mrs. Carter would not have been averse to carnal knowledge of him. But Eddie was too much of a gentleman to say so. He preferred to suggest she wanted to marry him.

cannot and must never try to do is portray youth. That nobody can get away with, and women have an even tougher time of it than men. No amount of makeup can make you *look* young; no amount of rehearsal can make you *act* young. Better—far better—to reconcile yourself to the character role.

It is not an easy reconciliation, particularly when, through electronic intervention, you are now faced with yourself on the late late show— your young self. I caught a glimpse of a man billed as Edward G. Robinson the other night on an obscure channel playing with Humphrey Bogart in a film called *Brother Orchid*. I thought both Bogart and Robinson overacted, shouted a little too much, and occasionally were very good indeed. Robinson would have played the character quite differently today; I suspect Bogie would have too.

It is oddly disconcerting to have performance made permanent; the only relics of those more than forty plays I did on the stage are yellowing notices. What I did on the screen is instantly available— and about 50 percent of the films I would gladly burn. I'm still proud of about 10 percent of them. But I really don't feel I had anything to do with them; they were played by a very eager young actor; they are now watched by a very critical old actor.

Well, this critical old actor thought nothing of taking what little savings he had after that engagement in *Stella Dallas* and going to Europe for the first time. I call it the first time because by this juncture I had almost forgotten the fact that I had *come* from Europe. It was silly and extravagant of me, but when it comes to money I have always been silly and extravagant. My grandmother's fault.

I remember that from the first we used to give her gifts—scarves, purses, handkerchiefs, lacy frilly things—and she would be grateful and put them away in her bureau drawer. We'd say, "Grandma, use them. Wear them. Put them on." And she would smile a little and nod her head, amused by our impatience, and say, "I'll wear them later —on an occasion. I'll save them for when it's necessary." Well, it never was necessary, and after she died, we found all those things in mint condition in their original packages. That's what motivated me— grandma's waiting for an occasion that never happened.

So I made my own occasion and sailed for Europe—first class! England was first, and I nearly went out of my mind with excitement —the plays, the restaurants, the world of Dickens, Westminster, Whitehall, and Parliament. You have never known a sightseer like me. I'd start out for the Tower of London every day and never make it because I'd go exploring down a side street first. And the galleries, the pictures! Wow! Those Rubens at Windsor; those Tintorettos; those Michelangelos; those Goyas!

In Paris I almost went berserk with elation. I haunted the Louvre and the shops on the Faubourg St. Honoré. My eye was dazzled by sketches by Michelangelo, Raphael, and Correggio—and Manet's *Dejeuner sur l'Herbe, The Portrait of Émile Zola,* Renoir's *Moulin de la Galette, The Hanged Man's House* by Cézanne, and Degas' *Bellelli Family.* I bought a hundred prints.

And would you believe it, I found a curious comfort and familiarity in Paris that I did not find in London. My French was only fair, but it worked in France. My English was, I thought, perfect, but it sounded strange and alien in England. In London I bought a homburg and a cane in order to melt into crowds, but I should have known —that external props do not create a character in life any more than they do in the theater.

I have an American voice, and I have never tried to assume a West End accent. It would be as absurd as an English actor trying to play an American (with only one exception: Peter Ustinov). We are cast by our own cultures and environments into roles from which we cannot escape. I can play and have played a variety of dialects—some good, some not so good—but the one thing I cannot play is an Englishman. As for a *young* Englishman . . .

Back from Europe, I played an Italian—Ottaviano, the Duke's cousin—in *The Firebrand* by Edwin Justus Mayer. It starred Joseph Schildkraut as Benvenuto Cellini and Frank Morgan, that most delightful of men, as Allesandro, the Duke of Florence. We all wore tights. Mine were red.

I am about to indulge in a spate of conceit. One of the critics said I had "the best legs in the cast." And I did not wear symmetricals.*

We were a hit even though the play was a very free exercise of the lives of the Medicis and Cellini. As a matter of fact, the author insisted on this note in the program: "For the historically minded playgoer: *The Firebrand* is a comedy rather than a document. Its author, Mr. Mayer, has utilized rather than chronicled Benvenuto Cellini."

Well, utilized or chronicled, the play was hugely successful, and the audience roared with laughter. The problem on stage was that we did the same thing. Frank Morgan (who loved his bourbon—more than once I had to make him up and guide him on stage where he would instantly sober up and play splendidly) was a wag. There was a scene in which he condemned Nana Bryant (I think it was Nana Bryant) to

---

* Symmetricals are leg falsies. They give the calf what nature has neglected. I plan to ask the publisher of this book to use a photograph of me as Ottaviano; I am inordinately proud of the way I looked in those red tights. (See photo section— *Ed.*)

death, and he would always break up, shattering the rest of us in the process. You cannot imagine what it is like to be shaking with laughter inside and trying to keep a deadly serious face at the same time. I have always been surprised that the audience never catches on.

After each performance I'd go for supper and dance with some gorgeous chick, take her home, and then commandeer a taxi to the Bronx.

Then I could endure it no longer. I took a flat at the Guilford, an East Side apartment building on Forty-sixth Street consisting of living room, bedroom, kitchen, and bath, then gathered all my courage to announce this startling fact to my mother and father and my brother Oscar.

The moment I had dreaded passed with very little drama; their resignation to my leaving home was at first silent, and then followed discussions of interior decoration. After all, Oscar was a cabinet-maker and Zach was an upholsterer. They helped me, and their passion for quality can best be demonstrated by telling you that I am now sitting in a chair originally made by Oscar and upholstered by Zach. It doesn't fit the classic definition of antique, but it's rapidly getting there.

Living alone for the first time in your life takes a bit of getting used to. Certainly there is joy in not having to check in, in bringing friends home, in doing anything at any hour at your own impulse. On the other hand, there's cleaning and dishes and polishing and laundry and garbage and having your suits pressed and your shoes shined and marketing, and the whole thing is boring and exasperating until you develop a routine (and even after). For me that was particularly difficult since those things had automatically been done for me either at home or at a hotel or a boardinghouse.

Nothing, I discovered, is an unmixed blessing. You achieve a long-sought goal only to discover that it is fraught with its own set of problems. And if that's true of domesticity, it's doubly true of career. Envy not the Broadway actor or the movie star; he has the same bellyaches as you. More, maybe, because his hours are so odd. Sleep late because you've been out till two or three in the morning, unable to dine with friends at a normal hour because at that normal hour you're shmearing makeup on your face. (And, in the movies, bed at nine o'clock because you've got to be up at half past five.)

The answer to a good deal of this for the actor is an understanding wife who will take care of all the chores and keep the household and social agonies away from you. But I didn't want a wife. I was thirty-one; I'd lived too long in my own monomanic world. I'd played the field; I'd been accounting for my movements too long to my family. I wished never to account again.

Living at the Guilford and egged on by Sam Jaffe, I began to cut something of a swathe in New York society. Certainly, by this time, I knew or had played with all the first-rate actors; I'd come to know a great many of the first-rate authors, and now I was beginning to meet musicians and artists and philosophers and publishers.

The top social royalty, of course, was the remnants of the Four Hundred—the Vanderbilts, Astors, Guggenheims, and Oelrichs. I never got a nod from them, though I think Miss Barrymore spent a great deal of time eating off their gold plate.

At the second level was the Algonquin crowd—Woollcott, Dorothy Parker, Neysa McMein, George Kaufman, Harold Ross, of *The New Yorker*, Marc Connelly. You know the cast: men and women of wit and substance who shaped what we all read and admired on a delightful but superficial level. (Lee Gershwin recalls there was a good deal of back-biting.)

I never lunched at the Algonquin Round Table. I was big with what we called the Paley crowd.

Emily Paley was Lee Gershwin's sister, and so automatically George and Ira were there. And so were Simeon Strunsky, a man of vast intellect and editor of *The New York Times Book Review*, and Walter Damrosch and Leopold Stokowski and Sol Hurok and Jascha Heifetz and Elman and Rubenstein and Gigli and Gatti-Cassaza and Frances Alda and Buddy da Silva and Sam Behrman and Pepe Schildkraut. How to describe it—the closest thing to a salon in New York: warm, turbulent, and brilliant.

And highly political, deeply aware of trends in society. Good talk and liberal talk and, as it turned out, prophetic talk.

But mostly music. Thus I bought a secondhand upright piano, which I played torturously, and eventually replaced it with a Steinway Ampico—an extraordinary invention born of the old-fashioned player piano—that would play transcribed rolls of the great pianists faithfully and beautifully. I had the piano so arranged that anybody coming into the apartment could see me at the keyboard and think I was playing Chopin.*

That was a prank I enjoyed and inflicted on my friends a great many times. Because, you see, by now I was entertaining others, returning all the wonderful hospitality that had been heaped on me. I

* The rumor that I was a piano virtuoso started then and ended when I was asked to perform at the Tanglewood Music Festival. It was hard to explain that I could play only a few pieces, mostly exercises from the lesson book by Czerny.

gave parties. Sherry did not cater them, and they were not as glorious as the one the Brothers Selwyn gave at the Hudson Theatre to celebrate the hundredth performance of *Under Fire*. But they were pretty good, and I enjoyed being the host. (I love it today, especially when my wife, Jane, handles all the details and all I have to do is go from table to table offering chit-chat and cigars.)

One of the best inventions, of course, is the aftertheater party because it really doesn't begin until about midnight and people have been to theater or the opera or a concert and they're full of excitement and gossip, and they're really hungry. Besides, you don't have to give them a sit-down dinner. You just do a buffet with lots of stuff from the delicatessen (I think Reuben's) and one hot dish and lots of coffee and Streusel cake, and there's always a buzz of conversation and somebody's playing the piano, and it's *gemutlich*.

To one of those particularly *gemutlich* evenings I invited a stockbroker who lived in the Guilford, and he arrived with a lady named Gladys Lloyd. What I felt when I first saw her has to be described in the phrasing that was not then cliché: I thought her a vision of loveliness. Tall, beautiful, aristocratic, contained, groomed, witty, and with natural charm Gladys was.

And In Love At First Sight I was.

I have always been jealous of my own privacy, and I've tried to keep my private life as private as possible. But I learned a long time ago that this is not *very* possible. From the moment Gladys and I began seeing each other regularly, we were the subject of speculation in the columns—Winchell, Sobol, Karl Kitchen, "Town Topics," and, of course later, Louella Parsons and Hedda Hopper. I sometimes wonder if this at first muted and later intense glare in which we lived was measurably responsible for our breakup and divorce. But here I am talking of divorce, and we are not yet married.

It took time for us to come to that decision. From Gladys' point of view, I think, there were few obstacles. She had been married and divorced, was the mother of a young daughter, was fairly successful as an actress, drew and painted in her spare time, and was ready for marriage again. We had a great deal in common: the theater, art, mutual friends; we were apparently moving in the same orbit.

But there were problems. Gladys was the quintessential American Protestant, a Daughter of the American Revolution, and I was Jewish. Was it possible for me to marry a non-Jew? What would mama and papa think? And what about Gladys' previous divorce and her child? Could I live with that?

I confess that her non-Jewishness weighed heavily, but not as heavily as the divorce and the child. Divorce was certainly a dirty word, and the prospect of ready-made fatherhood was scary. Added to that was Gladys' manner, her unpredictability—one moment loving and the next cool. She seemed to be using my love (infatuation?) for her as a weapon. Or was I merely seeking excuses—excuses I refuted because I wanted her so terribly—*all* of her?

It is almost too easy now to realize how instinctive my conflicts were. But my reflexes were so conditioned that what are very little problems now were very major ones then. There I was, caught between what I really wanted and a background that seemed to make fulfillment impossible.

It took two years to resolve the torture, though I think it was never totally resolved, and those self-doubts were time-released capsules of poison that eventually led to an ugly dissolution. But I could not have known that then, and had someone predicted the future, I would have scoffed.

For we were having a marvelous time. Lunch at the Colony and dinner at Voisin (when I wasn't playing) and the Met on Sunday nights. There were afternoons of doing the art galleries and parties and fun and, above all, a closeness I had never had with a woman. For that, I am forever grateful to her. I don't know if she shared that feeling, but you know something? I think so.

I cannot be sure, because—I must keep repeating it—some of Gladys was always an enigma to me. She held back, kept part of herself in reserve. Even in the love she gave there was something of a New England schoolteacher. I sometimes think she avoided, even disliked, my Jewishness. There was always a thin curtain between us. It eventually became a wall. Though we were married for more than twenty-five years, the wall never came down.

Thus, I never knew until I married Jane in the mid-1950s what a woman and a man could be to each other. Oh, surely, we have had our minor difficulties, but I never feel there is a private sector fenced off from me. And I fence nothing off from her. I often wonder how she stands it.

After *The Firebrand* closed (and because of Gladys I would not tour with it), the Theatre Guild came to me again and offered me the role of Caesar in Shaw's *Androcles and the Lion,* and I would also play Guiseppe in the curtain raiser, Shaw's *Man of Destiny.* I would not have hesitated a moment if they'd offered me the role of Napoleon in that play—but they did not; that was reserved for Tom Powers.

I've always wanted to play Napoleon (I'm the right height), and years later Jack Warner commissioned Emil Ludwig to do a screenplay of his own fabulously best-selling biography of Napoleon, but it didn't work out. The net result is that I've never played Napoleon, and that's a pity.

I hesitated a long time over the Guild offer: I had too many memories of those Sunday afternoon run-throughs, with the Guild committee making notes. And yet, what other producers were doing Shaw? So I agreed.

The play was designed by Miguel Covarrubias, and it was heaven to play with Henry Travers and Claire Eames (Mrs. Sidney Howard). It was equally wonderful to read those Shaw lines and to be menaced by Romney Brent's lion.

I am a Shaw lover, and while his reputation zigs and zags, it is my strong view that he will be remembered among the great playwrights of all time. When you think of *Saint Joan, Major Barbara, Candida*, and *Androcles*, how can you doubt it?

And a slight belated bow to Lawrence Langner, of the Guild, who persuaded Shaw to permit his plays to be performed here. If the Guild did nothing else, that entitles it to immortality. And I see that I have left out *Pygmalion*. It would be absurd to leave out *Pygmalion*.

I cannot say that I was altogether happy with the salary the Guild paid me or their treatment of actors, but I certainly was impressed with their tastes and their aspirations. They were always discussing repertory, in which actors would revolve roles,* in which plays would not be revived, but would continuously be in view.

Certainly I admired the fact that they were grooming young people. In 1925, at the Garrick Theatre, they opened for special matinees a little revue called *The Garrick Gaieties*, with a score written by two kids barely out of Columbia University—Dick Rodgers and Larry Hart. It was so successful and funny and witty that it went into regular performance, and the whole town was dancing and singing *Manhattan*. In the Paley crowd, in which Gladys and I were now regulars, we all knew the lyrics—the incomparable Larry Hart lyrics—our own twentieth-century Gilbert, a funny-looking, short, cigar-smoking imp whose theme throughout life was unrequited love.** He said it was a bore but that he had it awful bad.

God knows, *I* was not suffering from unrequited love—and what I

* One night you would play the lead, and the next night you would play the second lead, as Laurence Olivier and Tony Quinn did, years later, in the New York production of *Becket*.

** Ira Gershwin was more of a poet than Larry, and I think his work will outlast Larry's. But add Cole Porter and you have the three great lyricists of the twentieth century. Add Irving Berlin and you have four.

had was not a bore, and I had it awful bad. I wanted to marry Gladys, and she wanted to marry me, but I still couldn't do it.

So what did I do? I did another play for the Guild, Franz Werfel's *Goat Song*, which opened in January 1926—and that was the second time I played with Alfred Lunt and the first time I played with Lynn Fontanne.

Books and books have been written about them, and there is little point in discussing their talent and their well-deserved glories. But I *can* add something: They had the singular advantage of being married. After rehearsals were over for the day, we all went about our business. But not the Lunts. They kept rehearsing at home—refining, manicuring, probing every subtlety, mining every line to eliminate dross, and find pure gold. And God knows they found it.

They made it tough on the rest of us, yet it was also a challenge, driving us to refine our own performances (as Laurence Olivier made Michael Caine better in *Sleuth*).

And just think of the supporting company: Harold Clurman, certainly today one of the great figures of the theater, was practically a super. Lee Strasberg, the king and mentor of method acting, *was*, indeed, a super. And Philip Loeb, Blanche Yurka, Dwight Frye, Bela Blau, and Zita Johann. It was quite a group and, for me, an artistic challenge and a learning experience.*

Werfel had written a play about the trans-Danube countryside of the eighteenth century. To the sorrowing lady of its greatest house a monster is born—perhaps a curse, perhaps the seed of Pan. It is a creature so terrible, so unthinkable, that they can neither kill nor look upon him. After twenty-three years of being successfully hidden, the monster escapes. Revolution, terror, and violence sweep the land.

The subject was tremendously felt by Werfel—so much so that the play was undisciplined and uncontrolled, and it was evident that volcanic passion seethed inside the author, requiring clarification and sobriety on the part of the players and the director.

I played a Jew, a *kibitzer* (literally translated as a bird who pecks at other birds' nests), and I received hundreds of letters accusing me of anti-Semitism. I didn't feel the character was offensive, rather pathetic, if anything. But the letters disturbed me. As the play disturbed New York.

What did it mean? Was it symbolism? Was it prophetic? Was it satire?

---

* I use the words advisedly; a lot of these young players broke off from the Guild and formed the Group Theatre. They did remarkable plays and were highly politicized.

The Guild held three Sunday afternoon forums to which the cast, the press, and the Guild subscribers were invited to discuss the play. Nobody really could agree on Werfel's intent, and the guesses ranged from abstract platonic Good and Evil to political manipulation. Was Werfel pleading for Christianity and understanding or was he, indeed, pleading for Communism and Revolution? It seemed to me then that he was pleading for neither but was rather telling a folktale full of alarums and excursions and pure melodrama.

Or does it seem, in the light of having lived many years beyond *Goat Song*, that the monster hidden for twenty-three years was the National Socialist party of Germany? My God, could he really have known?

During the run of *Goat Song* I bought my first hand-painted oil painting. It was called *Cow in the Meadow*, and it portrayed a cow in a meadow. It cost two dollars at an auction, and I hung it at the Guilford together with my prints and reproductions of Rembrandt and Matisse.

I kept it for years, but it simply didn't belong with the pictures I subsequently was able to buy, so I exiled it to a back room of my house in Beverly Hills. Later when some burglars got in, they stole it, thinking that any oil painting belonging to me had value. It did, but purely sentimental, and I still miss my cow. I'm willing to pay a reward to have her back.

Gladys rather liked the cow too, and we talked about cows and art and plays and artists and were intimate and very rarely did we mention marriage. But it was clearly on her mind and mine. I still couldn't bring myself to do it.

10

In 1926 Jimmy Walker was mayor of New York, and the town was wide open. The bootleggers and racketeers were at the peak of their powers, and gang wars, shoot-outs, and black Cadillacs, manned by hoods carrying submachine guns, were probably everywhere. Al Capone, Dutch Schultz, and Owney Madden made the headlines. I don't think I ever met one of them.

I was reading a few novels: Sinclair Lewis' *Arrowsmith* and Ernest Hemingway's *The Sun Also Rises*. I thought Hemingway exciting and profound. I later changed my mind. It seemed to me that his bare bones style, while a breakthrough from the excessive description of the romantic novelists, was, after a steady diet of it, mannered and stultifying.

Eugene O'Neill, on the other hand, was neither. At a matinee I saw *The Great God Brown* and applauded his playwright's searching for a way to make the theater live beyond the proscenium. (Others who followed him seem to me to have gone too far.)

But, for a moment, back to Sinclair Lewis. In May he had been awarded the Pulitzer Prize but declined it, declaring that all such prizes tend to make writers "safe, polite, obedient, and sterile." Lewis urged all novelists to refuse such awards if they wished to remain free from constricting standards.

Sound familiar? George C. Scott feels that way about the Academy Awards. How do I feel? Well, it seems improper for me to comment, for I have never been nominated, certainly not for a Pulitzer Prize and never for an Oscar.* For me to say I wouldn't accept it would certainly be a case of refusing something never offered; for me to say I would, would be to ask for something I've never been tendered. My comfort is that neither Cary Grant nor Greta Garbo were ever tendered it either. Actually, I think there is something seriously wrong about this whole business of awards, but I can offer no solution.

Anyway, 1926 was a big work year for me—not so confining that Gladys and I didn't go dancing whenever we could—and the songs we danced to included *That's Why Darkies Were Born*. It's been a long pull from that song to *Shaft*. And if you think there hasn't been any progress, just consider the diverse social attitude of those two songs.

In a curious back flip, I think the social comments of the theater in the twenties were more pointed, more relevant than those of today. I do not put down Tennessee Williams, Harold Pinter, Edward Albee, John Osborne, or Samuel Beckett; they are men with important things on their minds, and they do the best they can to tell us about them. But it seems to me (with the exception of Albee's *Virginia Woolf* and the early Williams) the illumination is intended for themselves, not the audience.

I have made it a point these last years to see as much off-Broadway as I can, and I find a good deal of it self-serving, obscure, and almost deliberately trashy. And I am not talking about specific sexual acts, simulated or actually indulged in on stage; I'm talking of a use of the English language that dims rather than illuminates. I am not unaware of the custard pies that will be hurled at me for harboring these views; I am prepared for the barrage of my own trashy films that will be unearthed as evidence of my inconsistency. Still, I tell you, I've a right to speak; I've earned one.

A painting, a book, a play, must evoke response on the part of the observer or the reader; it is entirely conceivable that a young audience responds to what an older audience does not; but the true, the great work of art is so human, so noble that it makes a statement for all audiences—young, old, black, pink, or purple.

I have a piece of ancient African sculpture wrought by an anonymous genius that speaks to all men of the strength of the wretched.

The Chief Thing by Nicolas Evreinoff (a comedy for some—a drama for others) in which I appeared in March and April of 1926

---

* Note from L.S.: On January 9, 1973, the board of the Academy voted E.G.R. an honorary Oscar for his major contributions to the film.

for the Theatre Guild was not a work of art, but it was highly theatrical and stirring. Its sets and costumes had been designed by Sergei Soudiekinem, who had done those wonderfully brilliant settings for the *Chauve Souries*. The evening was, thus, vivid and colorful. While it owed a great deal to Pirandello, it had a charm and clarity of its own. The Russians have a curious affinity for theatricality; it is a land that begets great playwrights and great poets.

I wonder why it is now that the Soviet Union seeks to muffle the poetic voices that speak out of its greatest heritage.

(I learned enough Russian during World War II to be able to read some of these plays and poets in their original language. The imagery is intense; the language, while it sounds brutal and guttural to those who do not understand it, is actually rhythmic and graceful. I do not speak or readily understand the peasant idioms of Khrushchev; I am enchanted by the prose of Solzhenitsyn.)

The Theatre Guild, after all these years, had finally come to the point where they were about to launch their experiment in repertory. Already signed, or about to sign, were the Lunts, Helen Westley, Earl Larrimore, Margalo Gillmore, Henry Travers, Clare Eames, and Dudley Digges—all actors of commanding presence and undisputed talent (though, sadly, I'm not sure I can include Miss Westley).

The offer the Guild made to me was both tempting and unattractive. My salary would be reduced down to that same measly two hundred and fifty a week from the three hundred to which I was now accustomed. (If these figures startle you, that was top pay for a featured player in those days. In addition, there was no inflation; a buck was a solid buck.) To compensate for the cut, the Guild offered a twenty-week guarantee, which was really unheard of. The theater is a chance-cursed profession, and you could then—and still can—rehearse and knock your teeth out and close in one night.

So the Guild did offer a kind of security. More than that, however, they were full of glittering promises. As they had said years before, we would all alternate plays and we would alternate roles. We would eventually have a theater of our own. (And we did—the Guild Theatre on Fifty-second Street, terribly designed. You had to walk *up* a flight of stairs to the orchestra. As for the balcony, the poor creatures who had those tickets were winded before they ever got to their seats. The theater is now known as the Anta, and I advise you to take those steps slowly.)

I was wary of the Guild people until they came to me with the script of *Juarez and Maximilian*, the first production of their new acting company. It was a dramatic history in three acts and thirteen scenes by the author of *Goat Song*, Franz Werfel.

I read it and I signed. And we were an acting company that the Guild advertised so: "Next season, for the first time since its organization, the Theatre Guild will have a permanent company of its* own instead of being compelled, as heretofore, to engage outside actors for each production."

The serious critics hailed the Guild and wrote copiously of the hopes and problems. Walter Prichard Eaton summed up matters in the October 15, 1926, issue of *The Spur:*

> Within the memory of present theatregoers there has never been a successful repertoire theatre in America, and almost no attempts at one. We have known repertoire only from the traveling companies of a few ambitious and able actors like Richard Mansfield or Sothern and Marlowe. Granville Barker, during his season at Wallack's Theatre a dozen years ago or more, attempted repertoire only to discover that business at the box office at once slumped. The public did not relish the "confusion" resulting from different plays on different nights.
>
> Moreover, to play repertoire requires a permanent company of actors considerably in excess of the number demanded for any one play, unless you have one dominating figure to make the public forget shortcomings in the minor roles. With the public indifferent or even hostile to repertoire, and the cost of it greater and the returns less than those of long-run productions, it is not surprising that our 'art theatres,' like the Guild, have not been in a hurry to adopt the system.
>
> The Guild, however, like the Neighborhood Playhouse, has always had leanings that way, has long dreamed of a permanent company of actors trained to work together and a system of production which would enable them to play diverse parts and to mix and alternate these parts, thus avoiding staleness. Furthermore, the Guild has seen with regret its finest productions pass into the limbo of forgotten things, the actors scattered, the play put back on the shelf. It is only this season, however, that the directors have felt themselves in a position to work out the problem. The Guild now has its own ample and well-equipped theatre; it has a school of acting which can supply it with young players for minor parts, at need; it has the good will of the public, and a large list of season subscribers to insure it against loss. But the very size of this list, while it makes the Guild experiment possible, also greatly complicates it.
>
> If the Guild makes, as usual, as least five new productions in the season, each subscriber has to see every one of them. But it now takes about six weeks of eight performances a week to go through the subscription list. How, then, is the Guild to manage a repertoire program?

---

* I am painfully aware that, throughout, I should refer to the Guild as "it" instead of "they." You must forgive me because I thought of It as They, and I tend to chuck matters of grammar aside when I am dealing with matters of emotion.

A good question! And the answer: It didn't. All the good intentions fell apart, and in the ensuing years the Guild went back to its old way of hiring actors.

Perhaps that was the best way after all, because the Guild did go on to highly worthy work like *Idiots Delight, Elizabeth the Queen, Mourning Becomes Electra, Strange Interlude*, and *Porgy and Bess*.

Waiting for the Guild season to begin, I did a play called *We Americans* in Atlantic City. Because I had already committed myself to the Guild, I could not, unfortunately, continue with it. I tried to get out of the Guild contract because *We Americans* was bound to be a hit, but the Guild refused to release me.

Clara Langsner, a member of the cast, suggested a replacement for me, a young Yiddish actor named Muni Wiesenfreund. He, of course, became Paul Muni and my most potent competition. He played *Pasteur* and *Zola; I* could have. I played *Ehrlich* and *Reuter; he* could have. The Brothers Warner regarded us as two sides of a coin and did not hesitate to exploit the situation.

I disliked Muni and Muni detested me.

In July of that summer (waiting for the Guild season to begin) I was doing a play with Leo Carillo. It was called *The Stolen Lady*. While I had a bravura part as Colonel Virgilio Hermanos Barroso, it was so bravura that it was junk. And the play was junk. So, all right, blame me for trying to pay the rent.

In August I was in another rent-payer called *Henry Behave*, and the less said about that the better. Except for one thing. Gladys appeared in the play with me.

The truth about those months was that I was in turmoil; soon, it would be impossible to continue this relationship with Gladys without marriage. It was desperately unfair to her, and while she tried to behave sensibly, it was clear that inevitably we were approaching a decision. It was a decision I was trying to delay as long as possible.

Like about a month. It was an ultimatum.

So before 1926 was over, Gladys and I were married.*

Through the good offices of a lawyer friend of mine, Bill Justus, we located a justice of the peace in Medina, Pennsylvania, who never heard of Edward G. Robinson or Gladys Lloyd. When the ceremony

* Note from L.S.: E.G.R. indicated that in the early years of his marriage to Gladys his stepdaughter, Jeannie, lived with either her father or her maternal grandparents. As she grew up, I suspect she visited the Robinsons on a number of occasions. You will see later the three of them made a trip to Mexico. I do not know her, nor have I ever spoken to her. She is now, herself, a grandmother.

(*sic*) was over and I asked him, "How much?" he said, "The *legal* fee is ten dollars." I gave him twenty-five.

I did not tell my family. I did not dare. If my family knew, they did not tell me. They did not dare.

You are entitled to a poor opinion of Little Caesar.

11

In assembling these chronicles, I sometimes put myself in your place and debate which road you'd like me to follow. It would be easy to write of the social and domestic life of an actor and his wife in those last two years in New York before the crash; they were fairly good years and not entirely unhappy ones—though the secret I held from my family was gnawing—but I have not undertaken this journey to talk about parties and food and the minor irritations that erupt in the early years of a marriage, a marriage consummated when both its principals were mature. We may get into that later. I'm not sure at this point. I'll see.

So let us turn to *Juarez and Maximilian*, the Werfel play, with its glittering company—actors whose techniques were so honed that you could never see the machinery that produced the performances. Alfred Lunt played the Emperor Maximilian. Claire Eames played the Empress Carlotta, and I played Porfirio Diaz. Werfel never permitted Juarez to appear; he was an off-scene presence, and Diaz was his voice—the voice of liberalism, the common people, man in need, man in despair, the Mexican man, but to Werfel, *all* men.

I relished the role because it enabled me to say so much of what I believed; I think Alfred relished Maximilian for the same reason. Poor Maximilian, driven by a desire to do the best he knew how— only what he knew was pitifully inadequate. It was perfectly clear to me that Werfel had stacked the cards in Diaz's favor: Diaz was Werfel speaking.

In rehearsal, and in run-through, without settings, costume, or

91

makeup, the play turned from scene to scene with energy, poetry, and significance. When we got into Lee Simonson's costumes and sets (he called the scenes "pictures") the play seemed like a four-cylinder Model T trying to negotiate a steep hill. For one thing, the sets were so impressive that the audience looked at them, not us. For another, there was a buzz as Alfred appeared, looking exactly like Maximilian, and Clare, exactly like Carlotta. To change this heavy scenery, besides, there were at least sixty seconds between "pictures," and the play lost its cumulative force as the audience grew fidgety.

God knows, the critics were fidgety; they carped at us. I think, instead of carping, they should have been listening. What they should have said—and nobody did—was that Werfel's error had been in making Maximilian the central point of the play when the audience really gravitated to Diaz. Not *me* as Diaz; *anybody* as Diaz. Because Diaz was the dynamic figure. Whether he was in history is beside the point; he was in the play, and the audience, with that curious instinct audiences possess, felt cheated.

That was in October. In November, in line with the repertory concept, I appeared with Alfred Lunt in Sidney Howard's *Ned McCobb's Daughter*, playing Lawyer Grover for which I had to assume a New Englandish Boston way of speaking.

May I have a moment of pride? Most of the actors were native born Americans, some of them even from New England. But they were all trying too hard to do what John F. Kennedy did without trying to do at all—put an *r* at the end of North Carolina (Carolinar) and struggle with the long wide *o* of Boston (Baaaaahston).

Sidney Howard, attending a run-through, commented that as far as New England speech was concerned I most nearly approached the proper sound. I do not deny that I was flattered by this comment. I record it chiefly because I think I have something to say to my fellow actors—the young ones, of course. (If you're not an actor, you can skip the next paragraph.)

The trick of dialect is to do as little as possible; that is, merely *suggest* it. I ignored the *r* endings and the wide *o*'s; they were too obvious. What I did was to be occasionally nasal and sound a bit like Percy Kilbride in *Ma and Pa Kettle*. I used inflection, not imitation. Gertrude Berg, the incomparable doyenne of Jewish mothers, never once fell into the trap of using the vaudeville Yiddish accent; she merely rearranged lines so that the rhythm of the words would give her a sing-song. Most Jews or non-Jews playing with a Yiddish dialect would, on the other hand, put on too much accent, and if they already had an accent, they would put another on top of it.

Now let's get to the people who imitate me. The best of the mimics pretend to snarl and say "Nyaaah." The truth is that I never snarled and said "Nyaaah." I once appeared on a program with Jack Benny, and in rehearsal he asked me to imitate myself. I snarled and said "Nyaaah," imitating my imitators. Jack Benny did a long take and said, "You're not doing it right, Eddie. You don't sound like Edward G. Robinson."

He was right. I'm not nearly as good as the people who do me in nightclubs—or as lousy.

Next on the assembly line was *The Brothers Karamazov*, directed (as already noted) by Jacques Copeau. I was given the role of Smerdiakov, surely one of Dostoevsky's most extraordinary characters, and I was dazzled by the prospect.

Copeau undazzled us in short order. He had directed the play in French many times, and his vision of it was frozen in granite. Every entrance, every move, every exit was apparently dictated from the highest reaches of Parnassus. And the company, with its array of talent (Lunt, Fontanne, Eames, Henry Travers, Philip Loeb, Morris Carnovsky, and Dudley Digges) gave some of the worst performances (in dress rehearsals) I've ever seen in this vast, straggling skeleton of a masterpiece.

And so, as if by common consent, even though not in concert, we decided one by one to kick over the traces. And opening night was a sky rocket.

I mean I'm told it was a sky rocket. I don't remember it. I think I was transported. I know that my heart was beating a mile a minute and my blood pressure must have reached an astronomical figure. I recollect nothing except a doctor, after the performance, advising me to go straight to bed and stay there. Well, I couldn't stay there; I had more performances to play. This, I suppose, brings me to "the show must go on," an absolutely absurd sentence with which I do not agree. Except I always tried to obey it.

Two weeks in *Karamazov*, and the assistant stage manager did something between the acts he shouldn't have done; he told me there was a call from my brother. It was a devastating call. My father had had a heart attack, his second. The first had occurred ten years before, but he had recovered. This one was different. I was urged to get to the Bronx as rapidly as possible.

Should I ask the understudy to go on? Should I do that to him and the audience and my fellow players? No, I played the last act. Then, without even taking off my makeup, I took a taxi to the Bronx.

I was in time. I was in the room when he died.

Wrenched from Rumania, creating a new life in a strange land, true to his religion and his ethics, this man of compassion, under-statement, and deep love of family and adopted country had come to the end—living—and now dying—symbol of the hopes and ac-complishments of the New World. I held his hand, and I remembered the cafés in Bucharest and the smiles we had together. I couldn't cry. There are times when sadness is beyond tears.

The next week was torment. The funeral. The sitting *shivah*—that symbolic period of renting your clothes and donning sackcloth and ashes.*

My grief, surely, was heightened by the fact that I had never told my father about Gladys; additionally, I could not perform. I did not wear my crown of thorns lightly. Certainly, I could not respond to Gladys' heroic efforts to comfort me. I was ashamed for her; I was ashamed for my mother; I was ashamed for my father; God knows, I was ashamed of myself and, somehow, psychologically, immobilized.

But grief subsides. And then came another agony of Job.

In *Karamazov*, toward the end of the play in my role as Smerdia-kov, I played a highly emotional scene. Defeated, I dragged myself slowly and painfully up Raymond Sovey's staircase, which lifted from the stage floor high into the upper reaches of the Guild Theatre. It was my habit to grip the banister with my left hand as I made the journey up, and dramatically, it was effective. Once I reached the top I would remain in the view of the audience while the other players performed the coda of the play. At a Tuesday night performance I negotiated the steps, and toward the top my hand caught on an ex-posed nail on the staircase, ripping the flesh. In torture, dripping blood on the actors below, my own actor's instinct took hold, and I did not cry out or make a move.

Doctors came, eleven stitches were made, and I played another six performances with my left hand in a sling. But on Saturday matinee the pain was so intense that I could not manage to make the change between the first two acts. My understudy went on, and I was taken to the hospital.

It was my first time.

Cause or effect—I don't know—I developed bursitis, a pain, I am told, only slightly less severe than childbirth. All the furies seemed to

---

* From this time forward, with no exception, I have never missed the prayers or the anniversary of the deaths of my father, mother, Oscar, or the *Jahrtzeit*, which we must engage in with nine other Jewish males over the age of thirteen. From Kyoto I went to Tokyo to find the nine; geography never stopped me. It is *their* belief in it that is my compulsion; it is not for me. When I go, I expect no one to do it for me. I go further. I wish no one to.

possess me. At first I refused sedatives, but later I gave in. I think it was conscience over Gladys and my family that was devilling me, too; I was sick beyond my ability to understand it or to tolerate it.

Well, that was my first experience with hospitals and doctors. By this time, I am a candidate for a medical degree in cardiology, hypertension, abdominal surgery, cancer, and psychiatry—not only for myself but for my first wife and my son.

Of all the problems that plague the human being, the mental aberration, brain disorientation, is the worst, and through the years I have been unable to find a way out of the terrors of the manic-depressive and the alcoholic. I am neither; those close to me have been both.

I, myself, have had a heart attack in Africa, a hideous—almost fatal—automobile accident in Beverly Hills, a variety of systemic and malignant episodes, but I have always had faith in the ability of the doctor to heal; in the area of the mind I have little faith. Not little faith. No faith.

My wounded hand healed (the scar is ever with me) and the bursitis subsided and I went back to play *Karamazov*. It closed inevitably, and I continued with that small bit in *Ned McCobb's Daughter* and agreed (because, so eager was I to externalize my aggressions) to do special matinees for the Guild of Pirandello's *Right You Are If You Think You Are*. I played Ponza and Armina Marshall, Lawrence Langner's wife, played *my* wife. (I count Armina among my few and lasting friends.)

I enjoyed the play; I wish I could say I enjoyed the negotiations that followed with the Guild about the next season's acting company. I made an outlandish and impossible demand: I insisted on fifty dollars more a week. Let Ward Morehouse, in the New York *Evening Sun* of Monday, April 11, 1927, tell you what happened.

> Edward G. Robinson, who has been recurring season after season since he made his first Broadway appearance back in 1915 in the melodrama called *Under Fire*, and who has given many able performances in productions of the Theatre Guild, will not be with that organization next season. Negotiations between him and the Guild's Board in regard to a new season contract were under way for some time, but no agreement was reached. His association with the acting company will therefore terminate with the closing of the two pieces in which he is now appearing—*Right You Are If You Think You Are* and *Ned McCobb's Daughter*.
>
> Mr. Robinson's withdrawal follows that of Clare Eames, announced some weeks ago. . . .

Not quite thirty-four, I was beginning to get the stars out of my eyes. It was great to play Dostoevsky and Shaw and Werfel and Pirandello. But what was so terrible about making a buck?

It was necessary. I was married now with new responsibilities and an extravagant wife and, thus, bills from Stern's and McCreery's and Wanamaker's and Saks and, what's more, the apartment at the Guilford had a measly closet. So Gladys nagged at me and finally we took a flat at 15 West Eleventh Street on the periphery of Greenwich Village. Lower Fifth Avenue in those days was a kind of snobbery; Park Avenue smelled of the nouveau and kept women. I've been trying to think what we paid for that spacious apartment. I believe it was a hundred dollars a month, and that was pretty expensive.

Gladys and I both had a decorator touch, though our touches were somewhat different. I preferred the more solid, traditional look; she preferred the pastel, semi-art nouveau look. We had both in what was not exactly the most comfortable combination.

We were trying to compromise and merge our likes and dislikes. We sought to avoid quarrels, but they erupted, and then we each accepted the blame. It was not easy for two independent individuals to give up sovereignty. We *did* try, and to some extent we succeeded, but, I think, never totally.

In any case, the move did help; we weren't continually fighting about that miserable closet. In the new place we each had one of our own—a good thing for a marriage counsellor to bear in mind.

We also had walls—large, spacious walls, and those impressive but fake reproductions that were good enough for the sunless Guilford, were pretty sleazy on bright Eleventh Street.

I needed no further excuse.

During the period before our marriage, and certainly afterward, I'd made every effort to see as many pictures as I could, and many the time Henry Travers and Dudley Digges and I would cover the galleries, including Putzi Hanfstaengel's. Herr Hanfstaengel was always expansive, cordial, and delighted to see us. It was hard to believe that he closed his gallery and became one of Hitler's inner circle.

More than the public galleries and museums, I enjoyed viewing the private collections. The Alfred Barr, for instance, and the Lewisohn. You would write a letter and ask for permission, and an appointment would be made for you. I feasted my eye, and I think I trained it. Once, in the then unforeseeable future, a dealer was raving over and detailing the merits of a Pissarro, and I remember saying: "I don't need all that talk. Let the picture talk for itself." As I went from the private collections to Knoedler's, to Wildenstein, and Marie Harriman's in those days, that attitude began to develop in me without my consciously being aware of it.

Eventually I began to buy, out of instinct, impulse—all right, call it a sense of beauty. I bought the work of Twachtman, Winant, Robert Hosea, and Peter Brook. And once I even bought a Gilbert Stuart (I sold it soon afterward because I didn't like it) and ten Blakelocks. I still have those.

Do you wonder why I needed and wanted that fifty-buck raise from the Theatre Guild?

Gladys greeted my picture-buying with something less than enthusiasm and, even though she later joined in it (and later still sought to take credit for it), she was sensibly worried about my cavalier attitude toward money. We were living beyond our means, and it concerned her. We bickered and she was right and I was wrong, but when I look around my house today, I feel that maybe she was wrong and I was right.

I am not much of a businessman, and I really don't like talking about money, but I'd like somehow to explain why it is that so many people in show business, having once made large salaries, frequently end up broke. First, of course, are taxes. A prudent man is aware of them and puts the appropriate sums aside. But show me an actor who is prudent. He wouldn't be an actor if he were. Next come the levels of prosperity. You are entertained, and you entertain in return. Both occasions require clothes and apartments and lots of money spent at the local supermarket and/or delicatessen.

Then, in Hollywood, comes a bunch of dough and the feeling that it's going to last forever, so you buy a house and a car and another house and another car. It's all dumb, but that's how it is.

In the late twenties everybody was buying stocks—but not me, because all my available cash was tied up in pictures. So when the crash came, I didn't have to go scrambling about to rescue stocks bought on margin. Not for myself. But for all my brothers—and a great many of my friends.

The Summer of 1927 I was working, doing a play in Atlantic City called *The Kibitzer*. It was written by witty, intelligent, talented Jo Swerling, and for the first time I was given billing. The play was *with* Edward G. Robinson.

But with or without, it had a clever first act, a pedestrian second, and a *lox* of a third. The character I played, Lazarus, who owned a cigar store, was wonderfully wise and delicious—but the rest of the play was synthetic. We closed, and I urged Jo to rewrite—and he

tried, but couldn't, because, believe me, that's one of the most difficult things an author is called upon to do.

For months before I was being offered a play by Bart Cormack
called *The Racket*. The role was that of a gangster, and I didn't like
it. In order to play a part, you must have some kind of identification
with the role; I had little understanding of larceny and murder. I
would be forced to invent the gangster since I had no yardstick by
which to create him. I didn't want to do it, but when *The Kibitzer*
folded so ignominiously, I accepted with considerable misgiving.

Boy, did that play change my life. It was a smash!

We had a beautifully prosperous run in New York, and the producer had us booked into Chicago. It was a brilliant idea because the
play was all about crime in Chicago. What golden thinking on his
part. Except for one thing: Chicago refused to let us play there.

Mayor Thompson put his civic foot down; he would not permit
Chicago to be libeled. I have often wondered who sat in on the decision. Could it have been Big Al himself?

Since I was playing what I thought was a literary version of Big Al,
I must admit to a certain relief at Mayor Thompson's decision. I did
not relish what a great many of my friends solemnly predicted: a hail
of bullets. But our producer was not one to let so glittering a money-
maker as *The Racket* go down the drain. He accepted a lump sum
guarantee from a California theater man, Homer Curran, and we
were booked in the Biltmore in Los Angeles and the Curran in San
Francisco.

That's why and how the movie moguls saw me as a gangster. They
flocked to the Biltmore, and I was invited to all the studios.

The movies were still silent and still disagreeable to me, but both
Warner's and Fox were working on a system whereby the movies
would talk. They'd even produced some sound shorts. I considered
them eminently silly. I thought that most of the movie colony with
whom I had Sunday brunch on the porches of their Santa Monica
homes overlooking the Pacific were kind and polite and vaguely vulgar.

But I thought California wonderful. The scent of the orange blos-
soms, the palms (my first palms), the fabulous climate (smog not yet
invented), the marvelous red cars that hurtled you from downtown to
the beach, the funny motels (itself a funny word) that were done in
the shape of teepees or pyramids, the luxury of the Ambassador
Hotel, the pace of life slowed down to a human rhythm, the sense of
country and city combined—I loved California. A great place to
visit. Who would want to live there?

Nevertheless I had the opportunity. *Every* studio offered me a contract. It was all flattering and delightful, but I turned them all down. I was a New Yorker and a theater man, so thanks a lot for your silly movies, but no thanks.

So it was the last of 1928 and the beginning of 1929—for me a time in which I worked harder than I ever have, before or since. I returned from San Francisco to plunge right into Hugh Walpole's *A Man with Red Hair* in which, with a red wig, I played a maniacal masochist, a part in which I chewed the scenery and had a ball. He was gorgeous to play because he was first a wild character and then a lamb. On the Coast I'd gone to an animal farm on a Tuesday because the lions hadn't been fed on Monday. I saw the horse meat thrown at them and their ferocious pouncing upon it. Once fed, they became docile puppies. That's how I played the Walpole character—and we were a nervous hit. But then it was a nervous time.

The intelligent, like Roger Babson, were predicting a holocaust in the stock market. The owners of the stock laughed merrily as their paper profits continued to climb. Me, I didn't care.

I was hounding Jo Swerling to rewrite *The Kibitzer*. I knew there was a good play hidden in it somewhere. What it needed was a thrust that would lead to an unpredictable finish. Accordingly, while appearing in *Red Hair*, I conferred constantly with Jo. I would play out the parts while he sat at his typewriter and, in his very personal kind of shorthand, put down what I said, then amplify, add, and reject. Finally, we came up with a rough draft. I didn't see the title page until I'd read it all. Then he showed it to me, and it read: "*The Kibitzer* by Jo Swerling and Edward G. Robinson."

I would like to be able to tell you that I objected, that I said it was his work and my contribution was only incidental; I didn't. I was delighted. It was my first and only attempt at being a playwright, and we signed contracts with Patterson McNutt to produce it. Contained within the agreement was the right of Mr. Swerling to dispose of the subsidiary rights without my approval. If you saw the Paramount film of *The Kibitzer* starring Harry Green, you will know what exasperation that contract brought me.

Not that Patterson McNutt was the first producer we approached. Lewis and Gordon turned it down though I read them the play myself. Jed Harris kept Jo and me waiting in his outside office. We had the same experience with George Abbot, and I'll never forget what Jo said of him: "Abbot is like a hyena with saliva dripping from the jowls, ready to pounce on slightly ill plays."

While performing in one play, writing another, and trying to get a producer, I had little time for the movies. But one Sunday night

Gladys insisted that we go to see Al Jolson in *The Jazz Singer*.* It was the first feature movie with a talking sequence. I didn't want to go; I'd seen those talkie shorts—Will Hays, in his high collar and cataleptic stance, announcing the new era in the movies, and Marian Talley, the opera star, trying desperately to reach high C, yet not quite making it. But Gladys insisted, telling me that I never took her anyplace, and plunged into depression—one of her not uncommon ploys and certain to work with me—and so we stood in line to catch the Jolson film, which in some ways persisted in paralleling my own life. It convinced me of two things: Talking pictures were about to become a reality, and it was time to tell my mother and Oscar about Gladys.

They visited with us painfully on Eleventh Street, and Gladys was a model of sense, hospitality, and respect. So was my mother. It was all very awkward, but the marriage was out in the open at last, and I like to think that both the women in my life accepted the inevitability of each other.

I frequently say now that Gladys became my mother's favorite daughter-in-law, but I think that is what I wanted to believe, what I preferred to believe. This much I know to be the exact truth: They both behaved beautifully through the years, and neither ever confided her private thoughts to me. (My granddaughter, Francesca, Gladys' confidante, insists that my wife adored her mother-in-law. I think Francesca is trying to make me feel good.)

Walter Wanger, a Paramount executive, came to me with an offer to appear in a talking picture with Claudette Colbert. Obviously I could not accept. I was appearing in a play. There was no way I could go to Hollywood. Wanger, however, pointed out that Hollywood was not involved; the picture would be made in the Astoria, Long Island, studios, and the schedule so arranged that I could continue my performances in *Red Hair*, including the matinees.

I read the script. It was way below the standard I was accustomed to in the theater. Had it been a play, I never would have accepted it. But it wasn't a play, it was an annuity. It was fifty thousand dollars. I gave in.

Though my motives for doing the picture were venal, my professionalism asserted itself. It is scarcely pompous for me to say now that I was a highly tuned instrument and a technically expert actor, if only occasionally an inspired one. But I soon learned on the set in Astoria

* Note from L.S.: *The Jazz Singer* was a highly emotional story of a young man from a Jewish Orthodox house who deserts the synagogue for the stage, thus breaking his parents' hearts. The parallel was obviously not lost on Eddie.

that I must develop a whole new bag of tricks. Accustomed to projecting to the top of the second balcony, I discovered that I had only to reach the microphone. In the early days of the talkies the mike was planted in ferns, in Miss Colbert's décolletage, in the telephone—and we could move only slightly if we wished to continue to be heard. Until they invented a mike with a boom, the talking picture was doomed to be static.

When Wanger ran the rushes and I saw myself, I could hardly believe it. Was I really that short, stocky, ugly creature up there? And the voice! Did I speak with such affectation, such rolling *r*'s, such low, bass sounds? You never hear yourself speak; when you do, you're sure the voice belongs to someone else. Now that the tape recorder flourishes, a lot of people have come to understand this phenomenon; then it was a unique experience and a nauseating one.

The other problems were even more acute. To do a play out of continuity is unthinkable; in the movies it was standard operating procedure. I fought it then, fought it all the rest of my time in pictures, and remained deaf to the fact that the only financially sound way to make a picture was to do all the scenes that were laid in one set together, however long the time span between them.

I also had to stop mugging. That expressive lift of the eyebrow on the stage turned into a caricature in a closeup. The truth is you have to be more honest in films than on the stage. Today when you appear on the wide screen, your face is ten feet wide, so you cannot afford the slightest hint of mugging. Look at those early John Barrymore films and you'll see what I mean. Jack was one of the greatest on the stage; on the screen, he was almost a comic.

I think the Lunts recognized that pretty early; they made one film —*The Guardsman*—and never did it again.

I did it quite a lot.

I must admit I thought *Hole in the Wall* was going to be the stinker of all times, and I certainly did not accept the invitation to go to the preview. Claudette went, and she sent me a wire: "We weren't too bad, baby. We weren't too bad. Love, Claudette."

I take her word for it. I've never seen the film.

The Kibitzer opened and was a great success, even though the critics were grudging in their comments. After all, this was what was called—with a barely concealed sneer—an audience play. It was also a vehicle for me. Why not? I was the coauthor, and I gave myself all the best of it. It seemed to me I could play it forever—in New York for years and, on the road after that, for many more years. Every once in a while an actor finds a play that serves him well. Frank

Bacon did a play called *Lightnin'*, and, of course, Sarah Bernhardt and David Warfield and Duse all had their plays that were instantly revivable.

After all, what was the matter with what the French call "Le Thé-âtre du Boulevard"—the theater to make the ticket-buyers laugh and cry and relate? It is easy enough to treat a play like *Abie's Irish Rose* with contempt. Perhaps the contempt is deserved, but the audiences that thronged the Republic Theatre for five years saw something in it, *felt* something in it, that was out of the range of the critics.

I belabor this point only because that kind of theater was doomed with the advent of the talkies. The films took over the commercial theater's staples—the domestic comedy, the mystery (Mary Roberts Rinehart's *The Bat*), the simple-minded ethnic play (*The Kibitzer* was a prime example of the genre), and eventually even the musicals. To jump ahead of myself, the same thing happened when television came along—the Hardy families and the Charlie Chans were, in one guise or another, preempted by the tube, so the movies had to seek other kinds of stories.

But I did not know that then. I thought *The Kibitzer* would remain my insurance policy for years.

I did not count on the crash. It happened in October, and Broadway was in a frenzy of instant despair. Why single out Broadway? So was the rest of the nation, and soon the rest of the world.

Without my knowledge or prior consent, Patterson McNutt and Jo Swerling sold the film rights of *The Kibitzer* to Paramount. Though I shared in a minor portion of the author's loot, I was livid. I fought McNutt and Swerling. The matter was eventually brought to arbitration, and I lost.

Paramount made the picture instantly without me; the New York run was curtailed and the road wiped out. You could not appear in a live play for a top of $3.30 and show a film of the same play down the block for thirty-five cents.

To Patterson McNutt I never spoke again. The atmosphere between Jo Swerling and myself was glacial. I felt betrayed.

Now what?

To finance a new play on Broadway was increasingly difficult (so many backers had jumped from skyscrapers), and certainly the Depression was surfacing in many ways and forms—the bread lines, the apple-sellers, the empty stores on every street, the whole atmosphere of bust now that boom was irrevocably over.

And then came an offer from Irving Thalberg. I was hardly the only New York actor being wooed by Thalberg. Even in those early days the studios were beginning to realize that perennial favorites—

million-dollar movie stars—were being destroyed by the microphone.
Polly Moran and Marie Dressler, who had done yeoman service on
the stage, proved themselves capable of coping with the special demands of the new movies. Even Garbo was found to have a kind of
wonderful, charming, guttural voice. But William Haines, Ramon
Navarro, John Gilbert, *ad infinitum*, had voices that did not match
their faces or personalities. As a result, Hollywood was forced to go
to the theater not only for actors but for authors and directors as well.

It was the confluence of the Depression and the invention of the
talkies that permitted Hollywood to succeed. And one other untrivial
consideration: money.

A great big Broadway star might, at the peak of his career, get a
thousand dollars a week and perhaps a piece of the gross of the play.
But there was no guarantee. After three weeks of rehearsal, the play
could open and be a flop. In Hollywood, the picture might be a flop,
but the actor and all the other people connected with it were paid
before the picture opened. The success of the effort had nothing to do
with the remuneration. In the theater only success paid off.

These were considerations that were being debated all over New
York—at the Green Room Club, at the Lamb's, at Sardi's (newly
opened), in the Orangerie of the Astor Hotel, at Lindy's, in the Paley
house, and, above all, in my case, in *my* house. Pepe Schildkraut,
Dudley Digges, and Henry Travers engaged in the Broadway-versus-
Hollywood debate. And we came to a sensible conclusion: Take the
money and run! Expressed another way: Don't buy anything in California you can't put on the Santa Fe Chief.

It was a nice pragmatic decision, yet all of us hesitated to abide by
it. How could you make yourself say that junky dialogue? I was ready
to turn Thalberg down; Al Woods offered me star billing in a new
play he had already financed. I read it; the dialogue was junky. I
rejected it though I had no other engagement in view.

Then Thalberg sent me the script of *A Lady to Love*. It was
sensitive and intelligent and beautifully written—and not unfamiliar.
It turned out to be Sidney Howard's own screenplay of *They Knew
What They Wanted*, a resounding New York hit that had starred
darling Pauline Lord and immensely talented Richard Bennett.

It was to star me and Vilma Banky—I mean, Vilma Banky and
me. I really mean Vilma Banky *with* Edward G. Robinson.

Leaving Gladys behind, I got myself on New York Central's Twentieth Century Limited, spent some hours in Chicago at the Art Institute, boarded the Santa Fe Chief, was met at Pasadena by a black
Cadillac and chauffeur, was taken to a small inexpensive hotel at my
own request (I was going to save every buck), and reported at six

o'clock on a Monday morning to makeup, where I was turned into a fifty-year-old Italian.

From there I proceeded to a gorgeous dressing room replete with a bottle of brandy sent by Thalberg, a rather funereal type wreath from Louis B. Mayer, and a bouquet of flowers sent by Miss Banky, then into wardrobe, and finally onto Stage 9, where I was greeted with extreme cordiality by Victor Seastrom, the director, Robert Ames, an excellent actor I'd known in New York, and, finally, by the entrancing Miss Banky.

I was ready, of course, to read the play and rehearse. But there was no reading and no rehearsal. We plunged into the middle of the film, and it did not take long to realize that Miss Banky was seriously out of her depth. The glorious creature, playing a mail-order bride, complete with marcelled hair and a custom-made housedress and still the shimmering beauty she was with Ronald Colman in so many silent films, was seized with stage fright and inability. My heart went out to her, and I tried to help. Robert Ames tried, too. Mr. Seastrom didn't seem to try at all. He was as frightened as Miss Banky.

The cutter (one of the unsung heroes of films) managed somehow to find some passable takes of Miss Banky that showed her to her best advantage, and for the first time I came to understand a very significant factor in film-making—that your performance can be improved by a pair of scissors.

Unaware that could happen, I strove valiantly to bring reality, sympathy, tragedy, humor into my own performance. And each night, when I got back to the hotel, I felt exhausted, discouraged, and lonely.

Thalberg, however, was enthusiastic, praised the rushes, said we'd have a hit, and invited me to his beach house on a Sunday to lunch with his beautiful wife, Norma Shearer. On that occasion I met Hollywood royalty—Louis B. Mayer, Joan Crawford, Lionel Barrymore, Janet Gaynor, Charlie Farrell, the Town. It was all lavish beyond anything I'd ever known—more butlers, more wine (and Prohibition was still on the books), more caviar, and pâté, more diamonds, and more dames on the make.

They were hard to resist; I resisted.

Well, we wrapped up A Lady to Love, and I was looking forward to the Chief and Gladys and Eleventh Street when Universal contacted me with a script for Outside the Law. I didn't even want to talk to the Laemmles, father and son, but they offered me a packet, and I could only see those dollar signs in terms of paintings and a mink coat for Gladys. Besides, it was spring, and nothing would be happening in New York anyway, and wasn't Universal better than

Elitch's Gardens? The picture was on a short schedule—so, all right already, one more picture and back to Broadway, and good-bye to the palm trees and Hollywood Boulevard forever.

My experience with *Outside the Law* was a mirror image of *A Lady to Love*. Replace Victor Seastrom with Tod Browning, replace Vilma Banky with Mary Nolan, and it was the same agony all over again.

And so back I was on the Chief, heading straight for my beloved New York with that eminent actor Maurice Mosovich as my chance traveling companion, when the wires from Universal met me at every stop. They had finished a picture called *East Is West* in which Gene Hersholt (a gentleman of whom I was very fond) had played a Chinese, Charlie Wong. With his Danish accent he was less than credible, and the preview audiences had laughed long and loud. Would I be willing to reshoot his scenes? The offer was twenty-five thousand dollars in Albuquerque, thirty-five thousand in Kansas City, fifty in Chicago, and a hundred thousand by the time I reached Grand Central Station in New York.

Mr. Moskovitch said: "Don't be a goddamn fool, Eddie. Take the money. It's more than the President of the United States makes in a year!"

Gladys was clearly of two minds about my returning to the West Coast. She was enchanted by the offer (money being a high priority with her) but of two minds because it might mean that I would not be able to accept a play offered me by George C. Tyler entitled *Le Marchand de Paris* by Edmond Flege, adapted from the French by Winthrop Ames. Gladys' split opinion was based not solely on her preference for the theater, but also on the fact that there was a part in the play for her. She was not content with the role of housewife and/or hostess; she was chafing under my absences and her lack of personal identity.

Compounding her insecurities was the improbability that she could have another child. Her first confinement had left her brutalized; her physicians warned against another pregnancy. I assured her that the last thing I wanted was a child; I was fully aware it was not possible, and I swore passionately that I did not care. The truth is I passionately cared.

But *East Is West* was only the tip of the iceberg; I planned to keep the other neuroses submerged. I am not an expert at compromise; I had not grown accustomed to the need of having to consult with others about career decisions, chiefly because I think I made them from the seat of my pants. Still, I had to deal with Gladys' problems, and in the twenty-four hours before I boarded the Century again for the trip back to California, I read the play, liked it, talked with Tyler, got him to postpone rehearsal dates, soothed Gladys (not easy, because she was rigid and determined), and was on my unhappy way.

That trip across the desert in the mid-summer, on a train that had never heard of air conditioning, was torture. I wrapped myself in cold towels, held ice to my wrists, and suffered desperately, trying to breathe despite the equatorial desert air combined with the relentless soot of the locomotive.

At Universal City I did the retakes on *East Is West* directed by Monta Bell, playing opposite Lew Ayers and Lupe Velez.

A note on Lew Ayres: I had never met a finer young actor, and as the years passed and I came to know that he was a conscientious objector, who nevertheless risked his life as an ambulance driver, I saw in him a truly spiritual human being whose studies of Eastern mysticism were not, as they frequently are now, mere fad but sincere attempts to find the nature of man and the meaning of life. He is rare.

Lupe was rare, too, in quite another way. Sex was her game, and she played it on stage and off. On stage I could deal with her rubbing and roving hands; off stage I had my troubles. But I managed to elude her. Because she was a hot tomato and I was not a rock, it was not easy.

It was easier later to enjoy the takeoff that George Burns and Gracie Allen did on *East Is West* with Gracie playing Lupe and George playing me. It was one of their favorite movies.

Meanwhile, *A Lady to Love*, that horror I'd made with Vilma Banky, had apparently escaped the cutting room and was affronting audiences all over the nation. It was, though it beats me how, a success.

Irving Thalberg contacted my agents (I'd been in Hollywood long enough to use "contact" as a verb) and began negotiating a long-term contract with M.G.M.

The terms were fabulous except that no provision was made for my doing any work in the theater. The contract was exclusive, ran for three years, and called for six pictures.

The price was right—one million dollars.

I went to see Thalberg in his spectacular office on the Metro lot in Culver City. He kept me waiting that classic twenty minutes before I was admitted to his inner sanctum. It was a long walk to his desk. It is always a long walk to the desk of the head of a studio. In the books

I've read about Mussolini it is pointed out that it was a long walk to *his* desk; I suspect he picked up the idea from Thalberg.

Not that Thalberg was dictatorial. On the contrary. He rose, offered me a cigar, and couldn't have been more gracious—or tougher. What I proposed to him was one or one and a half pictures a year with suitable time off for me to do a play. He assured me that he well understood my devotion to the theater (he himself was a theater buff) but I must realize that it was, if not a dying art, certainly one soon to be replaced by the talking film. As for any proposed contract with M.G.M., it would have to be exclusive; the studio would use its best brains and guns to build me into a star. Obviously, it would be of some concern to them should I do plays on my own, risking failure and the destruction of that buildup. No, M.G.M. would have to make all the career decisions, don't you see? I did not see.

Visions of sugar plums and a million dollars danced in one part of my head; in the other was icy rage that this young man, whose credentials I considered inferior, would dare suggest that all decision would be taken from me, that I was some article to be packaged and merchandised. The temperature in his office was below zero. I compromised on some minor points, certainly demonstrating some goodwill. Thalberg compromised on nothing; he sat there, stern and immovable—the godhead.

I disliked him thoroughly. His eyes showed me that an actor was beneath contempt. My agent tried to intervene. I forbade him to.

It was High Noon. Thalberg's way or no way. Robinson's way or no way.

No way.

My agent and I abruptly left Thalberg's office. Then, trying to hide myself from the extras and executives in front of his building, I vomited.

I went back to New York and into rehearsal with *Le Marchand de Paris* (with Gladys in the cast) and with a great sense of relief. Hollywood was forever behind me.

Marchand was now called *Mr. Samuel*, and I enjoyed the rehearsals enormously. It was a good play, had been a success in Paris, and was certain to be in New York.

We opened at the Little Theatre on November 10, 1930. The notices were better than mixed. The second night there were fewer than a hundred people in the house. We ran eight performances to constantly diminishing audiences. Hal Wallis of Warner Brothers–First National was in one of those wretched little groups. He came backstage and said the Brothers Warner were ready to talk a deal.

I said to Gladys, on Eleventh Street, "I've been true to the theater, but who's been true to me?"

She replied, "I hear Hollywood's quite nice. I think I might have a career out there."

I didn't argue. Actresses with fewer gifts had made it. Though she had a minor talent, even she might.

When I stepped into the wings the last night at the Little Theatre, I did not know that I wouldn't set foot on a stage again for twenty-eight years.

12

I have been experiencing several bouts of ill health lately, and that's given me time to look at TV. Though most of it's grimly lower case, some of it isn't, and I'm not referring to Channel 52 out here which relentlessly keeps showing the Warner Brothers catalog in which I figure to no small extent. Mostly, I've been reading, and I'm astonished by the number of books about Hollywood. I leaf through many of them, trying to find one that reveals the movies the way they were. Occasionally, there is some truth, but mostly nostalgia and very little sense of the company town.

I'll try to reconstruct it, though I'm not sure it won't be a subjective view. Autumnal notes tend to be immensely personal.

Hollywood in the early thirties—and stretching out until perhaps ten years ago—could best be compared to the Holy Roman Empire or Germany prior to the unification and Bismarck. It consisted of seven duchies (Fox, M.G.M., Warner's, Columbia, R.K.O., Paramount, United Artists) each reigned over by a feudal lord in battle with each other and yet bound together by their common interest, which was simply to get as much talent as possible and pay as little as possible for it. Or, if it served their purpose, to pay as *much* as possible for it.

To help them, they had created monsters known as Agents. These were men like Milton Bren, Frank Orsatti, Myron Selznick, Frank Joyce, Frank Vincent,* Harry Edington—names that rarely appear in a history of Hollywood but are as important in some instances as

---

* A man I admired and loved. He is gone now, and I miss him—his integrity, his majesty of spirit.

the nabobs that ran the town. It was difficult, in my case, certainly, to tell whose side some of them were on—the client's or the studio's. Certainly, they had access to the highest reaches of power, and their manipulations shaped the course of your life.

None of these gentlemen acted as procurers (with the possible exception of one), but their underlings provided services calculated to make some studio personnel happy during their lunch hours. The casting couch was not as prevalent as it has been heralded, but there is little question that young female starlets—and a few male hopefuls —sang for their supper. When they weren't available or willing, the subagents had viable telephone numbers.

Because of these intimate relationships between top-echelon movie executives and agents, some agents were always able to play both sides of the fence. I found that out straightaway in my negotiations with Warner Brothers. I was caught in a crazy kind of deal that involved, for the first time, a raid on one studio by another. There had always been a gentleman's agreement (sic) that if M.G.M. or Warner's or Paramount had a star under contract, no other studio would offer him a better deal. Warner's broke that rigid rule and secured a number of stars whom Paramount felt belonged to them, hook, line, and sinker. They included William Powell, Ruth Chatterton, and Kay Francis. Warner's paid them astronomical sums. Since I was represented now by the same agent who had manipulated this expensive felony, I was to be offered to Warner's at a bargain.

I changed agents; I fought; I became a businessman; I looked at the small print; I demanded—and finally got—four months off each year to do a play. That I never used it is not Jack Warner's fault; it is my own.

But I realized I was in a web just short of being corrupt in which it was vital to protect yourself or you would become indentured labor— the Hollywood ideal!

The New York theatrical producer was hardly without warts, but even the least of them loved the theater, put up his own money, or went out and raised it, did plays because he believed in them (commercially or artistically), and took the risk along with the rest of us—playwright, director, actor. The studio head took no such risk and had no such love. For most of them had reached this high station quite by accident. They had been owners of stores in which nickelodeons happened to be tenants; they had been glove-makers or bouncers or disgraced members of city administrations or exhibitors or just plain lucky; they were mostly illiterate and, if educated at all, badly— and yet they were the ones who decided what America would see and hear upon its screens. Not only America—the world.

From the moment films deserted train wrecks for fiction, they became the lengthened shadows of the men who produced them—not the men who directed them or wrote them or acted in them, but the men who decided what story would be made and how. There was no conspiracy to lobotomize reality. There was no need to. Most of the early producers—and they had remarkable longevity—made films out of the moral training they'd received as children. That training was mostly Jewish and Catholic and only rarely Protestant, though that ethic was hardly different.

In the silent film virtue was always rewarded and sin punished. The favorite comics (Charlie Chaplin, Buster Keaton, Harold Lloyd, Harry Langdon, Snub Pollard, etc.) were pantomimists (usually plucked from the music halls and circuses) who were inevitably poor, downtrodden, despised by society, and yet always triumphant in the end. They became the dream fantasies of the immigrants who shaped them.

Women were treated as second-class citizens, rarely having any function beyond basting turkeys or bearing children. Mothers were very popular indeed—long-suffering mothers made of buckram between their shoulders and knees.

Younger women, to be successful, were pretty much always waifs: Mary Pickford, the Gishes, Marguerite Clark, Mary Philbin, Mae Marsh, all played variations on the same theme. Whether orphans or victims of stepmothers, they were wide-eyed, innocent, and put upon; by the fade-out they'd found a young man with a strong jaw and a Greek profile.

Note, too, how many—practically all—movies ended with boy and girl meeting each other and heading for the altar. Movies always said that marriage was the end of all *Sturm und Drang.* Anybody who's ever married knows it's the beginning.

There were whores, of course—but they were called dancehall girls or by some historical name. Pola Negri played Dubarry in *Passion*, Geraldine Farrar was the sexy and miserable mistress of Montezuma in *The Woman God Forgot* (note the implied moral criticism in that title), and Theda Bara and Louise Glaum, dripping eye shadow and breastplates, were fallen women who always got what they deserved —death, prison, infamy.

The western flourished and gave the world a crazy, distorted picture of the pioneer push westward. Indians were villains, cowboys were paragons of gallantry, the covered wagon was the very symbol of the American conquest of the plains and the Rockies. In only the rarest of cases did the filmmaker have the vaguest knowledge of the real facts about our western frontier. And except for an occasional film directed by John Ford, American history was distorted beyond recognition.

As was society. Remember all those swell movies in which the young man of the house on the hill wanted to marry the waitress in town, and she had to cope with Louise Closser Hale or Edna Mae Oliver as the young man's bigoted mother? Those pictures really knocked off the Four Hundred. And it was high fashion to prove (the millionaires doing the proving) that All Is Not Gold That Glitters. Money Isn't Everything. Poor but Proud, that's the ticket—and God-fearing alternates, literally called by competing ideologies, Opiates of the Masses.

As for the attitude toward minorities, all heroes and heroines were blond and all villains and roués were raven. As for Chinese, they were Fu Manchu and Charlie Chan. As for Negroes, they were Stepin Fechit or only occasionally Bojangles.

David W. Griffith, on the other hand, tried a little harder and made *Birth of a Nation*, which succeeded only in having lots of waifs, mothers, and profiles reactivate the Ku Klux Klan. Then he made *Intolerance*, which gave Cecil B. DeMille the way to show orgies and semisexual permissiveness on the screen as a horrid example of how not to behave.

There were exceptions to all of this, but by and large Adolph Zukor, Jesse Lasky, Louis Mayer, Harry Cohn, Sam Goldwyn, the Warners, Carl Laemmle, the Schencks, and the Skourases—whatever their own personal moralities—imposed their childhood moralities on the screen. And let us not forget the work ethic, the emphasis on success and getting ahead, the Catholic Church, and the jingoistic preoccupation with the armed forces. Ever recall a newsreel that didn't end with the S.S. *Utah* at sea?

I go into all this because that was the situation in which the movies found their tongue. In those first babbling years a revolution occurred. There were new actors (like me), new directors, new writers, but—and this is the essential point—the same old owners. Everything changed but the bosses. It's as though covered wagon drivers took on automobiles, railroad men flew aeroplanes, country doctors taught Einstein.

And they were seemingly imperishable; they kept their power for four decades after the movies found its tongue.

When Gladys and I first came to California to fulfill the obligations of the Warner Brothers contract, it never occurred to us to give up the apartment on Eleventh Street. This was to be an interlude; we were both New Yorkers and people of the theater, and we had no intention whatever of remaining here. So we took up residence in the penthouse of the Chateau Elysée, which was headquarters and command post for a great many of the New York expatriates.* Another branch of New Yorkers *manqués* was the Garden of Allah, but that was mostly occupied by the Algonquin crowd (Robert Benchley, Dotty Parker, et al.) and was a little fast for Gladys and me.

At first we were supplied with a car and driver. When that ran out, we took taxis to Burbank until it became obvious that we must buy a car. Only lately I failed a driving test (a dismal moment). Let me tell you that I was one of the most backward pupils my driving instructor ever encountered. The mysteries of the clutch I never fully conquered —and, it seems forever after, that driving was a time for musing, and musing is not a good thing to do when driving. When the freeways appeared, I thought motoring would be better; I negotiated them once and never again. Joan Crawford once told me that in trying to get on one she sat frozen with a hundred cars backed up behind her. When the cops came, she simply sobbed out her terror.

One can pretty much tell your status out here (except for Howard Hughes who always drove a beat-up Chevrolet) by the kind of car you drive. My first was a Ford upon which the Warner Brothers frowned; they got me into a LaSalle and then later into a top-echelon car, and I've stayed with it because they gave me a good deal. If you've got to be a movie star, you might as well take advantage of the fringe benefits. When I did appearances for Lux on radio, I got enough soap to wash my laundry for several lifetimes.

(I've just mentioned Howard Hughes. I met him a number of times. He was polite, well dressed, wore shoes, not sneakers, and never seemed in the least odd. I wish I could think of one exotic thing he did or one eccentric sentence he uttered. I just can't. He seemed a very pleasant gentleman, and that is not the stuff books are made of.)

I would prefer to forget the first picture I made under my new and highly rewarding Warner Brothers contract. It is a good thing the contract was rewarding because the picture certainly was not. I will not discuss the story; it was hokey-pokey and notable chiefly for its dependence upon coincidence. Notable, too, that it was called *The Widow from Chicago* and put its emphasis on Alice White. Now Miss White was part of the silent pictures—a charming part, indeed, but almost entirely without any acting ability. The director, Eddie

---

* It is now a home for the aged, luxurious, indeed, presided over by a Dr. Fifield, whose political stance is to the right of McKinley.

Cline, had a very minimum sense of the uses of the English language. Nice man, Cline, and I liked him, but I liked my mother better, and I wouldn't let *her* direct a picture.

I hate to appear so sour and disagreeable, and I must say I managed a cordial exterior, trying only now and then to inject a suggestion to Miss White or Mr. Cline and more than occasionally rearranging the dialogue. The actor has one certain way of getting the script changed: All he has to do is say that he isn't comfortable with a line or can't say it. Automatically he's permitted instant rewrite. (Between us, that kind of rewrite can change the whole meaning of a scene and throw everything out of balance. It should not be permitted, but I continue to do it.)

I was, let me admit it frankly now, full of self-doubt and self-hate and a bit of shame. What in the name of God was I doing playing a notorious vice baron named Dominic? What the hell did I know about a vice baron with a passion for nightclubs? Brother, was I tempted to go to Jack Warner or Hal Wallis and say "Get me out of this. Parole me. Pardon me! Here's all your money back!"

Naturally, I did no such thing. After each day's shooting, I'd take a look at the rushes and feel slightly ill, then hurry to my dressing room. Incidentally, I'd better describe that to you. It was an opulent suite consisting of a living room, dressing room, bath, a kitchen, and a patio—all done in terribly masculine dark wood and rather splendid English furniture. It was filled with fresh flowers, supplied, I expect, by the studio nursery, and my dresser (valet) would throw out any carnation that dared to wilt. I wasn't even allowed to handle my own makeup. Instead, Mr. Percy Westmore himself applied the yellow gook and lipstick and eyebrow pencil that made me fear to look into a mirror.

And weekly, on a Sheraton desk, in a manila envelope, was the check with all those zeros. How long is five years anyway? More and more checks would come, and then Gladys and I would get out of this horror and I'd play Lear and buy pictures and an annuity and forever farewell to ghastly people like Dominic and *The Widow from Chicago*.

I'm not sure you could call *Widow from Chicago* a success. The accounting procedures of film companies are so complex that unless success is highly, astronomically visible, like *Sound of Music* or *The Godfather*, you really never know what a picture earns. And earnings are obviously the clue to public approval. But I think *Chicago* made it; there really was no way for it *not* to make it under the release procedures then in vogue.

The companies had a thing called block booking, which meant that, good or bad, sick or ill, a film was assured of a nationwide release. In addition, many companies, including Warner's, had their own theaters and a goodie like *Widow* was bound to be played and even held over. And there was a third element that contributed to making movies a national habit: the Depression.

In 1931, before F.D.R. and the New Deal, with Herbert Hoover still advocating relief from starvation by private philanthropy (his remarks on this subject are still extant on newsreel film), unemployment reached new heights—or do I mean depths? Anyway, if you had a quarter before noon you could go to a Warner Brothers theater and spend the day. Not only was it warm against the winter cold, but it was a relief from the boring, benumbing process of seeking a job where none existed. Obviously, I am not including the desperately poor who didn't have the quarter, who lived in the Hoovervilles; I'm talking about the respectable, middle-class, white-collar workers who had used up their savings. As a small antidote to their hopelessness and shame, they could spend their days at the movies and go home at night and tell their families they'd been job-searching all day.

Clearly, block booking has gone out by federal court order, and in no small measure, the decline of Hollywood as a theatrical moving picture factory has ineluctably followed. Again by federal order, studios could no longer own theaters; that's like telling Chrysler and Ford and Buick that they're not allowed to sell their own cars or have showrooms. As for the Depression itself, it remains only in the memory of a generation that is fast approaching the non-membership of the Grand Army of the Republic.

Still, lots of us were unaffected—even some of us who found our first prosperity, even our first million, *during* those years. Was it any wonder that we, out of conscience or genuine concern, turned to social causes to ease the pain of our new-found security?

I said pain and I mean pain.

In late 1930 Hal Wallis asked me to his office to discuss my playing the role of Otero in *Little Caesar*—the best-seller by William R. Burnett, already recommended to me by Leah Salisbury.

Yes, I said Otero. Not Rico (Cesare Bandello) the lead, but Otero, a minor part.

To this day I think it was a ruse. I think Hal had always meant for me to play Rico, and his ploy was to soften my rigid backbone. I've never asked him.

May I say a word about him? Hal Wallis is perhaps the least known of the movie moguls because actually he is not a mogul at all. Unlike the rest of the boys, he had (and has) instinctive taste. He loves making a buck, and he loves meaning and significance as well. Through the years he has gone from pictures about Becket and Queen Elizabeth (historically accurate and beautifully devised) to Elvis Presley and Martin and Lewis.

Maybe he saw in Presley a *Nouvelle Vague* (which he most certainly was) or in Jerry Lewis a clown in the great tradition (which the French intellectuals passionately believe him to be). Whatever his reasoning or his intuitions, he is a great producer, and you don't find his like around much anymore. (He also has a stunning collection of paintings, with two thrilling Fantin-Latours. I had nothing whatever to do with his collecting, but he had a great deal to do with mine. The money that bought them came from Warner's via Wallis.)

But on that day in his office I loathed him. In his cool, offhand and peremptory manner he handed me the script of *Little Caesar*, pointing out that the part of Otero was exactly right for me. I took the script back to my dressing room, read it, and decided not only that the part of Otero was exactly wrong for me but that the script itself was a literal and undramatized rendering of the novel.

I catch on fast, and I could see that the movies were and, by definition had to be, visual and not dependent totally upon verbal communication. This was a strange conclusion for one who had always depended upon words and dialogue. But it was now amply clear to me that a closeup could convey inner thought, that the technique of cutting could provide the aside. And it also came to me, not in a vision, but after careful study of the new sound movies, that movies had to move.

And what occurred to me with the utmost finality was that if I were going to get anywhere in this new medium, I was not about to play bits. I did not ask for star billing; I knew that was a danger to be avoided until the public (and I) considered me a star—but I also knew that third leads and bits were a graveyard.

So back I went to Wallis and announced pompously: "If you're going to have me in *Little Caesar* as Otero, you will completely imbalance the picture. The only part I will consider playing is Little Caesar."

Hal was maddeningly patient, and I matched his patience. Rarely has there been so polite and well-managed double fury. But out of it I began to speak, to surface what I felt about the character in *Little Caesar*. It was not, I told him, merely a hokey-pokey cheap shot; it was rather a Greek tragedy. Inherent in it was the drama of the humblest, the most dispossessed, seeking to break his way out of the anonymity of ignorance, toward a goal in which he would be not one of many men but a man on his own. I even spilled some of my own longings that were parallel. Though Rico's goals were immoral and antisocial, and I had confined myself within stringent palings, we had this in common—somehow we would be different, above, higher. While I hoped the gods would not destroy me for my own ambition, they would surely destroy Rico, and in his death throes he would cry the eternal wail: "Mother of God, is this the end of Rico?"*

Hal listened carefully to my ravings, made a few notes, then reminded me that my contract gave me no approval of roles. Were I to refuse Otero, I could be put on suspension and no other studio would be able to use me—and no theatrical producer either.

Having made these points, thus asserting his contractual authority, Hal then said he would take the matter up with Mr. Warner, and within a matter of hours I was cast as Little Caesar. I think—and my memory may be faulty—that as a consideration I extended my contract. If I am wrong about this, I apologize to Hal. And I do now what I have never done before. I thank him for *Little Caesar*.

I am not at all sure I was ready at the time to thank him for Mervyn LeRoy, that cheery, bubbling, joking director assigned to guide me through this film. Mervyn was so likable that I distrusted him instantly. I have fears of professionals who make jokes of everything.

But I soon learned something about Mervyn that makes him special. It does not make him uniquely gifted or more than ordinarily talented, but it accounts for his long and successful career.

More than any director I know, Mervyn is the audience. He is the man who goes to the box office and plunks down his thirty-five cents (now three dollars or more) and loves or hates a picture through his own emotions. He is morally indignant about injustice, but the injustices must be large and blatant. He loves love; he loves children; he loves mothers; he feels deeply that in the end justice must be triumphant. I must say it again: He is the audience.

Add to this his technical proficiency, his command of celluloid, of lenses, of wild walls, of projection booths, of the million intricacies of manufacturing pictures, and you have a knowledgeable director —knowledgeable, too, of his own shortcomings. Never would he tell an actor how to read a line; never would he ignore a suggestion from any member of the cast or, indeed, from a grip** or prop man.

---

* That line, so often quoted, was actually shot two ways, and the way most of you hear it now on television and even in theaters then, is "Mother of *Mercy*, is this the end of Rico?"

** Note from L.S.: A "grip" is a generalized term for any stagehand, whether in the theater or in the movies—and now even in television.

Mervyn is no Ingmar Bergman or Alfred Hitchcock or John Ford or Ernst Lubitsch or Murnau or Jacques Tati or Buñuel; he does not sign his pictures. But he is a solid workman, and his films have made audiences laugh and cry. He is a special breed, and he is one of the giants (with a small *g*) that converted Hollywood from a sleezy suburb into a populist Athens, and it took me a long time to get used to him and it.

My God, what a time he must have had getting used to me. Oh, brother, I really wasn't very nice about the whole thing. The prospect of revealing my inner feelings and private behavior is repellent to me, chiefly because I think I've maintained a pretty fair facade of reserve. On the other hand, the Inquisitor who has been asking me pointed questions about those early Hollywood years has convinced me (after, I assure you, months of cajolery) that I should tell the truth— as exactly as I can put it together—about those first years in Hollywood. I'm assured it may serve some purpose for historians, and while I find that hard to believe, I am persuaded to risk sharing some of the seamier sides of my nature.

In the cast of *Little Caesar* there was a young man named Douglas Fairbanks, Jr. He was a fair and handsome young man indeed and the son of a well-known father. To try to chat with him about anything except Hollywood gossip was unproductive and futile. He was then married, I think, to Joan Crawford, and Gladys and I dined with them sumptuously and formally. I've never dined at Buckingham, but I think the young Fairbankses had more service plates, rare wines, and rare lamb than their Majesties.

The chit-chat at table was vapid—no less vapid when the ladies left while we gents had our cigars and brandy. *We* talked about the state of the industry, the importance of electing Herbert Hoover (in which I mildly did not concur), and the state of the Art, which meant what gross what picture was achieving.

Gladys reported that the ladies talked about the servant problems, the length of skirts, Bullock's Wilshire, Magnin's, and varieties of roses. A great many of the ladies believed all the flowers in a garden should be white. That, apparently, raised a few eyebrows among the other ladies who believed that all the flowers in a garden should be variegated.

For those of you who remember the headlines and movie magazines of an earlier and even contemporary period, let me assure you that among ladies and gentlemen both, the language was circumspect, unmarred by Anglo-Saxonisms; there was no nude bathing in swimming pools, no orgies, no anything. At ten o'clock sharp we would all depart via our Cadillacs, Packards, and Pierce Arrows because we all had to be up at an ungodly hour in the morning to make faces at the camera.

It would be less than fair for me to leave you with this view of the Fairbankses. Doug, as he grew and matured, became one of the most urbane and sophisticated men I ever knew; he also became a very good actor out of sheer grit. While politically he still, I think, leans in the direction of Grover Cleveland, in music, arts, and his concerns for the wretched, he has grown into a conspicuous example of susceptibility to growth.

Miss Crawford, of course, is a miracle. After divorcing Doug, she married Franchot Tone, whose political attitudes had been honed by the Group Theatre, and she went along. (You could hardly say *right* along.) Never did an actress work harder; never have I seen such improvement. I don't know how old she is; I *do* know she is virtually indestructible and that being in her company is sheer delight. Some of the things I liked about her least I now like about her most—her air, her grooming, her slightly imperious quality.

Those of us in *Little Caesar* who had come from the stage—Sidney Blackmer, Glenda Farrell, William Collier, Jr., and George E. Stone (for whom I felt a special affection because he was playing Otero, the role originally intended for me)—banded together. We were, I think, insufferable. *Our* conversation was a constant put-down of Hollywood, and our plans for our return to Mother Earth—Broadway. We were, I must admit, quite sickening.

For Gladys, all of Hollywood was sickening. Put yourself in her place. I would leave her at six o'clock in the morning, lolling in our Louis XIV, XV, XVI, Louis Phillipe, Barker Brothers, semi-Hispanic penthouse at the Chateau Elysée, and she would have the day before her. Off to Bullock's she would go, or Bess Schlank (then a haute courturiere) or Robinson's, which, while downtown, had the feel of Lord & Taylor's, and then lunch at the Derby or the French Room at the Ambassador, then a peek into the Dalzell Hatfield Galleries (the only picture dealer even worthy of the name), then perhaps to the antique shops on Los Feliz, then possibly a massage, a cup of tea with Rosalie Stewart or Pauline Lord (both ensconced at the Chateau) where they would talk of New York, then waiting for me to come home, not exactly a definite appointment, because, in those days, before the Screen Actors Guild got its two cents in, we would frequently work beyond six o'clock, six days a week. In Hollywood, Saturday was a weekday.

And once I arrived home, I was hardly a darling; the day might have gone badly; I would have to study tomorrow's lines; we would dine in the restaurant of the Chateau—only rarely accepting an invitation to a private home because the invitations were rare, and when they arrived, I was in no mood for the people or a black tie. So we were restaurant-bound, and while there were some good ones, there really weren't that many, and my palate, trained on Rumanian broilings and later on gourmet food, could find neither. You know, there wasn't decent delicatessen in Hollywood until after World War II. And since Gladys only suffered Jewish food, I could hardly take her to those out-of-the-way kosher joints in Boyle Heights or on Temple Street.

On Saturday nights (it I didn't have to work all night) we would join the swells and proceed jauntily to the Coconut Grove at the Ambassador where we'd have the regular dinner (salad was the first course) and then dance to the strains of Freddy Martin's orchestra. Occasionally Bing Crosby would sing. Or we'd go to Culver City to the Plantation, a garish roadhouse where George Olsen led the band and his wife, Ethel Shutta, would sing.

On Sundays there were no baseball games, no *New York Times Book Review*, no museums except a very bad one, no concerts or opera, no anything, so we'd drive occasionally to Santa Barbara, and even to Tijuana—actually Agua Caliente—where we'd gamble and drink a bit of legal booze, but sparingly, because we had that long drive back, and nobody ever called me Barney Oldfield.

Am I coming through loud and clear?

We were miserable.

13

Among the books I have been reading lately I've discovered a whole rash on the subject of the man nearing forty who apparently has it made yet suffers a diminution of the spirit; the more eminent the psychiatrist author, the more complex the diagnosis. As I read, I see symptoms that applied to me—but no more solutions now than then.

You have to provide your own solutions, and driving back and forth from Warner's, sitting in my dressing room between takes, trying desperately to sleep when no sleep would come, I reviewed the bidding. First, it was clear that I had had no childhood in the classic sense; furthermore, I had sown no wild oats in the even more classic sense. I was bound by moral considerations that were fast becoming passé; I was what I wanted to be—but so different. Movie star, yes, but that offered me nothing except celebrity and money. Since that was what apparently everybody else in the world wanted, why wasn't it enough for me?

God knows I should have been on my knees every morning thanking Him for my good fortune. The world was in chaos. Depression was withering away at America, and there seemed no solution; Hitler was gathering his brown forces in Germany; Spain was splitting at the seams; Mussolini was making the trains run on time just as certainly as he was abridging human freedom; the Soviet Union sat on the land between Europe and Asia licking its chops, waiting to pounce.

And I was miserable and bored in Hollywood? I should have had my head examined.

I did. Not by a psychiatrist but by friends—lawyers, wise people who suggested to me (as I suggest to you now) that you can't solve everything at once; you have to attack the problems one by one.

My first attack was to try to make my marriage work. Gladys was perishing of boredom, of uselessness, of having no discernible function. Oh, she tried everything—bridge, hostess at the Assistance League for the unfortunate, meetings to discuss mandatory school lunches in the Mexican neighborhoods, but, for the most part she devoted herself to Christmas.

Let me explain that as a child and in the early years before the theater Christmas was an embarrassment to me. In Bucharest, at the anniversary of the birth of the Savior, the Jews would huddle in their compounds, uncertain whether the celebrating Christians would, in their zeal, decide that harassing and killing Jews was more fun than decorating a tree—a form of community love of Christ that the Cossacks especially enjoyed in Russia though they were amateurs when compared to the Poles to whom the pogrom was equivalent to High Mass.

Later, in the theater, I rationalized that Christmas was a national holiday of joy, which, while its roots were far from secular, had managed to become a holiday for all people who believed in peace and goodwill. I was never really convinced.

But here I was married to Gladys to whom Christmas was so joyous and exciting a holiday that every December 26 she would immediately start preparations for the next December 25. For her it was a nonstop, year-long activity. I tried to join in, helping her wrap presents for some of her more obscure cousins, making lists, debating the size and form of the tree, even once agreeing to act as Santa Claus for one of her new charities (goodness knows, I had the figure for it), but backing out at the last minute because of a convenient and spurious case of tonsillitis.

But Gladys was no fool. She saw through me. The more enthusiastic my performance, the more certain she was that I was a phony, which, indeed, I was.

And so our marriage was rocky. Now it is the fashion to talk it out, communicate, touch, hold nothing back. In those days that was considered bickering and quarreling.

Well, out of bicker and quarrel, I came to know that Gladys wanted to work; she was an actress, had appeared in *Funny Face* with Fred Astaire, had even appeared with me. She *was* an actress, and she had a right to her career, but she was no longer Gladys Lloyd; she was Mrs. Edward G. Robinson, and if you think that made it easier, you're wrong.

I think more than anything in the world I hate asking favors. But I went to either Hal Wallis and Jack Warner (or perhaps it was a very nice casting man whose name I've forgotten) and suggested that in *Smart Money* there was a small part of a cigar stand clerk that was just right for Gladys; she had the characterization and looks for it. She got the job. And in *Five Star Final*, wouldn't she be just great in the part of Miss Edwards? Who could be a better Miss Edwards than Gladys? She got the job. As for *The Hatchet Man*, Gladys was absolutely perfect for bringing Fan Yi to life. She got the job. In *Two Seconds*, who better to play "Woman" than Miss Lloyd? She got the job.

These varied bits between 1930 and 1933 were at best stop-gap, but they enabled us to go to the studio together, and if she were given a dressing room far better than the roles warranted, that was just part of the gravy of being a movie star's wife.

Funny thing: Whenever I had to play a scene with her, not often and certainly not long, or whenever she stood on the set watching, I was suffused with embarrassment. I would look toward her for approval, and if she shook her head, I asked the director to make another take. That is the classic role of the stage mother; Gladys was in the ludicrous role of stage wife.

In any case, these small excursions by Gladys into the movies provided some easing of tension. And as our social life began to grow, the tensions decreased even more.

By this time the town was beginning to fill with friends from New York. Since *Little Caesar* had now raised me onto a pedestal, we were deluged with invitations. I was even asked to join the Hillcrest Country Club, but I refused; what the hell would I do in a golf club? I didn't know a mashie from a niblick. Later I joined because of the Sunday night buffets and the general *gemulichtkeit*, and it has become one of my favorite haunts.

But I was not interested in the country club fat cats then; I began to find friends with whom I could talk about the way the world was— and they were mostly writers. Included among them was the young man who is tortuously guiding me through the maze of these memories. He was a Democrat, and so was I; I was by way of being a movie star, and he was writing a picture with Erich von Stroheim. But we had a lot in common; his antecedents were partially, if not thoroughly, Rumanian, and while we disagreed on the recipes for eggplant and *pitcha* (his versions included garlic; mine emphatically did not), we both agreed that Hoover had to go and F.D.R. had to be elected.

While I have the most vivid memories of moments and incidents in

Bucharest, and he can tell you the names of everybody in his fifth-grade class at P.S. 167 (a school in Brooklyn, a borough of the city of New York which I view with certain disdain*), neither of us can recall the time or place of our first meeting. It concerned F.D.R.—about that we are quite certain. But where it took place and who else was there remain locked away. In concert we suggest that the paralysis of the McCarthy era is so pervasive that neither of us is capable of naming names.

There were mostly writers, of course, but a good smattering of directors and producers and only an occasional actor—though certainly the Gleasons and Helen Gahagan and Melvyn Douglas and Gene Kelly (the most forthright and decent of citizens) were bound to have been with us. Not to confuse you further, Lenny and I are saying that we're having difficulty sorting out the three F.D.R. campaigns on which we worked together.

By "work" I don't mean that we went out into the precinct and collected signatures. The stars (*sic*) were used to gather crowds; we were the political backers. The writers prepared our speeches, which, in my case, were forever bones of contention between Lenny and myself. Oh dear, not in terms of content; we were as one in our zeal for social security, T.V.A., the government as employer of last resort —though with due respect for the dignity of the worker—rural electrification, the whole New Deal philosophy.

The subject of most of our arguments was syntax. And the way out of that was to rehearse the speeches together as if they were the first reading of a play. Afterward, I would deliver them—never reading them—from memory as if I'd made them up on the spur of the moment. I have never been a spontaneous speaker; I sound like one, but it's pure fakery. I know every word by heart, and if the audience thinks I'm extemporizing, thank the American Academy of Dramatic Arts.

And thank the writers who have helped me. Not only Lenny, but Irving Stone, Ranald MacDougall, Allen Rivkin, and a great many others. I don't want to make lists of them; you never know about lists anymore. In the unfathomable future we may all be hailed in front of some as yet unauthorized government instrumentality to explain why we were so insistent on toilets for the migrant workers.

* Note from L.S.: I view the borough of the Bronx with equal disdain.

14

The years 1930 to 1933 were so full of new experiences, adventures, and events that I fear I'm getting ahead of myself and having difficulty sorting out the chronology. Actually, as in the best plays, the best life is that in which things overlap.

So let me back up for a moment and discuss some of the pictures I made. I hasten to assure you I've no intention of boring you with the details of the more than a hundred in which I participated. The most fun for me would be to tell you about the ones I hated; the most sensible policy for me would be to ignore them. Of course, if you're old enough, you can't ignore them; you paid to see them, and you're entitled to an apology. Forgive me if I think, from time to time, *I'm* entitled to an apology.

Still, let me talk for a moment about *Five Star Final*, a film taken from a beautifully written play by Louis Weitzenkorn and directed by Mervyn LeRoy. Since this was my second picture with him, I was far better equipped to deal with him, and he'd gotten my measure as well. More importantly, the play was about something. I played Randall, a city editor who is persuaded by his boss to pry into a twenty-year-old, long-forgotten murder case, causing a scandal that builds the newspaper's circulation and brings desperate ruin to the utterly innocent daughter of the murderer. As Randall, I first relished the heady joy of muckraking and sensationalism; as the play (picture) progressed, Randall began to see that a journalist has a responsibility beyond the cold statistics of how many papers are sold.

Consider this story in the light of those who today believe in the unabridged right of the press to print anything (and God knows I am among them). But Weitzenkorn posed a dilemma that has to be considered along with the First Amendment. Does freedom of the press not carry with it some freedom of compassion, some freedom concerning the rights of the innocently involved?

Okay. The ethics are one problem; the character I played is another. I loved Randall because he wasn't a gangster. I suspect he was conceived as an Anglo-Saxon. To look at me nobody would believe it, but I enjoyed doing him. He made sense, and thus I'm able to say that *Five Star Final* is one of my favorite films.

I'm able to say that the film that followed it—*The Hatchet Man*—is one of my horrible memories. *Two Seconds* is a mishmash memory. I adored *Tiger Shark* because I admired Howard Hawks, and I think the reason I admired him is because he let me chew the scenery. As the best tuna fisherman on the West Coast, with one hand already lost to a shark, a curly ebon wig and a flowing mustachio, I had the time of my life—though I was scared to death of the location.*

We shot most of it off Catalina, and the script called for me to fall into the sea quite a lot. When they cast me, they hadn't the foggiest notion that I couldn't swim, thus a lot of me in that picture is really an anonymous stunt man. Some of it *had* to be me, however, and I can assure you it did nothing to whet my appetite for boats or swimming pools.

I rather liked *Silver Dollar*, which was a biography (highly fictionalized) of Haw Tabor. While I worked very hard in it, my mind wasn't really on it. The world was too much with me.

In November 1932, F.D.R. was elected by a landslide, and we had what Noël Coward used to call a marvelous party. The only trouble with the party was that a great many of the guests kept saying, "It's all very well, but that house painter, Hitler (né Schicklgruber) is really coming up in Germany and look what's going on in Spain and don't discount Mussolini and all the big movie companies are in serious financial condition, and may go into '77B.'" I hardly dared admit that I didn't know what 77B was, but I learned: It's a form of bankruptcy, and it became very stylish.

Gladys was very interested in all these matters, and nobody can doubt that she was one of the most striking and lovely women at all the marvelous parties. But early in the campaign I noticed something in her that wasn't simply withdrawal; she had something on her mind —something very important indeed.

---

* If I sounded a bit like Holbrook Blinn in *The Bad Man*, do not put it down entirely to coincidence.

She had been going to a number of gynecologists and obstetricians (to this day I'm not certain which does what, though their functions have been explained to me over and over again), and there was disagreement about her ability to have another child. Mind you, I'd long since been reconciled to the fact that no child was possible; she'd told me often enough. However, neither of us had counted on the advance in obstetrics—or is it gynecology?

Imagine then the joy, the wonder, the fear, the whole jumble of emotions that beset me when, one evening in July, after I'd come home from work, Gladys, wearing a daffodil yellow negligee and glowing with excitement, kissed me and said, "Eddie, I've a present for you."

She was pregnant.

My first reaction should have been unconfounded joy; instead, it was terror. I'd been advised for so long that pregnancy, in her case, would be fatal. For so long I'd worried that some freak accident would occur and jeopardize her life, and I would be the murderer. But she calmed me; her new physician had assured her that her term of pregnancy would be normal provided she rested, stayed in bed most of the time, was not besieged by doubt or worry, and finally that the birth itself be cesarean.

Well, we did a lot of laughing and crying amid sips of champagne that night (Gladys assured me a small glass of wine would bring on no catastrophe), and we made plans. When the women's magazines later coined the phrase "togetherness," I always think of that night. Gladys and I were really together.

Or were we? I covered up, refused even to acknowledge what I was really thinking about. I would be in my fortieth year when the boy (it never occurred to me that it would be anything but a son) was born (and Gladys was not much behind me), and wasn't it late to be parents? Was it fair to the child? Was I really thinking: "Is it fair to *us?*" Could we manage it? Could we possibly give up the freedom of the childless? But I never mentioned it. Gladys never mentioned it.

Perhaps, as matters turned out, we should have.

In a day or two we had everything worked out. In New York there was a Dr. Pearson, the finest obstetrician (gynecologist) in America. Nobody else would do for Gladys—certainly not a doctor in Los Angeles, a yokel town. And moreover, my son would be born in New York. Gladys wanted to know why.

"I was born in New York," I said.

"Nonsense, you were born in Bucharest."

She simply didn't understand. The day I stepped off *La Touraine* onto the dock at Castle Garden was the day I was *really* born.

And let me add that from the vantage of forty years later that the whole business of a baby being conceived, turning from fetus into child, and eventually being born was a murky mystery to me. Brought up in a Victorian household with absolutely no real knowledge of the physiology, problems, or dangers of pregnancy (it was a word never even used in my childhood) or what the actual birth process entailed (I even hesitantly used the word "confinement"), I think more than anything I wanted friends around. I wanted my mother around. I wanted Gladys' family in the offing; I even wanted her daughter to be within calling distance. I wanted to share this experience; I did not want the responsibility of it alone.

And so it was arranged, after I completed *Silver Dollar*, that the two and a half Robinsons would undertake the Chief–Century journey again—even though the Brothers Warner were preparing the script of *The Little Giant*, about a beer baron who, sensing the inevitable end of Prohibition, decides to try to crash high society.

It was a comedy written by Robert Lord and Wilson Mizner, the wit to whom is ascribed the immortal line, "Hollywood is six suburbs in search of a city." However, I am now told that the line was not Mizner's but Arthur Caesar's. I would say that either was capable of coining it.

Roy Del Ruth was to direct, and Helen Vinson and Mary Astor were to be in the cast. Helen was to play a fake society girl, rolling in wealth, and Mary was to play a *real* society girl who is down on her luck "depression-wise," as it is badly put today. Bugs Ahearn (me) would engage Mary as his social secretary only to discover, in the end, that Helen is the fake and Mary is the real McCoy. Obviously, Bugs, knowing quality, chooses Mary over Helen, though why Helen chooses Bugs is not quite clear.

I talked to Mr. Wallis—or it could have been Jack or Harry Warner. I get confused about which of these three gentlemen I talked to, just as I am still confused about whether or not I was working for Warner Brothers or First National. To any rational person they would seem to be the same company, but to lawyers and the Internal Revenue Service they were, for reasons best known to Blackstone, fictionally, if not actually, separate corporations. It had something to do with taxes no doubt. In the end, something is always about taxes.

We had grim but gentlemanly conversations about my inability to do *The Little Giant*, though since a blessed event was the central issue, the conferences were subdued and cheerfully funereal. No amount of medical referrals could convince me that a Los Angeles physician could compare to Dr. Pearson (whom I'd never met). For my own purposes I envisioned Dr. Pearson delivering the children of kings, emperors, and Rockefellers. I described Gladys' physiological problems in so convincing a fashion—though I knew nothing whatever of them—that even to the Warner faculty it was clear that no one but Dr. Pearson would do. Being fathers themselves and Jewish and awed by childbirth, they could do nothing but agree.

Thus in November, after Mr. Roosevelt was safely elected (though I had severe doubts about Mr. John Nance Garner of Uvalde, Texas), the Robinsons, accompanied by a trained nurse, set out for the snug harbor of New York—but not to Eleventh Street, even though we still had a lease on the apartment.

If you will recall (as I do, but you probably don't because I never seem to realize how long ago all this must seem to somebody who's even forty years of age), in March of 1932 the Lindbergh baby had been kidnapped, and alarm rocked Hollywood, at least among the celebrated. Even though I had to pinch myself to realize that I was now among the celebrated, I did not have to pinch myself to realize that any son of mine could be a real target. Everybody was barring windows, hiring detectives and private police, and the children were guarded on the way to, in, and on the way home from school. I knew I'd have to do the same thing.

Add to that the fact that Eleventh Street could not accommodate a nurse (which Gladys needed in the last four months) or a nursery after the inevitable nastiness of a cesarean, and you will see that Eleventh Street wouldn't do. While Eleventh Street had a doorman and elevator attendants, that didn't seem safe enough. After consultation with experts we chose the Essex House on Central Park South and rented a gargantuan suite high above the park. It offered luxury and security.

Get a load of the kid who'd lived in the Bronx for such a long time. He kept the apartment at the Château Elysée, was paying rent on an apartment on Eleventh Street, and was shelling out golden bills to the Essex House as well. On top of these items add an allowance to mama for her flat and disorderly amounts of money to my brothers who were suffering, not by their own devices, from the bitter fruits of the depression and, by their own devices, from bad investments. Also add that I was an easy touch, and I'd been helping out lots of actors with whom I'd played during the years.

I was not strapped, but God knows, an easy buck I didn't have.

Safe in New York at last, Dr. Pearson went ahead and probed over Gladys and announced cheerfully that all would be well—that is, all would be well if Gladys remained in bed and was not subjected to worry. Meanwhile, he assured us that a cesarean was nothing to worry about. He did not say it was no worse than a bad cold, but I have the clear notion that that was the impression he was trying to leave with us.

At the Essex House we were treated like some vagrant Middle European royalty which was a good thing because we were deluged with flowers, invitations, and visitors. My own mother, wise in the art of bearing children, was a comfort, except that her advice was in contradiction to Dr. Pearson's. The good doctor advised minimum weight increase; mama considered pregnancy with thick cream, malted milks, doubly strengthened chicken soup, custards, meringues, and her own Rumanian version of the French *milles feuilles* for which the haute chefs of Saulieu would have taken refuge in shameful suicide.

There were, of course, inevitable meetings between mama and Gladys' New England family, a prospect I viewed with considerable alarm until I realized that they shared the same formula for pregnancy: heavy cream and lots of it.

What was I to do? There was no sense during this waiting period to remain staring at Gladys in bed all day; less sense in attempting to discuss diet and dilation—dilation being a concomitant of accouchement and a subject leaving me with a vague feeling of nausea.

Still, I had many friends, and my Warner's contract allowed me four months' time to do a play. Obviously, that was the ticket.

As I made the trek down Broadway and my old haunts between Thirty-eighth and Forty-eighth streets, I felt little change inside myself, but the change outside was geometric. I was mobbed for autographs. I didn't mind that so much, but I certainly was distressed by the young (frequently sodden) men who approached me with: "Tough guy, huh? Little Caesar, huh? Well, let's see how tough you are. I can knock you into Tuesday!"

The point was undebatable. They certainly could have knocked me into Tuesday. I sought refuge in office building lobbies; I pleaded with walking patrolmen for assistance; I gave up walking on Broadway.

I bought dark glasses in an attempt to achieve disguise and anonymity; they merely added to my troubles. Dark glasses were a signature. I took taxis, and the taxi-drivers assured me I knew nothing of the gangster world; for a price they would show me. The usual tip of a dime on top of the fare would be thrown back at me, a quarter was reluctantly accepted, and a dollar seemed required.

So I got one of those Carey Cadillacs with a chauffeur out of the need for survival, and he'd wait for me as I lunched at 21. Even there I was treated as some kind of gangster demigod, sometimes by the drunken stockbrokers at the bar who wanted to square off and show they could knock the shit out of Little Caesar. (The word is theirs; not mine.)

Over those 21 lunches I was offered a variety of excellent dramas —far, indeed, from the garbage I was playing at Warner Brothers. And I was so sorely tempted that I was ready to make a deal. The producer was delirious with joy and assured me there would be no problem about billing. My name would come above the title in letters as large as the Chesterfield ads on Broadway across from the Astor. There would be a three-and-a-half-week rehearsal, four weeks playing the Stations of the Cross, Philadelphia and Boston, and after a year's run, we could tour.

I told him I had four months.

Four months!

That meant, after rehearsals and out-of-town dates, that there would be only four and a half weeks in New York. Then he laughed. Of course I was joking; matters could certainly be arranged with Warner Brothers. Besides, he was offering me a thousand a week— okay, fifteen hundred a week and 10 percent of the gross. What would Hal Wallis say when he heard that? I knew exactly what Hal Wallis would say—and he said it.

It was clear I'd made an uncalculated error. That four-month clause was ridiculous. And fifteen hundred a week—a sum formerly so astronomical it was beyond imagining—now seemed paltry. So much for the theater.

I had a ball with all my old friends, but there weren't so many of them now. A whole bunch was in Hollywood. The ones in town were talking a curious language—new plays. And I hadn't seen the old ones. When I caught up, the conversation was easier, but as for next year's gossip, I was uninformed. Who'd play what and who was doing it with whom? And their interest in Hal Wallis was minimal. The only thing they really wanted to know was what Greta Garbo was really like, and I had no answer because I'd never laid eyes on her.

Thank God for Sam Jaffe. Together we'd have a look at some paintings. I could afford sketches by my friend Averbach Levy and caricatures by my even better friend Abe Birnbaum, but the stuff at Knoedler's and Marie Harriman's—a Pissarro costing as much as twenty-five hundred dollars for a medium-sized oil—was out of the question. As for the Gauguins and Matisses at Wildenstein, forget it! Who could pay ten thousand dollars for a picture?

Who could pay the bill at the Essex House?

Where the hell was my salary check from Warner's?

Let's get it straight. I wasn't put on suspension or anything indelicate like that, but I was taken off the payroll because I wasn't performing. Oh, they understood, and the time out would be added to the end of the contract, but surely I did not expect to be paid for nonperformance.

Dear Mr. Robinson, you understand, we're a business and not a charitable institution, and the way things are. . . . You *do* understand, Mr. Robinson, don't you? While we wouldn't dream of your coming back to make *The Little Giant*, still, if Mrs. Robinson were beautifully taken care of and we could manage to do all your scenes in a lump and thus shorten the schedule so you'd be certain to be back in time for your son's birth, I'm sure financial matters could be arranged entirely to your satisfaction.

How's about it, dear Mr. Robinson?

Dear Mr. Robinson regarded this conversation with indignation. On the other hand, Emanuel Goldenberg figured what could be the harm in looking into the matter. Listen, to echo my grandmother, logical is logical.

Well, I had a long conversation with Dr. Pearson, and he dropped his bedside manner and let me have it between the eyes. Had he been consulted in an earlier stage of the episode (that's what he called it—an episode), he most certainly would have recommended terminating the pregnancy. (Never once did he use the word "abortion.") By this time, however, causative factors would make termination a grave risk. Besides, even in view of the edema (I had to stop him and find out what edema was—it's fluid retention), he was cautiously optimistic that this would not be a breach case or a forceps one, and he was, you can be sure, a great believer in twilight sleep (scopolamine) despite what others might say about it. He was, of course, minimally anxious about postnatal hemorrhaging; he even half smiled when he said that, as if to assure me that in his hands I was not even to consider the possibility.

To my direct question: "Would it be all right if I left my wife for approximately eight weeks but returned in time for the birth?" he answered: "My dear Mr. Robinson, you serve absolutely no purpose here. Your job as father was accomplished, I suspect, one evening, and that's absolutely the last you have to do with it."

"But what?" I insisted, "about the psychological effects? Will she feel abandoned, deserted? Will it appear that I don't want the child?"

"My dear Mr. Robinson," he said, "to predict the psychological reactions of a pregnant woman is to wallow in quicksand, but if you'd like my opinion . . ."

I would.

"My opinion is that you irritate her a bit, fuss over her, tend to treat her as made of alabaster, causing some melancholia. No, my dear Mr. Robinson, your going may do no harm and, indeed, may do a great deal of good." Then, grinning, he asked, "How are you bearing up under your enforced marital deprivation?"

"Very nicely," I said, flushing to the roots of my hair.

"My dear Mr. Robinson," he said, "that can be a trial for some men whose rhythmic conjugal habits are disrupted. There are, of course, many substitutes which, ethically, I do not recommend but which, as a fellow man, I understand."

"Thank you, doctor," I said. And I rose to go.

"Just a moment, dear Mr. Robinson," he said. "Could you do a little something for me? My wife's sister is a great admirer of yours. She's asked me—it's hideously embarrassing and idiotic, isn't it—if she could have your autograph."

"Delighted," I replied and asked her name and wrote: "To Corinne with warm regards, Edward G. Robinson."*

By the time I got back to the Essex House to discuss my possible return to the Coast, the doctor had already called Gladys—and we had a strange confrontation as *she* suggested that my going would not bother her at all and would, as a matter of fact, make things easier for her. Apparently she'd been worrying about my worry, and she was delighted that I'd be occupied during the final months of pregnancy. For a moment I was irritated with her, which goes to show that the role of a husband is a very difficult one to play. The wife so rarely utters the right dialogue.

But there were a couple of days before I had to go, and I was conscience-stricken and full of guilt, so I thought I'd get rid of the guilt by buying Gladys a present. I did the usual Tiffany and Cartier looking, then wandered over to Knoedler's. There I saw a Renoir nude that cost less than a pair of earrings. I wasn't too certain of it and went on to the Durand Ruel Galleries, and there was another Renoir, more expensive but less red. Do you realize that red pictures are not very popular? I like them, however, because in its own shouting way a painting in red is a great and mighty thing.

But I knew Gladys was not a red-lover (I mean literally, not figuratively), and so I had the Durand Ruel people send the Renoir to the hotel. Then, to really cheer and amuse her, I had Knoedler's send the redder Renoir. I put one on each wall, and in the few days before I was to return to the Coast I asked her to make a choice.

---

* If you ever get to be a movie star, remember nobody ever wants an autograph for himself. It's always for his sister-in-law, and most of them have unspellable names. Further note: Edward G. Robinson is far too long a name to sign.

She had that curious woman's inability to make up her mind. I had that curious man's ability to get my own way. I bought them both.

I wouldn't tell you what Buddy de Sylva eventually paid me for the slightly inferior Renoir.

Off I went on the Century again, stopping long enough in Chicago to have another look at the brilliant pictures in the Chicago Art Institute and, luckily, to meet the sensitive and gifted architect Sam Marx.*

At that point he was already well-known, but in the years that followed he designed such monuments as the Pierre Hotel in New York, the Alexander Hamilton Memorial, the Pump Room of the Ambassador East in Chicago, and other very distinguished buildings. Chiefly he was not only an architect but had the deepest possible interest in painting. Accordingly, from our very first meeting we had very much in common.

What was most important to me was that he did not treat me as a movie star or as a moron; many people tended to equate one with the other. If you were in the movies, how could you possibly know anything about art or music? Conversely, if you knew anything about art or music, how could you possibly be in the movies?

Sam Marx accepted my movie stardom with hardly a comment. He was deeply interested in *my* comments on the Fauves, the Impressionists, and the Postimpressionists. The only time he ever mentioned the fact that I was in the movies was when he apologized for never having seen *Little Caesar*. He did, however, compliment me on *The Hole in the Wall*—the picture I made with Claudette Colbert. That made us even. As you know, *I* had never seen that.

He was fascinated professionally by motion picture and stage sets and had a vast knowledge of Gordon Craig, Ellen Terry's son, who had brought a whole new dimension to theater design. I was more interested in his opinion of Frank Lloyd Wright; our conversation between trains was absolutely absorbing and fascinating.

At the time, I had no need of his professional services; it never occurred to me that I would ever require them. In later years I called on him to help me, and I live now in a house graced by his talent.

It was hardly an accident that he came out of Chicago; it is the most underrated of American cities. Some of the best American art is held there, both in public institutions and in private hands, not the

* A number of people confuse this Sam Marx with a very well-known Hollywood figure of the same name. They were both good friends of mine. Sam, the architect, is gone. Sam, the producer, I see from time to time.

least of which is owned by the Leigh Blocks. Mary Block is the daughter of Albert Lasker; her stepmother, Mary Lasker, is also a very distinguished collector. The two Mary Laskers are sometimes confused; they shouldn't be. They are both women of exceptional taste, and American art owes a great deal to both of them.

Even though I had had a very bad experience with Chicago as far as *The Racket* was concerned, I always find it a rewarding and surprisingly beautiful city. It seems to me that it should really be the center of American art, that it should have a thriving theater, out of its uncorrupted sense of the American past. (Can't we simply forget Al Capone?)

There was a time when people would go coast to coast by train, when they would always stop off in Chicago. I suspect that the airplane has left Chicago to its own devices, and from an artistic point of view, this may be a very good thing. As the New York theater grows less and less palatable, one of the few predictions I dare make is that its renaissance will come in Chicago.

I know this sounds disloyal to Los Angeles. I'm sorry, but theater can only flourish in a downtown area. Los Angeles has its three theaters at the Music Center and a new Shubert in Century City and a few in Hollywood, but they do not make up a theatrical community. Also, the audience is mostly subscription. When you've known for a year you're going to see a play, it's bound to be disappointing.

Broadway reigned once because all its theaters were bunched together; London has Shaftsbury Avenue with all its houses chop-a-block on top of each other. Los Angeles missed its opportunity to create a Rialto. Chicago still has the chance, if it would only recognize it. It still has a theatrical heart to its city; the question is whether it will be retained and, more important, *sustained* by the Chicago audience.

So I got on the Sante Fe Chief and returned to do *The Little Giant*. It was not an unpleasant experience—or perhaps I was now getting used to making pictures. In any case, I cannot pass it by without saying a word about Mary Astor. She had then all the attributes that make for greatness in an actress: beauty, poise, experience, talent, and, above all, she did her homework. She has been vastly underrated, and it's a great pity. The George Kaufman episode and its attendant publicity was an even greater pity. I'm told Mary's more or less retired and writing. I wish she'd come back to the screen; we can use her dignity and her knowledge. (Remember her in *Dodsworth*?)

While we were fast coming to the end of *The Little Giant*, Mr. Roosevelt was inaugurated, and that auspicious event was immediately followed by an executive order closing all the banks. Though I can't recall whether the next event preceded or followed it, the studios asked all the creative personnel to take a 50 percent cut in salary.

What I did in that situation was to agree to take no salary at all—to work for nothing—but to have a contract prepared that would give me all my back pay when the studio was again solvent. Most writers accepted the 50 percent cut—and most players, extras, directors, and grips as well. It was not long before we learned that the only ones who had not been chopped in half were the executive producers and the releasing arms of the studios.

The selective paring of the payroll—or what some called perfidy—led to the beginnings of the unions in the studios, though, as artists, the word "union" seemed inappropriate, and we settled on a less lower class description: "guild."

Writers, directors, and actors began forming guilds and making demands, and the studios reacted predictably. First they ignored us, then they threatened us, then they fired the ringleaders (only to hire most of them back because they needed them), and eventually in the late thirties came the reluctant recognition of the guilds due to the passage of the National Labor Relations Act, called, more personally, the Wagner Act, and the studios were forced by law to sit down and negotiate.

How reminiscent it all was of the days when Actors Equity struck Broadway and George M. Cohan never forgave us. We are, I think, not totally forgiven yet, even though the various guilds brought order out of chaos and actually made working conditions more tolerable for the bosses as well as the workers.

I was deeply engaged in discussing the possibility of unions with writers, actors, and directors in March of 1933, and late one afternoon I left the studio and attended a meeting at the old Writers Club on DeLongpre with such eminences as Governeur Morris, Rex Beach, and Don Marquis.

At one minute to six there was such a rolling and thundering as you wouldn't believe. The chandeliers swayed, and we were all sick to our stomachs; cities like Long Beach and Compton practically crumpled to the ground.

I rushed back to the Chateau Elysée and tried to put a call through to New York, but all the circuits were busy. I must also remind you that long-distance telephone calling in 1933 was not as easy as it is today. It was midnight before I could get Gladys, who, by that time, had heard on the radio that Hollywood was devastated. I tried to reassure her and tell her that I would get back to New York as soon as I could.

Through the next few days, while we finished the picture, the after-shocks continued, and if you ever see *The Little Giant* on the late late show, you may from time to time notice a curious rocking motion in the film. It had nothing to do with the cameraman. It was that God-awful earthquake going on and on and on.

As a result, when I returned to New York, believe you me, I was determined never to return to California.

A few days after my return to the Essex House we took Gladys to the hospital. The joy of a cesarean, according to Dr. Pearson, was that you didn't have to wait for nature to make up its mind; you could decide when and where the baby could be born. Dr. Pearson tried to make me a party to the decision, but I copped out. It was a matter for him and him alone to decide.

However, there was another matter that Gladys and I had to decide along with him, and that was the engagement of a pediatrician. Now, in whatever stupid a light it puts me, when it was first mentioned, I thought a pediatrician was a chiropodist. I now know that a chiropodist is a podiatrist and a pediatrician is a doctor who takes care of infants and young children. It seems silly, so many years later, to quarrel with the English language, but if you think about it, pediatrician would seem a very logical label for a foot doctor.

In any case, off Gladys went to the Doctors' Hospital, and need I tell you she had the very best possible room and special nurses round the clock? And need I also tell you that I paced that waiting room all the time she was in surgery? At last Dr. Pearson came down—it was very early of a March morning—and told me that I had a fine and healthy son.

I rushed wildly to see Gladys, but she was still under the anesthetic and didn't know me. Then they gently guided this shaking new parent to let me peer at my son through a glass partition. My son seemed very red and quite hairy, and he was crying; I thought he was prob-ably the single most beautiful thing that God had ever devised.

My son! I was so proud and so happy and so excited that I almost went out of my mind. Of course, it was an excuse to buy boxes of the best Havana cigars and give them out to chauffeurs and bellboys and room clerks and all my friends. It was an excuse to go to Cartier's and buy Gladys a diamond necklace.* It was an excuse to have Sam Jaffe and the Paley crowd up for champagne. It was an excuse to go to Thorley's and the House of Flowers and send hundreds of orchids and

---

* Warner's had come through with the back pay, but I didn't need it because I suddenly discovered my credit was good. Up to now I had never charged anything or bought now and paid later. It became a habit I sorely regretted, but I became addicted.

roses to Gladys. It was an excuse to go to Marie Harriman's Gallery on Fifty-seventh Street and, since I couldn't offer her a cigar and had no bottle of champagne with me, I let her celebrate with me in the best way that I could: I admired the group of French Impressionists she'd bought from a woman in Philadelphia. Then, to mark suitably the birth of my son, I bought a good sized Degas of two dancers and a lovely Pissarro—oh, such a lovely Pissarro—for $2,500 and a Monet painting of some willows for another $2,500. The next afternoon, in my heady and nutty joy, I bought still another Pissarro.*

And so I had a gorgeous new son, the most beautiful wife in the world, a Degas, a Monet, two Pissarros—and no place to put them. Obviously, the apartment on Eleventh Street was out of the question; it was equally out of the question to remain at the Essex House, which was not only expensive but hardly the place for a baby, a nurse, diapers, bottles, formulas, cribs, toys, Bathinettes, and potties.

The thing to do, I concluded, was to rent a big New York apartment. Yet, that didn't make much sense because I still had some years to go on my contract with Warner Brothers.

It was middle spring now, and the weather was filthy. While I was taking Gladys and the baby and the nurse back to the Essex House, Gladys looked out of the limousine window at the bleak streets and all the "for rent" signs and said: "You know something, Eddie? I miss California."

Suddenly, in a crazy, cockeyed way I realized that I missed California too. I might have missed it less were I able to do a play; I certainly would have missed it less had I been a part of the actors, producers, directors, and all their marvelous gossip at Sardi's. However, as I learned on my previous trip to New York, I was no longer a part of it. I was no longer a part of them.

The temptation was to hire a lawyer and get myself out of the Warner Brothers slavery act. But it was a temptation I could not indulge in because my expenses were now so enormous, and the bills on the first of the month broke my arms.

I should think, by this time, that you've a pretty good idea of my folly about money. It was merely something to use to make everybody comfortable and happy and delighted. Money in Hollywood was easy; money on Broadway was hard. It was not only the depression; it was New York rapidly coming apart at the seams.

I agonized. New York blustered and clamored and challenged. New York was home, its streets as familiar as my right palm. I was

* A little down and so much a month. It was depression time, and Mrs. Harriman was delighted to make suitable arrangements.

somebody in New York, not with the masses but with the people I respected. And I was afraid of the movies—snobbish about them, if you like—fearful that eventually they'd run out of stories for a short and far from handsome leading man.

Gladys sensed this in me, yet I think she wanted me away from my old friends. Try as I did, I could not make her a real part of my friends, or perhaps she resisted them because they *were* my friends. Inevitably, Gladys and I had a long conference, holding our enchanting son, now called Edward G. Robinson, Jr., and it was Edward G. Robinson, Jr., who made the decision. It would be better to raise a child in California.

Let me say that calling him Edward G. Robinson, Jr., was Gladys' choice and not mine. I opposed it. Calling a son by his father's name and adding "junior" is not a Jewish custom. As a matter of fact, I think some place, in one of the commentaries written by a learned rabbi, it is expressly forbidden. But in New England, from where Gladys came, it was the accepted thing to do.

Jews honor the dead by calling the new child after a favorite deceased relative, and I wanted to call my son by my father's name. But Gladys wanted him to be Edward G. Robinson, Jr., and when she grew gloomy and moody over my objections, I withdrew them. I was always worried and concerned when Gladys grew moody.

She had gone so far in her choice of names that had it been a girl she was determined to call the baby Manuela. I think it was the only way she could get herself to say Emanuel.

15

While all this was going on, Warner's (or was it First National?) was preparing another script for me, to be called *I Loved a Woman*. In it I was to have two leading ladies, Kay Francis and Genevieve Tobin, and the studio was making the familiar noises about my coming back.

The New York office sent me the script, and I liked some of it because, again, it was about *something*—about the crimes of Chicago meat-packers, both during the Spanish American and First World wars. But I wanted changes, and this time I intended to have my way.

And so the die was cast; I would return to California, start the picture (after they fixed the script), find a house, and then return to New York to bring back Gladys and Manny.*

I Loved a Woman was based on the book by David Karsner, who had also written the book on which *Silver Dollar* was based. Charles Kenyon and Sidney Sutherland had done the screenplay, and I found it inadequate. The characters were sharp and clearly defined in the book but vague and poorly motivated in the screenplay. I wanted these matters sorted out and improved.

I admit now, with some dismay, that from that picture forward I achieved a lousy reputation with writers; I was always arguing about scripts, but so were Bette Davis and Bogie and Jimmy Cagney and

---

* Even though he was christened Edward G. Robinson, Jr., I called him Manny and so finally did his mother and so eventually did everybody else. I even think *he* thinks of himself as Manny.

—I'm certain, over at M.G.M.—Crawford and Gable and, I'm told, at Universal, so distinguished a literary figure as Deanna Durbin.

Let me make the case for all of us. It was the system of making pictures we were fighting. In the first place, a book or a play or an original story would be read by somebody in a reading department, synopsized, and then distributed among the associate producers at the studio. If one of them glommed onto it and Hal Wallis and/or Jack Warner and/or Darryl Zanuck liked it as well and it was castable (which is to say if one of the so-called stars with name above the title was suitable for it) and the price could be negotiated, it was bought.* Then it was assigned to an associate producer, or supervisor (interchangeable terms), and he would engage a writer. Now, the writer would seek to dramatize the work to satisfy the associate producer, whose hope was that *he* would satisfy the executive producer. And, of course, there were strict guidelines—the happy ending, for one thing, a certain degree of action and violence, and the star triumphant in the end.

With the first talkies there had been insistence on lots of dialogue; now the pendulum was swinging back in the other direction, and there was insistence on a minimum of it. Add to this the fact that the picture was aimed at a total audience—that is, it was intended to please both American urban and agrarian populations, as well as the English and French and Japanese.

Having achieved a script that fell within these guidelines, the associate producer would hand it to the executive producer, who would seek changes within his own spectrum. Sometimes they were improvements; more often they were ways of cutting the budget. At this point (the budget and shooting schedule having been laid out by the production department and those gentlemen having made their own literary contributions) a director was assigned, usually somebody under contract to the studio so that his arenas of dispute were already within well established parameters.

Do you think Alfred Green, for instance, would tell Jack Warner that a script stank? What he would gingerly do would be to ask for certain changes that he thought obtainable—and back down instantly if Wallis/Zanuck/Warner tapped a collective foot.

Then and only then did the actors get it. By this time it was entirely possible that there had been more than one writer assigned to the

---

* Somewhere at this point in time Wallis ran First National and Zanuck ran Warner Brothers. Then they merged. In a year or so Zanuck was let out and Wallis became head man. Zanuck took to Twentieth Century, which merged with Fox, and Wallis left to form an independent company with Joe Hazen at Paramount. I leave the dates to the researchers of trivia.

subject. I'm told of cases where there were more than twenty. If so, the script was in a number of styles and thus did not represent one man's vision.*

So there it was, fait accompli, and we were expected, by our very presence or box office appeal, somehow to put flesh on bare bones, add motivation where none existed, and bring self-inflicted character-ization to the cardboard characters we were to play.

So you can see it was not against the writer that we were making the fuss; it was against the system that had produced 120 pages of mimeographed inconsistency. The truth is we were on the writer's side. And in the years that have passed the system has changed, and the writer is more and more the star. In some cases, of course, the star is more and more the writer and the director is more and more the boss.

But, then, the troubles the producers had with actors were practi-cally always about the script. And Warner's had more than its share, believe me. Bette Davis and Olivia de Havilland made public and legal issues out of this problem; I tried to solve the problems quietly and in the privacy of an office. Sometimes I succeeded and sometimes I failed. Just as I must candidly admit that sometimes I was right and sometimes I was wrong.

But my problems about scripts were hardly secret from the members of the Screen Writers Guild, and I am told I was regarded as a cur-mudgeon.

It's funny because socially I spent more time with writers than anybody else. Rummy they'd play with me; politics they'd argue with me; write scripts for me they'd only do for the money—and some of them not even for that.

In due course *I Loved a Woman* was fixed up and I made it. I saw it the other night on Channel 52 (the Edward G. Robinson network), and I was astonished to find it pretty good. Let me give a small bow to Kay Francis. Despite her lisp, despite her background as a model, despite her inexperience in the theater, she had that indefinable pres-ence that somehow enabled her to be convincing as well as beautiful. Another night, on that same relentless channel, I saw her play Florence Nightingale. You cannot imagine a more ludicrous piece of casting—Miss Francis with her Upper West Side New York accent playing an English nurse in the Crimean War and defying British field marshals. And, by God, she made it stick. Hurrah for her!

In the Kay Francis film I had a few days off, and I would use those

---

* John Stahl, in an Irene Dunne–Charles Boyer film, had twenty-seven writers. They all attended the preview in a bus.

to search out a house for my family. But what kind of house? My instinct was that it should be small, manageable, and easily sold should we change our minds and decide to return to New York. But the Lindbergh scare had hardly evaporated, and that was certainly a major consideration. In addition, I was torn by status. Yes, status. If you were large and authentic in the Hollywood hierarchy, it would not do to live in any but the large and authentic Hollywood ghettos of which Hollywood itself was the least desirable.

Not that it wasn't the most picturesque. Whitley Heights, where motion picture personalities like Rudolph Valentino and Burton Holmes, the travelogue man, had their estates, was still architecturally Mediterranean, high in the hills, and with commanding views of what would eventually be freeways. But it was distinctly unfashionable in 1933. Besides, there were no sidewalks; I could not imagine living where there were no paved streets. I also wanted drugstores and groceries within easy reach—highly practical requirements out of long memory of Broome Street and the Bronx.

Los Feliz was lovely, but nobody lived there except the Menjous, and I had no wish to live near the Menjous. (He never forgave King John for signing the Magna Carta.) Brentwood and Westwood (even with U.C.L.A. beginning to rise in a kind of bleak Romanesque architecture) seemed rural and hardly habitable bean fields. That left Beverly Hills, most of which, I later learned, was owned either by Miss Ruth Roland, a heroine of serials who'd made and kept a bundle, or Miss Corinne Griffith, not the one to whom I'd given an autograph but a silent star of breathtaking beauty who had put all her cash in Beverly Hills real estate. (I've been told, actually, that Beverly Hills is named after Miss Beverly Bayne, wife to Francis X. Bushman, both silent stars, but nobody's ever been able to authenticate that.)

I have not added the Wilshire district to this catalog of acceptable residential neighborhoods because while its houses and lawns and its Mount Vernon mansions were clearly to my taste (they looked rich, substantial, convincing, and permanent), there was still (as there had been since the early silent days) a secret protocol among the landowners—no actors or Jews.

The Wilshire Country Club, focal point of this section, was not as brazen; it merely refused to admit to its membership rolls anybody in show business which was simply another way of laying down ethnic rules. I have never been inside the Wilshire Country Club or the Jonathan Club downtown or the California Club, and I'm not suggesting they still have taboos against Jews. I suspect that, at best, they have an occasional club Jew for display purposes. Nothing so odd about that; Hillcrest, my own club, has a few Anglo-Saxons for the same reason. (One of them is George Seaton, and he gives Hillcrest stature and dignity; he also is probably among the five finest of our townspeople.)

Beverly Hills was the answer, obviously, so I got a real estate agent and began looking, and that was an unsatisfactory business.* The moment the owner of the house heard my name, up went the price and the demand for cash. I finally decided to rent instead of buying. After all, Gladys should be a part of the final decision on a permanent house. Until she and Manny got to the Coast, I'd put off buying. (Inner thought: Buying would mean that I was entering the ranks of the bourgeoisie—Bohemia and the theater, too, forever gone; the end of the second wandering. From Bucharest to New York, the first displacement; from New York to California, the second. I needed roots, and roots laid down at forty were, like forty-year-old trees, difficult to establish.)

But I had little choice. Gladys was already dismantling Eleventh Street and arranging to have everything shipped out here—the furniture and oddments to remain in storage until we had some place to put them. The pictures I'd bought were ready for shipment, too, but what good are pictures without walls?

I consulted an attorney, a good man who said renting a house would not be difficult. "It's the Depression," he said, "and everybody wants out. Just ride down any street. If you see a house you like, ring the doorbell and chances are superb they'll rent it to you on sight."

So I took his advice and piloted myself around Beverly Hills until I saw a house that, from the outside, looked exactly right—sedate, understated, and with walls and gates. I got out of the car, went through the unlocked gate and up the stairs, and rang the bell. For a moment there was no reply. Finally, a little peephole in the door opened and I saw an eye and heard a piercing scream: "There's a gangster outside!"

The door opened, and the lady was shivering in fright. Her husband, having grabbed an umbrella as a weapon, was coming to her rescue. There was a moment when even the husband thought I was Little Caesar, come to have him buy my beer or else, and then the embarrassment when he realized he was talking to a real, live movie star. I decided instantly I did not want the house.

But I did find one on Arden Drive that was owned by a daughter-in-

* Jack L. Warner and his wife have one of the most beautiful houses in America in Beverly Hills. Most of it's been imported from abroad, and it's exquisitely proportioned, indoors and out. It is truly a Great Mansion, and Jack Warner knows the pedigree of each piece of furniture.

law (ex, actually) of William Randolph Hearst. It was magnificently furnished, undoubtedly with some of the better leftovers from San Simeon, with great old masters on the walls (what I'd give to have *those* today), and it came complete with the 1933 version of Porthault linen on which you could put magnificent Waterford glass, Meissen porcelain, and coin silver. My attorney friend was right; Mrs. Hearst couldn't wait to rent it. I signed the lease then and there.

And so my family arrived—Gladys, Manny, a nurse, and—can you believe it?—my mother. Perhaps my granddaughter, Francesca, is right after all; perhaps Gladys and my mother did get along well. At the time I had a sneaking suspicion that my mother had achieved a rapport with the baby, and I thought Gladys would be jealous. On the contrary, she was delighted.

Mrs. Goldenberg (my mother had never changed her name to conform to mine) was the very essence of grandmotherhood. She not only didn't mind being a baby-sitter, she revelled in it. Not that Gladys did not love the baby; she did, with all her heart. I know that to be an absolute truth. But she felt clumsy and inept with him; the nurse made her feel like an outsider while my mother was patient and unfearful.

"Listen," she said to Gladys, "so the baby throws up. All babies throw up. So he has a little diarrhea. What baby doesn't? So he gets tangled up in the blankets of his crib and you're afraid he'll suffocate. Believe me, you'd be surprised how strong and clever babies are; they don't like to suffocate any more than you do. Don't treat him like glass. He's strong. He also is some *pisher*."

Gladys loved the house but immediately set out looking for one to buy. Mama, on the other hand, was a little cynical about all the luxury. I remember sitting in the garden with her on one of those gorgeous California mornings soon after she arrived.

"Like it?" I asked.

"What's not to like?"

"You understand, mama, I don't own it. I just rent it."

"Who's the landlord?"

"One of William Randolph Hearst's sons."

"Oh, Hearst, your hero. So why does he rent it?"

"They're divorced."

"So," said mama, looking around sadly, "what good is it to have such a house? Divorce, *oy vay*, what people do to themselves!"

What people do to themselves!

What I was doing to myself was preparing a new film for Warner's based on a flop play by George Kaufman and Alec Woollcott, *The*

Dark Tower, with the title changed, of course, to *The Man with Two Faces*.

I liked it not only because Mary Astor was to play opposite me but also because I'd be able to use a putty nose, a set of whiskers, false eyebrows, and a French accent. Archie Mayo was the director, a man out of the Mervyn LeRoy school, and the script, almost too faithful to Kaufman and Woollcott (the screenwriters in awe of those transcendent names), was not too bad.

But film-making, house-hunting, and baby-playing were no longer my real interests. I was taking an active interest in the newly formed Anti-Nazi League. I joined with some of the best brains and best names in films to try to rescue the victims of the Nazi terror, now achieving its full-blown shame—and we were managing to get out penniless refugees. Whether it was we or others who got out Thomas Mann, Franz Werfel, Lion Feuchtwanger, Arnold Schoenberg, Dr. Toch, the point was they'd gotten out, and most of them were brought to the Coast. I felt it a tragedy then and still do that we were concentrating on illustrious authors and composers, but that was as far as our reach would go.

Settled here, they became part of the scene, and their greatest friend was a writer named Sonia Levien and her husband, Carl Hovey.

I am not, at this point, going to discuss whether or not the members and the board of the Anti-Nazi League were Communists. Let me tell you that if they were pacifists, warmongers, Trotskyites, Stalinists, Quakers, Holy Rollers, D.A.R.'s, anarchists, or Republicans, I would have joined with them in some small way to fight against the black horror that was beginning to sweep Europe. Time enough later to discuss the accusations made against us, and I assure you I will give the accusers their due and their evidence. There will be no problem about that; I have reams of documentation of the evils of which they accused us. I will leave it to you to decide how evil we were.

But nobody, not the Tenney Committee nor even *Red Channels*, could ever accuse the Hoveys of anything but the greatest human compassion.* I don't know whether they subscribed to *New Theatre Magazine, The Nation, The New Republic,* or occasionally bought

---

* The Tenney Committee was named after Senator Jack R. Tenney, Chairman of the California Senate Fact Finding Committee on Un-American Activities. Senator Tenney was appointed by the Senate Committee on Rules: his report was issued on June 24, 1949, and I'm in the cast. *Red Channels* I've already mentioned. Its editors were self-appointed custodians of public morals and accused right and left, mostly left, without ever giving the accused the right to confront the accuser. I was in that cast, too.

the *People's World*, a San Francisco–edited radical newspaper that occasionally printed revealing pieces about the Nazis. (They may have been lies for all I know, but the six million dead in Dachau and the other German sanitizing points, certainly, in the years after the war, proved the *People's World* slightly more accurate than the *Herald Express*.)

I'm not sure if the Hoveys ever attended performances of the Group Theatre or gave money or old clothes to the anti-Franco forces or if, indeed, they were members of the Committee to Defend America by Aiding the Allies (Cochairpersons: Douglas Fairbanks, Jr., and Constance Bennett)—but to do a combination of any of these things was to have the Red label stuck on you by certain lady columnists and cowboy stars. I will not name them now; I will later bring to you in its entirety the case these patriots made when they formed the Motion Picture Alliance for the Preservation of American Ideals.

The Hoveys did not belong to that group or to any of the others. Sonia was a smallish, plain, unmadeup woman with an inner glow that belied the need of lipstick. She had been born in Russia, emigrated as a child, lived on the Lower East Side, took an active part in the life of the Henry Street Settlement House, went to college, law school, passed the bar, wrote for magazines, became associate editor of *Metropolitan* magazine, met Carl Hovey, its very New England non-Jewish editor, fell in love with him, married him, wrote short stories that were sold to the movies, became a movie writer, and the Hoveys moved out to California.

Sonia became one of the truly great movie writers (her credits go from *Rebecca of Sunnybrook Farm* to *Cavalcade*), and Carl continued to write for magazines and periodicals. Maybe one of the reasons they were never cited by Tenney and the Alliance is that their best friend was that radical president, Roosevelt. Only his first name was Theodore.

At Sonia and Carl's I met all the great German and Viennese refugees, to say nothing of Noël Coward, Zoe Akins, S. N. Behrman and Ethel Barrymore (again), Bob Sherwood, Max Anderson, and the Gershwins. I also think it was at their house—though it may have been somewhere else—that I met Toscanini, Stravinsky, and Otto Klemperer. The Hoveys had a salon, and it was *gemutlich* and homelike and easy and marvelous; Ira and Lee Gershwin had the same thing going, and Hollywood was not nearly so bleak, especially when George would visit Ira and Lee. Never have I enjoyed talking with anyone as much as George. And when he played his new stuff for me—what glory!

As a result, Gladys and I were not nearly so miserable. Or maybe it was that we were so miserable about the world and Hitler that Hollywood seemed an oasis.

Mama thought so, at any rate.* She stayed with us until we moved into our new house, an ersatz Tudor mansion in the flats of Beverly Hills that had lots of room, a badminton court, and no swimming pool. I still live there. That's a by-the-way.

Another by-the-way is that one day Gladys and Manny and his nurse and mama and I went out for a ride. When we first got to the Coast we were always going out for rides. I guess nobody does that anymore. But we all loved it—new streets, new neighborhoods, the sudden sight of the sea, the orange groves, the wineries (Prohibition was over, and the Virginia Dare people and the Guasti-Guili people were all tending their tender grapes again), and mostly for mama, the sun. Accustomed to the cruel winters of Rumania and New York, she could hardly believe the eternal sun, which, frankly, was beginning to bore me.

Anyway, one afternoon we were coming back from the beach and cruising along Pico Boulevard when mama said: "You know it's like nectar here, the air. Do you mind if I wonder something?"

"Anything you like, mama."

"Manny, tell me, is there a cemetery around here?" Her voice was very matter-of-fact.

"I don't know, mama," I said and looked quizzically at Gladys. She shook her head. She didn't know either.

"I guess people don't die in California," said mama, "but if it's not too much trouble, Manny, I'd like to see a cemetery."

It seemed a strange request, one which the nurse answered. Had we not heard of Forest Lawn in Glendale, a veritable masterpiece of a cemetery? But I hastened to say that it was a Christian cemetery and mama would not want to see that.

"Why not?" asked mama. "Dead is dead. A cemetery is a cemetery. Before I go home, sometime, Manny, you'll take me to Forest Lawn, yes?"

"Yes, mama," I said and stopped in the first gas station, not realizing why the station attendant blanched when Little Caesar asked the way to Forest Lawn. He gave me directions; I gave him an autograph and a tip, and this strange little band was on its way to Forest Lawn.

We entered. Mama got out and wandered among the flat gravestones. We let her do it alone.

---

* During her visit Gladys, to her eternal credit, maintained a kosher house— separate dishes for milk and meat, meat bought in a kosher butcher shop, everything in order—but Gladys and I never discovered whether swordfish was kosher or not. Mama enjoyed it, and if it be interdicted, let the sin be on my head, not hers.

I wondered why, in the midst of what we were trying to offer her—joy, opulence, luxury—she suddenly needed this rendezvous with death. Then I realized that so much of her world was underground—her mother, her father, her sisters, her brothers, her husband, one of her sons—and she was sharing with them again. In the midst of life there is death, and she wanted to say hello again to those she loved in a place that was devoted to them.

She came back and said, "Let's go home, please." She hadn't wept, she wasn't maudlin, and she never referred to it again.

May I tell the rest about Mama? She had to go back to New York because staying with us would not be fair to the rest of her children and daughters-in-law and grandchildren. We wrote regularly because she found conversations on the long-distance phone too harrowing; she was always upset if we talked more than three minutes.

Whenever I went East, I visited with her a great deal, and one day I said I'd like to have a portrait of her painted by a friend of mine. She agreed when I assured her the cost was minimal, and she would go daily and sit in the artist's studio in Carnegie Hall. But the artist was too thin for her, and she would bring him chicken soup and blintzes.

Do I make her sound the cliché comic Jewish mother, always dispensing chicken soup instead of penicillin? She was nothing of the kind. She was strong, independent, and utterly self-assured. She had wisdom, wit, pride, and a true native dignity.

She was proud of me, I think, and would be very modest about me with the ladies of the organizations to which she belonged. But modesty was simply the other side of pride.

"It's nothing," she'd say when they envied her son's stardom, "I've another son who's a dentist." But she knew very well that a movie star was some *yichis*, a word which I find so difficult to translate that I won't even try. Ask somebody Jewish if he knows what it means. It may take him half an hour to tell you.

My sister-in-law Rea, Willie's wife, tells me that mama would go to see all my pictures but that she'd never stay for the end because she couldn't bear to see me die. When I heard she was desperately ill, I took my first plane trip to New York to be with her. But, at the last moment, I, too, averted my eyes. I couldn't bear to see her die.

16

If you film buffs suspect I've skipped a picture I made called *Dark Hazard*, you're so right. Try hard not to see it on TV. I loathed it. And I wasn't very happy with the way *The Man with Two Faces* turned out. You couldn't exactly say the Brothers Warner were turning handsprings either. You'd think they'd have said, "That's it, brother. Good-bye. Good luck! Let's forget the rest of the contract." I personally would have danced the Big Apple.

The point, of course, was that they'd run out of ideas for this creature they'd invented. My gangster was getting to be a bore. God knows, he was boring me.

I thought that perhaps another studio, other intelligences, would be salutary. The Warners were not. They never personally explained their position to me, but I've come to understand the mentality of the studio system as it was practiced by all of them. I was under contract to them. If they lent me to another of the factories and the ensuing picture was a hit, it would mean the Warners were not as bright and clever as the new guy. This was common reflex behavior on the part of all the studios as far as their contract players were concerned; on the other hand, each one wanted the other's contract players. If it sounds contradictory, why are you surprised?

Well, Columbia wanted me, and I'm told that Jack Warner (or maybe it was Harry or maybe the casting department) said: "You're nuts. Edward G. Robinson is box office poison."

At least, that's what my agent reported to me. He said he'd gotten it from Harry Cohn at Columbia (or maybe it was Sam Briskin or their casting man). I also got it from Louella Parsons, who merely called to ask me if it were true that I was going to do *The Whole Town's Talking* at Columbia with Jean Arthur. I told her I knew nothing about it, but she printed it anyhow. *The Hollywood Reporter*, or one of its columnists, (or maybe it was *Variety*) denied it, and the publicity department at Warner's asked me why I was permitting my own press agent (I didn't have one) to circulate these rumors and lies.

I was terribly embarrassed; I always am when I'm telling an absolute truth. As a result I make it sound like an absolute lie. The only problem was that the absolute lie turned out to be the absolute truth. Warner Brothers loaned me to Columbia to make *The Whole Town's Talking* with Jean Arthur. The financial details of this bit of big business have never been revealed to me, but if there were any monies involved beyond the salary Warner's was paying me, you can be absolutely certain they did not accrue to me. It was not uncommon for the studios, in those trades, to make money on our flesh.

There was a matter involved with the Columbia picture that caused me considerable apprehension. The first script sent to me was quite good but not quite good enough. The title page had no author's name on it except that of William R. Burnett, the writer of the novel and, of course, the creator of *Little Caesar*. The revised version with blue pages indicating the rewriting was, by some mistake, sent to me with the name of the writer of the screenplay. It was Jo Swerling.

We had only nodded and smiled politely to each other since the episode with *The Kibitzer*. Was it possible for us to work together again?

It was. Our first meeting was altogether too jovial and almost idiotically convivial; then we had lunch, talked out the whole *Kibitzer* problem, and made up our differences. I realized that Jo had been pushed, cajoled, and dominated by Patterson McNutt. Jo realized how deeply hurt I'd been at losing the play to Harry Greene. I'm delighted to report we put our friendship back together again.

In all the unpleasantness I am forced to reveal about old Hollywood let me isolate a couple of characters for you. First, Harry Cohn at Columbia—gruff, uneducated, vulgar, dictatorial, swaggering, but also a showman of the highest order. And by "showman" I mean people like Barnum, Ziegfeld, and Belasco—that happy breed of producers who could do none of the individual things required to produce a film or a show or a circus, but could, through instinct, supplied by God or devil, put together all the individual elements. If you can understand ambivalence, let me try to tell you that I despised Harry Cohn at the same time I admired him. And that might be an excellent thing to put on his tombstone.

As for the director, John Ford, from my first meeting with him to the day the picture was completed I knew I was in the hands of the consummate professional. I felt safe and secure with him. If I argued a line of dialogue with him or objected to a bit of business, I can now assure you it was more to assert my ego than it was to attack him. Almost entirely throughout the film, when we clashed, it turned out he was right and I was wrong. The main point to be made is that he would sit me down and *show* me where I was wrong. He is a totally remarkable director and one of the few deserving a place in the Pantheon. I'm told he's aging now, and cranky; well, I'm aging now, and cranky, but I bet if the right script came along (and Jo Swerling were still around to write it), John Ford and I could knock the shit out of it.

This time *I'm* using the word.

While I was engaged playing two parts in the Ford film (I was a milquetoast clerk in a hardware store who bore a striking resemblance to Killer Mannion, public enemy number one—a plot line hardly remarkable for its originality, but in the hands of Ford and Swerling remarkably original and funny) Gladys and I were putting together our Beverly Hills house.*

The furniture shipped from Eleventh Street was hardly enough for the living room and bedroom, and there were—it seems to me now—dozens of other rooms. We needed sofas and curtains, nursery furniture, rugs, and a dining room set.

It is some indication of my deep-rooted middle-class background that I conceived it as a dining room set. It never occurred to me that you didn't buy the whole business as a unit in whatever style or period appealed to you.

But as at Barker Brothers and Robinson's and even Cannell and Chafin (the "ultra-ultra" furniture house) we looked at these sets, I realized there was something wrong. Furniture shouldn't come pre-packaged. If one had a sense of style and proportion (and papa had long ago supplied me with those), you could mix Duncan Phyfe and Chippendale—and they had to be either superb reproductions or the

----

* If you leave my house, walk half a block north, turn west for three blocks, you will come to Lucille Ball's home. I mention it only because in the cast of *The Whole Town's Talking*, if you have good eyes, you will see the following in the credits: "Bit girl . . . Lucille Ball." I have tried very hard to remember, but I do not recall the role. I think I recall everything else she ever played. I know her very little, but if it's any joy for her to know, she makes me laugh, and I don't laugh easily.

Here is Eddie as he looked when he was bar-mitzvahed.

One of the first photos Eddie had made to send out to his fans. It was retouched a great deal because the photographer tried to make him look as Anglo-Saxon as possible.

Eddie as he appeared with Rudolph Schildkraut in a Yiddish play called *Number 37*, at the West End Theatre, in 1912

In the Theatre Guild production of *Peer Gynt* at the Garrick Theatre in New York, 1923, Eddie played the part of the Button Moulder.

Eddie was always particularly fond of this picture (because he was proud of his legs). It reveals him in his role of Ottaviano in *The Firebrand*, by Edwin Justus Mayer, produced by Schwab, Liveright & Mandel at the Morosco Theatre in 1924.

Eddie as he appeared in the part of Smerdiakov in *The Brothers Karamazov*, produced by the Theatre Guild in 1927

Eddie in *The Man with Red Hair*, by Hugh Walpole, produced by Charles L. Wagner, at the Garrick Theatre, November 1928

In the 1928 Theatre Guild production of *Goat Song* Eddie played the part of the Jew.

Eddie is seen here with costar
Gena Rowlands in the play
Middle of the Night (1956).

An early photo of Eddie and
his mother at the Santa Fe
Railroad Station in Pasa-
dena, California

RIGHT: A moment of intimate
conversation with J. Edgar
Hoover. The inscription
reads: "To Edward G.
Robinson, a great actor, a fine
gentleman and a valued
friend, J. Edgar Hoover,
9/28/37."

To J. Edgar Hoover
a great officer, a fine
gentleman and a
valued friend
Edward G. Robinson
1/28/37

Eddie is seen here at one of the numerous Hollywood functions he attended. On the far right is his close friend Will Rogers.

Eddie in Mexico on visit with Diego Rivera
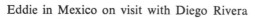

Eddie in *Little Caesar*, based on the novel by William R. Burnett, directed by Mervyn LeRoy, produced by Warners First National, and released in 1931 (© *First National Pictures, Inc. 1930, copyright renewed 1958*)

Eddie in *Dr. Ehrlich's Magic Bullet* in which he played Dr. Ehrlich
for Jack L. Warner and Hal B. Wallis, released by Warner Brothers
in 1940. The smaller photo (top, right) shows the actual Dr. Ehrlich.
(*Warner Bros. Pictures, Inc. 1940, copyright renewed 1968*)

RIGHT: Eddie poses with the cast from the M.G.M. film *Big Leaguer*.
Among the stars can be seen Milton Berle, Mickey Rooney, Jim
Garner, and Janet Leigh (1953).

Broadcasting from England in 1940

Oscar (Eddie's older brother) joins Gladys and Eddie in a family confab with mama.

A young Eddie with the young Igor Stravinsky

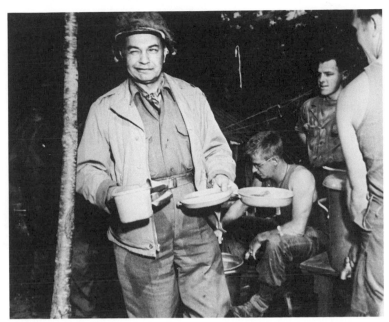

Entertaining the troops in Normandy, July 1944

Here Eddie can be seen among many of his Hollywood friends at a special White House reception given by Mrs. Franklin D. Roosevelt. Among the guests were Red Skelton, Pat O'Brien, Tyrone Power, Mickey Rooney, Ginny Simms, Judy Garland, and Jimmy Cagney.

Gladys and Eddie at home in Beverly Hills long before the divorce. He is pretending to play the piano.

Eddie had various musicians autograph the interior of his piano—after they played it. Included among the signatures are those of Jascha Heifetz, Toscanini, Vladimir Horowitz, Leopold Godowsky, and Sergei Prokofiev.

Gladys, Manny, and Eddie being painted by Edouard Vuillard at the
Plaza Athenée in Paris in 1939

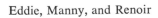

Eddie, Manny, and Renoir

Portrait of Eddie's granddaughter, Francesca, painted
by Eddie himself in 1965

A photographic view of Francesca, 1973

The real Eddie behind the beard and the goatee

Eddie at home with a couple of playful puppies

A joke from Ernie Kovacs

real thing. Believe it or not, the real things, the authentic antiques, were easier to come by in the thirties than the Grand Rapids stuff.

Many of the antique houses in Pasadena (and there were some great ones) were falling by the wayside and would hold distress auctions. There Gladys and I bought some of the furniture I still have— real treasures, the patina of the wood glossed by the centuries, at prices far below the equivalent at a department store.

The only trouble (as it continued to be a trouble for years) was that the moment I started to bid, the Little Caesar syndrome set in, and the bids around me would go up simply, it seemed to me, for the sole purpose of disconcerting me or getting the better of me.

Now, years later, I'm not sure that my assessments of these frustrating auctions are accurate; I am trying to tell you what I felt then. The truth could be that I was a bargain-hunter, and the other bidders knew more than I did. I may well have been overreacting. I've been known to do that.

I certainly overreacted to some other house decorating matters. Gladys wanted a decorator; everybody in the world (the world of Hollywood) had a decorator; I was far too egotistical to permit one. Thus, stripped of a decorator, Gladys wanted wholesale. I loathe buying anything wholesale. From the moment you walk into the wholesale house, you're under a curious obligation to buy, and then, if you are dissatisfied, you have no recourse.

While household hints are certainly no part of these chronicles, let me advise that in the matter of anything that can break (TV sets, radios, dishwashers, washing machines and dryers) go to the most expensive and reliable store and pay full price. When the appliance breaks—and, believe me, it will—you've got somebody to call up and shout at.

There was another problem, causing some dust between Gladys and me. I didn't really like the house. It was fakey; the fireplace was overblown, and the mantels and door panelings were cheap-jack. When we hung the good pictures I'd already bought, they were attacked by the gingerbread of the house. They looked uncomfortable, small, and degraded.

Add to them the Blakelocks and the Hoseas and the Alexander Brooks, and you had a small mishmash. A great mishmash developed when there arrived from the East five handpainted, enormous gilt-framed reproductions of Gladys' New England ancestors which she insisted on hanging. I hardly dared object; I simply wondered why Gladys could not see that these stern, badly painted New England faces were at war with Pissarro and Renoir.

Yet, Gladys was a Daughter of the American Revolution, and

these portraits were of sons and daughters of the American Revolution, and her pride in them overwhelmed her aesthetic judgment.

Which, of course, as you suspected it might, brings me to Grant
Wood. Chronologically, he should come in later; emotionally, he
comes in now.

In the late thirties I flew to New York (hating every minute of the
plane ride) to see about a school for Manny (I am not sure whether it
was because I had little faith in California education or because I
thought the Beverly Hills ambience was too luxurious and far too
separated from reality—or was it really because I wanted to get to
New York alone?), and on a Sunday I went museum-hopping.

By that time I had perfected my actor's ability to change my looks
so that people wouldn't recognize me. Instead of a trench coat I wore
an unfashionable McIntosh; instead of the gangster's inevitable fedora I wore a cap and sometimes a beret; I forsook dark glasses for
steel-rimmed ones with window-glass lenses; I altered my stance, and
most of the time it worked. Result: I was just another Sunday morning citizen of the Bronx out for a walk in the swell part of Manhattan.

The Museum of Modern Art had not yet built its edifice on Fifty-
third Street but was managing very nicely in a private house. Its
curator was having a good show—a French section with the greats
and an American section that was neither heavy, nor well attended.
But there were several good pictures, and I noticed they had all been
loaned by museums and private collectors. All except one. Grant
Wood's *Daughters of the American Revolution*.

I recognized it instantly; it was one of the most reproduced pictures
of our time and at the same time one of the most infamous. It was a
caricature in the manner of Daumier (in the figurative sense of
Daumier, not a copy—Grant Wood was far too great an artist in his
own right to copy anybody), but it seemed to be making a slinking
and miserable comment on American roots. The picture had been
called every dirty name possible by the American Legion and other
100-percent-American groups. It was treated not as art, comment,
observation, and a plea for understanding but as wicked, insolent,
radical, and unpatriotic.

Look at it today. It has majesty, breadth of vision, and the mark of
greatness. I looked at it then. To me it had majesty, breadth of vision,
and the mark of greatness. I stared, fascinated, and then I looked it
up in the catalog and saw that it merely said: "Courtesy of the Ferargril Galleries."

That meant that either it was owned by Ferargril and the gallery would or would not sell. I have rarely known a gallery that wouldn't sell a picture.

So the next day, no longer in my milquetoast disguise, I appeared at the Ferargril Galleries and asked immediately: "Is it for sale?"

The answer was yes. And I could see the gentleman offering it was overeager. I asked the price.

"Two thousand dollars."

I could hardly believe my ears. I bought it straightaway.

The price was so low because no museum—and practically no private collector—would have it.

I can tell you that through the years all the museums and private collectors kicked themselves around the block; I was offered any amount of money to part with it. Let me tell you some of its later history. After the McCarthy period it was sent to London and Paris under the aegis of the State Department. At one time Walter Annenberg, now American Ambassador to the Court of St. James, offered $100,000 for it so he could put it opposite a Gilbert Stuart portrait of George Washington.

He did not offer it to me; I no longer owned it. It was owned by a man named Stavros Niarchos, to whom it had been sold in order to arrive at a financial divorce settlement with Gladys.

Grant Wood, by now a friend, gave me a gift—the lacy bertha collar worn by the model in the picture and the china blue cup she held. Those I still have; in fact, I'm looking at them right now.

I've just walked out into the hall and gone up the first rise of five steps to look at my *Blue Picasso* of the death of a clown. I've done it because I can't wait to tell another story about Mr. Niarchos. That Picasso, too, was sold as part of the divorce settlement, and it almost broke my heart because I cherished it so dearly.

Later I'll go into detail about the arrangements I'd made with mutual emissaries of Mr. Niarchos and myself under which I would be able to buy back some of the pictures, at—I use the word advisedly —*elevated* prices. And I did secure some of them, but not the Picasso.

Then, one day a package arrived at the house; it was the Picasso, indeed. I was bewildered and happy and couldn't understand it.

The Knoedler people explained it to Jane. The picture was about death, and Mr. Niarchos hated anything that reminded him of death. Thus, Mr. Niarchos hated this Picasso.

When Knoedler couldn't sell it right off the bat, he had them return it to me. The price? Just what I'd paid him. Thank you, Mr. Niarchos.

On the open market I suppose it's now worth something in the neighborhood of a million dollars.* I don't care. Choose not to believe it, if you will, but I do not think of paintings in terms of their investment potential. Don't be ashamed not to believe me. Practically nobody does. However, it happens to be the exact truth.

Meanwhile, back at the ranch (or Warner Brothers, if you will) there was considerable glee that *The Whole Town's Talking* had the whole town talking. Andre Sennewald in *The New York Times*, Dick Watts in the *Tribune*, Eileen Creehan in the *Sun*, and Regina Crewe in the New York *American* all wrote rave reviews. They were handsome in their comments about me, but their raves were really for Jean Arthur—that curious, neurotic actress with so touching and appealing a nature that she really brought a new dimension to the screen. No curlylocks was Jean Arthur; hardly pretty by the ancient Hollywood standards, with a voice that grated like fresh peppermint, she seemed to me to be living—off and on screen—in a dream world of her own devising. She was whimsical without being silly, unique without being nutty, a theatrical personality who was an untheatrical person. She was a delight to work with and to know.

Miriam Hopkins, on the other hand, was a horror. I worked with her in Samuel Goldwyn's *Barbary Coast*. Well, you couldn't exactly say that. I *tried* to work with her. She made no effort whatever to work with me.

However, Sam Goldwyn, who denied absolutely that he fired me out of the silent film he'd made with the Selwyns (*Fields of Glory*), worked very hard to persuade the Warners to loan me out for *Barbary Coast*. While they were gleeful about the success of the Columbia film, they now thought me hot again and wanted me for their very own. What they wanted to put me in was quite another matter—more of that miserable gangster, a character of whom I was growing wearier and wearier all the time. The Goldwyn film, written by Ben Hecht** and Charlie MacArthur, offered good writing, a fascinating character, and a director named Howard Hawks.

I shall spare you the titles and the directors Warner's offered me

---

* Note from L.S.: In July 1973 the painting was sold in London on the open market for $650,000, the highest price ever paid for a Picasso.

** Ben Hecht was paid a fortune and insisted on getting his money in cash from Goldwyn at the close of each working day. I admired him, worked with him in innumerable meetings, rallies and dinners but fell out with him over his support of the Irgun, a radical Israeli group. His comments about his delight at the death of every English soldier sickened me. I thought him, at the very least, irrational. I never acknowledged him again.

and certainly the miserable scene that went on in the front office as I turned down every script and simply looked haughty when they mentioned suspension, that dread word that meant you'd not be paid and could not work for anyone else. While their other troubles with Bette Davis and Olivia de Havilland and, I suspect, Errol Flynn and Jimmy Cagney, were matters of public notice, I tried to keep my differences private. I had long since learned that you could do anything to Jack Warner except humiliate him. (It is easy to do; under that tough clown's facade he is easily hurt. Despite his wealth and power, I have always felt him to be insecure. I mean it as a compliment.)

Finally, after Goldwyn must have offered more than twice my salary, Jack let me go, assuring the newspapers the loan had been mutually agreeable, and even letting one columnist say that he was so concerned over my career that he had ranged over every studio to find something suitable for my talents. The inference was that, if not minimal, they were certainly limited. Jack Warner was always certain of the last word, and we talk of it often and laugh about it. Jack would rather laugh than anything in this world—except have the last word.

So off to the Goldwyn Studios I went, and I was delighted to discover that my old friend of *Under Fire* days, Frank Craven, had a dressing room nearby. Oh, what reminiscing we did, especially about the night I got drunk at the party the Selwyns had thrown eighteen years before.

I felt Frank had grown older—not old, but older—and a funny feeling came over me: the first realization of the passing of time and the parallel feeling that it could be happening to me, too. At forty-one you've passed the point of no return. You have fewer years left than you've already lived. My reunion with Frank Craven left me with a sense that youth had irrevocably passed, and I didn't like it.

Without consciously affecting the posture, I decided it was necessary to act younger than ever, more aggressively, more affirmatively, more conscious that each day must have meaning. Howard Hawks was the first recipient of that attitude. Or was it Miriam Hopkins?

It seems, remaining with me still were some of the remnants of my childhood—chiefly an almost instinctive reaction to people: from the very beginning, when I was introduced to somebody, or even saw him from a distance, I either liked or disliked him instantly. I have a psychoanalyst friend who tells me in a very scholarly way that this is not in the least unusual among the foreign born and minorities. They (we) tend to be suspicious of an attitude, a look, narrow eyes, thin lips, blond hair. I cannot agree that this is altogether a fact. If you will remember, when I discussed long ago the principal of P.S. 137 (whom I still think of as Mrs. Washington), she automatically had all the things I was taught to dislike. She was tall, Anglo-Saxon, thin-lipped, but at the same time she was warm and outreaching and friendly. Above all, she did not patronize me.

So I think my psychoanalyst friend is wrong. But people do give off auras—what Francesca calls vibes—and I respond to them automatically. It is not only with human beings that I have this weakness of character; it is also with paintings.

I remember that when I first saw the work of Rouault I disliked it thoroughly. I thought it cold and Gothic and satiric. I disregarded it. Then one day I heard a story about Rouault that made me want to examine his pictures again. It is a story that may reveal more about Rouault than myself, but it certainly does reveal that my first impressions are subject to change.

Vollard, the dealer, was a friend of Rouault and a man with an eye on the artistic buck. Rouault, painting those crazy, nonfashionable pictures, could rarely make a sale and thus could rarely afford to eat. Vollard, trusting his aesthetic judgment and feeling vaguely sorry for Rouault, agreed to support him on condition that all "completed pictures" would be given to and would be owned by Vollard. Thus, more than fifty paintings accumulated, and matters grew slightly complicated when Vollard died.

His estate instantly claimed that Rouault's paintings (now achieving some minimum recognition) belonged to the Vollard heirs. Rouault disputed this, and the matter was brought to court. There, arrogantly and utterly sure of their position, the Vollard attorneys displayed a written and attested document signed by Rouault, assigning title of all his completed pictures to Vollard.

Rouault did not dispute the document; in fact, he admitted quite readily to having signed it. The court was displeased with the artist; the contract was valid, and the Vollard ownership seemed to be clearly established.

"Except," said Rouault from the witness box, "for one thing: The contract provides that all *completed* pictures are the property of Vollard. Who is to say whether these pictures in evidence are completed or not? Only Rouault can say, and Rouault says they are *not* completed." In all justice then the court awarded his own pictures back to Rouault.

Because of this delicious story I went to see the paintings and found them not as stony as I'd first believed. I discovered humor in them, too, and arrogance and beauty, and I rather got to like them and then to love them. I bought one, then two, and then a few more.

Rouault is now among my favorite artists. So, you see, first impressions are dangerous indeed. Still I persist in going by them. Among the not inconsiderable number of flaws in my character it is one I am still unable to overcome.

At the time of *Barbary Coast* it was at its height. All of which, of course, brings me back to Howard Hawks and Miriam Hopkins.

Howard seemed to be patrician, aristocratic, and I sensed he was looking down his nose at me. I've learned to know him well since, and my initial assessment of him was wrong. His manner was concealing his own doubts, his own fears, his own insecurities at starting a new picture with a bunch of temperamental actors.

I do not propose to say the same thing about Miriam Hopkins. She was puerile and silly. There was one thing I recognized in her that could have made us friends: She, too, had come from the stage; she, too, felt that movies were beneath her. I had gone through the same thing; I had been graduated from that stage.

How odd, then, for me to be the recipient of the kind of snobbery that I, myself, had indulged in for so long! Even though I didn't know it then, it was clear (in the words I spoke over and over again on the screen) that I could dish it out but I couldn't take it.

In addition, the set of *Barbary Coast* was highly politicized. As I look back on it now, I really don't know the individual political stances of the company, but I'm sure of this: Hecht and MacArthur were liberals; Howard Hawks, Miriam Hopkins, Joel McCrea, Walter Brennan, and Harry Carey were not liberals. We were two warring camps, and that kind of deep dispute was going on in every studio and every living room.

Look at the times: F.D.R. was still in his first term, and antiadministration forces were calling the New Deal un-American, bolshevik, communist, and socialist. These inflammatory points of view were constantly being aired on the set, as indeed they were being aired all over Hollywood and all over the country.

There was a desperate fear of innovation, of change. The definition of a Communist supplied to me over and over by members of the cast was: "What's yours is mine; what's mine is my own."

The wealthy, the celebrated, the successful (and, realize, I could now count myself among them), saw F.D.R. as an enemy trying to change the fundamental fabric of the Republic. On the other hand, we saw him as a man trying to save capitalism by dealing with the fundamental inequities in the nation.

The arguments on the set were appalling; as a result, there was little socializing among us. There was a good deal of polite freezing and occasional bursts of rage.

This political sentiment took its toll in many ways. Miss Hopkins complained bitterly about every line, used every trick in the book to upstage me. I had long ago learned that these upstaging maneuvers (all of which I had learned well on the stage) would not work at all in films. The cutter could attend to them.

But when Miss Hopkins refused to stand on her marks, those little triangles of masking tape that set the actor within the proper range of the camera, it was too much. What was *really* too much was that Miss Hopkins, in period costume and headdress, was taller than I. When we did a scene together, Miss Hopkins wanted me to stand on a box. I refused, not only because it was undignified and made me self-conscious but because I was unable to play with any sincerity high on an insecure perch. My suggestion was that Miss Hopkins take off her shoes. When I think of it now, I suspect she could not play with any sincerity standing in her stockings.

There were other problems between us. In the making of a picture, frequently a scene between two people is broken up so that you get a closeup of one and then the other. When the closeup is of *you*, you play a love scene to a camera lens, and the other actor (actress) reads the off-scene lines from beside the camera. This is common courtesy in the making of a picture, and even the most illustrious of stars are willing to do this difficult chore. But Miss Hopkins was not.

When they did my closeups, I read my lines and Miss Hopkins' lines were read by the script girl. This infuriated me, and my revenge was to elaborately read the off-scene lines when it was Miss Hopkins' turn for a closeup. This taught her nothing.

Miss Hopkins is recently gone, and I'm sorry about that, of course. However, since these matters might help other young actors, I'm forced to proceed with them. The indictments:

1. Miss Hopkins was always late.
2. Miss Hopkins would never read a line precisely as it was written, thus not cuing me.
3. Miss Hopkins would make us all stand around and wait while she complained bitterly about her costumes.
4. Miss Hopkins indulged in every trick to delay, to confuse, to obstruct—and to prove that she and not I was the star.

Mr. Hawks tried to cope with these four lunatic types of behavior and, I'm sorry to say, I don't think Mr. Hawks coped very well.

As a result, one day, I told Miss Hopkins off. I shouldn't have done it, but I was fed to the teeth. I reeled off a litany of her mischief. In the first place I told her that temperament had gone out of fashion—that it had worked in the days of Fritzi Scheff, Mrs. Fiske, and Mrs. Carter but it simply did not have any place on a movie set. Then, thinking of her own good, I told her she was far too conscious of the camera; she hugged it and thus defeated herself. I showed her how, in her attempts to upstage me, she would back up on her own lights— and I did all this, unforgivably, in the presence of the cast and the crew. They remained silent.

The next scene we had to play was one in which I had to slap her. Slapping, to say nothing of hitting, punching, kicking, and general brutality in films is usually faked. I wanted to rehearse this fake scene with the lady. But she wouldn't have it. She looked me straight in the eye and spoke very loud so that the entire company could hear.

"Eddie," she said, "let's do this right. You smack me now so we won't have to do it over and over again. Do you hear me, Eddie? Smack me hard."

I followed her instructions. I slapped her so you could hear it all over the set. And the cast and crew burst into applause.

If you will examine the credits for that movie, you will see, almost at the end, the following: Sailor (thrown out of saloon) . . . David Niven.

Whether David applauded, I know not. I did not meet him for years. When it happened, we scrupulously did not discuss Miriam Hopkins or my atrocious behavior.

17

On my return from Goldwyn, Warner's was ready for me with another script called *Bullets or Ballots*, vaguely based on the life of the famous New York City detective Johnny Broderick. Detective Broderick was furious about the script, and so was I.

I agreed to do it after some minimal (I wanted maximal, but settled for minimal) changes were made because there were only three more pictures left on my Warner's contract, and, to tell you the truth, I didn't know whether to be glad or sorry. A contract is a strait-jacket; it is also assured income. In my heart I was not certain that once the contract was over anybody would want me—even though the facade I put up to my agent and Warner's was highlighted by bluster and insolence. Edward G. Robinson could have anything he wanted at any studio; Edward G. Robinson could even go back to New York and do Shakespeare, preferably Shylock. The world was Edward G. Robinson's oyster. But the Emanuel Goldenberg in Edward G. Robinson wasn't at all certain that this was true.

What he (I) was certain to be true was that Franco, Hitler, and Mussolini, between them, were conspiring, if not to take over the world, certainly to reform the world on an elitist basis. To me they were not only anti-Semitic but anti-Christ, and anti everything America stood for. And they seemed to be certain of conquest.

There were people in Hollywood who supported their views. "Oh," the thoughts went, "Hitler will forget the anti-Semitism; it's only a passing phase. And he *will* stop the spread of communism. At this point, that's the most important consideration."

I did not agree. I joined with all those who were opposed to the dictators and were supporting F.D.R. for a second term. I am listed as belonging to a great many organizations by the House Un-American Activities Committee—so many that I cannot recall lending my name to them. I readily admit belonging to those I do remember: the Progressive Citizens of America (I was even on the executive board), and certainly I was active on the American Committee for Protection of the Foreign Born.

Communist front organizations? Perhaps. I don't know. It never occurred to me. What occurred to me was that both groups were active in their passion for the deprived, the put-upon, the victims not only of Nazi terror but of our economic imbalance.

And we had meetings at my house even though I didn't like my house very much.

I certainly didn't like the bills. We had servants, a nurse for the boy, a gardener, two cars, and the expense of upkeep on a car for the nurse and the boy. There were contributions to charities and causes, taxes (not so high then but high enough), clothes for Gladys, entertaining expenses, and helping out my family and Gladys', and, well, money just seemed to melt away.

When you write about these things, it seems it was all worry and work and social consciousness. Those are the factors that stand out. Yet that's wrong because, actually, there were other things going on that were pleasant and joyous: friends, for instance. Lots of new ones, and people who ever after became very close—though I must admit we all shared the same political bias.

And music. Every Tuesday night, no matter what time I had to get up the next morning, Gladys and I would have the same seats for the concerts of the Los Angeles Philharmonic while I forgot the agonies of the world in the music of Beethoven and Mahler. And there were wonderful parties, too—and while I think I thought of them, then, as drags—incredible Hollywood premieres, with Kleig lights and adoring fans. It is my habit to say, "Phooey, I don't want to go." The truth is I enjoyed going.

I still do. Apart from the ballyhoo, which is not nearly as vulgar as has been advertised, I like to see a film (or a play or read a book) before the reviews come out. It's a little game I play with myself. What will my analysis be? Will the Pauline Kaels and the Judith Crists and the John Simons agree with me? A better question these days is, Will they agree with each other? And will Andrew Sarris and Vincent Canby agree with any of them?

I really don't keep score, but the last picture I saw before I was confined to house arrest for what I expect to be a light sentence was *Sleuth* with Lord Laurence Olivier and Michael Caine. Not having seen the play and thus not knowing the intricate joke, I had a gorgeous afternoon. Let me tell you those two actors really know how to act, and Joe Mankiewicz can direct me any time he wants to, *if* he wants to. The three of them display total and proud professionalism, and that's my distinguished service medal with three extra sets of palms.

I knew Joe's brother, Herman, well. (I knew him slightly when he was dramatic critic for *The New York Times*.) He was really something. You remember him for *Citizen Kane*; I remember him as the frankest, most outspoken wit of the time. I don't know whether or not we agreed politically. Herman, I think, would change his political stance just to get on the other side of an argument. We loved arguing the most. I frowned upon his association with the Screen Playwrights, that company union formed by the studios to combat the Screen Writers Guild. But in the end the Guild prevailed, and Herman and I forgot that bruising difference of opinion.

We'd meet, certainly, whenever there was a new play at the Biltmore. Well, not exactly a new play—rather a touring company—but a *good* touring company. The Lunts played there a lot, and so did Kit Cornell and Helen Hayes, who made a picture, won an Oscar, and then played *Victoria*. An opening night at the Biltmore could well have been considered the Broadway Government in Exile.

During the shooting of *Bullets and Ballots*, the head of the publicity department came on the set and said he had to talk to me privately about a matter of vast importance. He made me nervous—sounded as if I had committed some sort of moral turpitude and, though I knew I hadn't, that made no difference in those days.

If you talked to a young lady extra on the set, it was hardly a novelty for her to accuse you of being the father of her unborn child. It was a very popular pastime among certain agreeable young ladies, and while I had had no private relations with any of them, I was perfectly aware that that was a matter of insignificance. It would be her word against mine; there would be blood tests, lawsuits, glaring headlines, and, though you were as innocent as a seraph, forever after you would be regarded with knowing leers.

It was a measure of my innocence and chronic sense of impending disaster that I was convinced my publicity friend wished to talk to me about a paternity suit—that could not, under any circumstances, bear the slightest basis of truth. Yet, there was the maid Gladys had wanted fired; she was afraid to, and I went to her room, explained for fifteen minutes. . . . Oh, God, could it have been that maid?—though the only carnal knowledge we had of each other was that she tongue-lashed me for *daring* to fire her.

Memories of Fatty Arbuckle, Mabel Normand, and William Desmond Taylor kept crossing my mind. And more recent scandals about people whose names I will, of course, not mention. In any place but Hollywood, most of them would not have been given even the most minute credence. But out here, get a ticket for over parking, and you're a felon. And, if your relation to the film industry was as remote as the fact that you once rode a horse in a mob of extras in a western and, incidentally, if you killed somebody, the headlines would read: "MOVIE STAR MURDERS BEAUTY." and *Confidential Magazine* would do a piece on you implying frequent and chronic aberration.

Accordingly, when I sat my publicity friend down in my portable dressing room on Stage 17, I was prepared for anything and was mentally swearing my innocence to my unknown crime.

It *was* a serious crime. Their Majesties, the King and Queen of Rumania, had sent their ambassador to Hollywood; as a fellow Rumanian he wished to meet me, be photographed with me, present me with imperial and endearing photographs of the royal family, and was certain that I would respond by autographing a picture to the Royal House expressing my lovely memories of my childhood in Rumania and telling how much I owed to its culture and its educational system.

I refused. Since when does a refusal deter a publicity department?

The ambassador, together with his entourage, appeared on the set. Shooting stopped, and I was presented to the legation. I shook hands with the ambassador—I certainly could do nothing else with all the camera flashbulbs popping—and I mumbled something in Rumanian like, "How do you do," though I believe it's impossible to translate "How do you do" into Rumanian.

He thereupon presented me with the suitably inscribed photographs of Their Majesties (unframed because Rumania was such a poor country), and then he politely asked me for one of mine in return. I babbled in English that I didn't have a recent one, that I would eventually send one on. He was a pushy fellow, however, and insisted, so there I was, caught in the middle of a barefaced lie because the publicity man had a sheaf of them, practically all in the uniform of Little Caesar.

I wrote: "Very truly yours, Emanuel Goldenberg," then stomped off the set.

I think King Carol and Madame Lupescu might have had a good laugh. After all, I could have written it in Yiddish. Madame Lupescu would surely have understood.

Childhood in Rumania was certainly different from childhood in America. I was determined that Manny would have every advantage —a governess, the finest schools, the best possible education; he would be a brilliant doctor or a justice of the Supreme Court. He was a beautiful child, not quite three, and we would trundle him out whenever visitors came, and they'd admire him and play with him and adore him. In looks, he was a composite of Gladys and myself, more Gladys than I in young childhood; today, as he grows more mature, there's little doubt that he's my son. (Francesca, *his* daughter, who has Gladys' New England blood and her own mother's Scotch–Irish genes, turns out to be almost a replica of my mother. Go figure out heredity.)

Whatever differences between myself and my son that emerged later—and some of them made unpleasant and I truly believe unwarranted headlines—let me say to you and to him that initially the problems were of *my* making. I have read and reread all the books on bringing up children—especially in the vital areas of a son's superego being built upon his father. I have discussed these matters endlessly with analysts and psychiatrists, and I am prepared to admit, in the late afternoon of my life, that I did everything wrong.

Let us begin with my working hours. I'd leave the house before he was awake; I'd usually return when he was already in bed. I'd go up and see him, awaken him, kiss him, try to prove I loved him, but he was half asleep and I was exhausted and those sessions that should have consisted of my telling him a story usually lasted only two to three minutes.

On my days off—and that was only on Sundays—I tried to play with him on the badminton court next to the house. Play ball, that is. I cannot play ball. I am clumsy and self-conscious about a ball. So that came to nothing.

Meanwhile, Gladys and I, having no knowledge of the sins we were committing, would argue, scrap, and fight in his hearing. He would cry, and he had a nurse (or were we already calling her a governess?) who found a way to stop his crying; she would slip a few drops of Scotch into his milk. We fired her when we found out, but I guess it was too late.

I tried—God knows I tried—to be a proper father, but the only lessons I had came from my own father who was a strict disciplinarian out of the needs of a Rumanian semighetto and New York's East Side.

Those techniques were sadly out of place in Beverly Hills. And so I turned to bribery via magnificent and thoroughly unsuitable gifts: a shining bicycle when he was too young to use it, a set of electric trains that bankupted me at F.A.O. Schwarz; when he wanted to play baseball, a set of gloves and masks and bats and uniforms that the Yankees would have envied.

I confess it. I gave him everything but myself. I simply didn't know how. I don't think I ever learned.

There is a story that went around in the thirties, probably apocryphal, concerning Herman Mankiewicz' son, Frank, who worked so diligently for Senator McGovern. They say he was asked to write a composition in grammar school about his family, and he wrote, I paraphrase: There was once this very poor family with a very poor mother, a very poor father, a very poor brother, and a very poor maid, and a very poor governess, and a very poor chauffeur.

It's probably not true, but Manny could well have written it.

Bullets and Ballots finished, with two pictures left on my contract, and the year was suddenly 1936. Now I did not have to ask Warner Brothers to loan me out. They did it without my asking.

An English company, financed, I was later told, by the funds of British widows and orphans, had prepared a script called *Thunder in the City* for Columbia Pictures. It was to be shot in London, and, among others signed for it, were Nigel Bruce, Constance Collier, and Ralph Richardson, players of tremendous stature.

Columbia wanted me for the role of Dan Armstrong (obviously the all-American boy), a super go-getter salesman whose arrogant high-pressure tactics were dismaying to his employers; why they just didn't fire him I cannot imagine. Instead, they sent him to London to observe the less antic London ways of doing business. It turned out, too, that Armstrong had English relatives—Lord and Lady Challoner —to say nothing of friends like the Duke and Duchess of Glenavon.

Think you can figure out the rest of the script for yourself? If you can't, I'll tell you that Little Caesar ended up getting married to the daughter of the Duke and Duchess, Lady Patricia.

I was told by Warner Brothers to leave for London—first class all the way, limousine and the *Aquitania*, and a Rolls to the Savoy (River suite, of course) and, in due time, they'd even send Gladys and Manny over to be with me.

I was so sick of Warner's and social significance by this time that in the words of *The Godfather* (which is certainly my grandchild), it was an offer I couldn't refuse.*

And so off I went to London, leaving my family behind. That was how I really came to be an art collector—or, how art came to collect me.

You decide.

---

* That brings up Marlon Brando, and I have to say it: Easily, he has one of the keenest dramatic intelligences in the profession today. He is actor-born and almost "part-proof." But I grieve that he doesn't like being an actor. At least, that's what I've read in interviews. If I knew him better, I'd tell him that he could do more good for the world playing parts that elevate the human heart than he ever could do with his sporadic passion for the American Indian.

18

I don't plan to bore you with my arguments over the script of *Thunder in the City*; there was, however, a major breakthrough. The aristocratic London producers, deeply conscious of the sources of their money, wanted a big hit, and when I made my objections known (the script was obvious, predictable, on the nose, flat, frequently silly), to my astonishment, they agreed.

How to fix it? Well, I certainly do not believe it was an act of God that walking on Jermyn Street one day (I had so much time on my hands until they went on the floor—Anglicism for starting shooting—that I toured London, even saw the Tower, which I never got to see on my last visit), I ran across a gentleman I'd known on Broadway. How could you miss him? He was a very tall gentleman, and his name was Robert Sherwood. He was in London for reasons unknown—maybe something to do with F.D.R. and the British Government—but apparently time was not yet ripe for his negotiations, so he was at loose ends.

Twenty minutes after we met and had a cup of tea, he was no longer at loose ends—he was engaged to rewrite *Thunder in the City*. Imagine hooking a playwright of his status to work for the movies.

What he did was to turn it into a satire—tongue-in-cheek—transform idiot comedy into subtle wit. He really did wonders with the script—but not enough. It was a flop, and I apologized to Bob a thousand times for mixing him up in it. He was always very pleasant about it, said the money came in handy, bought some antiques and pictures with it.

Me, too. When it came to art and the buying of it, too many people are convinced there are metaphysical abstractions on which to base a decision. You sense it, they say; you feel it, others say; you just get a feeling about a picture. Nonsense.

What you get a feeling about is the subject matter and the skill with which the artist communicates it to you. What you are sensing is within *you*, not him. You must know what is in *him* to know if he speaks his own truth—not *your* truth, but his. I never have been able to.

I don't think I'm explaining this very well. But I think I can draw a parallel with a monstrous oversimplification. There is a magazine called *The National Review* edited by William Buckley, whom I have never met. I disagree with almost everything Mr. Buckley writes, and I know why I disagree. We come from different worlds; we can look at the same object or set of facts, and we will both, quite honestly, arrive at different conclusions. However, since I've never written a letter to him, this is the first he will know of it—even disagreeing, as I do, I love to read him. In the first place, I believe *he* believes what he's saying; and, indeed, he has something to say that needs saying even though I'm diametrically opposed; and, finally, he writes like a dream. What he does with the English language is pure joy.*

Now you can apply the same principles to painting. You must believe that an artist believes in what he is painting; he must have something to say (life stinks; life is a dream; I hate living; I love living—whatever); and then he must have the knowledge, the technique, the training to put it on canvas. He can distort that knowledge, he can twist that training to his purposes, but it must originally be there in its classic sense. And the same criteria apply to sculpture, architecture, and music.

But a word of warning. If *you* like it and it does something to you, ignore what I say and acquire it. You and the artist (or pseudoartist) have worked out a connection, and what's more important than that?

I myself have other considerations, and I might as well go into them now, because I intend to tell you how it came about that I became the owner (at least temporarily) of some of the world's great works of art.

First off, I am not Bernard Berenson. Berenson was truly an expert, the result of years of study and scholarship. He was a legend,

---

* For the same reason I am a devotee of Ezra Pound. Fascist and anti-Semitic, he was a magnificent poet. For those who insist on a distinction between an artist and his work (and that has been the eternal cry of the Left), I insist that it must work both ways.

and the great art collectors like the Morgans and the Fricks would seek out his advice to make certain that Duveen was not rooking them.

If you're going to buy old masters, and even new masters, do what Morgan and Frick do. Go to responsible dealers. But do not trust them when they tell you that the painter is in demand for his rarity. The demand for a painter is for his gifts; that his work happens to be rare is important only if you're a hoarder and if you're buying as an investment. If you buy as an investment, nothing I can say will matter to you, so skip these paragraphs.

If you're buying for beauty and to have something to come home to—besides a loving wife and family—don't buy legends; Buy what you see in front of you.

Even the most renowned of artists have painted dogs, and that goes for Rembrandt. Certainly it goes for Renoir, who has palmed off some pretty lousy work on the world. Before you buy the artist, therefore, it is wise to know his whole body of work. Is it a top picture or middling or fair or bottom of the barrel? You'd be surprised how many barrel-bottom famous names I see in museums.

I've been reading in *The New York Times* lately that even the New York Metropolitan is "de-acquisitioning" some of its master works. This means they realize some of the stuff they've bought or been willed is junk, even though it may be painted by a famous name.

It'll happen to you, too, unless you buy from a decent, respected dealer. It is not my plan to advertise the names of the galleries I trust, not only because there are certainly numbers I've not dealt with that are equally trustworthy, but because I've made some mistakes on my own. I've bought pictures that I liked at the time and came to find incompatible. The galleries from which I bought them always took them back, returning my money or at least giving me credit.

As an art buyer, I am a pain in the neck. I am also something of an egotist. I never take advice about what picture to buy; I never listen to anyone. Most dealers know it and no longer make an effort to talk me into buying a picture.

My usual rule (and in those days with the depression at its peak it happened more frequently than now) was that a dealer let me take a picture home and keep it for a month before making a final decision. At that point you could have a private little talk about the price. Once the picture was in your house, it was easier to bargain. And, I confess, I bargained.

Some people consider me sharp. Not true. I was never sharp. But I was always aware of the true market value of what I wanted and even more wary of schemes to build up certain painters into fad or fashion.

I got stuck once or twice, but I try to avoid it; I will not be a party to the creation of a false reputation.

Dealers were beginning to say to others: "Robinson's buying him." And to some they'd say: "Block's buying him." Or the Museum of Modern Art. Or the Whitney people. I learned to disregard that sales pitch about others. Disregard it about me.

In London the dealers Reed and LeFevre tried none of that with me—perhaps because I'd been given good notices to them by some people at the Tate. Because I was from Hollywood and they had seen me as a gangster, they did look a little alarmed when I walked in.

I was aware of this, so I used my best pear-shaped tones and company manners. I realized instantly that one did not immediately address one's self to commerce; one sat down with the director and had a cup of tea, even though one's eye was on a strategically placed painting, a master daub of Renoir's, *The Girl with Red Plume*. One did not even mention this, though one could hardly help feeling that the strategy of its placement and lighting were hardly accidental.

In the great tradition, one balanced one's tea cup and barely nibbled at one's *petits beurres* and one chatted about artists and their work. Very conscious of British manners, I hoped that the director would not notice that my hair had been dyed that morning in my favorite hairdresser's in Jermyn Street. (At forty-three I was beginning to have silver strands among the raven, and that would not do, certainly not for the film in which I was about to engage, nor in private life either. Movie stars are not supposed to grow old. At least, they must delay it as long as possible. But accustomed though I was to management of my hair, I was self-conscious this morning. It seemed to me it had never been as ebon.

The director, polite beyond measure, which, in the British way, may be considered a subtle indication of disapproval, pointed vaguely to a Vuillard, rather dim on the wall, and told me an anecdote about him.

As Dreyfus was being tried by the French Army for treason, Vuillard and a party of his painter friends awaited the verdict in a café in Montparnasse, probably the Dome.* When news was brought that Dreyfus was found guilty and would be sentenced to Devil's Island, Vuillard sobbed. He explained it by saying, "I weep not for Dreyfus; I weep for my country!"

I have managed, as a result of that story, to acquire a Vuillard here and there, and in his paintings I can feel the man who uttered that

---

* Pepe Schildkraut played Dreyfus in the Muni picture *Zola*. I tend to relate moving pictures to nonmoving ones.

line. But Vuillard was not the business at hand this teatime. Actually, nothing was. I was merely looking, browsing, feasting my eyes. I had no intention of buying anything.

I bought Renoir's *The Girl with Red Plume*.

It was manifestly silly. What financial logic was there in spending money on a painting when I had this one picture under my contract in London and one more in Burbank with Warner's? I was simply being profligate and silly. What would Gladys say? Should I not husband my resources? (How odd to use "husband" as a verb.)

Do you believe I even thought of any of those things? You can bet your last dollar I didn't. The director made lovely terms, and I became the owner of a masterpiece.

Heady with my new purchase, I left Reed and LeFevre, swearing I would stop in no other gallery. But Wildenstein was on the way back to the hotel, and what harm would it do to stop in and have a look?

The harm was evident. Immediately upon entering I was struck by a Berthe Morisot. How few women painters there were then—Rosa Bonheur, Georgia O'Keeffe, Suzanne Valadon (Utrillo's mother), Marie Laurencin, Mary Cassatt, and, of them all, certainly Berthe Morisot, the reigning empress.

The Morisot picture was titled *Avant le Théâtre*, and a note appended said it was thought to be a portrait of Madame Hisnes. I wanted it so badly. I could hardly bear it.

I had another cup of tea with George Wildenstein while he told me something of the *provenience* of the Morisot. He explained that it came from the collection of Oscar Schmitz, a world-renowned Swiss collector, and the Morisot was simply a token. The main body of the collection—indeed, the entire collection—was on display and *on sale* in the Wildenstein Paris Gallery.

I did two things. First, I bought the Morisot. Then I went to Paris.

Wildenstein then was at 57 rue la Boétie. In its muted, severe, yet utterly sumptuous gallery the pictures of Oscar Schmitz shimmered and glowed in the light of the afternoon.

Schmitz? Who was he and how did he come to these treasures? The catalog says (I have it in front of me in the original French, and I'm translating it into my original English):

> The collection of Oscar Schmitz of Dresden was one of the glories and one of the major attractions of that ancient Saxon capital. It was the work of a man whose name must be, in the twentieth century, among the greatest amateur patrons of the arts.
>
> The Medicis of Italy, the Doges of Venice, the Dukes of Ferrara, have taught us how the collector of the art of his times, out of his taste

and personal preferences, can evolve our tastes and how the choices of a collector can influence the artistic climate of a milieu, of a city, of a country.

Such was the role of the Schmitz collection in Dresden and in Germany of our period. In his private Baroque Museum, half-villa, half-gallery, he kept so many precious masterpieces of ancient art, to which he added rare examples of modern art, including Degas and Van Gogh. He reached out to them by a historical progression that included Corot, Manet, Monet, Sisley, Renoir, Cézanne, and many others, the entire collection starting at the beginning of the century, enabling Schmitz to bring together the diverse lines of the art he loved, French art, above all . . .

He was born in Prague in 1861; he became a Swiss citizen, which he remained until his death in 1933. He left Germany in 1931.*

As a young man he worked for his father in the cotton business and was a graduate of the School of Commerce. He had great success in this enterprise in Le Havre. But at the age of forty-two he retired from business to install in the suburbs of Dresden, in his charming villa situated in a pine forest, the pictures he had been collecting.

That collection started in Paris in 1890. From his first days in Paris, he made friends and enjoyed cordial relations with amateurs, artists, collectors. Many became devoted friends. In their company, and as a result of their long conversations about art, he began his artistic education. The amateurs did little more than reinforce the originality of his mind and his artistic instincts. Artists confided in him . . . dealers like Durand-Rouell, who were pioneering the work of the Impressionists, guided Schmitz and gave him wise counsel.

Finally, he dared to express himself and to buy.

In this new era of his life, his gifts as a business man were not forgotten. And we can recognize, without false shame, that he bought not out of caprice but as a merchant, served by an inner and intuitive sense of the real value of the works he was buying. . . . He was deeply impressed by the masters of French Impressionism, and he bought them, even though, at the time, their work (and his choices) were considered audacious.

Thus, it was a profession of faith on the part of a man. For him the role of amateur was not simply a luxury. Buying these pictures was at the same time a stroke of business and an act of dedication. Each purchase required double criteria—first, that of quality. Then, the questions he always asked himself. Is it a good picture? Is it a star in the heavens of French art?

After having at first bought only the Impressionists, not only the most perfect but also the most significant and the most important, he

---

* There are those who say that Oscar Schmitz felt and sensed the advent of Nazism. There is nobody left either to prove or disprove this. In any case, he did take his pictures out of Germany in 1931.

began to acquire the works of their predecessors. All the fragrance of the nineteenth century in the works of Corot and Delacroix led to the birth of the twentieth century and the fragrance of Van Gogh and Cézanne. Between these two periods came the Impressionists, whose work is not understandable without the help of what came before and what they caused to happen after.

The collection gathered together by Schmitz contained only the most powerful and best quality pictures. Thus, it offers a portrait of a great epic of art. In this resides his principal worth as a collector and as an aesthete.

I immediately felt, as I read this, though I dared not utter it aloud nor even permit myself to give it more than an instant's thought, that the role of collector had been given a definition I'd been striving to find all my life. A man who is not an artist yet is impelled to support, encourage, and, in effect, subsidize the artist—to make his work available to the public eye—what is he? An egotist? An investor? An exhibitionist getting his kicks by displaying not himself but his ownership? No, said the catalog, a man who "can influence the artistic climate of a milieu, of a city, of a country."

Was it possible to do it with movies? No.

Was this the goal I had been seeking despite autograph hunters and Warner Brothers? I still do not propose to answer the question because I have no answer.

Schmitz had one. Not one. Sixty-two. Sixty-two Boudins, Daumiers, Géricaults, Monets, Lautrecs, and Van Goghs—and every other now-famous name.

I looked at every one of these sixty-two pictures with lust. I did not want, nor could I conceivably afford them all. Some instinct told me (and I was wrong) that one or two of the Daumiers were fakes; I was not interested in Corot, but the rest, ah, the rest. If only I could . . . but why think about it? I did not ask prices; I could pretty well make educated guesses, and the guesses and my bank balance were in glaring contradiction.

Still, would the Gauguin *Fleurs de Tahiti* break me? Certainly I nodded to the Wildenstein man, not asking how much. And a small Daumier, that was sure to quicken the heart. And the Géricault, so ignored an artist, so powerful, so pulsing. I nodded again.

And the Cézannes. Good God, which one? *Paysage à l'Estaque?*— though it was not the Cézanne I really wanted. That was the *Black Clock*, and it was not in this collection.

Memories. George Gershwin and I in a gallery in New York looking at the *Black Clock* and drooling and debating whether we could pool our resources to buy it. More memories: George Gershwin and I looking at *Père Tanguy* by Van Gogh, the drooling even more evident.

But neither the *Black Clock* nor *Père Tanguy* were for sale in the Schmitz Collection. I bought the Gauguin, a Daumier, a Berthe Morisot, another Renoir, a Cézanne landscape, and the Géricault—and, I think, a few others.

The cost was far beyond anything I could afford, but Wildenstein offered excellent terms and shipped the pictures to London.

I moved into a large suite in the Dorchester where I could hang the pictures I'd bought from the Schmitz Collection, and Gladys and Manny came to join me. I cannot tell you now whether Gladys was appalled or overjoyed at seeing these pictures on the walls of the Dorchester. I suspect the best analysis is to say that she was both. She was excited by them but appalled at the cost.

We both went to lunch with George Wildenstein and then dropped in at his London Gallery where, to my astonishment, I saw that the *Black Clock* was for sale. On the spot I offered George a deal. Would he exchange the Cézanne landscape for the *Black Clock*? He would, and he did, and I now owned the picture I wanted more than any other in the world.

Gladys, Manny, and I went to Paris, and, of course, I took her to see the rest of the Schmitz Collection. She saw the Corot, and suddenly she, too, was fired with enthusiasm. I told her that I'd wanted the Corot but that at the last moment I felt I simply couldn't afford it. She reminded me that since we were living beyond our means, we might as well go whole-hog, so we bought the Corot.

Those pictures, together with those I already possessed, became the nucleus of—forgive me for saying so—one of the greatest collections of French Impressionist art ever assembled by an American.

Now Fate, or The Man Upstairs, or God, or Allah, or Buddha—or whatever you want to call that force—took a hand in my fortunes.

Here I was, with this insanely splendid collection of pictures, returning to America with no idea how to pay for them. Here I was, complete with wife and child, returning to the United States in all the luxury of the Cunard Line, to debts and mortgages and a wife who was suddenly in a terrible depression about the whole thing. The entire trip was punctuated with her visions of bread lines and the poor house.

Have you forgotten that I'd made a picture called *Bullets or Ballots*? God knows, I had. It was an eighteen-karat, walloping wowsie of a hit.

The critics raved. And Douglas Gilbert in the New York *World-Telegram* said:

> The role of Johnny Blake is a natural for Edward G. Robinson, and it is a tribute to his art that he tosses his studio differences into the ashcan and throws himself wholeheartedly into the part for a performance unequalled since his *Little Caesar*.

Studio differences? Don't be silly. To Jack Warner I was the second coming. And he wasn't exactly unhappy with Humphrey Bogart either. He was, of course, terribly unhappy with Bette Davis and Jimmy Cagney, both of whom, he told me tearfully in London, were trouble-makers, demanding more money and script approval. Did you ever hear of such appalling nonsense? Such ingratitude?

When he came to my house (can you imagine!) to discuss a new film with me (a script of *Kid Galahad* under his arm), he was all smiles and darlingness.

Jack Warner possessed every hallmark of the superb businessman except one. He did not, nor did he ever have a poker face. It is, to mix a metaphor as far as you can go, his Achilles' heel. It was very clear when we sat down in the patio and had a cup of coffee that his merry face was to set me up for a deal.

We went through the usual *pavane*—houses—mine was jammed with new paintings, and I was considering altering it; he suggested architects and ways I could get everything wholesale. We discussed again (boringly) the difficulties he was having with Jimmy, Bette, and Livvy (need I bother with last names, or do you want the feeling of what it's like to be on the inside?). I told him that he treated actors badly. At this point he nearly sobbed, and, by God, he was sincere about it.

Who were these people? Nobodies that he'd transformed into stars, arranged for them to have money, deference, houses, international fame. And how was he being paid back? They were nailing him to the cross.

I reminded him that we had had the identical conversation in London and that I had told him then—and was telling him again—that just as he had done so much for them, so had they done a great deal for him. I repeated my advice that the New York producer was an arbitrator, a compromiser, a repository for talent, not a slave master; I advised Jack L. to share the wealth, that an actor did not necessarily mean money by wealth; he also meant some determination in his own fate.

I was pleading for all of us in what I have previously called and still do, this chance-cursed profession.

But Jack L. dealt me out. I was different. Oh, we'd had our differences, of course—I being sort of a perfectionist when it came to scripts (and he made "perfectionist" sound like some dread disease). However, except for an occasional leak to the newspapers (planted by his men) *our* differences had always been kept behind closed doors. He was a private man, and so was I, and that's why we got along so well together and that's why we'd have so many more happy years together. And he got up to go.

"Sit!" I said. And he sat. "What happy years?" I asked.

"The years we'll be associated together from now on, Eddie. You shall have everything you want."

"For my one last picture?"

"What one last picture?"

"There is only one more picture left on my contract."

"Formality. Formality. Just tell your agent what you want and it's yours. Within reason, of course. After all, we're both reasonable men."

I instantly decided to prove that I was not a reasonable man, but he wasn't listening. He was advising me that he, personally, cared nothing about my political activities, but did I have to champion Roosevelt so visibly? After all, he and Louis B. Mayer were for Landon, and L.B. was the California man on the Republican National Committee and a great friend of Herbert Hoover's. While J.L. *hated* Hitler, wasn't it true that the Anti-Nazi League was full of dirty Bolsheviks?

I was, I think, in complete control (though inwardly seething) as I tried to fill Jack Warner in on the facts of life—Spain being used as a testing ground for German and Italian weapons; Hitler's gestures toward the Rhineland and his mutterings about the Sudetenland, England's wavering posture; France's dependence on the Maginot Line, which many of my French friends, especially Léon Blum, had told me was an archaic monstrosity; the Japanese posture in Manchuria; the growth in the United States of a body of men who posed as pacifists but were actually (I put it as mildly as I could) pro status quo.

I tried to make Warner see what men like Harold Laski in London and Madariaga of Spain and Winston Churchill in England were seeing all too clearly—that the world was on the verge of Armageddon. I told him of the hideous concentration camps in Germany, though at the time they were not clearly visible nor widely known, the fears among the Jews of Europe, and the fears, too, of the non-Jews in Czechoslovakia, Poland, and the Eastern reaches.

What I was saying to Jack Warner, I must admit in all deference to his intelligence, was known to him—but he was caught between an unreasoning fear of communism and a not altogether yet congealed dread of fascism.

I assured him there was still another way, and I'm afraid I used all the clichés: the American way, self-determination, the democratic process, the rights of *all* men to—oh, yes, I said it—life, liberty, and the pursuit of happiness. But Jack, like so many self-made millionaires, spent most of his time with bankers, brokers, and Republican politicians who believed in the impregnability of the Atlantic, the concept of Fortress America, and George Washington's warning against entangling alliances.

Let me admit it was not a very intelligent political discussion. I pride myself on being reasonable, but I am not really very reasonable when my basic assumptions are being challenged. On Jack's behalf, let me say that his major interest was not in the state of the world but in signing me to another contract.

What he offered was simple enough: a huge raise in salary, which he considered the crowning argument and, of course, those four months off every year to do a play. He was safe enough there. I had never used them; it was apparent to him that I never would. Jack Warner knew four months wouldn't make it.

As far as he was concerned, the matter was practically settled although he suspected I might have some minor points the way a child might have some minor points with daddy.

I had some minor points. One was story and script approval.

Jack Warner almost died. Did I not realize that a studio like Warner's surrounded me with the very best brains as far as material was concerned? Did I not know the sorry results of actors choosing their own material? He quoted Charles Ray, a silent star, who had insisted on playing Miles Standish and as a result had gone bankrupt. Did I not recall how Clark Gable had refused *It Happened One Night* and had to be forced to play it, achieving, as a result, immense stature?

He quoted the errors of Gloria Swanson (*Madame Sans Gene*), Mary Pickford (*Taming of the Shrew*), Norma Shearer (*Romeo and Juliet*), Clark Gable (*Parnell*), George Arliss (*Old English*), going on and on with a catalog of stars who saw only their own role in a film and guessed wrong. I had to admit that some of his indictments were accurate, but again I pointed out that an actor is not a puppet.

He wanted to know my terms exactly. My terms were that I would sign for as long as he wished, one year, two, ten—*as long as he wished*.

I could sense him figuring out my life expectancy.

"If . . ."

"If what, Eddie?"

"If the stories and scripts are mutually agreeable."

"To whom?"

"To you and to me."

"Suppose," asked Jack, "you like such and such a story and I don't?"

"Then you don't have to make it."

"What'll you do with it?"

"I might acquire it and take it to M.G.M."

"Over my dead body you'll take it to Mayer."

"Then you have a simple decision; you can take my judgment and make it."

"All right," he said, "that part we could work out. You're a decent man. You're not as hard as a rock. If there's something I don't like, you'll listen?"

"Of course, I'll listen. I may not agree, but I'll listen. If you're right, I'll do more than listen. I'll make any rational changes you request."

"Good. Now let's put the shoe on the other foot. Suppose *I* like the script and you don't."

"I won't play it."

He played his trump card. "So then I could give it to Bogart who is going to be a very big star, or Cagney, who is already a big star, or Muni. Fox ruined Muni. I'm giving him a whole new life. You think you know more than Muni?"

"Yes."

"Okay, Eddie, that's all."

"No, Jack, not all. I want something on a platter."

"For instance?"

"I don't want to carry a picture by myself. I want other stars with me. Like they do at Metro."

He hesitated, then he grinned. "I can get you Miriam Hopkins."

We both laughed. Hollowly.

It took weeks of haggling with lawyers and agents examining the dot over every *i*, every comma, every clause, most of which were couched in double and triple negatives. And let me add that the fine print, known in the trade as boiler plate, is the thinnest of all ice. The simplest of phrases, apparently innocent and innocuous, can knock out the whole contract.

What I could not get out was the morals clause—that extraordinary paragraph that forbids you to do or say anything that might subject you or the studio to low esteem. I made a counteroffer: I would sign it if the studio or Mr. Warner agreed to do the same thing—if Mr. Warner or the studio were forbidden to do anything that might subject me to low esteem. My lawyers and agents talked me out of this gambit.

So there we were. I was back at Warner's and a potential millionaire (if I liked the stories and didn't die) and I could turn my mind to more pressing matters.

Before I do, let me tell you something that went on between Humphrey Bogart and myself. Bogie had a manner, a personality—yes, an immense talent—that has made him almost immortal. Working with him, I think I understood it better than his fans. For all his outward toughness, insolence, braggadocio, and contempt (and those were always part of the characters he played, though they were not entirely within Bogie), there came through a kind of sadness, loneliness, and heartbreak (all of which *were* very much part of Bogie the man). I always felt sorry for him—sorry that he imposed upon himself the facade of the character with which he had become identified.

I knew him through a series of wives; in the end, he met his match and his comfort in a woman as spirited as himself, Lauren Bacall.

She was all hardness and rough on the outside, but she was mush in her heart. She was even—and she'll kill me for saying this—dear and warm and utterly devoted to her husband, her family, and her nation. But, brother, she shellacked and varnished herself so that no one would know it. I knew it. I still know it, and at the risk of embarrassing her with a word she'd hate, I think she is lovable.

Anyway, Bogie and I carried on a charade in each picture. Almost inevitably both of us would get killed at the end of the films in which we worked together. Because we were both rotten, we had to get our just desserts. Will Hays and his successors said so in the motion picture code. The charade followed a precise pattern. When I was the reigning star, Bogie would be slain first, and I'd live another reel before I got it. As the years passed and Bogie became the reigning star and I was demoted to character roles, *I'd* get the bullet first and Bogie would live out another reel before he was struck down for his sins.

Check that one out, film historians!

19

I guess I would be drawn and quartered if I passed *Kid Galahad* without telling you that its leading lady was Bette Davis. In any case, I may, of course, be drawn and quartered for what I'm about to say of her. Let me assure you, early on, that it is not what I had to say about Miriam Hopkins.

On the contrary. Miss Davis was and is every inch a lady—polite, mannerly, gracious, even self-effacing. But by today's standards she could never have gotten a job in a high school production of *East Lynne*. I know it's goatish of me to say it, but Miss Davis was, when I played with her, not a very gifted amateur and employed any number of jarring mannerisms that she used to form an image. In her early period Miss Davis played the image, and not herself, and certainly not the character provided by the author.

Though I cannot recall talking to her about this and thus having no personal knowledge of her feelings, I can only assume by reason of the difficulties she raised with Jack Warner that she was thoroughly aware of her problems. She was the victim of the movies' attitude toward women.

It was impossible for her to play a waif because there was too much steel in her; it was absurd for her to play a creature over whom men swooned because there was nothing about her to make you swoon. She was far too independent and self-assured to be a convincing whore, though she brilliantly played some unconvincing ones. The fact is she was not an ingenue or a comedienne or an inconstant wife when those were the roles reserved for actresses.

Had she remained on the stage (and she had had some minimal experience there), I think her development would have been quite extraordinary. She was not unlike Pauline Lord in her own way, or even, to make no odious comparison, like Sarah Bernhardt. The unpretty woman of the stage required meaty roles, deep in emotion, and filled with scenes of frustration and despair. Katharine Hepburn was in the same boat, but she was either luckier or more determined than Miss Davis; she also had more humor. She also had the fortune of finding Spencer Tracy as a costar, and romance between them in the movies seemed not only plausible but welcome. She grew and grew, and wonderful parts opened for her.

Then, of course, the same thing happened to Miss Davis. It began early on, I think with *Jezebel*, and came to flower in *All About Eve*. She deserted the mannerisms, laying them aside, I should think, with unbounded joy.

Too late? For male actors it is possible, though not easy, to slip gradually from leading man into character roles. For me, it just came naturally, since I was never Tab Hunter; my unsymmetrical face grew more lined, and I was able to continue, the parts growing smaller, but the range (and, forgive me, the eminence) remaining. For a woman, it is extremely difficult. The day an actress agrees to play a mother is a turning point in her life. Where does she go from there? What does a pinup girl like Betty Grable do with the rest of most of her life? Or a Rita Hayworth?

But they were simply sex pots. Bette Davis never was. You know what I think? I think her best days are ahead of her. I think she'll give up those horror movies (that she played simply, I would guess, to make a living) and turn to the classics. To the Greeks and Ibsen and Lady Macbeth—to the classic parts where the role is ageless.

When I played with her in *Kid Galahad*, I did not admire Bette Davis; I admire her now.

The new Warner contract was so arranged that I would have a certain degree of financial probity. Any sane man with a family to support, the owner of a house and fabulous pictures, the possibility of security assured, would have done the sensible thing: Save the money and look forward to a nice old age on a country estate with time for golf and tennis and no pressure to have to make a buck. Such an idea never entered my mind.

The pictures, bought from the Schmitz collection, joined with the potpourri of art we already possessed, were in constant battle with the house in which they were hung. Half the pictures were masterpieces, and they were upstaged by a silly, junky fireplace. The phony Tudor ceiling depressed the Géricault. The carpet fought with the Morisot. The sofas defied the Pissarros.

I have often said in interviews that great pictures are tyrants, that they will not tolerate surroundings alien or hostile to them. Well, that kind of comment is great for an interview, an article, or a speech. The truth is that the unhappiness was in me, and in Gladys, too.

We realized that we either had to sell the house and find one in which the pictures could be the stars and the rest of the house was underplayed—or make the alternate choice of remodeling this very house to achieve the same result. We chose to remodel.

I remembered Sam Marx, the architect. I went to see him in Chicago. He showed me a house he had done for a financier named Epstein who owned many old masters and indicated how it was possible to have a house you could live in on a day-to-day basis and still make the pictures preeminent. It was interesting, too, to discover that Sam Marx was himself a collector of paintings, though his tastes were far more avant-garde than mine. I thought the stuff he owned was wild and radical. The stuff he owned was painted by Picasso and Braque. My eye had not yet come to accept the Cubist or Postimpressionist school. But my eye certainly assured me that Sam Marx was the man to redo my Beverly Hills house.

How long would it take? What would we do with everything in the meantime? And where would we live? Because, as Sam came out, looked over the house, and he and Gladys and I discussed plans, made little drawings, decided to change one room, then two, then the entire joint, it became absolutely clear that we'd have to get out of the way of the wreckers and carpenters and electricians.

Through an attorney friend of mine I had long been interested in a little farm in the hills above Beverly; it seemed to me to be an ideal place for Manny to grow up—an informal, rough and ready rancho where he could have his friends and whoop it up. So I bought it, and it was there we decided to move while the main house was being redecorated.

I used that word advisedly because what we were going to do could hardly be called redecoration; we were really rebuilding and refurnishing.

Speaking of my little country house in the hills, I no longer own it, and it is no longer the country. The city reached out through the years and engulfed it. I really couldn't care less; living in the country those two and a half years that Sam Marx was plunging me into bankruptcy were not pleasant for me. I do not much care for the outdoors unless it is carefully manicured by a gardener.

We were constantly in consultation over the shape of the house and its furnishings. The wall coloring would be beige, certainly, so that the pictures would stand out; there would be no tall piece of furniture to fight them. And there came a point where we almost decided there should be no windows. How else could we achieve walls long and important enough for a large Monet canvas? Now it is manifestly absurd to have no windows, yet art galleries have few.

I should never have said that, because all at once, to the three of us, the same thought occurred: Why *not* have a gallery? We had the ground for it—the badminton court—and the pictures to put into it. So we decided on it, not knowing that the Beverly Hills City Council or Zoning Department or whatever would view the idea with disdain.

Gladys plunged into severe depression when our plans were turned down, a melancholy out of all proportion to the problem. It was a symptom to which I should have paid more attention—the beginning of an illness then unrecognizable to me as anything but bad temper. Even when, by altering the setback and the plans and purchasing fifteen more feet from my next-door neighbor, Beverly Hills gave us permission to build the gallery, the depression did not leave her. Then one morning she awakened bright and happy and gay and full of excitement, with more plans for another suite in the attic—for Manny, of course. These odd switches in mood angered and bored me, but I did not consider them serious.

Nor did I bring Manny into the planning. Today I know what I should have done; I should have made him a partner. I should have told him I was sending the pictures to the Los Angeles Museum until the house was ready; I should have said the remodelling was for him as well as for us; I should have asked his opinions. But who asks the opinions of a five-, barely six-year-old, child? Anybody with any sense does. But neither Gladys nor I had that kind of sense; we thought he had everything; we could not begin to realize his fears, his insecurity, his hostility at losing the badminton court.

When it came to the emotions and doubts and wonders of a small child, we dismissed them. We did not know, *I* did not know what I know now: that a small child is an adult in miniature, and those early years are filled with terrible nightmares and fantasies of abandonment and desertion and loneliness.

While the plastering and bricklaying and carving were going on, Warner Brothers offered me one script after another, all of which I turned down. I think the scripts were all bad. However, if I am to be candid with myself and you, the truth is I was setting up my independence of action with Warner's. It seemed necessary to exercise the clauses in the new contract that gave me approval; I had to show that I meant it.

It would be understandable to you if I turned down the Warner Brothers script in order to play *Othello*. I can well understand that you must think me demented that I turned them down to go over to Metro to play a picture called *The Last Gangster*. I, who had demanded script approval, hoping never again to play a gangster, now agreed to play an aging one. I, who had insisted upon others sharing the burden of the film, played it with a young man, hardly having achieved stardom by then—James Stewart—and my costar was the compelling Rose Stradner (an eminent European actress) entirely unknown to the American public.

It seemed to me that I was doing the right thing. I know now that the decision to accept the Metro offer was made out of bad temper, anxiety, and the evermounting costs of the remodeling of the house. Money was the overriding consideration, not art. And it's rather a relief to be able to admit that thirty-five years later.

Or is it thirty-five centuries?

20

Last night I went to bed and scribbled some notes about M.G.M. "Thalberg dead, Mannix, Thau, Nick Schenck—retakes . . . perfectionism . . . how different from Warner's. . . ." Then I was suddenly very tired and thought I would sleep and tried and couldn't. For me, the greatest pill is television. That's why I have one of those postage stamp Japanese affairs next to my bed. I turned it on. It was only nine o'clock, and it said: somebody's movie of the week, and it was, if you like, *my* movie of the week or, more exactly, Steve McQueen's, and I watched it through.

This may be considered rambling, but I don't consider it rambling at all; there must be a special word for the experience of an ancient actor who lies in his own bed and sees another himself as once he was, dredging up memories and astonished at his own performance and what only *he* knows as revealing.

Let me admit that one of the unexpected rewards of watching a movie in which I appeared is that I can manage it without wearing my hearing aid. I can read my own lips, and that is a unique experience denied to most of you. Nor is my preoccupation with it this morning all that much of a detour, for *The Cincinnati Kid* was made at M.G.M. in 1964, and what a different M.G.M. it was from the studio of 1936. How different *that* M.G.M. was from the one of 1931. And in the autumn of 1972 I made *Soylent Green* at what was left of M.G.M., and how vast a difference that eight-year span made. Gerontology is not only a tragedy of man; it applies to corporations as well.*

Let me point out in a sardonic historical sense that the film *The Cincinnati Kid* was written and publicly credited to Ring Lardner, Jr., who had, some seventeen years before, been held in contempt by the House Un-American Activities Committee. He had been sentenced to a federal penitentiary, served his time, and was out.

Now here he was back, accepted again, the prison episode forgotten, the town mostly ashamed. How can shame make up for a year of a life?

He collaborated on the script either together or one was put on top of the other (one never knows about these curious writing arrangements) with Terry Sothern, whose previous work as a novelist would have given Louis B. Mayer cardiac arrest. The film was not strictly produced by M.G.M. at all but by Martin Ransohoff, an independent leasing through M.G.M.—a kind of picture arrangement that would have also given Nick Schenck cardiac arrest. It was directed by Norman Jewison,** almost fresh from television, which would certainly have given Eddie Mannix cardiac arrest, and it starred young McQueen, whose beautiful–ugly face would probably have pleased Benny Thau.

In the film I played Lancey Howard, the reigning champ of the stud poker tables. I was over seventy as I watched the screen, and the man on the screen was over seventy, bearded, contained, groomed, self-confident, and with the eyes of an eagle. Steve McQueen played the Cincinnati Kid, all jaw muscles, contained, not well groomed, self-confident, and with the eyes of an eagle.

It seemed to me that once I had been the young Steve McQueen. I had played the same kind of part with that same virginal sense of character, that same undercurrent of sex, subtly motivating the most unsexual of acts (though gambling for high stakes is either a form of or replaces eroticism); I strongly identified with McQueen. ("Heavy," he said.)

I could hardly say I identified with Lancey; I *was* Lancey. That man on the screen, more than in any other picture I ever made, was Edward G. Robinson with great patches of Emanuel Goldenberg

---

* Two-thirds of it were sold to Leavitt for another town, and all the props were sold at a heart-breaking auction.

** Norman directed the film version of *Fiddler on the Roof*, and some Jews, considering the film a Protestant version of the *shtetel*, felt he should have changed his name to Norman Christianson.

showing through. He was all cold and discerning and unflappable on the exterior; he was aging and full of self-doubt on the inside.

From those first days on the stage through *Little Caesar*, the Schmitz Collection, the war, the divorce, the Red-baiting, the two serious illnesses—that now bearded face was a living step-by-step relief map. And only I could know that.

The Kid and Lancey play an all-night poker game. At one period they rest for an hour. There is a scene in which Lancey, in his hotel room for this intermission, sinks to his bed, tired, exhausted, the facade of egotism and assurance crumbled, and he is old and almost finished yet not ready to give up. It was not hard to play that moment; Jewison did not have to direct me. It was *real*.

Even the final session of the poker game was real. God knows I'd read the script. God knows I understood that it called for me to win with a diamond straight flush, beating out the Kid's full house, aces up, but I think Steve and I played that game as if it were for blood. It was one of the best performances I ever gave on stage or screen or radio or TV, and the reason for it is that it wasn't a performance at all; it was symbolically the playing out of my whole gamble with life. (I play poker like a dummy; in the film I played like Canfield even though I knew it was a cold deck set up by the prop department.) *

Finally there was a line I had to Steve: "As long as I'm around, you're second best; you may as well learn to live with it." I could hardly speak the words. I knew they weren't true. It was I who had to live with it. He was the star. *I* was second best.

A word to and about Steve McQueen: He comes out of the tradition of Gable, Bogie, Cagney, and even me—but he's added his own dimension. He is a stunner, and who knows what glory the future holds? But surely he is already an honorable member of the company of players.

But we must back to *The Last Gangster* and 1937.

I had always known that M.G.M. films had a very special hallmark on them, discounting my bad experience with *I Loved a Woman*, but I'm prone to think now that a great deal of that was my own fault. As an institution, a manufacturer of film, M.G.M. had no peer. Tiffany's, if you like.

---

* Note from L.S.: Jane tells me that one night, when E.G.R. came home from the set during the filming of the poker game of *Cincinnati Kid*, he said, "Toughest thing I've had to play. No movement. No action. I have to play the entire role with my eyes."

Bosley Crowther, one-time critic for *The New York Times*, wrote a book on M.G.M. that I read with interest, and, while it offers many facts, it leaves out something very important: Let's call it flavor.

Louis B. Mayer, since Thalberg's death, had developed an empire. He was, of course, emperor, but beneath him he had kings, princes, and dukes. Nothing but the best (within his own definition of what was best) would do for Louis B. Say what you will of him (and, to many, he remains the quintessential caricature of the Hollywood producer), he had style, *panache*, and the ability—the need, I think—to make pictures that were his ideals of what life should be. That it wasn't always the best was not his fault; he believed in beauty, glamor, materialism, and the star system; he believed movies should be an escape from the ugliness of the world and should contain no messages except that love and fieldstone houses and gorgeous women and manly men were, in sum, God's true purpose.

He also believed in making money for himself and his stockholders and his employees, and through the creation of stables of writers and actors and the ability to buy the best stories and plays (if they weren't controversial), he succeeded.

What was he like as a man? I have no way of psyching him, except to tell you that on my first day at Metro, having been shown my Federal dressing room with all the amenities of the suite I had at Warner's and with a set-dresser anxiously asking me for suggestions (I had none; the rooms were so perfect that I dreaded to think that, neat as I am, I would certainly mess them up), I was escorted by the director of the film, William A. Wellman, a chilly, knowledgeable, 100-percent American, to Mr. Mayer's office.

No long walk to Mr. Mayer's desk. On the contrary. Ida Koverman, Mr. Mayer's righthand executive secretary (an aging, but clearsighted lady who had lately worked for Herbert Hoover), explained graciously to Mr. Wellman that Mr. Mayer wished to see me alone, and Mr. Wellman humbly remained outside as I went in.

Mr. Mayer, standing almost at the door, welcomed me with evident pleasure. He suggested we sit not at his desk but in two very comfortable armchairs, and we chatted.

For openers, he wished to welcome me as a new member of the M.G.M. family, not remembering that I'd already done a film there with Thalberg. He sighed about Thalberg, told me how much he missed him, speculated briefly on the shortness and unpredictability of life, and cleared his throat.

This was what I was waiting for: a discussion of my political bents. I knew that Mr. Mayer had supported for governor of California the Republican candidate against Upton Sinclair. Mr. Mayer knew beyond doubt that I had supported Upton Sinclair. I had refused to make a contribution to the Republican campaign, though we all—secretaries, grips, readers, writers, stars—had been gently reminded that the election of Upton Sinclair would destroy the industry.*

I was also waiting for Mayer to comment on the fact that I had joined with others in opposition to the then pending Neutrality Act, prohibiting the export of arms and ammunition to belligerent nations. While on the surface it looked as though we were, in this pose of neutrality, trying to preserve peace, I felt that it was directed against the Spanish Loyalists and the Czechs, threatened by Hitler. I was also tensely waiting for Mr. Mayer to throw a few darts at Eleanor Roosevelt, social security, and unions.

Mr. Mayer never mentioned any of these matters; rather, we discussed the difficulty of film-making and those involved in it. Though M.G.M. was solvent (unlike many of the other film factories that were hovering or were already in 77B), even Mr. Mayer's resources were limited. In terms of his Family, human wills, he sighed, were unpredictable and the human emotions even more so; interests conflicted, but all must be met and heeded and compromised. He, L.B., was the great compromiser, and he wanted me to understand that if any great conflicts arose, in my case in the making of *The Last Gangster*, he would always listen with enormous sympathy and understanding to my side of the story.

I must confess that not for an instant did I discern hypocrisy or untruth in what he was saying. He meant every word, and whatever the battles that prompted his eventual downfall, I found him to be a man of truth. As far as others were concerned, I do not know. I will say that it was clear that behind his gutta-percha face and roly-poly figure (contained in some of the best tailoring I've ever seen) it was evident there was a man of steel—but well-mannered steel, the very best quality steel, which meant the hardest and most impenetrable steel.

Our chat finished, he ushered me out of his office to his private elevator and up to the fourth floor. Here there was a delightful dining room table at which all the executives sat—Mr. Mannix, Irish, bluff, second in command; Benny Thau, in charge of talent, whose chief

---

* Through the years we also were asked to make contributions to the anti-daylight-saving campaigns on the grounds that as long as the sun didn't set, people wouldn't go to the movies. That may or not have been an accurate estimate of the situation, but as soon as a studio asked me to contribute to something, I sensed its political implications. I, of course, exempt the Motion Picture Relief, which is one of the greatest, best run philanthropies in the nation, and I have always contributed a portion of my salary to it.

credential was that he spoke in so low a voice that you were instantly disarmed because all your energies were consumed in trying to hear him; Joe Cohen, head of physical production and a genius at it; Marvin Schenck, a dear soul of whom it was said that his job was to sit at his window keeping careful watch on Washington Boulevard so as to report instantly to Mr. Mayer of the coming of a new glacier; L. K. Sidney, one-time exhibitor and vaudevillian who dealt in labor relations; Sam Marx (not the architect), in charge of story purchases and their eventual transformation into scenarios;* and a pride of producers like Hunt Stromberg, Bernie Hyman, Sam Katz, Harry Rapf, and a great many other names that can't possibly mean anything to you but made the pictures you or your fathers and mothers saw—and, no intention to demean here, they were very good pictures.

As we entered, everybody made a fainthearted attempt to stand, but Mr. Mayer, with a wave of his hand, would have none of it, and I was directed to Mr. Mayer's right. He suggested the chicken soup with matzoh balls, and I had it and found it excellent. Then we had filet mignon and excellent coffee, but no dessert because everybody, including me, was watching his weight. It's time to tell you that everybody in Hollywood, then and now, was and is watching his weight. It is and was the one thing that everybody in the town had in common. We were all cholesterol-conscious long before we ever heard of the word.

After lunch Mr. Mayer introduced me to a chiropractor, a genius with backs, who had an office on the fourth floor. Everybody in Hollywood had back trouble. It was not that most of us were satyrs and nymphomaniacs. Rather, it surely was that most of us were hypochondriacs.

If medicine flourishes in Beverly Hills, it is because Mr. Mayer and his fellow executives, not only at M.G.M. but through the city, imported the very best doctors from the Mayo Clinic, the Menninger Clinic, and Johns Hopkins. Later, Bedford Drive in Beverly Hills became Freud Street.

But back to lunch. The conversation, at first general and concerned with cigars, baseball, film grosses, and rather gentle gossip about the eventual fate of some of the studios, later took on a harder edge, and I heard some acid comments on Eleanor Roosevelt, Harold Ickes, and Mrs. Perkins. I also felt, in some quarters, a disposition for the supporters of the New Deal to keep their mouths shut. By "some

* By this time there were well over a hundred writers under contract to the studio, and the list read like the membership roles of the Authors' League. There were young writers there, too, who, it seemed to me, were doing the bulk of the work, receiving salaries less than the makeup men.

quarters" I suppose I mean myself; I had long since grown to know that luncheon arguments about a world heading into war would change no one's opinion.

And so I made *The Last Gangster* at Metro and found that it was politically the most schizophrenic of lots. The executives, almost to a man, were antiliberal; the writers and lesser executives were fellow members of mine in organizations to oppose the Nazis. Thus, the commissary, where we all lunched, divided itself into tables where political differences were minimized.* The writers' table was a hotbed of progressive thought; those writers who didn't agree ate with the directors, whose table was a hotbed of people who longed for the reincarnation of Calvin Coolidge.

The sound and the fury of diametrically opposed political and social views were so loud that the waitresses could hardly take the orders for green goddess salad, which was supposed to be low in calories but wasn't. The screams of rage as writer would confront director on the subject of Hitler's entry into the Rhineland made it quite impossible to have a bacon and tomato on whole wheat toast in peace.

Eventually I resorted to having lunch in my dressing room; it is quite impossible to do justice to a role after you've spilled your guts out on the subject of the Sudeten Germans.

I returned to Warner's to make *A Slight Case of Murder* from a play by Damon Runyon and Howard Lindsay.** I had absolutely no fault to find with the script because it was beautifully constructed and written and it was very funny.

Nor did I object in any way to *The Amazing Dr. Clitterhouse*, which I made next.

This was all during 1938 and 1939, and what was happening in the world made the making of movies seem almost absurd: Anschluss with Austria; the Russian invasion of Finland; Munich; Chamberlain's peace in our time; the Russo-German Pact; The War.

I have made no bones about the fact that I belonged to and sup-

---

* Mr. Mayer also had a small private dining room here so that he could lunch with prime ministers and senators and thus give the employees a small view of his eminence. Kings and queens were usually given large luncheons on Stage 16.

** I knew Mr. Runyon only slightly, but young Boswell, who is ridding this book of dangling participles and split infinitives, assures me that the famous line attributed to everybody: "If I want a message in a picture, I'll send for Western Union," was uttered by Runyon. The only personal note I have on Runyon is that he was absolutely unlike the characters he invented; he was soft-spoken, reserved, and never once did he utter a Runyonism.

ported every organization that was opposed to Hitler. I not only gave money, I went to meetings and sat through them and let my name be used on letterheads. More than that, I worked actively with some of the groups. I am no fool; I knew that some of the people with whom I was involved were pro-Stalin and pro-Soviet Union, but I thought then, and I kept thinking it for a long time, that those political motivations were secondary to their concerns about the German tentacles that threatened Europe and the world. If communism was a way to stop the brutalization of the world, so be it. I would deal with that later. The first and prime consideration was major and undiluted opposition to the Third Reich.

Soviet aggression against Finland shook me deeply. Explanations that Mannheim was a potential supporter of Hitler and that the Russians had to protect their flank left me unconvinced and with a sour taste in my mouth.

When Molotov went to Berlin and concluded the Russo–German alliance (or treaty or devil's agreement), I was shaken to the core. I watched my friends—suddenly former friends—burbling; they explained the cleverness of it, the strategy of it. The cleverness, the strategy to join with Hitler!

I can recall no event in history that gave me greater pain. I was suddenly the enemy of people who had been my friends.

I resigned right and left.

Meanwhile, it was unfortunately true that in the summer of 1939 Gladys and I took Manny to Europe, together with the governess. In Paris we stayed at the Plaza Athenée, and despite the war talk, we visited the museums and galleries, *Guide Michelin* three-star restaurants, and, more importantly, the cafés in Montparnasse. One evening, while we were there, I met Vuillard, the painter, learned he was eager for some money, and had a brainstorm. Would he paint a picture of Manny, Gladys and me? Family (*sic*) portrait.

He would and did. My six-year-old son hated sitting for him, but the old man persisted, and the painting was completed. It is short of a masterwork. Paintings on commission usually are. But it beats hell out of a Kodak snapshot.

By now the acrid smell of war was in the air, and as it grew closer, I began making frantic efforts to get us all back to safety. We had return tickets on the *Athenia*, but apparently our reservations were canceled out.* Quickly, we all decided to get out of Paris and went to Deauville, somehow believing it safer.

---

* Luck, indeed. The *Athenia* was one of the first passenger ships to be blown out of the water by the Nazi U-boats.

In Deauville the prospect of war seemed dim indeed. The casinos were filled with the wealthy of the world playing chemin. (I tried a bit of it and grew to like it; in fact, I still take a seat at the chemin table at Las Vegas now and then.) By the end of August and into September the war talk began to infiltrate this Victorian spa, and I was on the phone trying, along with thousands of others, to book passage on any ship to get us out. Even steerage would have been acceptable.

George Wildenstein did the best he could; he arranged for us to get to Le Havre. (I remembered another such trip to this identical port so long ago.) He even got us on board the *America*, of the United States Lines. The plan was that we would sleep in the main salon and do our best with the public toilets. But being a movie star has its benefits. The purser gave up his cabin to Gladys and me, and the ship's chief nurse decided she would sleep in the infirmary and abandon her quarters to Manny and his governess.

Aboard the *America* was Mrs. Sara Roosevelt, F.D.R.'s mother, and her grandson John, and we knew she was an inevitable target. Two days out, we all felt as the passengers must have felt aboard the *Lusitania*. Would there be a war? Would a submarine challenge us?

Deep in my heart I would have liked to remain in France. I felt like a coward leaving. I wanted to join the French Army, help man the Maginot Line and even made a stab at it. I was not laughed at—at least, not in my presence.

Then came the night in the grand salon when we could barely hear the news that Hitler had marched into Poland and Warsaw was levelled, followed by equally crackling words of Chamberlain declaring war—and then Daladier. The ship's band, not knowing quite what to do, played *God Save the King* and the *Marseillaise*.

A close friend of mine on board refused to stand. We all turned our backs on him. Ten years later he told anybody who would listen that I was a member of the Communist party.*

I had no hard proof then about his own affiliations. You will learn I had proof later.

You will learn that two die-hard conservatives saved my reputation: Cecil B. DeMille and Sam Yorty.

I do not propose to continue along this line until the full effects become apparent. But I think you should have some sense of the fury

---

* What point in mentioning his name? He's dead now. He thought he could clear himself by naming me; he was blacklisted and irrational and driven to the wall by the loss of his career. He was a victim of the witch hunt. He was also a louse.

Note from L.S.: To the day he died, Eddie never told me the name of this man.

of the accusations. It is only fair to give Gerald L. K. Smith his say about me, though he did not say it until June 8, 1949, at the Embassy Auditorium, Ninth and Grand streets, Los Angeles, California. A shorthand expert covered the meeting, and I have his report in front of me. He mentioned others than myself, but I will not do so. This is what he said: *

> ——— and Edward G. Robinson are communists. Robinson's real name is Emanuel Goldenberg. These were the men who led the picket line to get me out of Hollywood. Robinson is one of Stalin's main agents in Hollywood. ——— is part of the Stalin machine in Hollywood. Edward G. Robinson should be put in a Federal Penitentiary. . . .

I believe part of Mr. Smith's displeasure with me was a picture I made for Warner's in 1939. (He has kept railing at me since then, but it was only in 1949 that I was able to procure a verbatim report of his accusations.) In any case, the picture was *Confessions of a Nazi Spy,* and it is inconceivable that Mr. Smith gave it a rave review.

A Slight Case of Murder, on the other hand, received very favorable attention in the press. "Little Caesar has died hard but his passing shouldn't grieve Mr. Robinson unduly if he can get more scripts like this one," Howard Barnes wrote in the New York *Herald Tribune.*

I was overjoyed because it was a script on which J.L. and I agreed, as we did on *Clitterhouse.* Unfortunately, that had been played on the stage by Cedric Hardwicke, and all the New York reviews gave him the better of it by far. It is a curious thing that sometimes by not appearing in a picture, you get the best reviews. Ask Ethel Merman, Celeste Holm, and Gertrude Berg. The roles they created were filmed by other players, and the reviews were devoted to *them.* (You might enjoy trying to figure out the names of the pictures.)

Anyway, the new contract with Warner's was working very smoothly, indeed.

And so, finally, was the remodeling of the house. At first it had all been destruction; now, at last, it was beginning to take some shape and form. My early feelings of despair and concern had dissipated,

---

* Gerald L. K. Smith was the moving force behind the Knights of the White Camellia, an avowed anti-Semitic and antiblack organization. His group was listed as subversive by the Department of Justice. I believe he was convicted and jailed. I do not know if this is true. I will waste neither time nor energy researching it. It was Smith yesterday; this was followed by Father Coughlin, and the breed will hopefully eventually die out. I doubt I will live to see it.

and I was beginning to believe that Sam Marx was not a total idiot.

Of course, Gladys and I were chafing, living on the little ranch, but Manny seemed to enjoy it. I'm afraid we left him alone a great deal during this period. I was working; Gladys was going to meetings—we both attended them at night—and there were concerts and the San Francisco Opera, and parties (now all given for something under large tents with braziers to keep the cold out, which they never did) and, most of all, there were paintings being offered us, some by local dealers, others by catalog. Those catalog pictures I'd put in offers for (if they were being sold at auction) and you'd be surprised how many I bid on.

Gladys was alternately happy and furious when we won a painting —I never could be certain what her attitude was going to be. She took to blaming me for the length of time the remodeling was taking. In turn, I blamed her. We both were victims of that insane disease that afflicts anyone building or rebuilding a house—making some more changes. I made more than Gladys. Hers were, it seemed to me, unreasonable; mine were, it seemed to her, insane.

Moreover, Gladys had taken to writing a column for a weekly Hollywood magazine, Rob Wagner's *Script*. I did not approve since it contained not only her own views on Hollywood but information gleaned from our friends. I thought the column infamous and unwise and frequently badly written. But she would not give it up; here again was an example of her overriding and consistent attempt to achieve her own identity.

I fully understand the need for it now. How is it possible I simply could not understand then? The upshot is we were constantly battling.

21

Meanwhile, I was battling with Warner's to make *Confessions of a Nazi Spy*. When for reasons best known to themselves they decided to postpone it even though they owned it and a script was in preparation, I turned down everything else they offered. Then, under the provisions of my contract, I accepted a script sent to me by Columbia and written by my again friend Jo Swerling. It was called *I Am the Law*, and I played a law professor turned special prosecutor who takes on the rackets à la Tom Dewey. The scene was New York, and the prosecutor so able that he might eventually have been elected mayor of New York. (As a matter of fact, he was. The name of the character I played was John Lindsay—a fictitious John Lindsay, of course.) The *V* was obviously left out in the process by which life always follows art.

The film was clearly a potboiler, but at least I was on the right side of the law for once and survived; up to now, it seemed to me, I had died in every picture.

But it was all making faces at the camera and not really acting. As a result, when I got home (to the little ranch) after a day's work, I was silent and reserved and retired to my room; I didn't want to go out. I was sick to death of political parties and political arguments. I wanted to be doing something about the world, not sitting around and talking about it.

This attitude exacerbated my relationship with Gladys, and I realized I had to do something about that. So, when Hal Wallis assured me that within a month or two they'd be ready to go with *Nazi Spy*, I suggested as a peace offering that Gladys and I take another vacation.

She was absolutely delighted, and we were both full of self-recrimination and apology as we considered the alternatives, severely limited by the world situation. Since Europe was clearly out of the question, Mexico seemed the most tranquil of possibilities. One of the best arguments for Mexico was that I had bought a number of Diego Riveras, the dean of Mexican painters. He had visited California, and I'd found him a warm and charming man. It would be good to see him again and visit his studio.

Gladys agreed. She also said that she wanted to take her daughter along with us. I did not object, though it did not please me too much. My wife's child by her first husband was a pretty, pleasant, charming girl, but we never took to each other. I've never asked an expert in these matters, but I think we were both vying for Gladys. In any case, it's all a long time ago, and Jeannie is now certainly a mature woman, and I hold her to no account for any troubles between her mother and myself. Quite the contrary. I think I may have caused Jeannie some very traumatic moments. Human relations are easily sorted out in retrospect; when they occur, it is the moments that are difficult, not the days.

But the trip to Mexico was pleasant enough; we all held our tongues. We visited with Diego Rivera at San Miguel outside of Mexico City, and I was enchanted with his pre-Columbian ceramics, my first real introduction to these incredibly beautiful primitives. All three of us were overpowered by his proletarian murals and his paintings of peon and worker. I selected several.

But that did not entirely please him. He was much more intense about his wife's work. Curious about her: Freda Carlo; she painted dolls because she was unable to have children herself. I think I was the first American to buy her work.

But we were eager to see more of Diego's things, and he opened a cupboard where he kept watercolors, a medium in which he rarely worked. I found them so beautiful that I selected several. He stared at me in astonishment and then at his wife. "You've chosen," he said, "all the pictures I painted for my wife."

Gladys and I thought them too private to buy, but he insisted we have them as gifts. Then we had coffee in the bright sunshine and discussed politics. He was an ardent Marx-Engels classic Communist, and his hatred for Lenin and Stalin was so intense that he kept heaping curses on their heads. He believed that Lenin and Stalin had betrayed the whole theory of Communism; his hero was Leon Trotsky—and Trotsky lived only a short distance' away. The co-author of the Russian Revolution, in exile at the time, was guarded constantly from the threat of assassination because Stalin considered him his greatest enemy.

For those who wondered at the break between the Soviet Union and Red China, a little reading would have shown them that from the beginning the Communists were far from monolithic. Trotsky, the high priest of communism, was at this point in time an avowed enemy of the Soviet Union, and the leaders of that nation were doing everything in their power to murder him.

Would we, asked Diego, like to meet him? Would we, indeed!

Diego arranged it. It was to be at a certain time of a certain day, but we were not told the details. We would be called for, and we were to be ready. Precautions were necessary.

I prepared myself by going at once to a bookstore where I found five volumes of Trotsky's works. I bought them; I wanted them autographed. The clerk, who spoke little English, showed a surprising amount of interest in this purchase, and I immediately grew suspicious. What if he followed us? Was he an agent of the anti-Trotskyite group? I had obviously played too much melodrama.

Early one morning a car came for us. Diego was not along. Only a driver. Jeannie, Gladys, and I were put in the back seat and driven to a point where we changed to another car that took us, by a circuitous route, pretty much back where we had come from.

Eventually we arrived at a walled villa surrounded by guards with rifles and Alsatian dogs. We were admitted. Diego was inside the wall. We made our way through the patio into the hacienda and into a room where Diego introduced us to Leon Trotsky, then left.

Trotsky, except for his piercing eyes, looked like a retired Brooklyn waiter. His English was Brooklynese; his Yiddish was excellent. His greeting to us was cordial and thoroughly bourgeois. (He was flattered by my request that he autograph his books and returned the compliment by asking for my autograph.) He offered us cigars and cigarettes. For Jeannie there was cocoa; for us beer or coffee. The room was neat and filled with mementos, photographs that looked like stills from a Sergei Eisenstein film. There was no indication that, to use a phrase out of every gangster film, a contract had been given out on him. No indication save one: A pearl-handled revolver lay on the paper- and book-covered desk.

He was a considerate conversationalist and talked about the weather, the charms of Mexico, and his friends in the United States. Then he stopped himself. He wished to mention no names.

He wondered about Brooklyn. Had I been there lately? Brownsville, Pitkin Avenue, places of his childhood and early immigrant times. I confessed I knew little of Brooklyn except for that one excursion across the Williamsburg Bridge to see my ancient Hebrew teacher. He was impressed. So young a boy to seek out an inspiration. Inspiration had been the moving force of his life. He had been inspired by Marx–Engels to destroy the despicable capitalistic system —*and*, the even more despicable Soviet system (*sic*).

Lenin and Stalin were latter-day tyrants. Thus, Trotsky felt the deepest attachment to the anti-Soviet forces in the United States— including the Burton K. Wheelers, Lindbergh, and the other America firsters. They were playing each other's game—the Far Left Trotskyites and the Far Right anti-Stalinists. Together they would prevail. All of this was not for attribution and quotation, of course.

For two hours he talked. One day he would return, he told us, and be the big boss and unswervingly begin anew the true march of Marxism. He was not the least surprised that Stalin and Hitler were brothers in arms. Indeed, they were logical brothers in motive, planning to divide the earth between them. But they reckoned without him, Trotsky. He would wreck their plans if he could but outwit the monstrous traitor, Stalin—and, never fear, he would.

But enough of this talk. He wanted to chat with Jeannie, for he loved and missed most the young! He wanted to know what it was like to be young in America in the thirties. Did youth care about the state of the world or was it still doing the Tango? We all laughed at that; nobody had Tangoed in years. But Trotsky kept seeing America through the same eyes that had once beheld it with loathing; he seemed, despite the fact that he said he read American papers omnivorously, almost totally out of touch with American political thought. He knew only of the divisions; he warned Jeannie against the American Communist party. "Thralls," he called them. "Leaches. Slaves." His decision was that J. P. Morgan was far more trustworthy than Earl Browder. You could hardly believe your ears.

And Gladys started making notes. He looked at her fiercely. She told him about her column in Rob Wagner's *Script*, while I could hardly keep my temper. Icily, he suggested that if she would submit questions in writing, he would answer those he could, again in writing. He was not prepared to be quoted out of idle conversation. And she would have to use his answers verbatim.

I tried to change the subject. Did he ever see the movies? He loved them, he said—Chaplin, Keaton, Snub Pollard, Norma Talmadge, Constance Talmadge, and me, even though he'd seen very little of me. Once in a while a print of one of my pictures—undoubtedly showing America in its worst possible light—had been pirated into

Moscow. I tried to make the point that no other country made pictures of its worst features; that this was a testament to American freedom. He brushed the statement aside.

In any case, he was eager to see films, but he could not go to a public theater. I told him I would arrange to have the Warner Brothers Mexican office send him a sixteen millimeter projector and print of some films, including one or two of mine.*

He was delighted and invited us back. Gladys, meanwhile, had her questions, and his answers were innocuous and temperate.

We talked again, but it seemed like a rerun of our first conversation. He was exiled not only physically but, it seemed to me then, in his thought processes as well.

We left him, promising to come for a longer visit the next time we were in Mexico. "Or," he added wryly, "perhaps you will be among the first American guests at the Kremlin when I am living there." He turned to Jeanie. "More likely, you." Neither in Mexico nor Moscow did we ever see him again.

I have in front of me now Gladys' article about our meeting with Trotsky. Since it differs from mine, I think it not insignificant. Here it is:

> I was told he couldn't be interviewed in the first place. Other reporters had tried and failed. But I had an introduction and I used it.
>
> We knew the Diego Riveras because my husband, who has a notable art collection, had bought many of his paintings and we had become friends. When Trotsky came to Mexico, we went there as the guests of the Riveras, and I asked about the possibilities of an interview for *Script*. *Life* magazine, you know, had failed, and all others had failed because Trotsky was afraid, at that time, of the Stalinites. But Diego made the appointment.
>
> We went, one bright Mexican morning, up the little road to Trotsky's house, a pink stucco hacienda, guarded by bastilles and monkeys, pronged cacti and sleepy donkeys, Mexican flower beds in blazing patterns. It was quiet and colorful and bucolic. We didn't know at the time that the place was also guarded by guns.
>
> Trotsky's aide greeted us. He was a tall, impressive-looking young American, and around his waist he wore a cartridge belt and two Colt .44's.
>
> We entered Trotsky's study. He stood up and greeted us warmly. He is a small man, and his once famous black beard is now white. But his eyes blaze and sparkle with the cold, steady blue of the Swiss

---

* The Warner Mexico City Exchange reported by wire "prints returned in dreadful condition." Apparently, each frame was examined to make certain it contained no secret explosive. Rewinding was not an art known to his projectionist.

lakes—or of sharp steel. He prefers to speak French, but can speak excellent English. I might add that a very shining revolver lay on his desk between us.

He was especially interested in my young daughter, who is studying to be a singer, and told her that the future lies with the young people. He invited her to sit by him as he talked.

I'd come prepared so I shot questions at him. I asked him about Mayor Hague, about Roosevelt, about Democracy, about the future of Europe, about Russia, about his plans. He was tired, but he was dynamic. Something hypnotic leaps at you from this small, and really very amazing man. Now I couldn't be a Communist, not ever, but I believe Leon Trotsky could hypnotize anybody to his way during an hour's conversation. You would leave feeling that he was right about everything, and only recover when you had time to think it all over.

It was a beautiful interview, and I had a scoop. Trotsky rose and bowed, ever so politely.

"You understand, of course, Madame, that you can't print any of this."

"Can't print it!" I was aghast. My scoop spoiled, my trip worthless. I protested, I pleaded, and I have to confess, I almost wept.

Trotsky's aide intervened. "You may submit your questions in writing, and Mr. Trotsky will be happy to answer them tomorrow," he said.

And so that was how we did it. It was better than ever, for he answered fully everything I asked, and signed the statement—a very valuable keepsake for me. When I returned to the United States, I emphatically refused to sell the story and gave it to *Script*, exclusively.

Note the differences in our versions. They really signaled the differences between us. We were both at the same place at the same time, yet we did not hear or see the same things.

I feel pangs of conscience in revealing these diametrically opposed memories; I wish Gladys were alive to tell her side. Believe me, I have no anger about her taking the leading role; I offer it only as evidence that despite marriage and a son, we remained separate people. We were two egos, congenitally incapable of merging into one, and, if we didn't live in a state of siege, it's because I can't think of a better word for it.

I accept my share of the blame—51 percent of it. I should have been more compassionate. At least, more clever. With Gladys I was neither.

And I went back to do *Confessions of a Nazi Spy*.
Only the script wasn't ready.
Only Warner's couldn't get the director they wanted.

Only the studio was so busy, there were no stages available.

Only—well, you know what was going on; they were scared to make it. Not Wallis, not Warner's, but that mysterious all-powerful influence in Hollywood called New York. Whenever there was a crunch about any matter in any studio, New York, that faceless city, was always the villain.

And New York did not want to have anything to do with a movie about the Nazis.

It seemed to me then that the film as the most widely disseminated medium should concern itself not only with entertainment—its basic function—but from time to time with the problems of society, the threats to liberty, the miseries heaped upon the minds and bodies of fellow human beings. As an almost-octogenarian with considerable time to muse, consider, and evaluate, I wonder if that isn't a fair definition of propaganda. And I wonder, too, if I am all for propaganda when it expresses my own views and all against it when it expresses diverse views. Suppose R.K.O. or United Artists (theoretically, of course) had been preparing a film that was pro-Nazi, or pro-isolation. What would my attitude have been? What course would I have taken? Certainly, I would have opposed it vigorously.

That is the true dilemma of propaganda in a democracy. The even-handed approach is the only one possible, except that it's *impossible* in the movies. The time lag alone is against it; it takes a minimum of a year between the assignment of a script and the preview; in that year even-handedness, certainly relevance, can become as old-fashioned as the hoop skirt. Events, unpredictable and catastrophic, can turn a film from a serious investigation of a social phenomenon into a ludicrous farce.

Take Chaplin's *Dictator*; he started out to make a farce, to show Hitler and Mussolini as idiots. By the time the film was released, Hitler and Mussolini were hardly idiots; rather, they were potential inheritors of the earth. I've often wondered if Chaplin did not add that last oration, so inconsistent with the rest of the picture, at the last moment. I've always meant to ask him.

The theater and the novel, much more quickly and easily produced during this period, obviously could and did deal with social and world problems. Odets and Sherwood wrote meaningful plays; hardly a novel appeared that did not in one way or another have its characters mired in Spain or Germany, or the deep South.

Later, of course, the Nazi, the storm trooper, became a staple of all the media. Since the days of Von Stroheim the bull-necked German Junker general was a villain easily translatable to the screen. In his uniform and hauteur he was the instant enemy.

On the other hand, once the Russians ceased to be grand dukes, they made deplorable villains. Twentieth Century made a picture called *The Iron Curtain* in which the Bolsheviks were portrayed simply with baggy and unpressed pants, and the Slavic face, without a monocle and wearing a cap, seemed not a plausible enemy but a Bowery bum. To those who complained through the latter years that we never made anti-Soviet films, let me say we did, and they all bombed because, try as we could, the ladies always came out Garbo or Mrs. Khrushchev while the villains, whatever their dialogue, were simply badly tailored.

The Chinese, of course, we'd goofed on long ago. What Red Chinese general could ever be half as venal as Fu Manchu? The movies also found it tough to make the Japanese look anything but ridiculous; we were so accustomed to the Lafcadio Hearn land of fans, kimonos, and community bathtubs that we never were able to make a convincing Tojo out of a Chinese actor. And all the actors who played Japanese in our war films *were* Chinese because we'd banished the Japanese population to the Santa Anita racetrack, our simplistic version of Dachau.

Early one morning I received a call from the studio. *Confessions* was to be made immediately. New York had apparently gotten round to reading the newspapers, or perhaps some executive or banker had had a nasty experience in Yorkville. Whatever the reason, all my arguments prevailed; we'd make the film with no holds barred, a phrase current at the time which meant that some hold would most certainly be barred.

The picture was based on a book by Leon G. Turrou, *The Nazi Spy Conspiracy in America*, and the screenplay was by Milton Krims and John Wexley. Directing was Anatole Litvak, surely one of the most urbane, sophisticated, gourmet, haut monde anti-Nazis ever known—and one of the most talented. He approached the film with zeal and commitment; that it was less than an artistic triumph was due to the fact that the participating actors, including myself, were too familiar to be taken seriously.

Three beautiful actors, Paul Lukas, Francis Lederer, and George Sanders, playing Nazis, were just about as believable as myself as a G-man. The picture suffered from the familiarity of its cast and the inevitability of its denouement; nobody, obviously, was going to outdo G-man Edward G. Robinson, and by no stretch of the imagination could the Nazis win. Had the film been made, as so many are now, as a semidocumentary with unfamiliar faces, it would have carried credibility.

I think the vogue for foreign films is based entirely on the fact that we do not regard the players as actors but as real people, and since we do not understand the language, we are incapable of knowing whether the dialogue is excellent or hackneyed.*

During the filming of *Confessions* and in the months of its subsequent release, Warner Brothers were deluged with threatening mail. I, myself, received obscene letters and phone calls threatening me and my family with death. The studio put me under guard. I put Manny under guard, and while I tried lightheartedly to dismiss the whole thing, I was worried. I suddenly could understand Trotsky's situation.

A few years later when I was invited to London to broadcast in several languages to the nations vanquished by Hitler and some of the Allies well (Russia being one), the British government, as a result of *Confessions*, provided me with more than ordinary wartime precautions. I was, at all times, surrounded by Scotland Yard and army personnel. It was thoroughly inhibiting, and when I see films today of the President or political candidates with this kind of constant protection, I wonder how they can endure it. Going to the bathroom is probably one of the most difficult maneuvers when you are under security; my bodyguard told me it is one of the favorite targets of assassins, and I point it out only because it is an entertaining topic for dinner parties.

Dinner parties went on during that curious period when, though Poland and Warsaw were gone, Hitler seeemed to be waiting. It was not long before we discovered what he was waiting for; he marched on the north countries; then the low countries; then Belgium, Holland, and France. Forever graven on my memory are the newsreel shots of the Luftwaffe marching under the Arc de Triomphe and Hitler dancing his little dance as he looked at the Eiffel Tower from the broad veranda of the old Trocadéro.

I found that I was involved with new wartime enterprises— Bundles for Britain, Committee to Defend America by Aiding the Allies, headed here by, as I think I've already mentioned, Constance Bennett and young Fairbanks. I was also part of Fight for Freedom, a national group that, to use a precise term for it, was warmongering. We lobbied and shouted for Lend-Lease and for fifty ancient destroy-

* I find English subtitles a terrible problem because I frequently understand the language of the film, and it's almost impossible to translate argot. Still, I prefer it to the dubbing process, though I must say it has achieved the position of a minor art. A year ago I heard and watched myself speaking Japanese, and the language was almost perfectly lip-synched. What I was saying I haven't the foggiest.

ers to be sent to Britain. Even in these matters we were opposed and branded Limousine Liberals or Parlor Pinks by the Hollywood branch of the national isolationists.

Then, of course, Hitler turned his legions on Russia instead of trying to invade England after the Battle of Britain, and for a while we were all together. Talk of strange bedfellows.

I was working not only in the movies, but on the radio. As long before as 1937 attorneys and agents had come to me with a proposition that I star in a radio series. I turned them down. Then, when they told me the format (I would be the editor of a big town paper and there would be ample opportunity for me to deal with pressing social matters), I agreed.

You want the truth? It was the money.

I starred as Steve Wilson in *Big Town* from 1937 to 1942, aided and abetted the first few years by Claire Trevor (a smashing lady) and later by Ona Munson (an equally smashing lady). I did not have to ask the permission of Warner's to do this; the contract said nothing about radio.

Why did I work so hard? I said money, didn't I? But I'm trying desperately to make sure there weren't other reasons. There were. Work was my crutch; work had always been my crutch. When I worked, nothing else mattered—the world, my home, my family, my own doubts and fears and ambitions. Work was what I'd been brought up to do; work was my career and my hobby and my golf. Work was all I knew. Work was all I was good at.

I have not been well; I look forward to returning health only because I want to work again.

Is it that, in the work of an actor, I am many other people and not myself? I read that in books about actors. It seems silly to me. Maybe it isn't. Do I really not want to be me?

Do I really not want to be me? I repeat that question because it's been befuddling me. I wish I could say it's arrant nonsense, but it isn't. Playing characters, particularly on stage, is a transcending experience. You are, indeed, not yourself but that other fellow you're pretending to be—but only if the words have become part of your consciousness and you do not have to struggle for them. The moment you must try to remember the author's words, you're you, trying to remember the author's words.

In films, of course, where you play in fragments, you are very rarely anybody but yourself—yourself with spectacles, yourself with beard, with wig, with accent, with a Falstaffian belly—but yourself.

What the psychologists—and the actors who write their autobiographies—are trying to say is that frequently, in playing a character, you can rid yourself of aggressions that you would not dare manifest during the course of a normal day. It can be—this playing a part—a purging experience, and on the other hand, it can fill you with new frustrations.

No, I don't think I'm an actor because I don't want to be myself. I'm an actor because it is my trade, and when I first apprenticed to the trade, the disciplines were rigid and totally demanding. Now the trade has been split up so that you can be a dark scoundrel on the set all day long and a darling on a talk show at eleven o'clock at night.

Can you imagine Maude Adams or Sarah Bernhardt or David Warfield or Greto Garbo on a talk show? As for Mrs. Fiske, I have a letter from her in which she speaks of retaining one's privacy so as not to reveal the human being beneath the actor while, at the same time, she urges the actor to remember that being a human being is far more important than being an actor. I'm not sure whether she wrote the letter to me personally or whether it was copied in whatever they called mimeographing or Xeroxing in those days and sent to the student body of the American Academy of Dramatic Arts.

Returning to the subject of the radio show, *Big Town*, I actually thought of ignoring it when I started these memoirs. But how can I ignore a show that was heard by almost as many people as heard Jack Benny? Would you believe I'm proud of that? And I'm particularly gratified because, nominally, I was only the star. In point of fact, I was everything—producer, director, casting man, Final Word.

Had television not come along, radio might have become one of the fine arts. Except for phonograph records, nobody before had ever been asked to listen and not see. Listen the radio audience would and, through the voice of the actors (and quickly I add the script), cast the show—invent faces for the actors, build their own sets, involve themselves with relationships they could only invent, and thus become part of the creative enterprise. The ear became the sole line to the brain. The eye had been used to that for a long time—in reading, painting, sculpture, you use only your own eyes, but you can go back and reread and relook. In the silent movies you used only the eye and not the ear. In the theater, talking pictures, and TV, you use both.

But to have only the ear as an instrument of communication! For the actor, how marvelous! No makeup, no wardrobe, no moving about. Only his voice to worry about, a voice that could make you cry or laugh or scare you to death—but subject to the most perverse and hidebound censorship I have ever known.

To play a city editor and vent your spleen by saying "Darn it!" was unbearable. You could say "Darn it!" on the stage or screen and your face could be saying the vilest of words. On radio, "Darn it!" with whatever inflection you used to give it meaning beyond the phrase, only came out "Darn it." To express joy with "Hot ziggety!" or "Whooppee" was the norm; to seek other ways of expressing joy like "Thank God" was forbidden. I have never been in a medium where so many words were forbidden. Even "Go to blazes!" instead of "Go to hell!" was subjected to the closest scrutiny. And "son of a gun" was admitted only if the censors were certain you were not saying "son of a bitch" in your head.

As for subject matter, the city editor of *Big Town* was concerned almost exclusively with larceny, arson (if its methods were not disclosed), pickpockets, civic scandals (if they covered poisoning the water supply of a city—and even that was not to be frightening), and national corruption only in a mythical republic.

Thus, how could I do this week after week, with summer vacations in Mexico, under all these restrictions? By fighting, that's how. I fought over every script and rewrote them myself (oh, dear members of the Radio Writers Guild, forgive me!), and eventually, by repetition, I invented code words and code phrases that made the audience understand that I was saying something beyond the actual words I was using.

The proof: From radio listeners I got not just plain fan letters—obscene, unsigned threatening scrawls—but meaningful letters discussing the problems posed by the program; signed letters, intelligent ones, enormously helpful ones. Once I had a researcher collate them and discovered they were coming from the blind, the shut-ins, the invalids, the ill in hospitals. It was an audience that at that point in time could be reached no other way. They were not fans of mine; they were faithful fans of the program, and their hearing was so acute that they would complain bitterly at inconsistency in character; at the same time, they appeared to grasp every subtlety. I did not always enjoy the chore of *Big Town*, but I enjoyed the letters with all my heart.

However, by 1942, when we were involved in the war, the irrelevancy of *Big Town* became so obvious that it had to be abandoned; it had outlived its usefulness, however minimal.

22

Prior to Pearl Harbor, Warner Brothers brought to my attention a subject so fascinating and compelling that I quaked with eagerness to play it. When I say Warner's, I really mean Wolfgang Reinhardt, son of the immortal Max. Reinhardt was attempting to prepare a script on the life of Dr. Ehrlich, the man who worked with such energy and devotion in an effort to find a cure for syphilis.

Syphilis! It was hardly a word current in the American vocabulary. Venereal disease, though rampant, was mentioned to and by decent people only in the most hushed and reserved terms. And Reinhardt wanted to make a picture out of it!

The mind boggled! Hal Wallis didn't. He gave Reinhardt the money and the impetus to proceed—with, I am sure, all kinds of caveats.

I waited breathlessly for the script but not so breathlessly that I did not agree first to do another picture at Metro entitled *Blackmail*, to be directed by Hank Potter. I hated the script and sat in on a story conference with two handsome and intense young writers, William Ludwig and David Hertz, chilling them with my criticism and having no effect whatever on them. I could not understand why, until young Ludwig explained in very precise and legal language (turned out he was a member of the New York bar), he and Hertz had nothing to do with the drivel I had read. They were there to rewrite the script. I apologized. I did a lot of apologizing in those days.

They worked like fiends and came up with a reasonable facsimile of a good script. They could do no better because I was on payroll and the shooting date could not be set ahead because the precise terms of my agreement with M.G.M. spelled out exactly when I was to be returned to Warner's. Accordingly, we did one of those pictures that pleased few, entertained many, and somehow got its money back and made a few shekels for the stockholders.*

I can only tell you that in the movie I was in prison for a crime I did not commit (wearing that black and white striped prison costume), that I escaped, assumed another identity, and became rich, successful, and married. Only years later. . . . But do I have to go on? Surely, you can write the plot yourself.

In 1940 James Stewart won the Academy Award for *The Philadelphia Story*, and Ginger Rogers won the best actress award for *Kitty Foyle*. *Dr. Ehrlich's Magic Bullet* won nothing. Had it, I'd have made an acceptance speech thanking with all my heart Jack Warner, Hal Wallis, Wolfgang Reinhardt, director William Dieterle, writers John Huston, Heinz Herald, and Norman Burnside, and the whole cast, with a special bow to Ruth Gordon, Otto Kruger, Donald Crisp, Sig Rumann, Albert Basserman, and Maria Ouspenskaya. Oh, especially, Madame Ouspenskaya.

Among all the plays and films in which I've appeared, I'm proudest of my role in *Dr. Ehrlich's Magic Bullet*. I played Paul Ehrlich, a Berlin doctor who insisted on telling patients the truth. The rest of the time, with the backing of Dr. Robert Koch, Ehrlich experimented with a chemical staining process. He contracted tuberculosis and went with his wife to Egypt. On his return to Germany, the government cut off his research funds. He was helped by Frau Speizer, a philanthropist, and Ehrlich, after 605 miserable failures, came up with formula 606, a cure for syphilis. He released the compound prematurely, which resulted in some deaths, but he was vindicated. In the end he died with the final plea for truth and justice in science.

It was, I think, one of the most distinguished performances I've ever given. I say that not only because the critics said it and my mail and the box office said it, but most of all because that inner voice, that inner self, that captious critic Emanuel Goldenberg said it.

And others said it, people who, in the end, meant the most: Dr. Ehrlich's family.

One day the Screen Actors Guild called (since it would not give

---

* Note from L.S.: Bill Ludwig tells me, with pardonable pride, that a year later he and David Hertz received quite an ornate plaque with an inscription in Spanish that read: "To the authors of *Blackmail*—a film which did the biggest business in Buenos Aires on a third Thursday in November!"

out my private number) and said a lady with a thick German accent and an unpronounceable name wished urgently to get in touch with me. For a moment I was afraid it was one of those Gerald L. K. Smith kooks but not so afraid that I was not curious. I asked my agent to find someone who could speak German well to call the number she had left. It was, of course, the former Fräulein Ehrlich, the doctor's daughter, and her husband.

First I asked them to the set of *Brother Orchid* and embraced the young lady as if she were my own daughter. Then I took her and her husband to the studio to see the film. God, I was nervous, but they were complimentary, if a little polite. I asked about their mother. She was in Geneva with hardly enough brought out of Berlin on which to live. I hesitantly offered help; they absolutely refused. They did not refuse to come to the house to dinner—and they continued to come and became excellent friends. I was gratified by their good eye for art. As for their mother, would I write her and enclose some of my stills made up as her husband?

I wrote immediately, enclosing the pictures of her children as well and gingerly asked if perhaps she had some small memento of Dr. Ehrlich—a scrap of paper with his name on it—anything of his I could hold in my hand.

I received the following letter—written in German, from Switzerland—in her own hand. The brackets in this and the following letter are the result of my own feeble translation and my inability to read some of the handwriting.

                                                            June 15th 1940

Most esteemed Mr. Robinson:

Please receive heartfelt thanks for your friendly lines, which especially do one's heart good in these [trying] times. I would have answered same long ago, but as the result of the current stress and strain [excitement of the soul] I haven't been feeling well at all, and wanted to write you in a favorable moment.

Meanwhile, I have so much to thank you for. . . .

For the excellent photographs which portray you in the role of my husband, and which are uncannily resemblant; for the snapshots taken with my children at your house; for your warm-hearted annotations on the photographs. My daughter and son-in-law couldn't say enough about your magnificent home and the carefully nurtured art collection therein; above all, they praised the warmth with which you received them, and they told me that for the first time in a long while, they felt "at home," these poor, uprooted transplants. . . .

Their get-together with you will be an unforgettable event for them.

Meanwhile, I received from my children not just their enthusiastic report of your enchanting reception, but I also gather from their letters that your film portrayal of my husband made an indelible impression on them; they speak of a direct, touching resemblance in the portrayal; the only explanation for this lies in the very facts my daughter Stephanie writes about *YOU*; how you have immersed yourself in his personage far beyond what one would normally expect from a great artist's portrayal . . . and how this is deeply rooted in your own humanism.

Now I await the film's showing in Switzerland with great trepidation.

Have already received newspaper clippings about the openings in Italy and London; what a great pity, though, that this production comes in such unholy times here, and how good that the film came out in America in a quieter period.

At my daughter's request, I am forwarding a handwritten note from my husband. It was difficult for me to find this note because in my exodus from Germany I packed everything, even his writings, in as yet unopened crates.

Besides, my husband *dictated* nearly everything, so I only possess but a very few letters in his own handwriting; moreover, I only packed but a very few of our family letters, and am sending you one of these —but promise to send you later a letter with a more interesting content.

Now, I come to you with a question and a request. My grandson wonders whether the Warner Brothers Film Company could give the Ehrlich family a print of the film as a memento. Is that possible?

I am, unfortunately, not at all technically cognizant, and really don't know whether such a thing is feasible. It would be most kind of you to look into this matter for us, and represent our family's interests in this request to Warner Brothers. Hope that you will not be importuned by my asking this of you.

With warm greetings and renewed gratitude for everything, I remain, in sincere admiration. . . .

Your,
Hedwig Ehrlich

And this was the original letter from her husband to her, which she enclosed:

Beloved Hedwig:

Today I wanted to write to you in all haste between my return from the sessions and my departure (8.24 PM) for Copenhagen— that here everything went according to my wishes.

I spoke for about a half an hour, and Apolauf [a colleague] three quarters of an hour.

What pleased me most in this conference was that the other pathologists almost unanimously dwelled upon the theme of the great meaning our discovery held for human pathology.

From various sources, it was also observed that SARCOM [sic] acted as a palliative on carcinoma [cancer] of *humans*, a fact heretofore unknown; we are, therefore, right in the mainstream [threshold?]!

I have decided, after long and careful deliberation, to undertake the journey to Copenhagen. *Perhaps* it will serve a purpose, and I wished to seize even the smallest chance to try.

Eugenia [Professor Fraenkel, Hamburg] was also present here— and not at all in accord. . . .

We will be lunching today at Anincke's the local, very capable clinical researcher [?] who also happens to be a very nice fellow. He was Frerichs' former assistant.

Don't let yourself get blue, and try to amuse yourself as much as it's possible to do so in Frankfurt. . . . It pleases me much that you find distraction with our dear Hanschen [grandson].

With best greetings, and the hope of a very good reunion, your devotedly loving . . . Paul.

I must pack now.

I have no idea whether scientists ever followed up on Dr. Ehrlich's hope that compound 606 might be a palliative for cancer, but my own recent doctors, Oscar Magidson, Ronald Thompson, and Marvin Levy, have explained that while there is no certainty, there is considerable evidence that some cancers are viral in nature.*

They also tell me that Ehrlich created the new branch of medicine called chemotherapy. It is one of the odd coincidences—or is it planned?—that if certain symptoms I now have multiply, I will be treated by chemotherapy.

When could he have written that letter to Hedwig? The only certainty is that it was before 1915, for that is when he died.

---

* "Ehrlich's work may be classified in three groups: (1) the application of stains to the differentiation of cells and tissue for the purpose of revealing their functions (1877–90); (2) immunity studies (1890–1900), and (3) chemotherapeutic discoveries (1907–15). In 1907 he discovered the dye known as trypan red, which, when injected into the blood of animals infected with trypanosomes, effected the destruction of these organisms. This led him to try to treat other diseases by chemical injections and culminated in his famous discovery in connection with venereal diseases. It was announced in 1910 that he had prepared an arsenical compound, known as salvarsan or "606," which was a cure for syphilis. The name was given because it was the 606th compound that he had tried for the purpose. Ehrlich also did important work on problems of immunity. In 1908 he shared with Ilya Mechnikov the Nobel Prize for Medicine."—from the *Encyclopaedia Britannica*.

After World War II I tried to find Frau Ehrlich in Geneva, but by this time she had joined her husband. I should like so much to hear from their daughter again. I have had no word from her in thirty years.

Ehrlich, chemotherapy, and I! Is it part of some divine plan?

Rot!

Playing Dr. Ehrlich was for me a quasi-equivalent of lying on the couch. I was three years away from fifty, a watershed birthday so painful in prospect that it cannot be imagined by those who do not contemplate it. Those who have know that it passes; the next grimness to dread is sixty. As for seventy, ludicrous! And eighty? Who knows about eighty?

While doing *Ehrlich*, the world outside seemed to vanish, or at least diminish in importance. During the filming I kept to myself, studied the script, practiced gestures before the mirror, read about his life and times, studied pictures of the man, tried to put myself in his mental state, tried to *be* him.

As we shot the film, I realized more and more that I was being a highly idealistic version of my father. Had my father been German, had he been a doctor, had he been passionate about science, I think he would have been a Dr. Ehrlich. So what you see now on the television screen (and you don't see it nearly as often as the gangster films) is Emanuel Goldenberg, via E.G.R., playing his father, if his father were Dr. Ehrlich or, conversely, if Dr. Ehrlich were his father.

The world inside the sound stage seemed real; the world outside, hostile, terrifying, and dangerous. Gladys and I were still manipulating the remodeling of the house with Sam, and I was pretty much of a lamb. Buying lighting fixtures and exactly the right desk and dining room table was fun, expensive, and not worthy of too much argument. Some argument, yes. A husband and father must maintain his authority; like the head of a studio, he must not give in too easily even though he knows quite well, at the beginning of an argument, that he is going to give in at the end.

As for the war, as yet unnamed but soon to be called World War II, I stopped carrying a portable radio around with me. A portable radio in those days was hardly portable in the transistor sense, but there came a time when the Hitler hordes sweeping over Europe became impossible to listen to. The news was ingloriously and consistently appalling.

This is a point in time at which I went to no meetings but, on the set with a secretary, answered appeals for help from all over the country. I refused to crawl or slither out of anything; any committee with a title that seemed to me to suggest help for England and France against the Nazis and which contained on its letterhead the name of a recognized figure, I responded to—usually with a check. Later I responded by making speeches.

I was now not living; I was in the midst of a series of obsessions.

Work: Warner's was belaboring me to make more and more films.

My family: I was trying desperately to make life with Gladys easy and comfortable. For the most part, I held my tongue, and God knows she tried. Still, we fought constantly, *never* on major issues like the state and fate of the world, but about plumbers and whether to have a hedge around the driveway. Indeed, whether to have a driveway.

My son: I wanted everything for this seven-? eight-? nine-year-old boy, and I thought a decent world in which to live was the most important. I was wrong; what was most important was to play catch with him or go fishing with him or try to see things from his point of view. Instead, I complained about his marks: I wanted straight A's, and I was cold and disciplinary when he got less. I thought any son of mine would be an intellectual—highest standing in his school. When his grades were less than A, I blamed the schools and began the process of changing *them*. That was among the most serious mistakes of my life.

My house: Would it ever, ever, be finished?

My pictures: I bought more. I was hooked on art—an addict. The only thing real in the world seemed to be catalogs from dealers, galleries, and museums.

As a result of *Ehrlich* I expected a rash of offers from every studio in town—parts with substance, characters of maturity: scientists, politicians, Supreme Court justices. Nothing happened.

There can be little question that in the front offices of the studios and particularly "New York" a decision on high policy had been formulated: Keep 'em laughing!

Consider that throughout the depression very few pictures had been made dealing with the Troubles. Yes, at Columbia *Hatter's Castle*, which was honest and true, flopped like a gangster's body encased in cement and thrown into the sea. And Darryl Zanuck, of all people, did Steinbeck's *Grapes of Wrath*, a picture so admirable in intent, so excellent in execution, that it found an audience despite its subject matter. It was helped by the fact that it was a best-seller; helped, I think, mainly because it dealt with the rural depression and urban audiences could view it without feeling involved or guilty.

As for the rest, there were depression-funny pictures like Universal's *My Man Godfrey*, with William Powell playing a man of wealth forced to become a butler; or Paramount's *Three Cornered Moon* in which once wealthy Mary Boland and her daughter, once wealthy Claudette Colbert, discovered the hilarity of being poor. Add the two Capra films: *Mr. Deeds* and *Mr. Smith*, both simple, indeed, almost anarchistic, versions of Man against Society. Add a film here and there about dirty Nazi spies, and there you have it all.

I can hardly add as a footnote something that should be in upper case: The anti-Communist accusers screamed and shrieked and bellowed that throughout this period films were loaded with Stalinist propaganda. I am no researcher for the American Film Institute, and certainly I did not see every picture made in this period, but I consider the charge hysterical and unfounded.

It really was impossible for it to have happened. It would have required that executive, writer, director, and cast all believe in the same propaganda or device. If any individual held these views, it was more than certain that a higher-up would delete them.

It was later true, of course, that Hollywood made pro-Soviet pictures, but that was at a time when the Russians were allies, and even Army films, closely scrutinized by a bureaucratic microscope, were calling Stalin "Uncle Joe." It was even at a time, I suppose, that Hedda Hopper might have given a quarter to Russian War Relief while she was railing against a second front. But here I go, getting ahead of myself.

Would you believe the picture I made after *Ehrlich* was *Brother Orchid*, a kind of burlesque of gangster films in which I (as still another version of *Little Caesar*) learned the joys of an idyllic life in a monastery. Bogie (noted somewhere long ago in these pages) was in this one, too, and you would think that the two of us would be at each other's throats. Not at all. He was a pro in the best meaning of the word and put the play above himself. We got along splendidly. While the script called for us to snarl at each other, between takes we would discuss the world and the war as friends. We were never close friends, but we respected each other.

As did Ralph Bellamy and myself. When you need an actor to play *anything*, get Ralph Bellamy. His range is limitless; his abilities unparalleled; his ego, barely ever ruffled. He is the kind of star that made it possible to make pictures. Never getting the girl is a difficult role; it enables an actor to grow old gracefully. I cherish Ralph. I could not say the same about *Brother Orchid*.

I was prepared to put on my private walk-out act on Hal Wallis and Jack Warner when they came at me, like gangbusters, with two new scripts: *A Dispatch from Reuter's** and *The Sea Wolf*. No actor could ask for more—no actor nearing fifty, that is. I enjoyed them, and perhaps it is not mere coincidence that the associate producer on both was a man named Henry Blanke. Dieterle directed *Reuter's*, which seemed, underneath its somewhat flossy rendering of a great man's career, a plea for the freedom of the press; Michael Curtiz directed *The Sea Wolf*. It was pure Jack London, and the character I played, the famous Wolf Larsen (remember how long ago I'd read the book?), was a Nazi in everything but name. So both films seemed to have relevance to the world about me, however attenuated.

A few notes: John Garfield was one of the best young actors I ever encountered, but his passions about the world were so intense that I feared any day he would have a heart attack. It was not long before he did.

Michael Curtiz, a Hungarian (Hollywood had a wild passion for Hungarians), provided me with some of the juicier malapropisms and crazy stories. They could fill a book. Even if I did not suspect you'd heard them all, I long ago decided that I would not bore myself or you with Curtizisms, Pasternakisms, Goldwynisms, or Gaborisms. Too many writers have made a cottage industry of reporting the misuse of the English language by Hollywood people.

I followed *Sea Wolf* with *Manpower*, in which I played with Marlene Dietrich. You are by now certainly aware of my less than generous habit of assessing people by first impression. My first impression of Miss Dietrich made me nervous, because, to carp, she appeared to have such arrogant self-assurance and security. I had never met her before, though I had seen all her pictures and was aware that she was sexy, temperamental, demanding, beautiful, and perhaps the synthetic creation of Joseph von Sternberg.

Playing with her, I learned that we shared a common passion: work. More than that: Be on time, know the lines, toe the marks, say the words, be ready for anything. God, she was beautiful—and still is—but I don't think it interested her very much. Beauty, that obsessive sexual thing she had, and her superficial self-confidence were simply instruments to help her bank account and her art.

One of the things about her that astonished me most was her knowledge of the technical side of motion pictures. She seemed to know everything. She constantly watched the camera and the lighting,

* In any pecking order of my preferences, I name *Reuter* as my number-two favorite.

and she would politely superintend, make suggestions to the camera-
men and gaffers so subtly and so sexily that no one was offended, and
she got precisely what she wanted. (I didn't mind; what possible difference could it make which side of my face was photographed? Both
sides were equally homely.) She was one of the first actresses I ever
knew to have her own makeup table and mirror placed in the same
lights in which she would have to play—a trick she told me Von
Sternberg had taught her. Between takes she was constantly in front
of the mirror, adjusting her hair and her makeup, and the instant the
director called her, she was ready.

She came to my house often, loved the pictures, understood them,
knew many of the artists personally, and wearing some of the most
breathtaking gowns on record, would come off as an intellectual,
which, indeed, she was (is).

We never became friends, but we became close acquaintances. If
that requires an explanation, I am not able to give one. I know Marlene; I see her every so often; I know nothing of her personal or
private or semiprivate life; she knows nothing of mine; we will always
keep it that way.

My view of her as an actress? I am not sure I would call it talent; it
is something beyond that—mystery, unavailability, distance, feminine
mystique (before those two words got to mean something else). I
gladly risk the sneer of Germaine Greer: I like the Dietrich mystique
better than the Greer. Certainly, while Betty Friedan may be more
intelligent, I'd rather spend my time with Marlene, who, by the way,
is one of the best gourmet and family cooks about and certainly could
and should be called Ms. Kleen. She is the quintessential sex goddess;
she is also the quintessential German hausfrau. She is mother as sex;
sex as it was intended. She is rough and tough—and absolutely and
uniquely and gloriously herself.

I cannot say Dietrich and not say Garbo.

I never played with Garbo. She was as mysterious and unreachable
to me as she was to you—except that one day in the remodeled house
the bell rang, and against all my principles, I answered the door
myself. There, through the peephole, I saw a lady with a floppy hat
holding a package. And the lady said: "Is Mr. Robinson in? My name
is Garbo."

I opened the door. She came in, shook hands with me stiffly in the
European manner, asked my pardon for intruding, but there was a
matter of some importance she wished to discuss with me if I could
spare her a moment or two. Greta Garbo in my house! I was overwhelmed, awed, and as nervous as a cat.

I took her into the living room; she glanced at the pictures on the wall approvingly but did not look at them closely. She refused to sit down, toyed with the string on her package, having some trouble with the knots, refused to let me help her, and finally unveiled a painting.

Was it worth buying?

It was a landscape by an artist I had never heard of. It had quite a decent feeling about it, though far from masterly. It could be called a daub except that it was brooding and sylvan and rather like her—or at least the image that you and I had come to have about her.

"Is it worth——" she started to ask, and I interrupted, I hope, politely.

"Don't tell me the price yet," I said. "Tell me if you like it."

"I do at night," she said. "In the morning I am not so sure."

"Then," I said, "live with it for a few weeks before making up your mind."

"But it is necessary," she insisted, "that I make up my mind today."

"Do not be forced into a decision you might regret."

"You are right, Mr. Robinson," she said. "I do not like to be forced until I am certain. Yet, he needs the money."

"The artist?"

"No, the man who bought it from the artist and now needs to sell it in order to eat."

"In that case," I said, "you are not buying a picture; you are giving charity. How much charity does he want?"

"Two hundred dollars," she said.

"For two hundred dollars," I told her, "you are getting a very nice picture. And if you find you do not like it, you can always give it away or put it in a closet."

"That is excellent advice, Mr. Robinson," she said, "but two hundred dollars is still quite a lot of money. Can I take it off my tax?"

"I don't know, Miss Garbo," I said. "I suggest you talk to your accountant."

"He will charge me," she said. Again refusing help, she wrapped the picture again. "I will buy it. It is nice. It is about forests. And I like forests."

She started for the door. I followed her and opened it for her.

"Thank you very much for your time, Mr. Robinson," she said, and then suddenly she smiled that *Ninotchka* smile. "You also have nice pictures. Very nice. Thank you. Good-bye."

I never saw her again.

I'm wrong. Once again. On Fifty-sixth Street. She didn't know
me.

Back to *Manpower*. A lot of it was inane, yet Dietrich and I (I say
this in no immodesty but rather as a fact) were a stunning combination, and our joint presence was tough box office. Add George Raft,
and you had showmanship casting. Bad—but showmanship. Raft was
touchy, difficult, and thoroughly impossible to play with. He threw a
punch at me, and I was ready to walk; Hal Wallis had to act as
peacemaker.

I was in the hospital lately, and the first flowers I received carried a
card that read: "Get well, your pal, George Raft." I guess he forgave
me for whatever infraction caused him to clop me on the "chops"—
an expression for which I am indebted to Damon Runyon.

23

So off to M.G.M. and a picture called *Unholy Partners*, directed by Mervyn again and, I think, best forgotten by both of us.

Then back to Warner's for *Larceny, Inc.* And before we finished shooting, the Robinson family moved back into the remodeled house. It was the end of November 1941.

How to describe the joy? Each painting in its assigned position, each one at peace with its neighbor. The furniture was muted and secondary to the pictures. The whole house was a kind of museum and the gallery attached was indeed a museum. Gladys and I were ecstatic, but almost from the beginning we rarely used the great room for ourselves. We retired upstairs to our private rooms—and that's the way it was until the divorce and Manny went off to live on his own and I married Jane and somehow she made this museum house into a home. I'm not sure how she accomplished the miracle, but she's great with needlepoint, and she redid the chairs and the rugs; the ashtrays were no longer so forbidding that you couldn't put a cigar down without feeling you were committing sacrilege.

But that last week in November and that first week in December I was in ecstasy. I had reached the peak in my life. All the money had bought this. It was mine, and I was *le grand seigneur*, lord of everything over which I reigned. I felt surges of happiness and expanded ego.

Then one Sunday Gladys awakened me hysterically. Who, in my age bracket, does not remember where he was that Sunday or what he was doing? Who does not remember where he was or what he was doing the day F.D.R. died? Who does not remember where he was or what he was doing when he was told Kennedy was assassinated?

Those are the three graven dates. The first, that Sunday, was Pearl Harbor.

I had extremely painful decisions to make about this era in my life. The temptation to gloss over them has been compelling; it is time, I think, to lie no longer. For years I believed that psychiatry and aberration were two words that meant people were crazy, and craziness, to me, meant snake pits and asylums and bedlam. I could not accept mental illness as illness—curable illness—and the words used about mental sickness made me angry.

I lied about Gladys' illness as long as she was alive; I was worried, fearful, and deeply heartsick about it; I was also, in my heart, ashamed.

I tell the truth now, since Gladys sadly died last year and cannot be hurt by my words; because Manny, I think, has always known the truth; because Francesca deserves to; and because I would like to help people who felt as I do. Mental illness is nothing to be ashamed of or hidden; it is treatable; there are drugs today that are emptying institutions. Science has learned to deal with almost all aspects of aberration, especially depression. That was what Gladys had. She was, according to the minimum technical term, a manic-depressive.

Where this comes from, how it happens, from what source it derives, I have no way of telling you. If I had known some of these things, perhaps I would have noticed the symptoms earlier; perhaps I would have had her treated earlier. Perhaps we might all have been saved the terrible consequences of this disease. And please try to understand that it *is* a disease and treatable and, these days, curable.

In any case, Gladys' reaction to Pearl Harbor was manic. She was prepared to go out and die for her country. She raged against the Japanese, predicted a squad of marines would destroy them in a few days. She was prepared to fight the war single-handed.

A few days later she was in such utter abysmal despair that it broke your heart. When she was manic, she thought I was the greatest man in the world. Not only *she*, but *I* could win the war. In depression, I'd started it all. It was my fault. She was measured in her comments, but maybe if it hadn't been for the Jews, there would have been no Hitler, and hence no Pearl Harbor.

For the first time I realized these were unbalanced ravings. I called in our family doctor. She refused to see him. He came on social pretext and then called in a psychiatrist who again appeared to be there simply for a cup of tea. They consulted with me and recommended a sanitarium in Pasadena and shock treatments.

When it was suggested to her that she go to this lovely place for rest and to calm her nerves, she absolutely refused. That afternoon I was called by an attorney and told that Gladys was suing me for divorce.

I immediately ran up the stairs to her room. She was in a negligee, studying a pile of papers. When I dared to ask her about the divorce, she merely referred me to her attorney, a man whose name (I'm not sure of this) was Robert Freston. She then told me as if nothing were wrong that she was planning to devote a great deal of her time to war work, the USO—entertainment for American troops. Did I think this a good idea? And was it a good idea for Manny to be in military school? Her conversation was so strange and inconsistent that when I collected my wits, I did not know which to call first, her lawyer or her psychiatrist.

I decided on the lawyer. He told me that he was as surprised as I, that she had phoned him, had asked about community property, and learned that half of everything I owned was legally hers. She had asked him to prepare the papers, suing me and asking for large alimony and more than an equal division of assets. He said he had not yet done so, would not until he had had a personal conversation with her, and urged me to repair our marital differences.

I told him that I had no knowledge they had taken so serious a turn, and Freston suggested that he was certain that mention of the Pasadena sanitarium had led her to believe I wanted to be rid of her.

I called the doctor. He was not surprised at her action, told me he preferred it to other measures she might have taken. *What* other measures? I insisted on knowing. He was vague, and then he said, "Self-injury; self-imposed way out of her inner devils."

"Suicide?"

And he said, "Yes, suicide." Then he advised me to wait for a few days. In those few days she forgot everything, certainly the USO, and was in so grave a depression that we were able to engage two nurses and carry and drive her to Las Encinas, the Pasadena sanitarium. I waited, pacing the floor, while they administered shock treatment over a period of weeks.

I brought a perfectly delightful Gladys home—a Gladys who remembered nothing of divorce, suicide, USO, or the sanitarium. I was to learn in the episodes that followed that this was one of the classic results of shock treatment—loss of memory of the immediate past.

It is so painful to go into specific detail about the next six or seven years, that I'll lump it all together.

Gladys' pattern remained the same. When she was manic I was Jesus Christ; when she was depressed, I was the meanest son of a bitch that ever lived. Or it may have been the other way around. My mind seems to block out the details, but a look at my papers and letters reminds me.

She was hospitalized again in 1944 for the same ailment. Same shock treatments. Same threat of divorce prior to treatment.

In 1946, the same.

In 1947, the same.

In 1949, the same—with one major difference. This time she gave the story of her suit for divorce to the papers. It was front page news. I was besieged by newspapermen.

She wasn't. She was in Menninger's.

As for me, between and during these bouts my mind was on the war. Of course I made another picture, *Tales of Manhattan*. It was in five parts, and I appeared in only one of them. Was it good or bad? I don't know. I didn't much care.

I'd come home at night and sit in the living room and look and touch and (maybe it's my insanity) talk to the pictures. I was stern with Manny and his marks. I tried to keep the house running. I was in mortal agony.

But so was she. So was she.

Thank God for the Office of War Information. I had tried desperately to do something in the war effort, but I was almost fifty and beyond the draft age, and Frank Capra and his Signal Corps film group in Washington had nothing for me. Nor the O.S.S. Nor the Navy. Then I got a wire from the Office of War Information, headed by Elmer Davis, and was asked if I'd fly to London, broadcast to the British, and even to the Germans and Rumanians and the French, because in my letter I'd said I could speak all those languages.*

SR 136 132 DL GOVT-WUX WASHINGTON DC 29 616P
                                         1942 SEP 29 PM 3 48

EDWARD G ROBINSON

    BEVERLY HILLS CALIF-

DEAR EDDIE: WE HAVE CLEARED WITH OUR LONDON OFFICE ON THE PROPOSAL TO HAVE YOU GO OVER THERE FOR A FEW WEEKS THEY ARE MOST ENTHUSIASTIC ABOUT THE IDEA SO ARE HIGH AUTHORITIES IN THE ARMY AS YOU KNOW THEREFORE IF IT IS CONVENIENT FOR YOU TO DO SO WE WOULD LIKE TO ARRANGE TO SEND YOU AS A SPECIAL REPRESENTATIVE OF THE OFFICE OF WAR INFORMATION AT THE EARLIEST POSSIBLE DATE IT IS A GOOD IDEA TO GET OFF SOON BECAUSE AS THE SEASON ADVANCES TRANSPORTATION BECOMES MORE DIFFICULT PLEASE TELEGRAPH ME WHEN YOU THINK YOU

* Note from L.S.: I have found among E.G.R.'s papers the following telegram:

CAN COME EAST TO TALK THIS OVER AND ARRANGE ALL
THE DETAILS WE ARE MOST GRATEFUL FOR THE OFFER OF
YOUR SERVICES AND BELIEVE WE CAN MAKE EXTREMELY
GOOD USE OF THEM VERY BEST REGARDS-
            ROBERT SHERWOOD.

They wanted me! And I never wanted to do anything so much in
my life.

Help the war effort, of course. But get away! That was the important thing. Get away!

Get away!

Can a movie star?

Let's go into that whole thing right now and be done with it. It is
1942; we are in the middle of a war; my ability to contribute to it
is based on no other factor than this: I am a known face. There is
little or no inquiry into my knowledge of facts or strategies; I am a
puppet whose features and voice are known to millions of people in
the western world. Therefore, that face is to be fed words to speak—
and that voice is to say nothing that does not hew to the line. With
that I agree. I am Punch without Judy, and Punch will do and say
anything that the government requests.

I flew (ugh!) to Washington on high priority, was met not only by
government figures but by Warner Brothers press people. Warner's
was going to get as much mileage out of this as possible, and who
could blame them?

I met with Robert Sherwood, Philip Wylie, Milton Eisenhower,
and Elmer Davis. I was treated with respect and gratitude. I gave
autographs to hundreds of secretaries who lined the halls; I was entertained privately at Georgetown houses by famous hostesses and despite the guest list, which was composed of ambassadors, senators,
cabinet members, congressmen, and an occasional journalist, I was
the Lion of the Evening. I am not going into the whole absurd question of how and why, in the middle of a war, a movie star takes on a
sheen and patina that outdazzles the people who run the war; I am
only going to state that I felt ridiculous and embarrassed.

When asked what I was doing there, I clammed up because I had
been warned over and over again that my mission was top secret and
that I was to tell no one where I was going or what I would do when I
got there. This added an air of mystery and suspense, and I heard
speculations that came right out of the movies I'd been in. The fiction
I'd played seemed to have more reality than the nonfiction being
spread about me.

The truth: I was to make morale speeches to the British and broadcast in as many foreign languages as I could to the occupied areas of

Europe. That was the sum and substance of it. The speeches were prepared for me, and as you shall see momentarily and officially, even my ad libs were to be made within certain well-defined parameters.

Actually, I was more interested in the process, the way of my going, than my eventual destination. I was deathly afraid of flying, and when I was told that I was to fly in a clipper—arranged with a berth—to Greenland first, then to the Azores, then to Bristol, that my time of departure was secret, that the reason for the secrecy was to keep the enemy from knowing where I was or what route I was taking, I can tell you I felt fear in the pit of my gut.

I was taken to an Army camp on Long Island, put up in bachelor officers quarters, dined with aviation personnel, and was regaled with stories of how clippers belly-whopped on landing and could possibly break in two. Then I was given an envelope marked "SECRET" and told that I could open it once we were airborne.

At last, at four in the morning, we were airborne, and I opened the envelope. Its contents too were marked "SECRET" and dated October 13, 1942. That is over thirty years ago, and the word "secret" still scares me. I've tried to call Washington in the last few days to find out if it is okay to release this secret document (after all, I know the fuss that was raised about the Pentagon Papers), but there is no longer any OWI, and the man at the State Department did laugh a little when I read the document, so I give it to you for your edification, at the risk of being prosecuted under the Espionage Act. Here is the secret document, verbatim:

OFFICE OF WAR INFORMATION

WASHINGTON

October 13, 1942.

MEMORANDUM

To: Mr. Edward G. Robinson

From: Irving Pflaum, London Desk, Outpost Bureau, Washington.

Subject: Suggestions for talks in Great Britain.

1. To the British people on the subject of "Hollywood is not America".

        American people go to the cinema for amusement and relaxation just as do the people of Great Britain. American films, therefore, indulge in anything but realism, unless realism can be depicted so as to amuse, relax and, incidentally, educate the audience. Americans are not deceived or misled very much by the romanticism and glorifi-

cation of ordinary everyday living that goes on in the cinema, but
in Great Britain and elsewhere abroad, the people do not have the
same reality to hold on to.   So many of them may be deceived by
American films into believing that American life is portrayed
accurately down to the last detail. Some sections of American
life is portrayed in every film, but it often is only a segment
of America and it seldom is representative of any large section
of the people.

    Something about the size and diversity of the United States,
our dialects, our climatic differences.

    Something about that certain common factor that makes residents
of the United States Americans despite diversities mentioned above.
An example of the leveling or common factor — our public school
system, our common history books, and our deep, though short-lived
tradition as symbolized in famous battles, Abraham Lincoln, George
Washington, America the Beautiful, Songs and Dances.

    Some mention of films, old or new, that went a long way toward
giving an accurate picture of American politics and of the people.

            Talks through the BBC *to* the continent of
Europe in the various languages in general follow the
oral and written suggestions of Mr. Wallace Carroll
and his staff in London and in addition bring out
cinema industries attitude toward the war. Be careful
not to overstress lack of government control of film
industry in America. Probably refer to other film
stars and their part in the war effort with descriptions
of a personal nature. Some emphasis on theme of film
people of European origin succeeding in America, stress-
ing their continual interest in Europe and European
reconstruction. Anything to show that ordinary American
is overcoming Isolationism and will not pull out of
Europe at the end of the war.

I plan no comment on that urgent secret dispatch from OWI; it
speaks for itself; it speaks for the immense naiveté of people engaged
in the art of war.

I was met in Bristol by OWI people stationed in England; we were
put on a train to London, and I was given a suite at Claridge's—a
moment of self-doubt for me because I had already planned how I
was going to live in an Army camp. Since this seems to be turning into
a matter of record, let me tell you that the autograph hunters in the

lobby of Claridge's equaled, if not exceeded, the zeal of those in the lobby of the Waldorf in New York. As a matter of fact, I had no idea of the impact of this ancient Rumanian face; I was besieged by fans wherever I went.

I went first to a dinner party, where I met Lord Beaverbrook, Winston Churchill, Anthony Eden, and various members of royalty.* I was briefed on the bomb damage; I was not surprised at the austerity of the banquet, though I was surprised at the elegance of the service and the number of French wines.

(Note for the gourmets: Everything was strictly rationed. I never went to or saw or was advised of a black market restaurant—*but*, at Fortnum and Mason's and Harrod's in the grocery department you could get not necessities but incredible luxuries: plovers' eggs, mandarin oranges in grenadine, snails, occasionally fresh Scottish salmon, Dijon mustard, bottled Périgord truffles—no pâté—capers, a whole assortment of White Rose canned goods, brandied peaches in ancient and slightly rusted cans, and an assortment of meats—mostly whale, venison, grouse, pheasant, and partridge—thoroughly riddled with gunshot.)

I made an incredible number of jingoistic speeches from Broadcasting House in an incredible number of languages. And since the Soviet Union was now an ally, I kept taking Russian lessons.

I then went to Scotland and made speeches there—God, how the Scots loved *Little Caesar*, which it seemed to me was in first run— and I entertained our own troops, now stationed in England.

I must go into this matter with some thoroughness because it brings up the whole problem of a straight actor (straight in terms of profession, not in terms of his sex life) trying to find a way to entertain troops. I was announced, I appeared, and the ovations were beyond anything I'd ever known. What was I to do? No singer, I. No stand-up comic. No entertainer.

Well, I'd been forewarned. What they wanted was not Edward G. Robinson but Little Caesar. Accordingly, I had worked out, before I left, with the help of Jack Benny, whole idiotic routines, inevitably beginning with "Hey, youse guys," and including "Buy your beer from me or else." I even took along a felt hat and a trench coat, and it didn't work very well until I remembered whole speeches from *The Racket*, a play in which I'd appeared. When I played them—and thank God, I was working as an actor with lines engraved on my

* Can you believe this? Mr. Eden said he dared not go home without my autograph for his wife.

consciousness—I was a smash. A sweaty, shivering, shaking, heart-throbbing smash—but a smash.*

Back in London, before my return via ship—a saga you will not be spared—I met with the loyal opposition to His Majesty's Government—Ernest Bevan, Clement Attlee, Harold Laski. I saw G. B. Shaw for a few minutes and Noël Coward for an entire evening. What a man, that Noël Coward. What a wit! What a patriot! He was the Englishiest Englishman I ever met in my life.

I met the young Princesses Lillibet (does anybody else remember that that's what the Queen used to be called?) and Margaret and all the British theater greats who weren't in uniform on a variety of fronts. I ate tons of mandarin oranges and potted hare. I never wish in my life again to eat another mandarin orange or see another dish of potted hare.

I was all set to sail for home when an urgent inquiry was made of me. Could I speak German? Yes, I could. Would I? Yes, I would. To whom? To the Underground in Germany—anti-Nazis who had secret radios. Would I be bound by another secret document? I would. Could I have the secret document? Yes—but only in a secret broadcasting room. And so I now risk prosecution under the British Official Secrets Act, but here's the document, dated December 1942. The exact date has faded in the ensuing years.

Just before you read it, remember I was asked to compose six five-minute speeches, talks, orations, chats—God knows what to call them—within these guidelines:

PhD/CD/A2/s   POLITICAL WARFARE EXECUTIVE   SECRET
                                                      COPY No. 6

ANNEXE II

THROUGH GERMAN EARS.

(Prepared by Mr. H. Carleton Greene, B.B.C. German Editor, from personal experiences of jamming when listening in stockholm to B.B.C. German programmes. This bears out listener-evidence regarding jamming elsewhere in Europe. His recommendations, which are of general interest are directed to German language broadcasts.)

* I remember the opening of one of my earlier speeches at an Air Force base in the north of England. I began by saying: "I am happy to be here, the most privileged moment of my life to see the men who are defeating Hitler." I have never laid so big a bomb in my life. I could sense the audience despising me. So that crazy actor instinct took over, and to stop the buzz of their boos and Bronx cheers, I ad-libbed, "Pipe down, you mugs, or I'll let you have it. Whaddaya hear from the mob?" There was an instant burst of high laughter and applause. What they didn't know was that I wasn't laughing; I was crying.

Listening in through really heavy jamming is a nerve-wracking experience. To catch what is said the listener has to sit with his ear right up against the set and he gets up after the transmission half deafened, with his ears singing, feeling rather as if he had just got out of an aeroplane which has come down quickly from a great height. Intense concentration is required and his nerves are on the stretch all the time. If an obvious mistake is made, or something is said in an obscure and long-winded way, he is apt to get so angry that he wants to smash the set. Then he misses several minutes before his concentration is re-established.

That describes my reactions to listening through jamming.

The reactions of a German listener whose nerves are probably in a very bad state are likely to be even more exaggerated.

GENERAL CONCLUSIONS

1. Always remember that you must not worry your listener. You need not think of a listener who is conscious all the time of risking his life (in Germany at any rate I do not think that this thought is constantly in listeners' minds) but of a listener who is under very great nervous strain.

2. It is impossible to "think" while listening. The only part of a transmission which does any good is the part which is remembered afterwards. Try to provide your listeners with pointers which will stick in their minds and help them to remember the rest of what they have heard.

3. Be simple and straight-forward in the way you tell a story. Do not try to be "clever" or to get the last ounce of propaganda out of a story. Let the simple facts speak for themselves. Don't invert facts merely as a trick of presentation. Begin a story at the beginning and end it at the end.

4. It is very hard to appeal to the emotions of an audience listening in these conditions. It is better to aim at making your audience think by a simple and clear method of presentation.

NEWS

Every news bulletin should begin and end with a news summary. The news summary at the beginning, is useful because jamming often doesn't start until two or three minutes after the transmission has got under way.. A summary at the end of a transmission is useful for the many listeners who will have missed part of the transmission. It will also help the memories of those who have heard the whole transmission.

There is no place for "smart" leads in or any other tricks of that sort. Give the facts one after another in their natural order. Write in short sharp sentences with as few subordinate clauses as possible. Prune your story for excrescences (unnecessary adjectives and adverbs, false picturesqueness, repetitions, etc.) and as these will inevitably sometimes creep in in the English, prune the translation over again.

Remember that short stories or long stories divided up into sections with changes of voice help to maintain the listeners' interest.

TALKS

Much of the above applies to talks but a strong personality can hold the attention for 5 or 6 minutes even in bad jamming conditions if his talk is full of facts or if he is discussing a subject which really interests his audience.

There is no place for rhetoric which gives the listener nothing new to think about. He will simply switch off. (This was what I did after two or three minutes vain attempt to concentrate on the transport talks.)

PRODUCTIONS

The effect which a production will have on a listener, depends on what can be remembered afterwards. It is hard to create an emotional atmosphere through heavy jammers. In those circumstances the main purpose of productions should be to present facts in new and attractive ways but as simply and straight-forwardly possible. The question and answer form and the "illustrated talk" are particularl suitable because they make things easy for the listener.

The use of actuality noises should be reduced to a minimum. In most cases if they penetrate the jamming at all, they only add to the din which in flooding the ears of the listener and do not help to create atmosphere. Such tricks as the superimposition of one voice on another, several voices talking at once, or voices talking on the telephone, should be avoided. They are merely confusing. In a recent actuality piece at the Duesseldorf raid the only noise which came through at all was the sound of the heavy bombers passing just overhead. Great care needs to taken with the use of music.

The use of music merely to create atmosphere should be avoided. It will not create atmosphere. Tunes which are so well known that distortion does not matter (to take a recent example: "Wir fahren gegen Engelland" and "Bomben auf England") can be used with good effect. It should also be possible to plug a new tune for so long that it would become well known. The use of too many voices in a production may become very confusing.

Producers should use all their ingenuity to find the most simple and straight-forward ways of putting across their ideas.

VOICES

The best voice for penetrating jamming is a resonant voice which gives the listener the impression that is is echoing back from an invisible wall behind the microphone. Low-pitched voices seem to have this quality more often than high-pitched voices. This also applies to women's voices; a deep voice is much the best. The three most important points for the announcer to remember are:-

1. Enunciate every word
2. Keep an even pace
3. Go slow.

An announcer who may seem good in English listening conditions may be very poor when heard through jamming if he swallows some of his words and changes his pace from sentence to sentence.

In our German bulletins the system of having two announcers reading alternate stories thoroughly justifies itself and helps to hold the listener's attention. It does not make listening more difficult.

FINAL CONCLUSION

There are two main recipes for defeating the jammer.

1. Chose resonant voices.
2. In news, talks, production, simplicity, simplicity, simplicity.

Nobody listening through jamming cares a damn about clever phrasing.
Say "German" every time you mean "German". Cut out such words as "the enemy"
"invaders", "the oppressors". When the listener hears words like that he has to
think for a split second before he knows what they mean and before his concentration
is re-established he will have lost several sentences.

I pleaded for a moment of rehearsal to test my German, but that was impossible. These broadcasts were made on fixed schedules so the German possessors of illegal radios would know when to listen—listen, indeed, at the risk of their lives. For what seemed like hours my voice shook so that I was scarcely audible because I kept seeing those poor wretches listening in barns, in cellars, in caves, lookouts posted against the gestapo, and then I remembered Christmas and Easter in Bucharest, and my family's breathless waiting for a pogrom that never happened but one we feared nonetheless.

The thoughts that flashed through your mind were incredible: I kept screaming to my insides that my German must be absolutely German and have no taint of Yiddish, which is enormously difficult because the slightest umlaut or ablaut changes one language into another. I remembered somebody telling me that Yiddish and German both derived from Middle High Gothic, and I thought perhaps I should tell them that. That seemed idiotic, so I ended up by saying in German that we were all behind them and that we were certain of the eventual victory—a sentence I uttered with no conviction.

The gentleman in charge said I would go on the air again in five minutes, then added shamefacedly, "Would you mind, Mr. Robinson, if I make a suggestion?"

"Please."

"Your German is excellent, but occasionally it is *Hoch Deutsch*."

Me, *Hoch Deutsch*! Me, High German!

"If you would speak a little more gutturally, Bavarian, colloquially . . ."

To me, in the next speech, I sounded as though I were playing in Yiddish with Rudolf Schildkraut.

Did I get through? Was there an Underground in Germany that listened? Was I talking into thin air—jammed thin air, at that? I did not know for years. Then, when the war was over, I began getting letters from Germans who praised my wartime broadcasts, told me I had given them hope, and wondered (some of them) if I would communicate these sentiments to the War Crimes Commission. Don't ask me if they were copping out, using me to prove they had always been anti-Nazis.

I don't know the answer. Except in one case.

I had a letter from Heidelberg from a Karl Mayer. I read one day in the *Times* that he was sentenced to life imprisonment for his work in the ultimate solution—Buchenwald. The best way for me to sleep is to think that there were two people by the same name. After all, Karl Mayer is the German equivalent of John Jones.

So, in January 1943, I sailed back to the United States on a huge liner that I think was the *Queen Elizabeth*, though it may well have been the *Queen Mary*. All identification was blotted out. I was certain the ship would be empty. I was wrong. It was loaded to the gunwales with wounded British contingents going to the States for training in radar and the Norden bombsight. There were gun crews on board and a good deal of rehearsal. There were sixty-six guns, and I was allowed to fire a round. The crew gave me a blue thing to wear in my buttonhole, and I've searched all over for that blue thing, which made me an honorary gun crew member, but I can't find it.

Also on board were young Douglas Fairbanks and Alexander Korda, merchant marine survivors, members of the R.A.F., and loads of brass, and they all shared troop accommodations. Except me. For reasons best known to the readers of *Photoplay* magazine, I was given a room by myself.

We zig-zagged across the Atlantic, avoiding submarines—and during the zig-zags I was called upon to entertain—and I went into the sickbays and there was that same odor and horror I'd found after World War I, and I said: "Pipe down, you mugs, or I'll let you have it. Whaddaya hear from the mob?"

Obviously, they'd heard nothing.

There was only silence.

24

I returned to a Hollywood that was at war. Gladys, seemingly recovered, was indeed working her heart and brains out for the USO. Not only that; she took on some of the toughest jobs, particularly the care and entertainment of troops somewhere south of San Diego—desert battalions. When she would come home, she would refuse to tell me their eventual destination; she was, it appeared, in possession of top secret information. She said she couldn't even tell her darling husband.

I was so glad to be her darling husband again that I told her all my top secret information, which would not have enabled the German High Command to take another inch of ground. Let's face it. I really knew nothing. Every move made in the war was as much a surprise to me as it was to you.

In the next two or three years I made a lot of pictures: *Destroyer* (in which I had a higher rank than ever I did at Pelham Bay); *Flesh and Fantasy*, directed by a marvelous French refugee, Julien Duvivier; *Tampico*, with Victor McLaglen, a natural born actor with immense Irish sympathies, which I refused to let myself think of as pro-German; and *Mr. Winkle Goes to War*. I felt they were all, at the very best, trivial. Yet, deep in my heart I was grateful that anybody could find a role for a fifty-one-year-old man.

Anyway, the fifty-one-year-old man was busy with other matters. Socially, my lovely house with Gladys as generous and brilliant hostess was the scene of an incredible number of luncheons, cocktail parties, dinners, and meetings for Russian War Relief, USO, American Women's Voluntary Services, N.A.A.C.P., Desert Battalion, Assistance League, County Museum of Art—and, well, if you want the list, which includes every contribution I ever made to anything, I refer you to the printed record of the Committee on Un-American Activities, House of Representatives, Eighty-first Congress, Second Session (October 27 and December 21, 1950), obtainable, I would assume, even now from the Government Printing Office, Washington, D.C. The number of the document is 75514.

I do not propose to go into the matter now; soon, however, I will attempt to treat the matter at some length. There are other printed government documents, as well, to which I will refer. You might as well know the full extent of—shall I call it perfidy? I call it by an equally unfashionable word—patriotism.

I did a picture called *Double Indemnity** with Fred MacMurray and Barbara Stanwyck for Paramount. It was, in fact, the third lead. I debated accepting it; Emanuel Goldenberg told me that at my age it was time to begin thinking of character roles, to slide into middle and old age with the same grace as that marvelous actor Lewis Stone. Gladys was hospitalized again, and I had empty night hours to debate the decision. In the end it came to this: Wherefore was this night different from any other night (a question asked at the Passover seder table by the youngest celebrant in regard to the anniversary of the Jewish exodus from Egypt)? Wherefore was this picture different from any other picture? I was never the handsome leading man; I could proceed with my career growing older in roles that would grow older, too. And (forgive me for being mercenary) there was, instead of a decrease in pay, a slight hike. The decision made itself.

It was in this period that I took to prowling the house to find comfort and strength from the artists who had painted my pictures. Do I hear myself saying *my* pictures? Forgive me. They are *your* pictures; they belong to the world. One possesses them only for a fraction of time; inevitably, they go to humanity.

During these years I was trying to show them to as many people as possible. The USO arranged tours, and every day the house was filled with soldiers, sailors, and marines, looking at them, some blankly, others with interest, and a few with intense pleasure. I tried to be the tour guide myself, but I soon realized I was more of a distraction than a help. Besides, I had a fellow working for me (I find it very hard for me to call him a butler, but you may if you like,

---

* One of my favorite films.

because I guess that's what he was) who listened to my spiels and finally got them all down pat. *He* became the guide.

Whenever I came home in the late afternoon (I'd taken to playing gin rummy at Hillcrest with such worthies as Jack Benny and George Burns, and, even now, millionaire bankers and builders, each of us smoking Havanas, the cost of the Uppmans matched by the stakes; in the end, I neither lost nor won; I played with enormous caution and no luck whatever), I would see lines of buses or cars about the house. I'd enter by way of the service gate, pass through the kitchen, and hurry up the service stairs to my room.

Sam Jaffe, having sadly lost his wife and bewildered, though staunch with grief, came to live with us. He occupied the third-floor apartment that Gladys had insisted Sam Marx add. It had been intended for Manny, but Manny didn't like it. For Sam, it was a refuge.

For Manny, nearing twelve, the visitors to the house must have been a torment. But then it was only one of many torments for him— some of which I was conscious, others of which I either willfully or subconsciously ignored. Certainly he was bothered, upset, and diminished by his mother's episodes in various sanataria. I tried to explain her mental condition, but my supply of medical terms was matched only by my ignorance of what they really meant. Add to this my own sadness and anger, which made me explain these things abruptly and, I've now come to realize, unsatisfactorily.

He had other problems. He was a movie star's son, and I'm not prepared to suggest that I've even an inkling of what problems that must have posed. He was the son of Little Caesar, and the kids in the school emulated their fathers—most of whom belonged to the school of thought that I believed could be dispatched with the flick of a finger. Manny inherited this role of instant enemy; his classmates were aggressive toward him, tried to beat him up, determined to prove that Little Caesar's son was as much of a fake as his father.

He tried to tell me about some of those happenings. I brushed his agonies aside. It seemed to me that opposition made for strength of character, that the more the world was against you, the more certain you were to develop the backbone and inner strength to defeat it. That's what my father had told all six of us boys in Rumania and on the Lower East Side. It had worked for us; surely it would work for Manny.

It did not. Nor did religion.

I belonged to no organized church; I still don't. I am Jewish in my philosophy, outlook, and my palate; I am a gelding when it comes to God and immortality or the Old Testament.

And I wanted Manny to be bar mitzvahed. He would be thirteen in

1946, and to prepare for the bar mitzvah (the coming of age at thirteen; the admittance into the Jewish world as a man, as a viable congregant) required training. Could I deny him this? My rationalization was that once schooled, he could make his own theological decisions. But to make them with no background would be abdicating my role as father.

Gladys, however, was a Quaker, no more devout than I—but somehow terrified at the prospect of the bar mitzvah ceremony, and that terror would bring on her episodes of depression. Still, I was not to be dissuaded, and I could feel the hate in him.

Sometimes at night Sam and I would sit in the breakfast room and have a cup of coffee and some leftover dessert and smoke cigars (we rarely, if ever, had a drink) and *schmoosed*—a Yiddish word that means we discussed life and love and marriage and paintings and career and pain and death and immortality. To make the definition complete, add constipation, laxatives, who was sleeping with whom, and how ready people would be for a marvelous, peaceful world when peace came. Oh, God, how we kept using the phrase "*Win* the peace." It's almost forty years later, and that phrase is as hollow now as then. Can it ever be a reality?

After saying good night to Sam, I'd go upstairs and have a look-in on Manny, never sleeping soundly, but tossing and turning. I'd fix the blankets and wish he'd awaken so that, by some miracle, we could talk and settle matters, have a relationship—a meaningful relationship. That's the popular phrase now. Meaningful relationship. Father and son. Generation gap, they call it now. I didn't know that phrase then. It would have been useful.

For R.K.O I made a picture called *Woman in the Window* with Joan Bennett and Raymond Massey, directed by Fritz Lang, one of the greats in his declining period. Among the cast—guess their names— there was violent and accusatory anti-Communist talk. At first I defended my Russian War Relief friends, the believers in Uncle Joe, the defenders of Stalingrad, the strength and will of the Russian people. Then, having failed to convince anybody of anything, except that I was a Communist manqué, I retreated to my dressing room and kept my mouth shut.

I do not like keeping my mouth shut.

On my next picture I did not have to keep my mouth shut. It was written by Dalton Trumbo and was called *Our Vines Have Tender Grapes*. I'd known Trumbo for a long while; I knew he was hotheaded, wildly gifted, inordinately progressive, and, it seemed to me, intensely logical. My relationship with him professionally and socially became, not very many years later, a subject for official concern of the Congress.

I followed with *Scarlet Street* at Universal and hastened to finish it, so monotonous was the story and the character I played. So monotonous was I as an actor.

And I was in a hurry. The Royal Air Force Film Unit wanted me for a film written by Terrence Rattigan and directed by Roy Boulting. The script was solidly authentic; it was about the war; the role was wonderful—and I could get away. Get away!

So I went to London and thus was available to our own armed forces to be the first performer to visit the troops after the invasion on D-Day.

Dressed as a make-believe major (brevetted, I think it's called), I followed American troops through (I think) St. Lo and Caen (dying to have a dish of tripe à la mode du Caen, but there wasn't any), and, no fool anymore, I never pretended to be anything but Little Caesar. I worked out a routine and memorized it. Though it embarrassed me every time I did it, they loved it. I first did it on June 16, ten days after the invasion. To put it in vaudeville terms, it went something like this:

Pipe down, you mugs, or I'll let you have it. Whaddaya hear—from the mob?
                    (HOLDS OUT THE VIOLIN CASE)
I suppose you guys think there's a fiddle in this case. Who do you thing I am, Jascha Heifetz? Or Mischa Rubinoff?

That's what the USO Committee thought when they sent me over. I had to promise 'em I was going to play a little long-hair music, like maybe the finish of the Unfinished Symphony. . . .
                    (CASE FLOPS OPEN, REVEALING
                        A SUBMACHINE GUN)
But how can you play Beethoven on a Chicago typewriter?

This is the kid himself talking—Little Caesar. Remember? You'd better remember, because anybody who don't will find himself at the bottom of the East River with his feet in a cake of cement! I ain't kidding, neither.

Okay, now that we understand each other, I'm going to let you in on a little secret: I'm going to tell you why I'm here. The draft board—remember that little institution?—well, I was sap enough to want to get in this shindig, but they said nix to me. Wise guys. They didn't want me. How do you like that? I had a callous on my finger—from pulling the trigger so much. And besides, I was too old. So I said, "Okay, the hell with the Army if they don't want me." But get this: the Army better stay on the north side, see, or there's going to be an epidemic of lead poisoning.

> So General Marshall stays on the north side and I stay on the south side and everything is jake until I get to thinking about all the shooting that's going on all over the world and Little Caesar ain't in on it, and I get awful lonely, awful heartsick. So I goes back to the draft board, sticks my roscoe in the doctor's ribs and say, "Doc, if you say I'm 4-F again, I'll drill you fulla holes!" So what do you think he says? *"Five* F!"

That's only a sample. It went on and on for what seemed like a century but was actually half an hour. I memorized it all. After a couple of times I figured where the laughs came, where the self-abasement would make them yell with joy—and never have I had such respect for the stand-up comic. It is the single hardest performance in the world to give—all alone on stage in front of thousands of men who may be dead the next day.

In the end I tried to make some sense and spoke the line with which I had once bombed as an opening. It made a hell of a finish. Believe me, the finish, the end, the topper, getting off, is the hardest thing an actor has to do.

> I know a little bit about gangsters. I've played many of them. Remember how Little Caesar wound up? In the gutter with a bellyful of lead. That's how all the Little Caesars are going to end up in this picture that's being shot all over the world. Says who? Says you.
>
> This is the most privileged moment of my life, the opportunity to be here with you. I have seen the men who are defeating Hitler. I thank you, gentlemen, from the bottom of my heart.

That last paragraph is the only thing I really wanted to say.

25

I hope you got some enjoyment out of that bowdlerized routine to the troops. It was concocted by Jack Benny, Milton Berle, George Burns, and a whole gaggle of gag writers. I even wrote William Saroyan, enclosing a copy, asking for any jokes he had up his sleeve, but he politely turned me down.

You've had your fill of laughter, I'm sorry to have to report. From 1946 to 1954 the laughs are few, far apart, and at best, sardonic.

I made a picture called *The Stranger* for R.K.O., directed by Orson Welles. Orson has genius, but in this film it seemed to have run out. It was bloodless, and so was I.

Socially, of course, I was—or rather, Gladys was—Elsa Maxwell. We had everybody under the sun to the house including all the great musicians—Toscanini, Schnabel, Stravinsky, Prokofiev, Elman, Godowsky, Molinari, Iturbi, and Horowitz—and I devised a little plan. Each would play a few bars on the enormous Steinway, and then— and *only* then—autograph it. I've just opened the piano and looked at all these sentiments and signatures, and they've either faded or my eyes aren't as good as they used to be. I'm going to have a sharp-eyed photographer in with a camera and Kleig lights and see if the inside of the Steinway can be photographed. I personally doubt it. L.S. says it can be done. But he thinks almost anything can be done. Ah, youth!*

Once, when I was out of town, Gladys had a dinner party for

* Note from L.S.: *Some* youth!

Senator Claude Pepper. You will find the matter thoroughly examined in the Un-American Activities Committee reports.

But, before we get to that, there's the matter of Manny's bar mitzvah.

It was the works at a temple with a party afterward. The whole town was there, and Harry Warner insisted on making a film record of it. I have a print.*

I was happy and excited, Gladys was polite and stonefaced. The guests had a marvelous time. Only some of those invited didn't come. There were a lot of sudden headaches that afternoon.

And so we get at it at last!

In 1949 the (California) Senate Fact-Finding Committee on Un-American Activities released its *fifth* report, which meant evidently that it had been engaged in tracking down, taking testimony about, and attacking a certain person or persons as present or past Communists. In that final report, "Repudiations and Denials of Communism," it listed those persons who had been included in that investigation. I was in that report, had been named over and over again since the beginning of the hearings, had protested, yet had never met my accusers, confronted them, or testified verbally before the committee. I have a massive file of letters to prove this point, but in all fairness, that accumulation of paper proves only that I protested my designation as a Communist: I readily admit it does not prove anything else.

How do you prove you are *not* a Communist? Your word obviously means nothing, because to belong to a political party that has as its very point the overthrow of the government by force means obviously that lying would be the least of your sins.

This, according to the published document I have before me, was the list of my sins:

> *EDWARD G. ROBINSON:* Prominent actor, frequently involved in Communist fronts and causes. Following are citations from recent reports by California Senate Committee:
> Listed in circular as a leader of Progressive Citizens of America.
> Signer of call for P.C.A. organizing meeting.
> Cited as listed in two C.P. fronts by House Committee.
> Elected to Executive Board of P.C.A.

* Note from L.S.: It was completely restaged for the purpose. Harry Warner, having recently lost a son, made Manny his godson and wanted the film as one-third of a series that would include Catholic and Protestant services. Somehow it didn't work out, but Harry Warner (according to Manny's book) always gave the boy his friendship.

Affiliated with American Committee for Protection of Foreign Born, a Communist front.

Sponsor, American Committee for Yugoslav Relief, a C.P. front.

Listed on program of cultural conference sponsored by American Russian Institute, Inc., a C.P. front.

Cited as a supporter, who praised American Youth for Democracy, a Communist youth front.

Sponsor, China Conference Arrangements Committee.

Initiating Sponsor, National Congress on Civil Rights, in Detroit in 1946, from which was organized the major C.P. defense front, Civil Rights Congress.

Attended meeting of Communist front, Committee for First Amendment, at home of ———.

Member, Executive Committee, Hollywood Democratic Committee.

Star in rally staged by H.I.C.C.A.S.P., Communist front.

Member, Executive Council of H.I.C.C.A.S.P.

Initiating Sponsor, Independent Citizens Committee of Arts, Sciences and Professions.

Member, Executive Board, Los Angeles branch of Progressive Citizens of America.

I freely confess to all these charges. What I do not confess to is the constant reiteration of "A Communist Front," "A C.P. Defense Fund," "A C.P. Front," and other similar characterizations. I also freely confess that from the start of this attack upon me, including publication of pretty much this same series of affiliations in *Red Channels*, republication in Hedda Hopper, *The Hollywood Reporter*, American Legion magazines, and various publications issued by Gerald L. K. Smith and his successors, I refused to believe that anybody would take all these charges seriously.

Additionally, I was not alone. Many others—friends of mine, men and women of distinction and repute, even fame—were alongside me. These were men and women with whom I'd worked on committee after committee, people whom I respected and loved. Their names are a matter of public record, but you'll not hear them again from me. Even after all these years, even though the whole McCarthy era has long vanished, these accusations can cause pain and despair. God knows they caused blacklisting.

I had intended (at L.S.'s urging) to go into the whole dreary history of what I call a witch hunt and others call an effort to rid America of subversive characters. But I shan't. I can only tell you of matters as they appeared to me, how they affected my emotions and my ability to make a living, and most importantly, how they affected my self-esteem.

I was having, God knows, enough emotional traumas at the time *without* the Communist attack. Gladys had had another episode and had been taken to another sanitarium. She felt she was there under restraint, and she wrote me a letter in such agony and despair that my heart seemed to be torn from its body.

She was under the delusion that she was being incarcerated against her will, and, please, please, would I rescue her? And she added "love" eight times and promised to be an angel.

I am incapable of describing my emotions; I don't know which one to choose—heartbreak, terror, pity, guilt, despair. They all added up to a syndrome that made me grovel inwardly with self-hatred. I went immediately to the sanitarium to discuss the matter urgently with the doctor; he assured me that they were doing their best, that the letter was a symptom, that, of course, I could take her home (she was not committed legally in any way) but that I would be doing her irrevocable harm if I did what she wished.

I consulted by phone with New York and with the people at Menninger's, and every psychiatrist agreed that this kind of rest and treatment was indicated; to bring her home was definitely contraindicated.

Added to this was the fact that Manny was forever getting into trouble in school; and so I changed schools, always putting the blame not on him but on his teachers. He had parties with young girls at our ranch house—the police raided one of them. He drove a car without a license; he took to selling my cigars at a profit; and he sneaked drinks whenever he could.

I have reached a point in life where I make no judgments. Manny has written a book himself telling of these matters; sometimes I cannot believe we lived through the same moments. Whatever agonies of spirit forced him into these behavior patterns are matched now by my own agonies as I remember them.

In his book he remembers mama and papa. What he does not remember, what he did not know, was that papa couldn't get a job. Papa was blacklisted by the motion picture industry.

My agent, in the way of agents, went the way of all agents in dealing with a once hot and now cooling actor.

Phase 1: "Hell, Eddie, I've read a lot of scripts submitted for you, and there isn't one that's right for you. Nothing but the best for you, Eddie, baby. You know that."

Phase 2: "Business in lots of trouble, Eddie, baby. Postwar adjustment and all that crap. I've got something really hot cooking. Believe me, baby."

Phase 3: "Eddie, it's not so easy at your age. Character parts, you know. After all, you're not exactly a baby, are you, Eddie?"

Phase 4: "There seems to be some opposition to you, Eddie. I'm looking into it. Whatever it is, we'll fight it with every penny we've got. You know that."

Phase 5 (coming from the agent's secretary): "I'm sorry, Mr. Robinson, but Mr. B. is out of town. I'll give him your message. He'll certainly call you at his earliest convenience."

Phase 6: No earliest convenience.

What was happening was evident even to me. *The Hollywood Reporter*, in its "Tradeviews," written by its editor-publisher, Billy Wilkerson, was taking veiled potshots at my political activities. The American Legion put me on a list with a host of other undesirables. Other actors, writers, directors, and producers were going through the same six phases with their agents. And my mail was filled with letters like the one that follows. I chose it for posterity because it is among the most literate:

"WELL — WELL! — LOOK WHO'S TALKING! DIDN'T _YOU_ — CALL EVERYONE — WHO DID-N'T AGREE WITH YOUR YIDDISH IDEAS (DURING THE WAR) A "NAZI" — & LATER — A "FASCIST"? H — M — M? — WEREN'T _YOU_ THE GUY — WHO LED THE PICKET LINES (AROUND POLY, HIGH SCHOOL) OF A SCREAMING — HOWLING — HIDE-OUS YIDDISH MOB — WHEN A _REAL_ AMERICAN — GERALD L. K. SMITH — ADDRESSED A GATHERING OF _CHRISTIAN_ AMERICANS? DIDN'T _YOU_ & YOUR STINKING

YIDDISH RIFF RAFF — FROM STINKING EUROPEAN GHETTOS — CALL <u>HIM</u> & <u>HIS</u> FOLLOWERS NAMES — FAR WORSE THAN <u>YOU</u> ARE BEING CALLED TODAY? — DIDN'T <u>YOU</u> & YOUR WIFE — VISIT <u>TROTSKY</u> IN MEXICO — SHORTLY BEFORE <u>HIS</u> ASSASSINATION? WERE <u>YOU</u> — THE "FINGER MAN" — IN THAT — "RUB-OUT"? H — M — M? — JEW?

IT'S TOO LATE — JEW! — NOTHING THAT <u>YOU</u> & "CANTOR" — <u>ISSY ISHKOVITZ</u>! — CAN SAY OR DO — WILL BE ACCEPTED BY THE <u>CHRISTIAN</u> — AMERICAN PUBLIC! YOU & THE SKUNK — JEW — RIFF RAFF OF HOLLYWOOD — HAVE OVER PLAYED YOUR HAND! — WE — "DUMB GOIS" KNOW YOU NOW! — & WE'RE NOT GONNA REST — UNTIL YOU SCUM — ARE

DRIVEN <u>OUT</u> OF THE "ENTERTAINMENT" FIELD. — "EVERY DOG — HAS HIS DAY — SEE? — YOU KIKES — HAD YOURS — TOO LONG! NOW IT'S OUR TURN! — YOU WON'T <u>DARE</u> — GO TO COURT! — YELLOW! —

I would have my coffee and toast in the mornings with nowhere to go, nothing to do, idleness hanging heavily upon me, and having no capacity to deal with it. I'd take a little feather brush and dust the Corot and the Dufy and straighten the other pictures and wait for the phone to ring or the mail to come.

The phone rang quite a lot—crank calls (no use in changing your number, they find out somehow) or social calls, best attended to by Gladys, but Gladys was not there very much. After each visit to a sanitarium she'd take off for Europe or Marrakesh or some place as far away from me as possible, and I'd wait for the morning mail.

It was a mixed bag—letters like the one you've just read (others far more obscene) and then totally contradictory letters. For instance, from the American Legion, Department of California:

Dear Mr. Robinson:

   It is the desire of the Fourth Area, Department of California, The American Legion, to present you with a citation in recognition of the great contribution you have made through your personal sacrifices and efforts to bring cheer and comfort to our armed forces all over the world. We are holding our third and final Fourth Area Caucus on Sunday, July 15th, at Hollywood Post No. 43 Clubhouse, 2035 North Highland Avenue, Hollywood, California. Presentation of citations will be made at 11:45 a.m. on that date, to be followed by a luncheon for our honored guests.

   I sincerely hope you will find it possible to be present and anticipate with pleasure the opportunity to honor you before our Caucus.

                                        Yours very truly,
                                        Norman D. Dunbar, Commander
                                        Fourth Area

There was also a letter from the Federal Bureau of Investigation complimenting me on a performance I had given in radio on *Cavalcade of America*, playing a special agent for the F.B.I., that ended with "With best wishes and kind regards, sincerely yours, J. Edgar Hoover."

Radio! That seemed a possible way to continue living as an actor. For the record, I made four appearances, one in 1946, one in 1947, and two in 1948. And those came after long discussions with C.B.S. executives on my precise political coloration. They were doubtful but embarrassed. On N.B.C. I appeared only once, and they could hardly prevent that because all I did was act as an unpaid narrator on a segment of *The Eternal Light*, a religious program.

I read a great deal during these empty days, read and mused and considered the future, which in the ordinary sense of things would mean economizing, living on a fixed income, or selling the pictures—three equally grim alternatives. But I was spending money at a fast rate on the household (which continued to flourish as if I were still a working stiff), on Gladys' medical bills and her voyages to North Africa and Paris, and on the boy—his schooling, psychiatrists for him, and getting him out of scrapes.

I found the Hillcrest Country Club something of a haven; I even tried to play golf a couple of times, but it's a game that requires a whole series of concentrations and coordinations. I was capable of none of them.

There I lunched one day with Sol Lesser, a veteran producer who at one time had been, among other things, head of R.K.O. He had a story by Delmar Daves; I'd be perfect for it. I was all set up and excited until he told me that we'd have to form a production company, that he was certain that with my name and my scrounging a little, we could get financing and a United Artists Release. So that's how I became a producer (a role for which I'm totally unsuited) and Sol and I made a film called *The Red House*. It was a moody piece, got moody notices, but I think it made a few bucks.

Meanwhile, I was still waiting for the morning mail, expecting any day a subpoena from the House Un-American Activities Committee. It seemed everybody else I knew was getting one from J. Parnell Thomas, chairman of the committee. And the question would be asked: "Are you or have you ever been a member of the Communist party or any other organization or organizations dedicated to the overthrow of this country by force?"

Most Hollywood people expressed overt disdain for Mr. Thomas' right to ask these questions. They resented the fact that so many of us had been called subversive, pinko, disloyal—with no opportunity to defend our characters. While the committee had no punitive powers, to be subpoenaed by them was tantamount to accusation, trial, and condemnation.

And so the Committee for the First Amendment was organized in Hollywood by William Wyler, John Huston, and Philip Dunne. Dozens of Hollywood personages endorsed the committee's belief that "any investigation into the political beliefs of the individual is contrary to the basic principles of our democracy. Any attempt to curb freedom of expression and to set arbitrary standards of Americanism

With doorman at Claridges during the Robinson's London trip in 1966

On the same trip to England Eddie views a painting of Beau Nash at Bath.

Inside the Cathedral of Bath, England, Jane "shoots" Little Caesar.

On location in Kenya during the filming of *A Boy Ten Feet Tall* (1965)

Princess Margaret and her husband, Lord Snowdon, greet Eddie in the lobby during a Royal performance of *A Boy Ten Feet Tall* (1965).

Eddie with famous chef Henri Charpentier, orginator of crepe suzettes (*Sanford Roth*)

Jane and Eddie with Norton Simon, of Norton Simon Industries, also noted for his very fine art collection

On a trip to Japan Eddie strives for a quick fall with a wrestler who tops him by a few pounds.

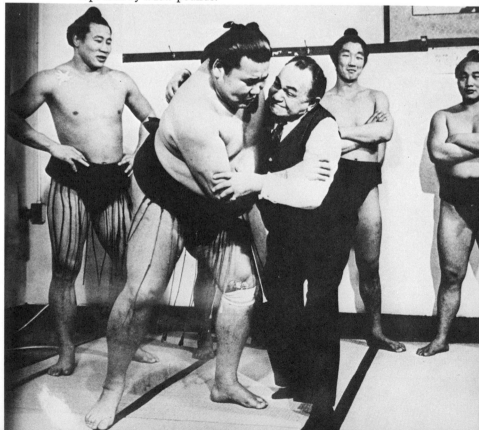

Eddie evokes smiles from some young Japanese fans.

Little Caesar in Big Caesar's Forum in Rome, 1966

Eddie with self-portrait inside his Beverly Hills home

Jane accepting the Oscar award for Eddie for his singular contribution to the film industry from Charlton Heston on the stage of the Forty-fifth Annual Awards Ceremony. Eddie had been informed of his selection for the award and until the end had hoped he could attend to receive his Oscar in person.

Jane with Leonard Spigelgass at the Academy Award Ceremony

Jane Robinson

Eddie is seen between two paintings of his art collection. "La Rue St. Honore" by Pissaro and "Nature Morte Aux Fruits" hung in a stairwell of his home. The former was painted in 1898; the latter in 1907. Eddie took time out from his acting chores on *Soylent Green* to allow photographers to shoot his famed art collection.

A painting by Eddie of his mother and himself

The garden is the scene for a chat with lifelong friend Sam Jaffe.

The library as it appeared before the second collection of paintings was sold

Entrance to Eddie's studio

Eddie is seen here reading over a script in his combined bedroom and study.

The Hatchet Man, 1932
(© First National Pictures, Inc. 1948)

The Sea Wolf, 1941 (© Warner Bros.
Pictures, Inc. 1941, copyright renewed 1968)

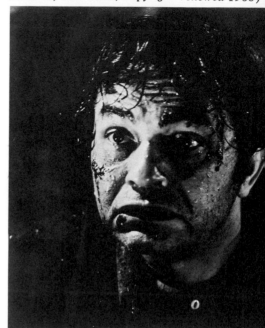

Tales of Manhattan, 1942

With Barbara Stanwyck in The Violent Men, 1955

The Ten Commandments, 1956

With Yul Brynner in *The Ten Commandments*

With Fergus McClelland in *A Boy Ten Feet Tall*, 1965

The Cincinnati Kid, 1965

With Charlton Heston in *Soylent Green,* 1972 (*M.G.M.*)

Here is Eddie in his first and 101st starring roles. He is shown (at left) in his 1931 portrayal of Little Caesar; he appears (at right) as Sol Roth in *Soylent Green,* a suspenseful, futuristic story set in New York City in the year 2022.

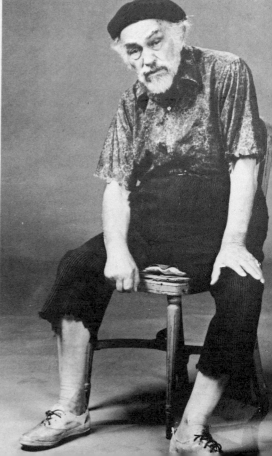

is in itself disloyal to both the spirit and the letter of the Constitution."

You can find the names in the record; I have no intention, this many years later, of stirring up hornets' nests for decent people who truly believed that the House Committee on Un-American Activities was itself engaging in the most un-American of activities. Some of them still feel that way; others do not. Time changes lots of opinions, including mine.

And I might as well air them. I was an original signer of the position of the Committee for the First Amendment. I was appalled by the behavior of that group, which came to be known as The Hollywood Ten at the Washington hearings. I was equally appalled by the behavior of some of the committee members whose insolence and arrogance seemed to me to be in the best tradition of fascism. I was sickened by the testimony of the Friendly Witnesses, by such people as Adolphe Menjou and Ginger Rogers' mother, who insisted that Hollywood was the center of a dedicated Communist cell to destroy the nation. (Words mine, distilled from hours of testimony.)

I waited to be subpoenaed. I was not.

It was almost worse not to be. Had they asked me the sixty-four-thousand-dollar question, my answer would have been easy: No.

It is embarrassing and boot-licking and sickening to me today to have to say, "No, I am not and have never been a member of the Communist party nor any other organization or organizations dedicated to the overthrow of the American government by force." But I wanted to say it then; I wanted to shout it from the housetops because then I would be able to say some other things as well. "How dare you suggest that only Communists care about the victims of the Nazis and Negroes, the Okies, the discrimination, Sacco and Vanzetti, Billings and Mooney, the (to use President Eisenhower's later words in a later context) corporate and military complex. How dare you suggest that a decent concern for humanity is communism!"

But nobody gave me a chance to say anything. The Hollywood Ten were cited for and convicted of contempt; and suspicion and gossip-mongering spread its clammy hand over all of Hollywood. The committee even came out here and had its Roman holiday.

If I am bitter, let me say in these waning years of my life that my bitterness extends from those liars who were indeed Communists to those 1000-percent Americans who were indeed Fascists.

One morning I received an invitation to appear on Monday, May 19, 1947, as one of the principal speakers at the Chicago Stadium, an event sponsored by the Chicago *Herald–American*, a Hearst news-

paper. I was delighted to accept. Here, at last, was a chance to speak
out in the presence of thousands and the other speakers: General
Kenney, commander of the Strategic Air Command; the governor of
Illinois, Dwight H. Green; Martin Kennelly, mayor of Chicago; His
Eminence, Samuel Cardinal Stritch, Roman Catholic archbishop of
Chicago; the Reverend Dr. Ray Freeman Jenny, president of the
Church Federation of Greater Chicago; Dr. Shimaryahu T. Swirsky,
representing the Chicago Rabbinical Council; and Joe E. Brown, Phil
Regan, Marilyn Maxwell, Bebe Daniels, Ben Lyon, and Dale Evans.
Oh yes, and me.

Five hundred new citizens were to be sworn in. It all seemed a little
corny and cliché, but I was glad to be invited because it was a
forum.

And then I received a telegram disinviting me. I was informed that
I was "not acceptable." Christ knows, I knew what that meant.

Attorneys advised inaction; agents suggested that any protest on
my part would only involve further unpleasant propaganda. By this
time I was sick and tired of that line of reasoning. Every time I'd
wanted to sue for accusation of a Communist association, I was advised it would only spread the virus, that I could not prove damages,
that, in legal fact, no one had ever called me a Communist out and
out, that the accusations were inferential, and that a suit to be rid of
them would make them more than inferential and give enemies a
witness box to denounce me and my record. And my record, according to the best counsel, was shaky at best, and incriminating at worst
—that is to say: The organizations to which I had belonged were, by
testimony, shown to have been infiltrated or partly infiltrated by
Communist party members. I was told to do nothing.

I did something. I remembered that I had a relationship with William Randolph Hearst—tenuous, long-ago, and one he probably
didn't even know about. But I wrote him the following letter: *

THIS WEEK I HAD AN EXPERIENCE INVOLVING THE CHICAGO HERALD-AMERICAN WHICH I FEEL
SHOULD BE BROUGHT TO YOUR ATTENTION.

A REPRESENTATIVE OF THE PAPER CAME TO HOLLYWOOD TO ARRANGE FOR THE APPEARANCE OF
A NUMBER OF MOTION PICTURE PERSONALITIES AT I AM AN AMERICAN DAY IN CHICAGO AND CALLED
UPON A MUTUAL FRIEND TO ASK FOR MY ATTENDANCE. AS YOU KNOW, I AM VITALLY INTERESTED

* Note from L.S.: It's clear that E.G.R. wrote first drafts of letters and kept
them. This is clearly such a first draft with corrections by E.G.R.

IN SUCH OCCASIONS, HAVE TAKEN PART IN THEM BEFORE, AND SINCERELY BELIEVE IN THEM. THE
PAPER'S REPRESENTATIVE ASSURED OUR MUTUAL FRIEND THAT MY PRESENCE WAS DESIRED AND I
MADE ARRANGEMENTS TO FLY TO CHICAGO ESPECIALLY FOR THE OCCASION, RETURNING TO MY WORK
HERE IMMEDIATELY FOLLOWING THE CEREMONY.

HOWEVER, THE FOLLOWING DAY I WAS NOTIFIED THAT I WAS "NOT ACCEPTABLE" TO THE
MANAGEMENT OF THE PAPER.

NOW, I KNOW, MR. HEARST, THAT I HAVE BEEN SMEARED BY NASTY RUMORS BECAUSE OF MY
SUPPORT OF PRESIDENT ROOSEVELT, BUT I AM SURE THAT SUCH SUPPORT IS NO MORE A REFLECTION
ON MY PATRIOTISM THAN MY CAMPAIGNING FOR YOU WHEN YOU RAN AGAINST MCCLELLAN FOR MAYOR
OF NEW YORK A ~~FEW YEARS AGO.~~ *some thirty years ago —*

AS A MATTER OF FACT, THIS EARLY INTEREST IN POLITICS ON MY PART WAS SOMETHING OF
A TURNING POINT IN MY CAREER. I WAS AN IMMIGRANT BOY IN KNEE PANTS HAVING ARRIVED IN
THIS COUNTRY ONLY THREE YEARS BEFORE. YOU REPRESENTED TO ME ALL THAT MY FATHER SOUGHT
WHEN HE BROUGHT HIS FAMILY OF SIX CHILDREN TO THIS COUNTRY FROM RUMANIA. I BEGAN
MAKING SPEECHES ON STREET CORNERS ON THE EAST SIDE AND I GUESS THAT ABOUT THE BIGGEST
THING THAT EVER HAPPENED TO ME WAS A CALL I GOT FROM YOUR HEADQUARTERS IN THE HERMITAGE
ASKING IF I WOULD SPEAK IN OTHER PARTS OF NEW YORK. AS A MATTER OF FACT, THE FIRST
AUTOMOBILE IN WHICH I EVER RODE WAS THE CAR SENT FOR ME BY YOUR CAMPAIGN HEADQUARTERS
AND MY FIRST APPEARANCE ON BROADWAY WAS IN THE AMATEURISH ROLE OF A CAMPAIGN ORATOR.

I HAD READ EVERY ONE OF BRISBANE'S EDITORIALS AND I AM SURE NO ONE WAS MORE BITTERLY
OPPOSED TO BOSS MURPHY THAN WAS I. I WAS A LIBERAL IN THOSE DAYS AS I LIKE TO FEEL I AM
A LIBERAL TODAY. I WAS OPPOSED TO BOSS MURPHY IN THE SAME SENSE THAT I AM OPPOSED TO
ANY AND ALL FORMS OF TYRANNY AND DICTATORSHIP TODAY—REGARDLESS OF WHAT "ISM" MIGHT AT-
TACH ITSELF TO THAT TYRANNY OR DICTATORSHIP. I BELIEVED THEN AS I DO TODAY THAT EVERY
MAN SHOULD HAVE A RELIGION AND THAT IT SHOULD BE HIS RIGHT TO CHOOSE THAT RELIGION; THAT
EVERY MAN SHOULD HAVE THE RIGHT TO SPEAK AND THINK FREELY WITHIN THE FRAMEWORK OF OUR
AMERICAN CONSTITUTION; THAT THERE IS NOTHING SUBVERSIVE OR UNAMERICAN IN DIFFERING FROM
ONE'S FELLOW MAN ON SUCH MATTERS AS PERSONALITIES AND POLITICS WHICH MAKE UP OUR AMERICAN
FORM OF GOVERNMENT. AND FOR THE RECORD, LET ME STATE THAT I THINK IT IS THE FINEST
FORM OF GOVERNMENT YET DEVISED BY MAN AND I INTEND TO SUPPORT IT WITH ALL THE MEANS
AT MY COMMAND.

I SERVED IN THE NAVY IN WORLD WAR I. I WENT TO ENGLAND IN WORLD WAR II AND SPENT
SEVERAL WEEKS THERE DURING THE "BLITZ" AS AN ACCREDITED OFFICER OF OWI. I WAS THE
FIRST HOLLYWOOD ACTOR TO FOLLOW THE TROOPS INTO NORMANDY. IT WAS MY PRIVILEGE TO
INAUGURATE ONE OF THE USO DRIVES WITH A CONTRIBUTION OF $100,000. MY WIFE DISTINGUISHED
HERSELF BY HER WORK WITH THE "DESERT BATALLION" WHEN MORALE BUILDING WAS SUCH AN IM-

PORTANT FACTOR TO THOSE TROOPS BEING TRAINED IN THE FAR WEST. ALL OF THESE CONTRIBU-
TIONS WE CONSIDERED BUT LITTLE DOWN PAYMENTS FOR THE PRIVILEGE OF BEING AND AMERICANS

I HAVE BEEN CITED BY THE GOVERNMENT, THE AMERICAN LEGION, AND MANY OTHER PATRIOTIC
ORGANIZATIONS ON NUMEROUS OCCASIONS. I LOOK UPON THESE CITATIONS MERELY AS CONFIRMATION
AND ASSURANCE OF MY OWN BELIEF IN AMERICA AND I AM HUMBLY PROUD THAT "I AM AN AMERICAN."
I CITE THESE FACTORS, MR. HEARST, MERELY FOR YOUR INFORMATION AS I AM SURE THERE IS
NOT A GREAT DEAL OF DIFFERENCE BETWEEN US IN OUR REGARD FOR THE FUNDAMENTALS OF AMERI-
CANISM. WE MAY FOLLOW DIFFERENT POLITICAL PARTIES AT THE MOMENT. WE MAY HAVE A
HEALTHY RESPECT FOR DIFFERENT POLITICAL LEADERS AND WE MAY CONDEMN DIFFERENT PRACTICES
WHICH HAVE GROWN UP UNDER OUR SYSTEM OF DEMOCRATIC GOVERNMENT, BUT I AM SURE THERE CAN
BE NO DISAGREEMENT BETWEEN US ON THE PRINCIPAL ISSUE—OUR BELIEF IN THE AMERICAN FORM
OF GOVERNMENT AS SET UP IN OUR CONSTITUTION.

I AM SORRY THAT MY UNPLEASANT EXPERIENCE IN CONNECTION WITH SUCH A FINE INSTITUTION
AS I AM AN AMERICAN DAY NECESSITATED MY BRINGING THIS MATTER TO YOUR ATTENTION AND I
HOPE THAT IT WILL MAKE FOR A BETTER UNDERSTANDING ALL AROUND.

RESPECTFULLY YOURS,

I had no direct reply from Mr. Hearst.

But Howard Mayer, a publicity man I had hired, did. He received the following telegram:

Charge to the account of _____ $ _____

WESTERN UNION

JOSEPH L. EGAN
PRESIDENT

1206

CHECK

ACCOUNTING INFORMATION

TIME FILED

Send the following telegram, subject to the terms on back hereof, which are hereby agreed to

MAY 16, 1947

SA408 DL PD—AM CHICAGO ILL 16 220P

HOWARD MAYER
6331 HOLLYWOOD LOSA—

PLEASE OFFER MY APOLOGIES TO MR ROBINSON FOR WHAT HAS BEEN AN UNFORTUNATE MISUNDERSTANDING.
I DID NOT UNDERSTAND THAT MR. ROBINSON WAS AVAILABLE OR WE WOULD CERTAINLY HAVE HAD HIM ON THE
LIST TO SAY THAT HE IS UNACCEPTABLE IS RIDICULOUS. I HOPE YOU CAN INDUCE HIM TO COME. REGARDS—

R. H. WILEY

It was not difficult for him to persuade me to appear. I went to Chicago; the *Herald-American* emblazoned my appearance in enormous headlines and printed my speech in full.

I have no intention of boring you with it. You've heard it a million times: "Love America with that special, special appreciation of millions . . . not born on this American earth, but who emigrated here. . . . This country and this people won't fail its destiny. . . . We want every last American to enjoy the fruits of this land—a home, work, education for the children . . . to worship in a church of his own choosing . . . tolerance . . . democracy . . . rights. . . ."

I was a smash.

Roy Topper, editor of the *Herald-American*, wrote: "Your message touched the hearts of everyone in the Stadium and today the reaction is one of overwhelming enthusiasm. . . ."

Okay, I now thought, that's that. I've made my position clear, and the horror is over.

It had just begun.

So back to work—in a picture of which I am inordinately proud: *All My Sons*, from the play by the great Arthur Miller. It was a part I played with such passion and intensity that the director, Irving Reis, told me constantly to take it easy. He also called me One-Take Eddie because rarely did I ever have to repeat a scene. And my passion imbued the whole cast. No need to imbue Mady Christians, a superb actress. No need either to imbue Burt Lancaster, playing in perhaps his second or third film but showing that animal vitality and suppressed volcano inside that inevitably made him a star.

Miller had written a play in which a father keeps a secret from a son. In my lonely domestic life I was keeping secrets from my son, not wanting to tell him of the inevitable estrangement between his mother and myself and the reason for it: mental illness. And Manny was keeping secrets from me—his liking for the bottle. Gladys was hospitalized or in Paris or some place, and her letters were, in turn, denouncements and endearments. It seemed to me I was being sued for divorce once a year, but she'd always change her mind.

Next time around, I thought, maybe I wouldn't change my mind—but not until the boy grew up. Oh, God, let's try to keep it all going until the boy finds himself.

Meanwhile, Warner's, thinking me absolutely clear of the Red smear, came to me with a script of *Key Largo*, produced by chubby, irrepressible Jerry Wald, directed by John Huston, based on the play by Maxwell Anderson, and with a screenplay by Anderson and a guy who's as feisty, individual, unpredictable, and honest as any man I've ever known: Richard Brooks.

A slight thing from my agent (now eagerly answering my phone calls again). There was "this-er-minor-er-sort-of-er-nothing problem." Could be straightened out in a minute. Didn't mean a hill of beans. I mean, what the hell is billing after all?

"Okay, what the hell is it?"

"Well, Eddie, baby, it's not like it was under the title or anything like that."

"Then what the hell is it?"

"Well, it's-er—you know, times change, and those crazy Warner bastards want to give Bogie top billing and you second."

The journey down. No suspense to this. I didn't even argue. Why not second billing? At fifty-three I was lucky to get any billing at all.

Let me tell you something about Bogie. On that set *he* gave it all to me. Second billing or no, I got the star treatment because he insisted upon it—not in words but in action. When asked to come on the set, he would ask: "Is Mr. Robinson ready?" He'd come to my trailer dressing room to get me. Lionel Barrymore was in the picture, and we both gave *him* the deference he deserved. Certainly we were all very conscious of Claire Trevor's position and dignity. But if you really want to know who got the A-one eighteen-carat bowing, it was Lauren Bacall; we were in the middle of romance, and that gets the highest priority always.

I followed immediately with a picture called *Night Has a Thousand Eyes*, unadulterated hokum that I did for the money. Then there was a picture called *House of Strangers* for Fox, directed by Joe Mankiewicz. I loved it.

Good thing I did, because suddenly the whole goddamn roof fell in again.

26

I remember one of the loveliest nights I ever spent in this house. The Arturo Toscaninis and the Vladimir Horowitzes came to dinner, and the six of us had a splendid feast in the dining room—white asparagus, chateaubriand, the finest wines, and a miraculous soufflé. The whole house was lit beautifully, and Gladys kept the conversation going splendidly. Afterward we went into the living room for coffee, and the pictures never looked so startlingly wonderful and alive. The Toscaninis were absolutely in love with a Berthe Morisot. As they stood there admiring it, my first instinct was to take it off the wall and present it to Toscanini with: "Maestro, for all the pleasure you've given me in my life, accept this as a small token of my esteem."

But Emanuel Goldenberg said to Edward G., "Give away a Morisot? Are you crazy?" And I curbed my generous impulse.

When Dalton Trumbo wrote me from prison (I am trying to find the letter) that his family, as a result of his jailing for contempt of Congress, was in serious financial difficulties and would I lend him $2500, I compassionately sent his wife a check.*

That brought the vultures down around my neck.

Let me give you a small idea of what happened. Victor Lasky, a newspaperman, publicist, and ardent antagonist of communism (a role he shared with George Sokolsky and Victor Riesel, both newspaper-

---

* Note from L.S.: We have not yet been able to find it, but I have another letter from Trumbo's wife acknowledging it; also, copies of E.G.R.'s letters asking for repayment.

men with large followings) came to me and chided me about my folly for having sent this check to the Trumbo family and clucked even more over my intensive affiliation with Communist front organizations. He was particularly miserable about my association with the American Committee for the Protection of Foreign Born, which he assured me was a Communist-dominated front, thus implying that its active members, including Reinhold Niebuhr, Dorothy Thompson, and William Allen White, were either Communists or dupes.

Dupes. Yes, that was the word. All I had to do to clear myself of all these charges, new and old, was to admit publicly and in print that I was a dupe. And he, Victor Lasky, would write it all out for me and secure its publication in some nice conservative journal like, I supposed, *American Legion Magazine*.

He prepared twenty-six pages of my dupedom. I only had to read one page to feel the urge to throw up.

I told Mr. Lasky politely and firmly that I wished no part of his attempt to set the world straight, though firms of lawyers I had engaged in New York and in Los Angeles were not at all sure it wasn't a good idea. The piece he fashioned made me out a fool who out of brainlessness and an overzealous consideration for mankind had been blindly led into organizations that wished to destroy America.

What was the real truth? In the Trumbo case it was very simple. A couple of human beings were in want; father and husband was in jail paying for his crime, if any; the deepest impulse to help the unfortunate drove me to write that check. Had I thought it wicked or indeed a secret and underhanded contribution to the Communist party, I could well have given them the money in cash, unrecorded, untraceable. No such thing. I did it openly.

How it came to be a matter of such public knowledge is puzzling, to say the least. I have some theories, and they are equally unpleasant —about the party and the antiparty groups. However, since I have no clear evidence, and there are proper laws concerning slander and libel, I will say nothing except that I think I was set up. By whom? I don't know. For what reason? I don't know. To what end? Oh, the answer to that one's simple: to destroy me.

And, of course, it almost did. I still had a few films left, one of them a guest appearance in an all-star piece of baloney called *It's a Great Feeling*, starring Dennis Morgan and Doris Day and with a whole bunch of stars playing themselves: Gary Cooper, Joan Crawford, Danny Kaye, and Ronnie Reagan. Imagine, Ronnie Reagan! (Of course, at that time, I think he was still a Democrat.)

Late in 1949 I went to London to make a picture in England. There it was called *My Daughter Joy*. In this country it was called

Operation X. In either country it should have been called unspeakable.

Then the drought set in. I became an absolute pariah. The only thing I could do if I wanted work was to return to the stage.

Go back on the stage? Could I? Dared I? No. It was out of the question.

Yet I was approached. Sidney Kingsley had written a play based on Arthur Koestler's *Darkness at Noon*, about an old Bolshevik called a traitor and imprisoned and condemned by the new order of Bolsheviks. I searched my soul. Could I do it? Or would it be too obvious for me to appear now in an anti-Communist play; would it be a kind of inverse confession, even though, God knows, I had nothing to confess?

After an agonizing reappraisal (a phrase for which I thank John Foster Dulles) I sent my regrets. Claude Rains, that beautiful actor, played it instead, and it was a hit.

What about Gladys and my son throughout all of this? Well, Gladys was suing for divorce, and attorneys were attempting to work out a settlement. Under California law the settlement would involve the sale of all our joint assets, and that meant the pictures and the house. I fought that, but it was like fighting shadows because Gladys was in a sanitarium and no further action could be devised until she was considered well enough to reach her own conclusions.

My son? He was out on his own now, wanting to be an actor and seeking solace from new friends and a new profession and, I suspect, a new bottle.

I turned inward. I searched my soul for the truth.

Was I a Communist? Really, Eddie, answer that one. Were you? Are you? And the answer always came out the same: No.

Then *somebody* must believe you. Somebody, anybody, some agency of government must be able to say loud and clear to the world: "This man is not a subversive."

Eventually I gained the right to speak three times before the House Committee on Un-American Activities, and I shall get to that in a short time, but first I think you are entitled to the case for the prosecution. There is so much anti–Edward G. Robinson material that I think it best if I simply republish a pamphlet entitled *Red Star over Hollywood* by Oliver Carlson, published by the Catholic Information Society, 214 West Thirty-first Street, New York City 10001. I have tried to get in touch with this publishing concern, but I am told it is long since out of business. I can see no reason why they should object to its republication since it is absolutely verbatim and I have not changed a word. It follows, edited only to avoid repetition. You can

come to no decision about me until you let Mr. Carlson have his
say.

Here it is:

Red Star over Hollywood
BY
OLIVER CARLSON

Every time the charge of Communist influence and intrigue in the
motion picture industry is made, there are the familiar outcries of
"red-baiting." But in addition there is a good deal of honest disbe-
lief, even among people who oppose Communism and know the extent
of its infiltration in American institutions. "How silly," they say in
substance, "to suppose that people who earn hundreds, and even
thousands, of dollars a week would have any truck with the Muscovite
movement!". . .

A mountain of facts is available today, with names, dates and
places given, to prove that the Communist Party has scored some of
its most notable victories in the movie field. This is not accidental.
Soviet leaders from the start recognized the value of the screen in
their worldwide propaganda and therefore made the conquest of
Hollywood one of their major objectives. . . .

During the gay 1920's and early 1930's, motion picture people knew
little and cared less about social, economic and political problems. But
by 1932, with the depression at its depth, the Communist Party finally
opened a few Hollywood doors. Its success was so easy that it followed
up in force. Top-flight Party propagandists were sent out to carry the
Red gospel to benighted California.

By 1935 "social consciousness," as it was called, had really hit
movieland in a big way. Always a sucker for the latest fads and
fancies, Hollywood embraced the Kremlin doctrines with rapturous
enthusiasm. . . .

There was a decline in the strength of the Red contingents in movieland in the 22-month period when the Hitler–Stalin Pact was in
force, though even then hundreds of Hollywood notables remained
faithful to the imported cause. But when Russia, by Hitler's rather
than Stalin's decision, became our ally, business boomed bigger than
ever for the comrades. . . .

Since the war ended, the Communists have managed to keep their
hold on the movie capital, though there have been some defections.
The anti-Communist trend felt in the rest of the country has been
exceedingly slow in reaching Hollywood.

* * *

What have the Communists gained in the movie industry?

In the first place, there is indisputable evidence that Hollywood
has been a gold mine as far as finances are concerned. The contributions to Red causes have been on a typically lush movie scale. In three

months, from May 14 to August 16, 1939, a single Red front organization, the Hollywood Anti-Nazi League, deposited $89,892 in its account. That gives the measure.

After careful investigation, a writer for the Hollywood *Citizen News* in 1940 declared that in his belief more than two million dollars had been drawn out of the city for Communist causes at that time. Personally I think his figure is decidedly an under-estimate. . . .

It is no secret that Hollywood gold made possible the launching of the Communist daily paper, *The People's World*, in San Francisco. Nor is it a secret that scores of Communists have been on the payrolls of numerous "front organizations, their salaries paid by Hollywood money. . . .

Names like Edward G. Robinson—to take a notorious example of an actor who has sponsored literally dozens of Red undertakings and organizations—gain for Red enterprises an audience a hundred thousand times greater than any avowed Communist can muster. And such names have been standard on all pro-Soviet and Red-dominated lists.

Naturally, the stars, movie writers, directors and the like who lend themselves to Stalinist purposes deny vehemently that they are Communists or fellow-travelers. Many of them, indeed, make the denial honestly; they have been sucked into the various causes and organizations without quite understanding who pulls the strings—under the tragic impression that they were thus being "liberal" and "progressive." . . .

. . . the Communists and their stooges have made serious inroads among the Guilds and labor unions in Hollywood. Job control in such a vital industry, affecting tens of thousands of workers, would be a major victory. Small wonder therefore that the comrades spare no effort in this domain.

In the last few years the Communists, though a small minority in terms of membership, have by their tactics and discipline succeeded in dominating the Screen Writers Guild, the Screen Publicists Guild, the Screen Analysis Guild; and have occupied a strong, though minority, position within the Screen Actors and Screen Directors Guild. The power and influence that can be wielded through such groups are obvious. . . .

So many special pressure organizations have been set up by the Communists and their victims in the last fifteen years that it would require pages just to list them. When an organization has served its purpose, it is scrapped and another takes its place.

Such was the case, for instance, with the Hollywood Anti-Nazi League, into which thousands of genuine anti-Nazis were drawn and hundreds of thousands of dollars were pumped. When the Hitler–Stalin Pact in August, 1939, obliged the Communists to cease their anti-Nazi work, this Hollywood organization, claiming 4,000 members, was quickly shelved.

Other organizations have included the Hollywood Film & Foto

League, the Hollywood Peace Council and Hollywood Peace Forum (creatures both of the Hitler–Stalin Pact period, used to sabotage American preparedness), the Hollywood Writers Congress—which in turn was part of the Communist-directed American Writers Congress. Then there was the Hollywood Independent Citizens Committee of Arts, Sciences and Professions; and more recently the Hollywood Writers Mobilization, and the Mobilization for Democracy, which at this writing is being used to rally Communist strength around Henry Wallace in California.

In addition, of course, there have been Hollywood branches of the nationwide pro-Soviet organizations, such as the League for Peace and Democracy, the American Peace Mobilization, the Council for American-Soviet Friendship and the rest. . . .

No serious effort to fight the plague was made until recent years. In 1943, however, there came into being the Motion Picture Alliance for the Preservation of American Ideals. From its inception this group was made up of people from every branch of the motion picture industry. There were lowly script girls and common laborers, along with top-flight writers, actors, and producers. There were Catholics, Protestants and Jews; native Americans and foreign-born citizens, employers and employees. They all united on a common dedication including this pledge:

> As members of the motion picture industry, we must face and accept an especial responsibility. Motion pictures are inescapably one of the world's great forces for influencing public thought and opinion, both at home and abroad. We refuse to permit the effort of Communist, Fascist and other totalitarian-minded groups to pervert this powerful medium into an instrument for the dissemination of un-American ideas and beliefs.

The Alliance counts among its members such well-known figures as Walt Disney, Clarence Brown, Sam Wood, Norman Taurog, James K. McGuinness, Morrie Ryskind, Clark Gable, Gary Cooper, Robert Taylor, Adolphe Menjou and a host of others who, as a matter of fact, are more representative of Hollywood than the pro-Communist contingent. . . .

The direct Communist influence on the screen, insofar as the output of pictures is concerned, has been limited to a handful of productions such as *Mission to Moscow, Song of Russia, North Star*, where the pro-Moscow bias is undisguised; and a few others, like *The Best Years of Our Lives*, in which the Communist "line" is fairly evident. . . .

The Motion Picture Alliance, in one of its bulletins, summed up the essential menace as it affects the screen:

> Communist propaganda is not done—as the naive imagine—by blatant slogans or appeals to revolution and violence.

> That comes much later. First, the groundwork has to be laid
> by making people accept the ideas, the basic premises, of
> Communism. This is done by making us swallow such no-
> tions as: all the rich are swindlers and exploiters, while all
> the poor are noble; every successful man is vicious, while all
> the incompetents are virtuous; anything done by an inde-
> pendent man is evil, but anything done by "the masses" is
> good; and, no man, life, emotion, purpose or motive has any
> value or right to exist, except those that serve a "social
> objective."

I prepared a list—thoroughly and totally researched—of every organization to which I had ever belonged. My accountants and I searched through every check to show every contribution I had ever made; I copied letters received by me for contributions and the use of my name; I attached thereto all my replies. This entire bundle of information I personally sent to J. Edgar Hoover in the hope that I would receive a letter from him clearing me or at least telling me of what other dire crimes I had been accused of by unknown witnesses, giving unknown testimony before unknown government bodies.

Do I appear to be making myself a martyr? It seeems that way to me now, too. Twenty-six years later I ask myself why I went to all that trouble, why I went through all that pain, so intense, I cannot describe it.

Maybe one of the reasons is that I received merely a form reply from Mr. Hoover's office. Maybe it was because I could get no work. Maybe it was because it appeared I might have to sell the pictures to live. Maybe because my passport expired and I was denied a new one. No passport, and no reason for not being able to get one—except to whom are passports denied? To traitors, that's who.

Hear me! Somebody! God in heaven, to whom do I turn? Call me as a witness. Probe me. Ask me questions. Swear me in. I will testify under oath.

The House Committee on Un-American Activities refused to call me. There were no accusations against me.

No accusations! What do you call *Red Channels* and *Counterattack* and *Red Star over Hollywood*? What do you call Billy Wilkerson's editorials? What do you term the things that Gerald L. K. Smith was calling me? What is the name for the slurs with which the Motion Picture Alliance for the Preservation of American Ideals was blackening my name?

I had lawyers by the score and public relations people. I have files stuffed with my letters and their answers. And still nothing happened.

In a report on *Blacklisting: Movies*, written by John Cogley for the

Fund for the Republic and as objective a study of the times as you can find, Cogley writes:

> By 1951 a number of prominent persons were begging the Committee for a chance to testify and the Committee had to disappoint some of them. There were, first of all, the ex-Communists, who by now looked upon the hearings as the only public forum open to them. If they wanted to prove to the world that they had broken with the Party, they had to testify. And until they did prove this, they were unemployable in the studios. The Committee welcomed them.
>
> But another class—persons who had never belonged to the Communist Party but suffered from unfavorable rumors—were also eager to go on record as anti-Communist. Many wanted to be heard but, according to [Raphael I.] Nixon, Edward G. Robinson, _____ _____ and the late John Garfield were the only three called where the Committee had no proof of Party membership, past or present. Robinson requested a hearing. Garfield and _____ were subpoenaed because they had been "the subject of considerable interest on the part of private organizations."
>
> At first the Committee wanted Garfield and _____ to testify in private sessions. "But," Nixon said, "we were catching it all over— from George Sokolsky, Victor Riesel and even from Ed Sullivan. No one came right out in print and said so, but there were intimations of payoffs. Mr. Moulder (Congressman from Missouri) was subjected to criticism for stating that he thought Garfield was "all right." Nixon also recalls that at the time some inexperienced anti-Communist groups were given to making loose, unsubstantiated charges, and the Committee drew fire for not acting on the "leads" these groups provided. From the other extremity, the Committee was attacked for "establishing blacklists."

For my chance to appear and testify I owe everything to Sam Yorty, mayor of Los Angeles. Through his intervention I first appeared in Washington in the impressive Hearing Room on October 27, 1947. Congressman Francis Walter of Pennsylvania was chairman. The committee included in its membership Congressman Donald Jackson, of my own 16th District in California.

For hours I was asked questions about every organization to which I ever belonged. Finally, I could stand it no longer, and in the end I became emotional. Mr. Louis J. Russell,* senior investigator for the

In January 1954 Mr. Russell was dismissed from his $11,600-a-year post by the Committee Chairman Representative Harold E.

* Note from L.S.: Mr. Russell died on July 4, 1973. His obituary, which appeared in *The New York Times* for that date, reads in part as follows:

> Belde, Republican of Illinois. His discharge was initially attributed
> to an internal struggle between factions of the Committee. It later
> developed that Mr. Russell had borrowed $300 from Edward G.
> Robinson, the film actor, who had appeared as a friendly witness
> before the Committee's inquiry into the Communist infiltration of
> the film industry.

committee, hammered at me, and I finally burst out: "You are the
only tribunal we have in the United States where an American citizen
can come and ask for this kind of relief; and after you have looked
over this rather exhaustive testimony that I have presented to the
committee, if you should like any further information, just the same
as I volunteered it to Mr. Hoover, I volunteer it to you; and if you
find me innocent, I would like to ask that you give these facts to the
American people because my name is very dear to me, above everything else. I ask in all sincerity that you do this for me because this is
the most vital thing I have ever faced in my life. I am sorry if I have
become a little bit emotional."

MR. WALTER: "It is perfectly understandable."

MR.ROBINSON: "Because I think I have not only been a good
citizen. I think I have been an extraordinarily good citizen and I value
this above everything else. . . . I think I may have taken money under
false pretenses in my own business, and I may not have been as good
a husband or father or friend as I should have been, but I know my
Americanism is unblemished and fine and wonderful, and I am proud
of it, and I don't feel it is conceit on my part to say this, and I stand
on my record or fall on it."

"Stand on my record or fall on it."
I stood and I fell.
Nothing happened. No doors opened. No jobs offered.
And so I appeared again before the Committee on December 21,
1950. It was a short session. Mr. Russell asked me a lot of questions. I
merely repeated over and over again that I was not and had never
been a member of the Communist party.
What the hell good was all that? In my view, looking at the situation from the vantage point of many years, what they wanted me to
say was that I was a dupe, a sucker, a fool, an idiot, that I'd been
double-crossed, that everthing I believed in was negated by the clubs
to which I belonged—that I was a tool, an unsuspecting agent of the
Communist conspiracy. I didn't say it because I didn't believe it.
The third time round, two years later, I said it.
My defenses were down and I said it. My judgment was warped
and I said it. My heart was sick and I said it.

At the end of my third appearance on April 30, 1952, Mr. Walter, chairman of the committee, made this comment: "Well, actually this committee has never had any evidence presented to indicate that you were anything more than a very choice sucker. I think you are number one on the sucker list in the country." A moment or two later the committee stood adjourned.

But in the two years between my second and third personal appearances in Washington this number-one sucker was faced with decisions so rocking and convulsive that only his rough Rumanian genes prevented him from suffering cardiac arrest.

27

Back in Hollywood, in 1950, there were clearly no more films; nobody would dare touch the sucker. As for radio, I made two appearances on the *Screen Director's Playhouse*, and that was only because the program was controlled by sympathetic and understanding people. But each appearance, let me tell you, was a hassle. Apart from that, nothing.

Oh, yes, there was something. Gladys was home in one of her rare periods of composure and security. No talk of divorce now. She was standing by. Was she cured? I could hardly believe it possible, yet it seemed so.

We had small dinner parties—small because I didn't want to spend the money on large ones. You'd be surprised at the names of the people who had other dates or headaches or appointments they couldn't possibly break. You'd be surprised, too, at the names of the people who came. I will name neither one group nor the other—the first because I understand their not wanting to be associated with a man called Communist, the second because their loyalty may, even today, cause them some trouble.*

Meanwhile, in New York Claude Rains had been appearing for over 150 performances in Sidney Kingsley's *Darkness at Noon*. He was exhausted and could not make the national tour. The Playwrights

---

* Note from L.S.: E.G.R. could not bear to think that friendship with him would cause others to be suspected. The truth is many of us rallied to him. Oh, "rallied" is a terrible word. We loved him, and since he asked me not to mention their names, I won't. But there were dozens.

Company, of which Robert Sherwood, one of my dear and good friends, was a member, sent me the script and begged me to take it on.

As a play it had one enormous virtue; if public relations were what I cared about, it was distinctly and thoroughly anti-Communist.

It had another virtue, which was at the same time a drawback; Rubashov, the lead, was hardly ever off the stage. It was a long and grueling part. I would be required to play an ex-commissar of the people, ex-member of the central committee, ex-general of the Red Army, bearer of the Order of the Red Banner, now disgraced, humiliated, imprisoned, and eventually sentenced to death. Arthur Koestler, who had written the original novel from which Sidney had dramatized the play, was, in a sense, prophesying the period in which Stalin himself would be made an unperson by the new heirs of the Soviet presidium. Even more certainly, he was writing of the great purge trials that shook the Soviet system to its base.

I read and reread the play and realized it was a great part. What I wondered in the dead of night as I acted it out, was—could I play it? Could I, after twenty-odd years, go back on the stage? And, if I were going to do this wrenching thing—this return to my first love—was it not insulting to do it on the road? They were calling it a national company, but I knew very well that it was a euphemism for road company. Had I not a thousand years ago decided I would be not a road actor but a Broadway actor?

I consulted with Gladys. Her mind was clear. If I intended to return to the stage, better to do it out of town and not face the New York critics. These new boys were bound to think of me as a movie star, and movie stars on Broadway were the kiss of death. That made sense. Besides, the money was good. And anyway, what else was there for me to do? At the age of fifty-seven–fifty-eight, could I open a candy store? Or could I answer Gletkin as Rubashov did on the last page of *Darkness at Noon?*

> Gletkin: Have you any last wish?
> Rubashov: To die.

> *Gletkin motions him to walk. Rubashov moves slowly out of the cell. Gletkin takes out his pistol, cocks it, and follows. The guard opens the gate to the cellar, a shaft of light coming up catches them. From all over the prison comes the hollowed muffling drumming which mounts higher and higher as Rubashov and Gletkin descend and the iron gates clang behind them.*

> THE CURTAIN FALLS

For me, the drumming reached a climax as the CURTAIN ROSE in Princeton, New Jersey. Yes, I had decided to do the play—since clearly there was no alternative—and had returned to New York to rehearse with the cast that had already played its 163 performances. Sidney Kingsley continued to be his own director, and he was politeness and kindness and civility all in one—except after the first reading.

It seemed to me he wanted me to give a carbon copy of the Claude Rains performance. I saw Rubashov differently from Rains; maybe I was bringing something of myself into it. Claude had not been born in Rumania; Claude was not a Jew; Claude could not possibly understand the agony of a world turned against him—and that was an experience I was still going through.

As a result, Sidney Kingsley and I had violent fights not only about the words but about the staging, the attitudes, the playing. I think the cast and Kingsley thought I was a stubborn, egomaniac movie star who wanted things my own way, and now that I look back on it, I can see that that was a strong possibility. In rehearsal I thought I was fighting for the play.

I will not say Sidney and I hated each other; hate is too strong a word.* God knows, we were at odds.

Then came the opening night in Princeton. What had worried Sidney the most, I think, was that I could not remember the words, that after twenty-eight years of fragmented motion pictures, I could not sustain. I was pretty certain he was wrong; all my actor training came back. I thought I was in command. I'd show him.

The curtain went up. I had my first speech. You couldn't hear me. I had a croak for a voice. I had laryngitis—psychological laryngitis. For ten minutes we went on like this, and I knew I was not courting disaster; the disaster had already occurred. A vision of the night I'd played in Yiddish with Rudolph Schildkraut came to me—the night I couldn't remember the words on stage and he'd sloughed it off with, "If you'd asked me, I'd have told you."

So I did the only thing possible: I stopped the action, went to the apron of the stage, and addressed the audience. I can't remember what I said exactly, but I think it was, "I'm having trouble with my

* Note from L.S.: Among E.G.R.'s papers, I found a warm and enthusiastic congratulatory wire from Sidney. I have not talked to Sidney about it, but I believe this playwright–actor feud was standard operating procedure—made worse by all those performances Kingsley had so carefully etched out with Rains—made even worse by E.G.R.'s eternal fear of returning to the stage. I have known the same problems when one actress took over from another. It is one of the inevitable crises of the theater—soon forgotten.

voice, but it's getting better. I think we're going to start the play all over again, if it's all right with you."

It was all right with them. The curtain rang down, I sprayed my throat, reassured the puzzled and terrified cast, nodded to the stage manager, and we began again. We went through to the end of the third act, and then I heard that noise that makes an actor a thousand feet tall: applause! Bravos!

I played *Darkness at Noon* for a year on the road. Let me tell you about the audiences, because in New York and Hollywood we get so involved with ourselves and our problems that we forget about the rest of the country.

Sure, there were crank letters accusing me of being a Communist —and even an occasional "Boo." But during that whole tour, do you know who I was? Edward G. Robinson, movie star, that's who I was. I was a ranking celebrity, entertained, adored, given adulation and deference, and it seemed to me that nobody had ever heard of the House Committee on Un-American Activities.

Gladys was there the opening night in Princeton and was wonderful. Later, during the run, she had another episode, was hospitalized, went to Paris, and finally wanted a divorce again. She was in Paris, and I was determined to see her. This time I was devil-bent on getting a passport, and a lady named Shipley, who was in charge of the government passport office for the State Department, refused me one. I was unacceptable for travel in foreign countries.

There it was all over again, the spring of 1952. Why not? McCarthyism was burgeoning; the cold war was in every headline; anticommunism was high fashion.

Who would say that I was *not* a Communist? There was only one body, though they denied they could make the determination—and that was the House Committee on Un-American Activities. Would they hear me again? Would they, this time, clear me and get me my passport?

Sam Yorty fixed it. What possible questions could they ask me that they had not asked before? It was the same grueling session, led by Congressman Walter, Congressman Jackson, of California, and Mr. Louis J. Russell. What they wanted this time, it seemed to me, was for me to say that *they* were right, that they had performed a patriotic service, that the criticism of *them*—now growing larger and more vocal—was unjustified. If I said that and I added that I had been a dupe—and, remember, a sucker—they would not clear me, but they would not *not* clear me. From them I was never to get a flat assertion that I had never been a member of the Communist party; the best I could hope for, if I cringed and wrung my hands and denounced people who had asked me to join organizations, was that I was a dupe.

So I was a dupe. So I made speeches admitting I was a dupe. So I said I was ashamed and embarrassed by my friends who had seduced me into Communist-front organizations. What the committee would have licked its chops over would have been names; I mentioned as few as possible, and never once (unlike others who testified in this period) did I name anybody—repeat, *anybody*—as being a member of the Communist party.

How could I? To this day, I don't know.

Through Mr. Walter's splendid assertion that I was a "sucker," through a letter of Sam Yorty's to Mrs. Shipley, through Yorty's taking me to lunch with George Sokolsky and Victor Riesel, through Yorty's insertion in the *Congressional Record* of my fine performance as an American citizen (despite my having been a—well, he never said sucker), I was cleared.

Yorty was an astute politician, and he knew well how to play the game. He got me my passport. I'm forever grateful to him.

I wish I knew how to play the game.

All the way to Paris to see Gladys and decide our future, I kept asking myself: "What game was I trying to win? Who was the enemy?"

It was clear the Congressional Committee was not my enemy; it was composed of essentially decent men, not very worldly, not very sophisticated, who sincerely believed the Bolsheviks were coming to America with bombs and free love, fanatically determined to destroy the capitalist system. I could sense in their questions their utter naiveté.

Not so with Congressman Jackson. I felt an ugliness in him—or maybe overambition, maybe a chance to make headlines and a political career for himself. I truly believed he'd try for senator or governor of California; I'm told he eventually ended up working for a South American nation as a lobbyist. But even *he* wasn't my enemy; he was simply beset with a bitter tongue and a phrase that could make a headline. In any case, I was certainly no Alger Hiss case—and Jackson was no Richard Nixon.

Then who or what was the enemy? Ignorance, my friends, ignorance. Insulation. Lack of education. Lack of knowledge of history. Fear of the unknown. Disappointment. Frustration. The atom bomb. Korea. The senator from Wisconsin.

Put together this potpourri, and you come up with something like the mood of a man or woman who has undergone what appeared in anticipation to be an ecstatic sexual experience and which turned out, in retrospect, to be disastrous and humiliating.

We had had the war; we'd knocked off Tojo and Hitler and Mussolini; Roosevelt was dead, but the United Nations was alive. Old enemy, Big Bear Russia, had been our ally. Here we were prepared for Utopia, a world safe for democracy (a phrase scarcely remembered), no more war, no more bestiality—and suddenly China was lost to the Communists, the bomb seemed ready to annihilate the earth, the draft was still taking the kids. Enemies! Everywhere! Who? Communism, of course. Rid the world of *that* scourge, undermining our youth with promises of sexual freedom, and . . . well, look at it all now, almost a quarter of a century later.

The Soviet Union has blue laws that make Anthony Comstock look like Rabelais. Richard Nixon, arch foe of Communists, visits with Mao and Kosygin. Stalin, the hero of The Hollywood Ten, in disgrace. Khrushchev, who disgraced him, now disgraced himself. Both are buried somewhere outside the Kremlin.

How quickly and thoroughly the personalized enemies have disappeared—and, I may add, the heroes, too. Today, to me, at the beginning of my ninth decade of life, it seems to me the world is ruled not by computers but by certified public accountants. And we will be destroyed not by ideology or -ism (two words that, once high fashion, seem to be no longer in use) but by air unfit to breathe and water unfit to drink.

Except—and the loveliest part of free government and free choice is the word "except"—that, yet unborn, or in kindergarten, or in some assembly district, or perhaps in a barrio, or in a Manchurian hut, or perhaps all together—a man or men will come and put it back together. Life on earth goes in cycles—five years for us common folk—perhaps five hundred years for mankind, and these cyclical highs and lows appear and disappear, and what seems hopeless at the moment, turns out to be the very basis for hope itself.

And, believe me, McGovern and convention quotas are not part of the answer. Neither are Nixon and Martha Mitchell.*

In Paris at the Plaza Athenée, Gladys had one of those lovely suites on the third floor. She couldn't have been more darling. The first thing she did was to show me her paintings—not in the hotel room

---

* Note from L.S.: E.G.R. said all that you just read *so* rapidly, *so* passionately, that I had extreme difficulty putting it down. The tears were streaming down his cheeks; but his voice was steady, and I have no doubt that the period in which he was accused of disloyalty was still weighing heavily on him and that he was seeking to make it meaningful. I thought perhaps not to use it; I think I must.

but in a Faubourg St. Honoré Gallery. She, like Berthe Morisot and Rosa Bonheur and Suzanne Valadon, was a painter. At last she had found herself. As for me, I was no longer to concern myself with the problems of Hollywood and Washington; we would live in Europe. Gladys had talked to many British and French producers; we would spend the rest of our lives in Europe. Expatriation was the only sensible thing for me—she was certain of that.

Expatriation? For the third time? Rumania to New York. New York to Hollywood. And now Hollywood to Paris. No, thank you. No, thank you very much.

We had a house and splendid paintings in Beverly Hills—two houses as a matter of fact, for we still had that small ranch. There was no need to worry about my official status as movie star; my agents, while hardly deluging me with offers, had come up with some more pictures. But, above all, there was the question of Manny, now almost twenty.

In his own book he tells of his teen years in his own words. They include drink, bad checks, arrest, probation, attempts to become an actor by going to the Neighborhood Playhouse School in New York (through the help of my friends Sam Jaffe and Gadge Kazan), living with a young lady, marrying her eventually, and having a daughter.

Francesca!

From the moment I saw her, I transferred all my own ambition and hopes for Utopia from Manny to her. And you know, I think they're working out—or will if she does her homework.

Anyway, I insisted to Gladys that we return to the United States. She gave in.

And so I entered the "B" picture phase of my career as a movie star—or former movie star, if that's a better way of putting it, or has-been, if that's still a better way. I got top billing, but in *Actors and Sin* second billing went to Marsha Hunt. In *Vice Squad* to Paulette Goddard. In *Big Leaguer* to Vera-Ellen. In the *Glass Web* to John Forsythe. In *Black Tuesday* to Jean Parker. In *The Violent Men*, for Columbia, I had third billing, playing character man for Barbara Stanwyck and Glenn Ford. In *Tight Spot* Ginger Rogers was the star. In *Bullet for Joey* George Raft was the lead. And so, on and on went the series of program movies that I did for the money and something to do, my own self-esteem decreasing by the hour. *Hell on Frisco Bay* I did, and it was hell in Beverly Hills. *Nightmare*, I did, and it was nightmare all around me.

Manny was getting a divorce and was in more trouble—and Gladys was having recurrent episodes and once again demanding a divorce as well. *Nightmare* wasn't a picture; it was a fact of life.

To go on, for a moment, with my "career," it was obvious that while I was forgiven my premature antifascism, I was doomed, both by age and former political leanings, to a slow graveyard. The top directors and producers wouldn't have me and while I'm grateful to those who did in the period and bow low to them for their guts, what I needed was recognition again by a top figure in the industry. I've already mentioned the name of that top figure—Cecil B. DeMille.

No more conservative or patriarchal figure existed in Hollywood, no one more opposed to communism or any permutation or combinations thereof. And no fairer one, no man with a greater sense of decency and justice. I'm told that when the part of Nathan was discussed in his new *Ten Commandments*, somebody suggested that I would be ideal but that under the circumstances I was, of course, unacceptable. Mr. DeMille wanted to know why, coldly reviewed the matter, felt I had been done an injustice, and told his people to offer me the part.

Cecil B. DeMille returned me to films. Cecil B. DeMille restored my self-respect.

Before that, however, an event, a meeting, occurred that is of some moment to these pages. Gladys had a passion for clothes. She also had a passion for buying them wholesale. The top designers in New York looked with some irritation on this practice but did it occasionally if asked by another designer. The Nettie Rosenstein group, approached by somebody to provide Mrs. Edward G. Robinson with the courtesy of a private showing, reluctantly agreed. The reluctant directrice who agreed was Jane Bodenheimer Adler.

Gladys bought all her clothes through Jane for a number of years. And in August 1953, Mrs. Adler, together with another executive of her firm, was in California on business. Gladys asked them over for cocktails to see the pictures; later they would dine at Romanoff's. (Cook's day off or something.)

Gladys told me about the date. Was I interested? I was not interested.

Mrs. Adler and her escort came to the house. Out of curiosity, I joined them. I found Mrs. Adler tall, attractive, graceful, witty, not in the least awed by me, highly knowledgeable about painting (although for years she has denied having any knowledge whatever except that which she got from me through osmosis).

The time came for the three of them to go to Romanoff's. I went along. We had a very good time.

Some years later, as you no doubt have already come to suspect, Jane agreed to marry me. There is a delicate irony in the fact that my first wife introduced me to my second.

Irony or plan?

It is what each man must conclude for himself. As hard as he tries, this man cannot believe in divine intervention. And still he cannot credit everything to happenstance.

Somewhere there lies an answer.

I hope one day to find it.

EPILOGUE BY
LEONARD SPIGELGASS

January 26, 1973

For twenty-eight days we had been pacing the halls and jamming up the waiting room of the fifth floor of Mount Sinai Hospital on Beverly Boulevard. My housekeeper, whose sister had suffered the same kind of tumor as Eddie, said to me at the beginning: "It takes twenty-eight days."

And on the twenty-eighth day of his hospitalization, at 4:55 P.M., Dr. Marvin Levy came down the hall and said to us (Jane, Francesca, the Simpsons, the Jaffes, the Karps, his brother Willie, and his sister-in-law Rhea): "It won't be long now."

I went into the waiting room thinking how ridiculous that Levy would say anything so corny, so boring, so uninspired. I looked out of the window. It was getting dark, and I thought it was already drizzling, but it was just the dirty window. I did not want to go back into the hall, and I didn't, so I didn't hear what Dr. Levy said, but I guess it was something like: "It's all over." I don't know that that's what he said, but that's his style.

I only know that somebody suggested using a back service elevator. It was crowded, and we got off; I stopped to light a cigarette. I was alone downstairs in the hospital, and I couldn't orient myself because I'd always used another bank of elevators.

I went out a door. The parking lot was on the other side, and I spun about trying to find it, but couldn't. Finally, a nurse pointed to it, but then I couldn't find my car. And I yelled: "Some dirty bastard's stolen my car!" I started shouting, and Sam Jaffe and his wife came up to me. Betty hugged me and cried and I didn't want her crying; I pushed her away and said the only sentence I seemed capable of uttering: "Some dirty bastard's stolen my car."

The parking man came to see what the trouble was. He was old and harried and, I think, used to people like me. I said the same brutal thing to him, and he gently took me over to my car. It had been right in front of me, but I was so angry I couldn't see it.

I drove home listening to a kind of Kostelanetz "Falling in Love with Love" on the radio and singing a bit of it. When I got to the house, I told my family, and they left me alone. I went into my office laden down with his manuscript and clippings and letters and scrapbooks and so much in Eddie's handwriting, and I grabbed a bunch of papers and I said "Sheeeeeeeeeyut!"

I told myself that nobody was going to make me work on this book one goddamn minute more, and I thought somebody would say: "That's what Eddie would have wanted." Then I thought, how in hell would *they* know what Eddie wanted? Suddenly I remembered how much he wanted to go to the Academy to receive his honorary Oscar and how he would have done so in a wheelchair, if necessary, and I thought I would have to finish this record, even if I did it in a wheelchair. Why was I angry? Angry! Angry! Oh, that son of a bitch dying on me. Oh, that magnificent son of a bitch!

February 5, 1973

And so, I continue—not in a wheelchair but in the third person—together with a fiendish memory and many notes, and in my own conviction there are more of his yesterdays you ought to know about.

I've decided that my first job is to put back some of the things he told me to take out. Maybe you'll get to know him in spite of himself. He didn't like being clever; he was clever. He was opinionated. He was funny. For instance:

ON BEING A STAGE STAR:
Its only virtue is that you get a ground floor dressing room.

ON VANITY:
I am vain.

ON BEING A STAR IN THE MOVIES:
You're as good as your picture before last. Three bombs in a row and you're through. Only *The New York Times* can rescue you by falling in love with a dreadful movie that somehow seems to appeal to

its critic. And, through the years, the movie critics of the *Times* inevitably fall in love with a "B" picture.

ON BEING A STAR IN TELEVISION:

I get "Special Guest Star" billing. That means you get a small salary but large billing, and nobody pays the slightest attention to it. At M.G.M. TV I did a piece of a series once in which there was a "Guest Star," a "Special Guest Star," and there was no way to bill me except as "Also starring special guest star Edward G. Robinson." It's what we used to call baloney. And while we now call it by a more explicit word, baloney is better. A bit is a bit no matter what the billing.

ON PICASSO:

He's the greatest bull artist in the world—and only occasionally the greatest artist in the world.

ON REMBRANDT:

Did it ever occur to anybody how boring his pictures are?

ON F.D.R.:

I'm told he's no longer a hero and he could have done more for the Jews, that he had a mistress. Well, count up the score. He turned the twentieth century around; without him, I think we'd be ruled by a commissariat.

ON AVIATION:

The most useless invention ever invented. Without it, we'd have had a lovelier world.

ON GOING TO THE MOON:

Why?

ON REMINISCENCE:

It is simply not possible to tell the truth about the past. My grandmother has become an angel; she couldn't possibly have been.

ON LINDBERGH:

The hell with his politics. He is our last, great hero.

ON VIETNAM:

A mistake we'll pay for, for a hundred years.

ON NIXON:

He may yet turn out to have greatness in him despite himself. I think his kind of ambition is indeed a grievous thing; now that he cannot be reelected, maybe he'll let his humanity emerge. There simply has to be more to the man than he lets us see.

ON XEROXING:

A script isn't the same. I prefer carbon copies or mimeographing. Then I don't feel the script has been broadcast to every actor.

ON WINE:

Either the very, very best—or a local red wine. Never drink an inexpensive white wine. Acid.

ON HUBERT HUMPHREY:

I love everything he stands for; I just wish *he* didn't love it so much. He needs a director to tell him when he's made his point. I think he'd have been a good President.

ON THE GREATEST PAINTER:

Titian, probably, or Goya. What a ridiculous question to ask!

ON DALI:

The most superb technician of the century—completely devoid of mind.

ON WINSTON CHURCHILL:

The greatest actor of the century, and lucky he was out of politics before TV. Like William Jennings Bryan, he could never have read from cue cards.

ON MOVIES:

They're just too goddamn long. After forty-five, a man must be able to relieve himself, at least once every two hours. I don't know if the bladder gets smaller; it certainly gets fuller.

ON MICROPHONES:

On the stage they are an abomination, and I think they're ruining this generation of actors.

ON CHAPLIN:

He should never have made a talkie. Once he opened his mouth, he ceased to be universal and became an actor. He is no actor; he is a figure. Being a figure is sometimes better than being an actor.

ON ENJOYMENT:

If you're a pro in the theater or movies, you'll enjoy few plays or pictures. The price you pay is that you'll be picking everything apart. If you don't, you can be sure you're looking at something wonderful.

ON TV COMMERCIALS:

Does everybody in America have a washing machine? And how can white be whiter than white? Also, what is advertised for hemorrhoids is useless for chronic cases. And for once, I'd like them to tell me *why* I should buy the product.

ON READING:

I always keep four or five books on my bed table, and each night I read a little of each; guess I can't concentrate on any one at a time. But I always finish them.

ON GEORGE GERSHWIN:

I knew he was sick. I thought it was a tumor. I went over every day and talked to him, and he didn't answer, but I kept talking away. I couldn't bear his dying. I just couldn't.

ON THE STOCK MARKET:

I think it should be declared illegal. I don't think we should gamble on wheat futures.

ON *Love Story*:

I hated every minute of it and couldn't stop crying.

ON HEARING AIDS:

Why is it I can hear a fire engine three blocks away and I can't hear the guy next to me talking?

ON ELEVATORS:

I'm scared to be alone in one and even more scared when there's off-key Muzak.

ON COOKING CHICKEN:

Cook it once, then cook it again.

ON ROCK MUSIC:

It's so loud it's beyond the capacity of my hearing aid, so I've never heard it.

ON GLASSES:

Where are they?

ON CIGARS:

Peace with Castro is required immediately so that I can have my Havanas. They are unequaled.

ON THE LEGION D'HONNEUR:

I was proud to get it, but I ceased wearing the red ribbon in my lapel when DeGaulle came to power; occasionally, I wear it.

ON WOMEN'S LIB:

My whole life has been lived for women, and I've never ceased being frightened by them. They have a weapon against which there is no defense—unpredictability. Whoever could have predicted women's lib itself?

ON HOMOSEXUALITY:

I never could understand why anybody would want to make love to a mirror.

ON PORNOGRAPHIC FILMS:

I went to see one. It did nothing for me. But I think that has to do with my age, not my morals.

ON NIARCHOS:

My greatest regret is that I never met him. I would have punched him right in the nose.

ON ONASSIS:

I get him mixed up with Niarchos.

ON MRS. ONASSIS:

Boy, that's a woman. I know it's the fashion to put her down; I find her admirable—not totally, but around 90 percent. Puts her in my top ten.

ON MCGOVERN:

I think he means everything he says, but he says it so badly that he sounds like a ventriloquist's dummy. His ambition was also grievous.

ON BASEBALL:

Sandy Koufax, come home!

ON BOXING:

I'd rather see Joe Louis punch than hear Mohammed Ali recite.

ON THE NEW LEFT:

There isn't a thing they want that isn't in the Constitution.

ON EINSTEIN:

He belonged to more causes than I did; I think I had a letter from him every other day asking for money. I always responded.

ON THE BALLET:

I love half an hour of it. The rest of the time I listen to the music, though ballet music is invariably reminiscent of Victor Herbert.

ON SHIRTS:

Manufacturers do not understand the human body. Why neck–sleeve sizes? The problems occur in the shoulders and the belly.

ON MANICURES:

One of my favorite things in life. Also pedicures.

ON DOGS:

All my dogs have Ph.D.'s and E.S.P.

ON DINING OUT:

The thing to do is to say you have stomach trouble right off. That way, you can find out the menu. I've never discovered a way to politely find out the guest list, but if I don't like it, I can always hark back to the stomach trouble and leave.

ON BEING ILL:

It's so boring and so humiliating.

ON MARGARINE:

It's the word I dislike, not the food. Give me a piece of bread and butter and I'll enjoy it. Now tell me it's margarine and I'll throw up.

ON THE FRENCH:

If I weren't Jewish, I'd like to be French. I can't imagine anything more appalling than being both.

ON SEX:

What we refuse to believe is that it was intended by nature as a manufacturing process. In order to make certain the race would continue, nature made it the most exciting and alluring of experiences; thus, we have turned it into a diversion and an entertainment. Nonetheless, it is a manufacturing process.

ON PHILIP ROTH:

I am not certain why I detested *Portnoy's Complaint*. It may be that it struck home. It may also be that it debased Roth's art.

ON EDWARD ALBEE:

I wish I were young enough to have played George in *Virginia Woolf*. I mean I'd like to have created the part, but I'm told Albee doesn't let an actor change anything. I wouldn't have liked that.

ON MARTHA MITCHELL:

I cannot tell you how much she sounds like Gladys.

WHAT IS ART:

I like Picasso's answer: "What is not?"

ON EUGENE O'NEILL:

He has never written a character I can play; his characters are not of Middle Europe—and they elude me—except *The Hairy Ape*.

ON SHAKESPEARE:

I quote him always when I tell young players that acting is not just "strutting and fretting" upon the stage. I've used a piece of that speech from *Macbeth* for the title of this book, turning it from plural to singular—thus accepting all the blame myself.

ON FREUD:

I think he, Christ, and Marx are responsible for the world being the way it is—and I confer my thanks upon all of them, as I withhold it.

OF DEATH:

I have some fear, but mostly apprehension.

OF LIFE:

I had no fear, but mostly apprehension.

ON GROWING OLD:

The first symptom is that hair grows on your ears. It's very disconcerting.

ON THE WORLD'S GREATEST MUSICIANS:

Beethoven—no contest. Tell no one I adore Strauss waltzes; can't bear Satie or Scriabin; tolerate Stravinsky; have a wonderful time with Tchaikovsky's *1812*.

ON EGYPT:

They wouldn't let me on the Sphinx or the Pyramids. Instead, they kept Jane and me in a customs shed until they could be rid of us. Don't they know that great works of art belong to everybody?

ON ART CRITICISM:

There has developed an extensive vocabulary among critics and catalog-writers that obscures meaning. One of life's joys is to reread criticism of five and ten years ago, when these boys tried to define abstraction intellectually. Some of them also tried to give meaning to Andy Warhol. How Mr. Warhol must have laughed! As an exercise in criticism, try to write out what you think Jackson Pollack had in mind. Or Kandinsky.

ON MUSIC:

All my life, whenever I saw an instrument that wasn't being used— a violin, a French horn, a guitar, a ukelele, a viola—I've tried to play it. Useless. The only beat I've ever managed is with a drum, and that belonged to my very young son. When I was very young, I never had a drum. I never had a kite. I never had a boy scout knife. I once had a magnet.

ON LAS VEGAS:

Hate turned to love. At first I couldn't endure it—plastic, neon, all those awful people seething with greed. And then, one time, it was the anniversary of my father's death, and I needed the men to make up a minyan, the biblical quorum required. Jack Entratter was alive then and operated the Sands Hotel. I told him my problem, and we had double the number of men needed. They didn't seem greedy at all.

ON TROLLEY CARS:

Francesca doesn't really believe that I remember distinctly when trolley cars were pulled by horses. In the summer they were open, and I liked to sit up front with the motorman. Can you believe I considered that a great adventure?

ON LEARNING A PART:

There's absolutely no sense to what I have to suggest, but sometimes it works: When you go to sleep, put the play under your pillow. Sometimes you wake up in the morning, letter-perfect.

ON PROPS:

No matter how big you get, check out all the props. Make certain they're where they're supposed to be. Guns that don't shoot are your worst enemies. In *The Racket* I was supposed to be gunned down. One night the poor actor shooting me had no blanks in his pistol, so I had no cue. Improvising out of sheer desperation, I changed Bart Cormack's play and died of a heart attack. It was simulated, but it was almost real.

ON LYNDON JOHNSON:

I think he was torn between two things—a humanity that derived from his childhood and his experiences as a schoolteacher in Texas, and a deep isolation from the world of art and the intellect.

ON VICUÑA COATS:

Jane gave me a hideously expensive one made by Stella at Magnin's. I went to Reuben's for a sandwich, checked it, and when I had finished the pastrami, went to collect the coat. They couldn't find it and gave me a miserable one instead. I had to spend some time at a police station where they couldn't understand how anybody would *dare* steal a coat from Little Caesar. I was insured but didn't claim anything because I knew they'd cancel the policy. For a vicuña coat, who needs to have the policy on the pictures knocked off? Now I never check coats; I put them always beside me. They hate that at 2 1, but that's their problem.

ON FREDRIC MARCH:

He played my part in *Middle of the Night*. How curious to watch

BY LEONARD SPIGELGASS   2 8 3

him, this man of near genius. He couldn't give the part life because he
was *acting* a Jew, not being one. Same thing with Roz Russell when
she made the film *Majority of One*. My heart bled for her. But even
more for Alec Guinness who probably can play any part in the world
except that of a Japanese.

ON CAGNEY:

One of the most extraordinary talents—that curious quality of
pugnaciousness. Maybe if you took that away from him, he'd be an
ordinary Mick. Some of my best friends have been Micks. I love
Micks. I use the word "Mick" with respect and affection.

ON RADIO CITY MUSIC HALL:

I may be wrong, but I don't think a picture of mine ever played
there. It was Tiffany's, and I played mostly at the Strand, which
wasn't exactly Woolworth's, but close.

ON DISNEY:

I don't know what it is with me, but animated cartoons make me
nervous. I loved bits of Disneyland, but it exhausted me, and for no
plausible or sensible reason, I felt it not anti- but non-Semitic. And I
think that's pretty silly of me.

TO LAURENCE OLIVER [When I told him that it was possible Sir
Laurence would give him the Oscar, this is what he said he'd say.]:

I'm breaking all the rules, but I have to say you have been my idol.
I admit being jealous of an actor. How I would like to have been what
you are. How I wish my career had approximated yours. You have
never deserted or failed to serve our noble profession. Sir, to be presented an award by you gives me infinite pride.

You, being a Lord, have raised me to a slightly higher position. I
don't feel that I'm quite such a commoner. But, more important, I'm
Eddie, and you're Larry. And how much easier that is.

TO JANE:

Pick up the Oscar for me, dearest one, and don't wear black.

TO FRANCESCA:

Do your homework, my darling.

TO MANNY:

All of us Goldenbergs live to our eighties. You've got forty-one
years more. Enjoy yourself, but make it work for you.

TO LENNY:
Be sure to keep the personal opinions minimal.

February 10, 1973—
April 23, 1973

The early and middle 1950s were a watershed in a life that had already, it seemed, achieved its full share. The first and overweaning change in Eddie's life occurred when Gladys again sued for divorce, and this time he could take no more of it. He was tired of her games; he was tired of this constant threat to whatever security he had left.

He wanted peace and love again. Was it possible? Was it Jane? It was Jane.

Gladys, who had been the instigator of all these divorce proceedings, now seemed to back away, and to delay the case, she went to Menninger's for treatment. As long as she was there, it was impossible for the case to come to trial.

Meanwhile, Eddie and his attorneys tried to straighten out the legal tangle the divorce required. Under California law, property is jointly owned by husband and wife. How does one divide a Corot? Does one cut a Morisot in half?

The ploy was to contest the divorce. Gladys' counterploy was to name Jane as corespondent. Eddie checked *that* game by withdrawing his contest of the divorce. Gladys withdrew Jane's name.

To wit: According to the attorneys, there appeared to be some simple solutions. The first and most obvious was that if Eddie could raise the cash, he could buy Gladys' interests out. But that meant there would have to be an evaluation of the picture collection, the house, the furniture, the bric-a-brac, and various other securities held by both of them. When this was done by hordes of accountants, the amount for Eddie was astronomical.

Additionally, Gladys, whenever she could be approached on the subject, refused this; she insisted that the pictures be divided among them. (He had already given her the Vuillard family portrait; she put it up for sale at Parke Bernet.)

Well, how do you handle this division? One Pissarro is not worth as much as another; do you trade off Rouault for a Segonzac? It isn't as though they were discussing pots and pans or shares of General Motors; those are all susceptible to division; works of art have ascending and descending values that fluctuate with the market. (How many owners of Buffets know that to their sorrow. Not *Du*buffet, Buffet.)

In the meantime Eddie spent his time doing something he preferred that I did not mention. But I see no point in not mentioning it now.

Throughout the Un-American Activities time, throughout his unemployment, he bought easels, brushes, oil paints, and palettes, and began to paint himself. He pooh-poohed his talents—said he had none, that he was at best a copyist; it was only a Sunday hobby. The plain truth, if you look at the pictures now, is that Eddie possessed more than minor talent as a painter. His work is, of course, Impressionist and borrows a great deal from the painters he admired, but it also has his own signature—and the signature is in the work itself, for, with one exception, he never signed a picture.

Today, after his second collection has been taken out of his house (bought by Victor and Armand Hammer of Knoedler & Company for $5,125,000), his own pictures hang in the living room where once hung Monet and Picasso. And Jane has done a curious thing to the room; she has changed it from a gallery into a home. I saw it last night for the first time, and I was frankly afraid to look, so long had I known that room with its masterworks; I was afraid my anger/grief would not be able to tolerate the room with other pictures—*his* pictures. Not only did I *not* feel grief/anger; I felt a sense of warmth and ecstasy; I think you would find it, as I did, a curious and odd aesthetic experience. I always thought Eddie was dealing in fantasy when he said pictures choose their own environment. Believe me, all those masterworks seemed remote and cold without him.

But smearing paint on canvases wasn't enough for Eddie. He cheered when Josh Logan sent him a script of Paddy Chayefsky's *Middle of the Night. Darkness at Noon* had given him courage to return to the stage; but the Kingsley play was set, not subject to rewrite. Of course, that didn't stop Eddie. He has already told you about his quarrels with Sidney Kingsley; but they were nothing compared to his quarrels with Paddy Chayefsky and Josh Logan. Eddie himself spoke to me a great deal about his feeling about the theater; he said that when a play is written, it is only half written; it is completed only when the actor brings to it his own sense of the character.

Chayefsky, of course, would disagree with this assessment as, I must confess, would I. Playwrights tend to believe (and I speak as one of them) that all the actors have to do is learn the words, that the director has to direct traffic, and that the written words are the only important things.

Josh Logan (with whom I have worked) takes quite another view. While he is an author himself and a Pulitzer Prize winner, and though he has enormous respect for actors, he believes it is the director's function to make the play work.

Well, you can see that you had three monumentally different points of view and three equally monumental egos. I was never present at a rehearsal of *Middle of the Night*, but I do know Nancy Pollock (who was a member of the cast in a play of my own), and during some of our own miserable waiting periods she told me of the agonies and the fights between Eddie, Paddy, and Josh. As a matter of fact, it was rumored all over Broadway (particularly in Sardi's after eleven o'clock) that *Middle of the Night* would never open.

I know Josh and Paddy very well, and I've been tempted to call them and ask them for their views; now it seems a fruitless exercise, for what went on during the rehearsals of *Middle of the Night* is actually standard operating procedure. And I speak with some emphasis on personal experience.

Nonetheless, despite the gossip and the inside dope, *Middle of the Night* did open, and it had what Eddie hated the most: mixed notices.

In the *Best Plays of 1955–1956* Louis Kronenberger gives the play its lumps:

> *Middle of the Night*, the first Broadway play by TV's star playwright, Paddy Chayefsky, was—even with Edward G. Robinson's fine performance to aid it—decidedly disappointing.

The other critics were perhaps a little kinder, or you might go so far as to say a little less kind. *Middle of the Night* did not look like a hot ticket, but in the curious alchemy and magic of the New York theater it became one and ran for 477 performances. (It should only happen to me!)

Eddie was a New York stage star again. There could be no doubt of it. I remember going to see it one night, and there were standees. When Eddie made his entrance, there was that marvelous, thrilling, round of applause, and my friend Eddie just waited it out, playing the character, ignoring the applause, and then proceeding with the play.

I went backstage afterward. He was taking off his makeup and was, I think, genuinely delighted to see me. Quickly he began dissecting the play and asking how I would rewrite it. I smiled to myself. The performance I had seen was close to the two hundredth, and Eddie was still not satisfied.

We went out and had a little supper with Jane, not at Sardi's, not at the Plaza, but at the Mayflower Donut Shop where nobody seemed to know him, though we'd had trouble with autograph hunters en route, and he told me some of the things that were happening to him.

When he left to do *Middle of the Night*, he had been very concerned about the paintings, and so he had decided for everybody's protection to send them, prior to possible sale, to the Los Angeles

County Museum, where they would be safe and, incidentally, out of Gladys' hands.

During this period, apparently, Gladys regained her mental health for a short period of time and returned to the Beverly Hills house only to find the walls empty. She was shocked and furious and demanded that the museum return the paintings.

The museum resisted. The exhibition had been an enormous success. There had been a record attendance, and Eddie had agreed with the museum that after the Los Angeles showing they could be sent to San Francisco. Since she could not get the pictures back, Gladys insisted at least that the catalog be changed—and the museum people agreed. Instead of being designated the "Edward G. Robinson Collection" it became the "Gladys Lloyd Robinson and Edward G. Robinson Collection." I have the two catalogs in front of me. The second billing was very distressing to Eddie.

In the end what was even more distressing was the fact that the only way out of this dilemma was to stall no longer and sell the pictures, then divide the money.

There was, heaven knows, no lack of offers. Eddie called them ghouls and vampires, all waiting to pounce on him and his pictures. Among them, Eddie believed, was Stavros Niarchos. Eddie was under the firm impression that Niarchos and his wife (who was Ari Onassis' sister) saw the collection in San Francisco. In any case, it was later clear that Niarchos had seen either them or the catalog and was deeply interested.

But when the San Francisco show was over, Gladys insisted that the pictures be returned to the house. She rehung them in their proper places—and then she had a great party and invited all the celebrities over to say good-bye to the pictures. Eddie told me this with such bitterness and such anger that I find I have no way to communicate it. It seemed to him the final insult—and the ultimate reason he decided on the divorce, no matter what the cost.

"Invitations to the good-bye party went out by the hundreds," Manny says in his book. "Apparently everybody wanted to come to see the end of an era, the dissolution of a royal house." As Manny and so many others have pointed out, movie stars were American royalty. "To be born in such a family," Manny goes on, "is to be raised like a prince . . . with all the rights, privileges . . . except the right of succession." The party was "the gayest funeral any family ever had."

Soon after this, Manny had a business meeting, had "one single scotch and soda," and late at night started to drive a girl home. Near

U.C.L.A. he was involved in a car crash; the girl was seriously in-
jured, and Manny was charged with drunken driving. "It was," he
writes, "another accident of fate that my first court appearance to
make my plea happened on the same day my mother was in court for
her final divorce decree. We met in the hallway, underneath the flashbulbs. The beleaguered Robinson family was back in the papers—in
tandem."

Prior to this, it is a matter of record, Eddie's own attorney made
arrangements with Gladys' attorney to give him a year to see whether
he could, himself, buy the pictures. He went to various banks and
many of the great collectors to try to raise a loan that would pay off
Gladys' half. Arnold Kirkeby, a Los Angeles millionaire, agreed on
condition that he could retain a majority of the pictures. Eddie refused. He had the same sort of proposition from David Rockefeller,
some French bankers, and Nate Cummings.* He felt they were arrogant, willing to lend him the money at vast rates of interest on condition that they could have the best of the collection.

An even more vexing problem was that Gladys was apparently
willing to sell *her* half of the collection (however that could be defined) at a much lower price than Eddie was willing to part with *his*
half. He tried to talk with her, to convince her that at least they
should stick together on the price. But he was dealing with a sick
woman—and she came up with a counterproposition. She was willing
to buy *his* half at their insured value. Of course, they had been insured at a figure far below their actual worth, so that proposition
came to nothing.

Eddie now told me in the most guarded terms about a potential
deal involving Roland Balay of Knoedler's. Balay had a buyer. The
price was well over three million dollars. The gentleman who was
buying the pictures really did not want them all; he would agree, after
a suitable period of time, to let Eddie have many of the seventy-four
paintings back for an agreed-upon price.

There was to be no written understanding. The same offer was
made to Gladys, but she wasn't interested. All she wanted was the
money. And the money she got. The pictures were finally sold to
Niarchos.

I cannot tell you whether Niarchos actually agreed to the arrangement to sell many of the pictures back; I can only tell you that Eddie
pursued Niarchos for a number of years, by mail and cable, even

---

* He now, by some convolution of fate, owns the Vuillard portrait of the Robinson family.

went to Europe to talk to him, but Niarchos evaded both his letters and his presence, and to the day he died, Eddie never met Niarchos. One of the things that made Eddie the angriest was that Niarchos put some of the pictures on his yacht—and you know what salt water can do to oil paintings.

Meanwhile, Niarchos was redoing his Paris house to install the pictures, and Eddie had a letter from Niarchos' secretary, permitting him to go and see the treasures he once owned.

Eventually, however, Eddie was able to buy back fourteen of the pictures at exorbitant prices from Knoedler, representing Niarchos, or from others to whom Niarchos had sold some of the pictures.

Thus, the world's greatest personal collection of paintings picked by an American went to Stavros Niarchos with the understanding that Eddie might buy back at a far higher price than the purchase price.* Apparently, he was financially unable to buy back the most expensive and important pictures in the collection, such as *Jane Avril Dancing* by Lautrec, Georges Seurat's *Le Crotoy*, Renoir's *After the Bath*, Renoir's *The Girl with Red Plume*, Van Gogh's *Portrait of Père Tanguy*, Gauguin's *Horsemen on the Beach*, Gauguin's *Tahitian Flowers*, Corot's *L'Italienne,* and Cézanne's *Black Clock*.

Nonetheless, there were approximately thirty-two paintings to be returned for appropriate compensation—in other words, more than Niarchos paid Eddie. This evidently was merely a gentlemen's agreement. Unfortunately, Eddie was only allowed to buy back a few.

Eddie wrote endless letters, spoke to his friends and Balay, and chased Niarchos from country to country. Niarchos left as soon as Eddie and Jane arrived. For Eddie, this was untold heartbreak.

The American collection, including Grant Wood's *Daughters of the Revolution*, Niarchos sold immediately but never offered them to Eddie.

Henri Matisse's *La Desserte* was a very personal thing to Eddie, but it was never returned to him. It reminded him of his mother, Friday night dinners, and the Jewish tradition. This has always remained a huge thorn in Eddie's side. His other particular love that he expected to get back was Georges Rouault's *The Old Clown.* To Eddie, as an actor, this represented every man with emotion and love. He told me without embarrassment that he cried two years ago when he saw it on exhibit in a European museum.

And there was another problem: Under the terms of the divorce settlement the house had to be sold and the money divided between

* This is Eddie's view of the matter. There is, however, no proof. The only one who knows is Niarchos, and I cannot get in touch with him.

Eddie and Gladys. Eddie almost went crazy trying to figure out what to do—and at the very last minute he, himself, bought back his own house.

When the divorce was granted—and, in those days, the decree took a year—Eddie and Jane were married. He had been seeing her all through the run of *Middle of the Night*, which is to say the most difficult period of the loss of the pictures and the house, and she had proved herself a rod and a staff. She gave him—and I speak with personal knowledge—the kind of esteem that renewed his own self-esteem and the kind of love he said he "had never known before."

When the tour of *Night* was over, they moved back to Beverly Hills, and Jane began restoring the house, not to its early grandeur but to a more comfortable place in which to live. Then together they began the life that for almost twenty years resulted in the purchase of a new collection of pictures, its base firm in the pictures Eddie had been able to buy back from Niarchos or his surrogates.

Eddie never again considered it a collection; he hated to use the word about it, considered it second class. It was not. Each picture showed the same regard, thought, and consideration that had gone into the amassing of the first collection. Jane not only helped but actually involved herself in the study of catalogs and sales. She once said she did not own a fashionable pair of shoes since her marriage to Eddie, so much gallery and museum walking did she have to do.

And they bought pictures.

Five years ago or so Jane and Eddie visited a major gallery and asked to see their best Impressionists. They showed many, but there were three that caught Eddie's eye. Two were quite large canvases—a magnificent Monet, a great Vuillard, and the third, a smaller pastel by Degas. It was love at first sight for Eddie, and he had to have them. In twenty minutes he had agreed to purchase all three.

Several museums were interested, but unfortunately for them, they had to consult their boards. Eddie consulted no one (not even his banker). He knew instinctively. As he said, the blood rushed to his head and that was that. Have them he must. Eddie said, grinning, "The Robinsons are always in debt to art dealers and always will be. Diamonds, furs, stocks, bonds, don't give us pleasure—only art. The pictures glow, the pictures have warmth, the pictures care. We glow, we have warmth, we care. You see, it is reciprocal."

So, they traveled the world and continually sought art. Unfortunately, or perhaps fortunately, since the younger generation had become aware of Eddie via television, he had a whole new group of young admirers. The Robinsons could no longer visit museums unnoticed; people were always asking Eddie who would be the artist of the future, in terms of money. He never failed to look at them with astonishment.

"Money and art are not one and the same," he said. "In fact, money is nothing; art is everything."

It may well be true that, as Eddie insisted, "Money is nothing; art is everything," but Emanuel Goldenberg was completely aware that to have one, you must achieve the other. He also knew that in his early sixties, parts were not easy to come by, though he grinned and contradicted himself:

> In a way, they were easier; you could play anything from fifty to a hundred—and since I'd been playing old men since I was a little boy, there was no wrench for me. I had a new sense of values, however; I was content with a part that had at least one scene that you could grab by the throat, as Matisse once told me. Of course, I'd prefer three, but I would be satisfied with one. What I would not do would be to hang around a picture supplying the exposition.

What else he would not do was join controversial organizations—not that there were many of them who wanted him anymore. The old Communist party by the beginning of the sixties was a kind of idiotic relic; the New Left was forming, and of that Eddie knew nothing. To picket, yes; to rally, yes; to march, yes—but to engage in sit-down demonstrations, to fire-bomb, to take over buildings by violence—none of this was in his nature.

"If I ever were a revolutionary," he said, "you might say I was a polite one, working within the system to change it. It never once occurred to me that Martin Luther King was wrong, and black militants right."

Was it age that was changing his political position, or the memory of how badly he had been burned? Was it the essential ingredient of growing older? No, it seemed to me as we talked that Eddie was the flaming liberal he had always been but that his liberalism had been overshadowed by onrushing events. Assassinations, murder, looting, burning, were so invidious he could not endure them. He mused aloud about this often; was he becoming a Republican as he grew older?

"No way!" said Eddie. "No way! I'm a devout Democrat!"

And so were his friends. Including Frank Sinatra.

The first picture he made after *Ten Commandments*, almost three years later, was *Hole in the Head*, produced and directed by Frank Capra and starring Frank Sinatra. The play by Arnold Schulman had originally been about a Jewish family; it is an interesting comment on Hollywood mores as recently as 1958 that in the Hollywood version the Jews became Italians.

"Jews are out of fashion," Eddie commented wryly. "The world is sick to death of their suffering at the hands of Hitler."

I think Eddie had only half the story; I suspect Columbia and Capra did not wish to show Jews as anything but excellent citizens. There was money-grubbing in *Hole in the Head*, and I can imagine the conferences in which Harry Cohn put his foot down. And from Capra's point of view, with Sinatra as star, an Italian family was closer to his own experiences.

I'm told that Eddie knew Sinatra long before this picture; surely on this set they became friends, and even greater friends when they discovered they shared a birthday, though Frank's was certainly more than twenty years later than Eddie's.

During the shooting there was a joint birthday party for both of them, and from then on they took to exchanging gifts; expensive ones, thoughtful ones. By 1964, when Eddie made another picture with Frank, *Robin and the Seven Hoods*, they were still doing it.

They continued to do it till Eddie's last birthday, last December, when Eddie proudly showed me a set of lapis luzuli cuff links that Frank had sent him.

But there was a coolness. In these last years Frank has changed from Democrat to Republican, has supported Nixon, has been very friendly with Agnew. Though only a few months before his death Eddie went to a party for Frank at which Agnew was one of the most distinguished guests, it was clear to me from his tone of voice and his disinclination to discuss it that Eddie did not approve of Sinatra turning Republican. The suspicion and hostility that young Emanuel Goldenberg had for the Middle America Republican was still in force.

Still, Eddie had fun with Frank—and lots of fun with Jack Benny, George Burns, and Groucho Marx. His house, now under the skillful and artistic management of Jane, was the scene of frequent parties, and they were not for causes. They were parties given simply to have a good time and eat and sip wine and talk and joke. I went to many of them. It was the way it used to be when we had company at our house long ago—only this company consisted of some of the most famous faces in the world, most of them beyond their time. Eddie once called the guest list a "wax works." He was wrong; the vitality and the talent were still there, though most of the cast was in retirement, except for an occasional television appearance.

Eddie was hardly in retirement. His old pictures were not yet being shown (the studios had not yet discovered what a gold mine lay in their ancient catalogs), but Eddie was all over *Playhouse 90, General Electric Theatre*, and *CBS Movie World Premiere*. Note C.B.S.— the last to forgive. HUAC was securely buried.

But not for Eddie; he still fussed and fumed over those terrible days; he was determined to retain his place in the social revolution (with a small *r*), he would accomplish it with the pictures and TV shows he did. *The Devil and Daniel Webster* was a particular favorite of his because Daniel Webster was saying all the things that might have come out of Eddie's own brain.

Three years ago Eddie came to me with a script. Archibald Mac-Leish had rewritten *The Devil and Daniel Webster* for the theater, and it was to be done on Broadway. Would I read it? Well, one thing you could say about it—it was long. To play this part eight times a week at Eddie's age (middle seventies) was nonsense. In any case, I didn't think it had much of a chance. The theater had changed so violently during the sixties that a thoughtful, serious literary play by MacLeish didn't have a prayer. Eddie worried over it. How do you turn down Archibald MacLeish? He did, on the grounds of health, and that was not entirely a falsehood.

I had been away for a while in New York, during which time Eddie had played himself in a film with Cantinflas called *Pepe* for which Sonia Levien and I had done the original story (with apologies to Besh-Fekete, who had originally done the original story, and with apologies to you who went to see Cantinflas and saw thousands of other stars instead). I thought I would see Eddie when I got back. However, after Mexico with *Pepe*, he was off to Japan to make *My Geisha* with Shirley MacLaine and Yves Montand. Then back to New York I went, and missed Eddie until he had finished *Two Weeks in Another Town* with Kirk Douglas. Thus, there was an interval of two or three years, and when I saw Eddie again, I felt much as he had when he saw Frank Craven after a long while.

I felt he had aged; he pooh-poohed any such thing. His health, he assured me, was the finest; he was indestructible. But he was heavier, still unbearded, and his eyes seemed tired. The old vigor was there when he talked about Japan, the wonders of the Far East, and his decision to travel. Whatever the picture, whatever the role, he would take it as long as it provided him with an opportunity to see parts of the world he'd never seen before—and its art.

Syd Boehm, the fabulous reporter turned screenwriter and now a constant gin rummy companion of Eddie's, shared with me the feeling that Eddie should take it easier. Neither of us dared mention it to Jane or Eddie, though, as matters turned out, Jane herself had some serious worries that she confided to no one.

Well, Eddie went on working—*Good Neighbor Sam* and *Seven Hoods* followed one on top of the other. Then Eddie did *Outrage*, the play Fay and Michael Kanin so intelligently and securely un-earthed out of *Rashomon* and out of which Mike Kanin and Martin Ritt made a movie. That was the first time I ever saw Eddie with a beard.

"I grew it for the part," he told me, "but I decided to keep it because it was a new man up there with the old Little Caesar peeping through. A beard would enable me to be rid of him forever."

Except that when John Ford wanted him for *Cheyenne Autumn*, he wanted the beard off—and "whatever John Ford wants John Ford gets." Clearly, to Eddie, John Ford had as much power as Lola.

Meanwhile, what of the house, the art collection? Flourishing, let me tell you—mushrooming by leaps and bounds and showing other interests as well. To his growing collection (a word he resolutely refused to use) of Sickert, Vuillard, Courbet, Redon, Rouault, De-rain, Monet, and Pissarro, he added a fine assortment of African sculpture; he'd bought the entire collection in one fell swoop within ten minutes after seeing it.

I have personally often wondered where Eddie got the money to buy all these great works of art—and I have to tell you that I don't know. The art market, when he first started, was uninflated. In the fifties and sixties the tax shelter bunch began to find that paintings were better investments than stocks. And so you began to read about all those fabulous prices at Parke Bernet and Christie auctions.

I suspect, though I do not know and I have asked no one, that Eddie made some pretty good trade-offs with dealers. He had a re-markable eye, and while he swore he was not a good businessman, I'll make bets that he bought and sold on the art market so that he had cash and credit available to buy what he wanted. And price, of course, was no object.

How strange, then, that he had such miserly habits about other matters. New decks of cards, for instance. He was never able to un-derstand why you couldn't use old ones. And turning off lights, for another. And not ordering new suits (he had to have them made to order; nothing off the rack would fit him). If this is beginning to suggest that he was getting crotchety, I think he'd be the first to admit it.

"Well, crotchety, maybe," he said to me once, "but I prefer to say I hate waste. I've always hated it, but growing older seems to synthesize feelings, and you grow more insistent, and that's what's called 'an old man's crotchets.' I consider them the rights of experience and wisdom." And then he added—I was going to say "ruefully," but he was never rueful—"I'm long on experience, and the jury is still out on wisdom."

It was not wisdom to accept the next script offered him in 1962, even though it was fairly well written, and the role was hand-tailored. *A Boy Ten Feet Tall* was to be made almost entirely on location in Africa, with Eddie playing a grizzled, bearded, warm-hearted diamond smuggler, with an obvious resemblance, in looks and manner, to Ernest Hemingway.

Off the Robinsons went to Kenya—and one night, while on location in the jungle, Eddie suffered a heart attack. He denied forever after that it was anything but an upset stomach, but doctors who attended him still assure me it was an infarct and very serious. And Africa is not the most advanced medical establishment in the world. Jane was beside herself—and took over.

The only people she knew in Nairobi were Jews, and the German doctor had forbidden her to call them on his phone. Fortunately, the other doctor who had taken care of Eddie was a non-Jew. Jane called him at four in the morning and asked that he get in touch with the proper medical people in Nairobi to fly in next morning to pick up her husband. They were there all right, but they forgot to bring any oxygen, and the plane wasn't pressurized.

It was a grim trip back to Nairobi; for a time it looked as if it would kill Eddie. At Nairobi the doctors and nurses and the supervisors were fine people. But Nairobi with its 9,000-foot altitude was no place to have a heart attack. The film people had an insurance doctor coming in from London. Would they hold the picture and wait for the return of the star? Jane knew that if Eddie were told that he would never act again, he would be much more of a sick man. Perhaps a dead one. Without acting he'd have little life left—or, indeed, income.

Dr. Somerville came from London. The doctors taking care of Eddie in Nairobi said he was considered the best heart specialist in England. Jane met him at the plane and told him that if the company wouldn't wait for him in the picture, Eddie would have another final heart attack. He went in to see Eddie. Later he announced his decision to wait for Eddie's full recovery. "He will recover; he will live to make the film. I have advised the company to wait for him.

However, location must be in England because we are up 9,000 feet here."

Jane contacted a New York doctor, Harold Brandalioni, who was a very good friend, and he hurried to Africa over the Fourth of July weekend with his wife. Brandalioni insisted that Eddie leave Africa, so Jane hired a hospital plane to transport Eddie to England, where Jane insisted he was going into the hospital for further recuperation. Eddie was angry at Jane, so she knew he was feeling better.

"How can you spend my money so foolishly!" Eddie said as he had to ride in a car from the hospital to the airport over a terribly kept road. He said to the doctor, "Don't worry, the old land rover will get there." The doctor didn't look too sure, but they got him to the plane alive.

After a long flight they arrived in London, and Eddie put up his fingers in a "V" sign for victory at the airport. There was only one photographer around, as they had tried to get in at five o'clock in the morning so that London wouldn't be aware of Eddie's coming to England as a sick man. (Incidentally, Winston Churchill was in the hospital at the same time as Eddie. They exchanged cigars later.)

Frank Sinatra was the first person to call when the world was aware of the fact that Eddie had had a heart attack. He offered Jane his plane and his aid to pick up Eddie. "Do you need money? Do you need anything?" Fortunately, they needed nothing but time for recovery. When they arrived at the hospital, Frank called Eddie. It was the only call that Eddie took for almost three weeks while he was there recuperating.

Art dealers in Bond Street who understood Eddie's character allowed Jane to pick up some fine French Impressionists from their showrooms, carry them to the London Clinic, and hang them so that Eddie would enjoy the walls of his hospital room.

The day Eddie was brought into the London Clinic, he said to Dr. Somerville, "When may I smoke my first cigar?" Dr. Somerville looked down at Eddie, still on the ambulance cart, and said, "Mr. Robinson, you may start to smoke immediately."

"Immediately?"

"Right now. May I light your cigar for you?"

He explained to Jane: "No further injury could happen. It would be far more disastrous to take his smoking privileges away. He has been smoking all of his sixty-odd adult years and it would make him twice as nervous, so just let him continue smoking."

The nurses had much more trouble trying to get Eddie to have a nightly drink to help his heartbeat. He really disliked alcohol.

When they got home, Jane said to me, "He still smokes, and his heart is fine."

Some fine. He looked great, acted animatedly, made speeches (rewriting them furiously), went to Israel, loved it, wrote about it. There's no date on what follows, but it'll give you an idea of his feelings:

"I have just returned from Israel. Let me picture for you the Jew as you see him there today.

"He has the face of all nations; and his features, hair, skin color, and physique, are those of all lands from which he has sprung. He looks like an Arab, Turk, a blond Bavarian, a redheaded American, a Pole, and all the other physical types you have ever seen. He speaks many languages or perhaps only Hebrew or no Hebrew at all but French, German, Yiddish, or Arabic.

"Let me tell you about only one of the many refugee camps I saw in Israel—one with Yemenite Jews in it. There are 35,000 of them. In the land of Yemen they were second-class citizens. When an Arab walked toward them on the sidewalk, they stepped into the street. Their culture is not Israel's; their language is Arabic, not Hebrew. The task of feeding them, building homes for them, training them to the skills Israel needs is immense. Bread and tea in their mouths means less for those already in Israel. Milk for their children means less for the children in the very kibbutz from which the milk comes. But Israel is a nation with a moral purpose. And for this reason the 35,000 Yemenite Jews were brought to Israel in airplanes sent by the Israeli government.

"The camp in which these Yemenites were living when I saw them was not where you would want to live, nor I. There were some old British and Israeli barracks and tents. The week before I arrived there had been unusually cold weather and a snowstorm.

"There is no technicolor in the romance they are living out, but there is brotherhood. There are two things you see in all these camps: a hospital, often staffed by other refugees; and nurseries into which the young children are sent to live.

"I saw brotherhood in those camps, and I saw brotherhood at any army post where I met the general staff. They had been discussing an urgent, human question—how to judge which soldiers and civilians should be given medals for heroism in their war of liberation. What did they decide? General Yadin, commander-in-chief—a man of only thirty-two, a native-born Israelite—told me: 'We decided to give no medals at all. We can't. How can you give medals when everyone has been a hero?'

"There is a vitality in this new land that has already produced five theaters and thirteen newspapers in Tel Aviv, that sees Shakespeare, opera, and new plays running at the same time. This is the vitality and awareness I even found directed at me when a man on a street corner pointed at me with affectionate interest and exclaimed, 'That's him— Aleph Gimmel Robinson!'

"Israel has brought to fruition a personal change in me that began some years before. I was not born in the United States. My parents were immigrants from Rumania. I was a very young child when we came across in steerage. What I was to know of life and of America I began to learn on New York's Lower East Side, in the streets and tenements.

"There was no Israel then, and in the ghettos of Europe, Jews knew freedom for a word but not a reality.

"In America they learned that there was at least one land where a Jew could live differently. There were no illusions, of course. It was not Utopia. There was still prejudice and bigotry. In the bricked-in piece of America in which I grew to manhood there were hoodlums who wrote ugly words on walls and sidewalks. But in America you could fight back. It was easy to love America, to cherish American freedom and to forget that, but for a steamship ticket, I might have been a harassed peddler in Bucharest.

"But when the Nazis came to power, I felt myself becoming a Jew again in a way I had not been for years. And seeing this nazi madness made me also a profounder American than I had ever been, more attached to the ideals of democracy and liberty.

"Out of those years, out of the concentration camps, the war, the murder, the gas chambers—came Israel.

"At Lydda airport, where I took a plane to return home, I stood with one of my new brothers. I said to him, 'Keep well and strong because you have a tremendous job ahead of you.'

"I saw a change come over his face, a sudden sobering, as though he had somehow been too busy to realize the immensity of the task he and his fellow citizens had undertaken. Our future is not separate from the future of that man."

Eddie insisted on being the architect of his own future; rest, retirement, the contemplation of the long and varied life he had led, his pictures, his books, were not enough for him. He denied the heart attack, continued to deny it even though the symptoms might reappear, and insisted on going back to work. He hounded his agents until one day they came up with the script of *The Cincinnati Kid*. He has already told you how dearly he loved that one.

If he was beginning to find contentment with a few good parts, his pleasant life—domestic and social—with Jane, and with the accumulation of a new art collection (why can't I stop using the word he detested so much?), there were other things in his life that were, to use his son's word, "beleaguering" him.

Manny had divorced and married again. Eddie's granddaughter—the precious Francesca—of course lived with her mother. But, as time passed, it became clear that the ex-Mrs. Robinson, Francesca's mother, suffered from a debilitating mental problem. I personally had no knowledge of this, and I assure you Eddie never discussed it. The other day, however, Francesca came over, and we chatted. Suddenly, without my questioning her, she began to tell me of her life and with it, necessarily, of her mother's life and her father's (as much as she knew) and her grandfather's and her step-grandmother's (Jane) and Augustine and Mattie.

Augustine and Mattie?

The name Augustine I vaguely remembered; she had been young Manny's governess, and now apparently Francesca was living with her. But Mattie?

Mattie was Gladys. Gladys' daughter, Jeannie, had two children who couldn't manage to say "grandma." Somehow it came out "Mattie," and Francesca went along with it, and so her account of her own years is filled with references to Mattie. I'm going to have to translate it to Gladys before we all go a little nutty. Francesca told her story in fits and starts. Let me try to put some order to it.

First, by the terms of the divorce settlement, Gladys was to receive, in addition to half the proceeds of the pictures and the property, a healthy percentage of whatever Eddie would make for the rest of his or her life. I'm told 25 percent; others tell me one-third. The amount really doesn't matter. I think the only fact worth mentioning was that Gladys, by whatever percentage, had a considerable income.

Eddie told me, and Francesca agrees, that one of the first results of the Eddie/Gladys divorce was the tendency of their friends to take sides. Only a few people remained friendly to both Eddie and Gladys, and Eddie could not understand that. Since *he* was the noted one, it was obvious that more people would remain with him than with Gladys, and Eddie found this unconscionable. Still, there was nothing he could do about it, but as the years passed, these social matters sorted themselves out.

Gladys helped by taking an apartment in Beverly Hills, eventually in the very chic Century City Towers, but spending most of her time abroad. Seven to eight months a year she lived in London or Paris,

Francesca tells me, and would return to California only to check into financial matters *and* Francesca.

The child was living with her mother. The mother continued from time to time to have mental problems and was eventually put in the hands of the psychiatric department of the Superior Court, which recommended rehabilitation at a state hospital.* Francesca seems to think that the diagnosis was manic depression, but she isn't sure, and I refuse to discuss the ironies of fate. Eddie believed that such ironies are no more than coincidence, and I agree.

Francesca's mother had a family living in Florida, and that's where the baby was taken. Manny, diligently trying to find work either as an actor or in any other way, helped with her support. But it wasn't enough. Accordingly, Gladys helped, too. And, of course, Eddie and Jane.

But Francesca was brought back to the West Coast, and her mother tried to remake her life with a social group that all the Robinsons found unacceptable. Gladys, on her return to America, instigated a custody suit to be made guardian of the child. This made all sorts of newspaper headlines, most of which featured Eddie and practically all of which played fast and loose with the facts. Eddie cared only for the child's future and fought the custody suit—and Gladys dropped it.

Francesca's mother was eventually sent away for five years. After incredible heartbreak for all of them—Gladys, Manny, Eddie, Jane, and God knows, certainly Francesca—the courts decided to name Augustine as the child's legal guardian.

I have met Augustine only once—at Eddie's funeral—and she is an aging lady with compassionate eyes, and I think she was exactly the right person for Francesca. Gladys was, of course, far too old to raise a young child. Eddie and Jane wanted her, but Gladys never would have stood still for that. Manny was remarried and did not have the resources. The best I can make of it is that Eddie and Gladys, separately and apart, supported Francesca, and Jane helped, too, on the side. Hers, of course, was the most difficult of roles. But Jane came to love Francesca, and they have achieved by now an adult and loving relationship.

I debate my own role at this point. This is a book about Eddie, not Gladys—but I cannot leave the rest of her story untold.

She painted (she was pretty good); she was surrounded by new friends in Europe; she became the patron of many new artists; she

* The former Mrs. Edward G. Robinson, Jr., is in excellent physical and mental health today.

became perhaps what she'd always wanted to be—a person in her own right.

In the late 1960s, even though she was beginning to suffer from mild heart seizures, she took Francesca to Paris for a holiday, and Francesca talks about her times with "Mattie" with such joy that it's very hard not to blubber. The Café de la Paix, the Tour d'Argent, the ballet, the opera, the great galleries—they did them all together. The next year they both went off to Hawaii; Francesca remembers those days as some of the happiest episodes in her life, as she does the three weeks she spent with Jane and Eddie and her other trip to Paris with Jane after Eddie's automobile accident (he insisted on it).

Then came the time of her graduation from Marymount at Palos Verdes. This was a day on which all the Robinsons were as one in their joy: Eddie, Jane, Francesca's mother, Gladys, and Manny. They all were so proud.

The event consisted of a religious gathering followed by a brunch. The baccalaureate ceremony was scheduled for the afternoon. Francesca and Gladys, together with their friends, were to attend the whole affair; Eddie, Jane, and Manny planned to come only for the graduation proceedings.

At lunch Gladys went to the ladies' room and suddenly collapsed. Augustine informed Francesca that Gladys was ill. Panic. Ambulances. Doctors. Francesca was certain it was a heart attack; it was a stroke. Francesca wanted to go to the hospital with her grandmother, but wiser heads prevailed. What Gladys wanted most was for Francesca to be graduated. And so, tearfully, Francesca remained.

Eddie and Jane came, were told the news, comforted Francesca, took her and Augustine home with them. Says Eddie, Francesca wanted to go to the hospital to see Gladys, but the stroke had left her unable to recognize anybody. She lapsed into a coma and died.

Eddie and Francesca and Manny, of course, went to the funeral. Jane waited at home and tried to provide solace.

Death brings forgiveness; death brings guilt and regret; death pales out dissension and leaves only the good memories.

Jane saw Eddie through the custody fight and the subsequent arrangements for Francesca—and the inevitable problems with Manny —for where did the money come from to sustain the younger Robinson? Eddie was the only solvent member of the family. In the end all matters were settled—painfully and with enormous publicity.

I am not prepared to discuss Eddie's relationship with Manny. I know young Robinson only slightly, and I feel a terrible sadness in him, but I have been too close to Eddie to have an objective opinion.

It is certainly a major tragedy for both of them that they never could manage to reach each other—and for me to assess fault would be unproductive. I think young Robinson suffered from competition with a father; I think the father tried to raise the child in an unhappy household, on a moral level created by his own father.

During the times Eddie was in the hospital, his son haunted the corridors, but each member of the family seemed to be alone in his apprehension. Jane and Francesca, it seemed to me, worked out a relationship that seems capable of enduring love. The boy was an outsider, and my heart ached for him—and for them, too. This is hardly a moral judgment; certainly, it's an emotional one.

The custody battle marked a tough time for Eddie and Jane; though the matter made front pages, you'd go to their house to dinner or a party and not a word would be said of it. They maintained their privacy, and that kind of privacy leads to ulcers in the young.

In Eddie's case it led to something much worse. On June 8, 1966, while driving his car, Eddie either blacked out or had a seizure—or could it have been simply that he was musing?—and at high speed his car careened into a tree a few blocks from his house.

His injuries were massive—penetration of the stomach wall and the spleen; his face was marred. He was in intensive care for weeks. There were moments when doctors despaired of his life. We all paraded that same fifth floor corridor at Mount Sinai.

And then he was out, recuperating, convalescing—and dying to make some more pictures.

He made nine more. He did twelve television shows.

He appeared regularly at the Passover Israel Convocation at Madison Square Garden. He bought more pictures. He sold none. He smoked ten thousand cigars.

He rewrote every speech we worked on together. He played with his dogs in the garden. He made contributions to the Democratic party.

Meanwhile, he was looking for one good, last starring role. Most of the movies involved small parts and were filmed in Italy or France. That wasn't enough for him. It was suggested he write his autobiography. He refused.

Now I am about to do something that is neither conventional nor the way of biographies or autobiographies. I'm going to tell the absolute truth. When, as you will soon discover, Eddie agreed to do this book, he was as nervous as a cat, and when he reread the first sixty pages, he was even more nervous. He took to rewriting them again—

and then he insisted on a preface. This is the preface I wrote in October 1972 at his urgent request. He loved it.

A Note on How This Book Came to Be Written

I have as little patience with the "as told to" or "with" school of books as most people. They are usually fan magazine puffery or glossy reminiscence.

Edward G. has had his fill of puff and gloss. At seventy-nine he has a secure reputation and scant need of press agentry. On the contrary, what he cherishes above all is privacy.

Thus, despite the most flattering offers, suggestions, imprecations, and contracts offered by various publishers, both here and in England, he has consistently declined to write his memoirs.

The reason, I used to suspect, and now I know beyond doubt, is that biography requires assigning motives to decisions, obscure at the time they were made, evident only in retrospect. To find the truth, you must turn inward, and that can frequently be painful—the great moments, perhaps, even more painful than the desperate ones, because great or desperate, they are both populated by phantoms. And in bringing them to life, you must make certain they are real and not curios—true and not laminated with pious memory. Not exactly easy to do.

Why, then, this book?

Well, Edward G. and I have been friends for a good long time, and over endless gallons of coffee we've talked. In talking, I've learned a great deal about his views, his positions, and his career. None of that surprised me. What continues to surprise me is his modesty. Oh, he can be tough as any number of managers, producers, and art galleries can attest; but, essentially, he is modest. Not self-effacing, but modest. Not shy, but modest. Not self-abnegating, but modest.

He persists in minimizing himself. You have to get used to that and realize it's a part of the machinery he has developed to cope with his sometimes burdensome public self; it is very difficult to be a star; it is even more difficult to be a star who is, at the same time, a participating citizen and one of the great patrons of the arts.

Still, why this book?

Well, in the sixties, and now past the last election campaign, he has been assessing the discontent, frustration, and change about him; the Broadway he knew is a shambles; the movies he knew are franker and more realistic than the ones he made; words he never uses are common coin on the stage and screen; the America that gave· him his celebrity and his Picassos is disputed by the young—at least the more vocal young.

His own life has been a pageant of the twentieth century; he has been involved in most aspects of it; he has been in Theodore Roosevelt's words, "in the arena"—and the ultimate decision to consider writing about it was not in terms of himself but in terms of the society to which he quite obviously owes everything.

When, grudgingly, he consented to *think* about this book, I asked him if he had any documentation. We went upstairs to his bedroom (riding on that staircase elevator that always scares me to death, but which he navigates as though it were the *Mauretania*), and we began opening drawers, cabinets, and hidden recesses. Out poured early scrapbooks (he kept every program, every notice, every comment about his work until he went to Hollywood), photographs, stills, speeches, letters, documents, citations, awards, testimony, and books. It is a bibliography, certainly, of Edward G., but even more certainly of the times in which he lived.

So we talked and consulted the scrapbooks, and I took notes and wrote furiously. His memory blossomed (and bristled) with vivid accounts of his life (his recall is not total, but almost), each account led to another, and altogether they began to form a coherent picture filled with emotion, instantly tempered by humor. He never speaks in chronology because a major decision in 1916 leads to the memory of a major decision in 1952.

Thus, the "with" in the authorship of this book indicates that I have put matters in order. It does not mean that the language is mine; in large part it is Eddie's. It is written in the first person because it was revealed in the first person. I think, as the months went on, he has come to enjoy the revelation very much.

I know I have.

October 1972
L.S.

January 1, 1973
I didn't love it. And so, when he was hospitalized at the end of December, and I thought it temporary, I decided I'd write an addendum and perhaps, one day, timidly ask for his approval. This is what I wrote then:

What you have just read is not entirely true. Eddie asked me to write it out of his dislike for show-biz biography. He wanted it made certain that no one would think him guilty of egoism. He went over each word and gave his approval, as he did to most of this book. And why not—since most of it, indeed, is his own language. But he imposed severe restrictions on himself: He would say nothing mean-spirited about anybody, except mildly in the cases of Mrs. Leslie Carter, for instance, or the Theatre Guild or Ethel Barrymore or, perhaps a little less mildly, in the case of Irving Thalberg. But by and large, he would not—except to me—reveal his dislike of people or his insights. Then why write it at all?

In 1970, after what he believed to be a routine physical checkup, his doctor found something that was hardly routine: cancer of the bladder. He was subjected to the maximum number of sessions of cobalt treatment, and to all outward indications it appeared that he had made a remarkable recovery.

While he was hardly the aggressive, vital man he had been before, still he was alert and vigorous enough to play in one last film: *Soylent Green*. The producers gave a party on an M.G.M. stage to honor him when it was over, and a great many people who appeared in these pages attended, drank champagne, and heard Eddie make an impromptu speech that was funny and touching and which we had written and rehearsed together for hours.

Simultaneously, indeed before, a well-known publisher had asked Eddie to do an autobiography, and Eddie seemed interested. We all dined together, and I knew it was an occasion because Eddie produced a great bottle of wine from his cellar. It had been a precious cellar for many years but lately gone to pot, and that bottle was one of the few of premium vintage he had been hoarding.

I knew that night that he was interested in doing a book. When we were alone, he asked if I felt there was a book in him. I was not altogether convinced.

I had written many of Eddie's speeches; he was an actor who would not appear on any public platform without a script—and he furiously edited every sentence. He said he could not write himself; I testify to his ability to rewrite. Additionally, as homage to him, I had done a capsule biography for a book called *Edward G. Robinson's World of Art* and a piece on him for Roddy McDowell's *Double Exposure*. So I was blooded; I knew how difficult this would be.

We agreed to talk, and he began telling me things I already knew —the early days, the East Side, all of that. We had a tape recorder switched on, and Eddie finally said he didn't want it; it made him self-conscious. "Give me a mike and I use pear-shaped tones," he said.

"That's only part of the problem," I forced myself to say. "What you're doing, Eddie, is giving me an interview. I've read all this stuff a thousand times. It's guarded and comes out of you by rote. If you persist in putting up all these roadblocks, there can be no book."

He nodded. "I'm so used to interviews; I've made up so many glib sentences to guard my privacy that they come out of me mechanically."

It was then I suggested documentation. As a result he did, indeed, give me many of his papers and scrapbooks. In looking over them, the artificial barriers began to break down. He had not seen some of these things for fifty years; he regarded them with delight, sorrow, and humor.

Still, he did persist in speaking at length of his boyhood and his family, and I think that if he had had his way, he would have devoted hundreds of pages to his grandmother and those early years in Bucharest and the East Side.

I tried to get him away from the early period, and he would make some curious transitions to the theater and Grant Wood and Matisse and Toscanini and Bette Davis—for all of which I now thank God, because had we proceeded in chronological order, there would have been no book.

After a month to six weeks of this, I myself began to develop some excitement—and my excitement was apparently what he had been waiting for. Our afternoon sessions became fun and productive. We'd meet every day at two and work until six, and he spoke so fast that I could hardly keep up with him. In the mornings I'd write up the notes and put them in some shape, then give them back to him, and he'd go about editing.

Later he agreed to meet with the publisher of this book, and they liked each other. And so Eddie agreed to sign a contract.

I will not dwell on his examination of the publishing contract except to say that in his own words: "Anybody who's been offered a contract by Jack Warner or Harry Cohn learns to read the small print." Well, he read the small print and analyzed it and demanded changes—and got them. I have rarely seen him as robust and forceful as when he discussed the contract for this book with the agents and the publisher. And I have never seen a publisher so warm and understanding.

As we now continued officially, one day Eddie would be clear and precise; the next, he would wander and ponder his life, and without realizing it, reveal his deepest feelings and the private events that engendered them. We would sit in the breakfast room while he smoked endless cigarettes and I wrote endless notes, injecting now and then a question that more often than not he would refuse to answer—and then, the next day, he would answer it as if he had thought it up himself.

Then, suddenly, he seemed depressed. The doctors said he was right; it was severe depression. I thought the memories were contributing, but the doctors said the book was giving him an interest in life. One said it was giving him something to live for. Jane thought it was more than depression; so did I. When he was the most mentally alert, he was the most physically feeble. It was as though there were two people—the classic young Edward G. Robinson struggling to get out of the wreck of the body of the old, sick Edward G. Robinson. But, of course, it was more than old age. It was the cancer again.

And, as I write this, he's in the hospital, struggling for life without any possibility of making it. I stand the watch with Jane and some devoted friends. Occasionally he says he wants to see me, and I go in and talk with him—and he wants to know where I'm at in the book and have I reached the part about the Un-American Activities Committee and did I rewrite the part about his grandmother and I'm not to worry because he'll be out soon, and we'll finish.

I never got to show it to him. But I was able to show him something else.

On his second Tuesday night in the hospital the Academy of Motion Picture Arts and Sciences voted him an honorary award for his massive contribution to films, with the following words:

TO EDWARD G. ROBINSON, WHO ACHIEVED GREATNESS AS A PLAYER, A PATRON OF THE ARTS AND A DEDICATED CITIZEN . . . IN SUM, A RENAISSANCE MAN. FROM HIS FRIENDS IN THE INDUSTRY HE LOVES.

Dan Taradash, president of the academy, called me at midnight and asked whether E.G.R. would be able to attend the Oscar ceremonies. I lied (or at least I burbled), and Dan Taradash, smart in these matters, said perhaps I should tell Eddie and sent an unmarked Oscar over to my house.

I was at the hospital the next morning, consulting with Jane and the doctors. Should we tell him? Would it indicate how ill he was, how hopeless his condition—or would it perhaps give him a reason to arouse himself from his listlessness? The decision was made that I should tell him.

And so, crunched by his bed—his hearing aid off—which made it even more difficult, I told him. He waved his hand in denial and refutation. Then I showed him the Oscar and said, "Eddie, have I ever lied to you?" He shook his head and held the Oscar tightly to him and wept softly. Then I said, "Eddie, you've got to make a press statement." He agreed, and he was all full of writing zeal, and laboriously he dictated the following statement—not actually the following statement because I shouted it back to him, and he rewrote it quite a lot.

> It couldn't have come at a better time in a man's life. Had it come earlier, it would have aroused deep feelings in me. Still, not so deep as now. I am so very grateful to my rich warm creative talented intimate colleagues who have been my life's associates. How much richer can you be?*

I saw him every day from then on till the end: He was able to read about the Oscar in *The Hollywood Reporter* and *Variety*, the trade papers he had once despised.

Once he asked about this book and said: "Don't you worry about me. Take care of yourself. You're very precious to me; we'll finish the book."

And two days later he died.

---

* Jane, in a performance unequaled for its dignity and guts, accepted the Oscar for Eddie on March 27, 1973, and used these very words of Eddie's. You might have seen her. A quarter of a billion others did.

APPENDIX A
NOTES ON ACTING

After Eddie's death Jane and I went through his papers, and we found two extraordinary speeches he made. One is about art and what it meant to him, and what he thinks it should mean to you. The other is about acting. I don't know when he spoke it or wrote it. There's no date on it. In his own hand there's just this notation: "Reinhardt." Which to remember him by? The notes on art? Or the notes on acting? Easy decision. Acting. He was an actor. He was proud of it. That was his trade. This is what he felt about his trade. This is his testament. I include the notes in his own words, just as he prepared them.

L.S.

Today the theater is struggling for its life. It is suffering from the poorness of its blood. In the noise and rush of the great cities its peculiar, festive beauty, its enchanted playfulness, has been taken from it. It is not organically rooted in the new growth of the modern metropolis. The stream of dramatic literature flows meagerly. In it our truly dramatic epoch is mirrored faintly. The creative power of mankind passes through other channels. For the present. But we are living in the present.

The salvation can only come from the actor because it is to the actor and to no one else that the theater belongs. When I say this, I do not mean the professional actor alone. I mean the actor as director, stage manager, musician, scene designer, and first and foremost, the actor as playwright. All the great dramatists have been born actors—whether they actually exercised this progression or not.

Shakespeare is the greatest, the most incomparable stroke of good fortune that the theater has had. He was playwright, actor, and producer in one. He painted landscapes and built whole cities with his words. Of all men, he approaches closest to God. He has created the most wondrous, the most all-embracing world; the earth with all its flowers, the sea with all its tempests, the light of the sun, the moon, the stars; fire with all its terrors and the air with all its spirits—and in the midst of this, human beings. Human beings with all their passions, their humor and tragedy, beings of elemental grandeur, and at the same time, utter reality. Shakespeare's omnipotence is infinite, unfathomable. He was Hamlet and King Claudius, Ophelia and Polonius in one person. Othello and Iago, Brutus and Cassius, Romeo and Juliet, Falstaff and Prince Henry, Shylock and Antonio, Bottom and Titania, and the whole retinue of merry and sorrowful fools lived within him. They all were part of his inscrutable being. Over them he hovers like a godhead, invisible and unknown.

The theater, once it forsakes its true vocation, can become the sorriest business, the most miserable prostitution. But the passion for seeing theater and acting in the theater is an elemental impulse of mankind. It will always again draw forth the actor and the spectator to play together, for the part of the spectator is as important as that of the actor. The audience must participate in the play to bring about the true art—the oldest, most powerful, and most immediate of the arts, combining the many in one.

In all human beings lives more or less consciously the longing for transformation. Every one of us bears within him the possibility of all passions, all destinies of life in all its manifold forms. Nothing human is foreign to us. If this were not so, we could not understand other people, either in life or in art. But inheritance, upbringing, and individual experiences impregnate and develop only a few of the thousands of potentialities in us. The others gradually wither and die.

Bourgeois life today is narrowly circumscribed and poor in emotional content. And of its deficiencies it has made virtues, past which it tries to squeeze its way as well as it can.

The average man generally feels once in his life the full happiness of love and once the joy of freedom. Once in his life he hates bitterly. Once with deep grief he buries a loved one, and once, finally, he dies himself. That is too little for our innate capacity to love, hate, enjoy, and suffer. We exercise daily to strengthen our muscles and sinews that they may not degenerate. But our spiritual organs, which were created for a lifetime of full activity, remain unused, undeveloped, and so, with the passing years, they lose their productive power.

Yet our spiritual (like our bodily) health depends upon the uninhibited functioning of these organs. We feel unmistakably how a hearty laugh frees us, how weeping or an outbreak of anger relieves us. Often, indeed, we seek such emotional outbursts with subconscious longing.

But our upbringing works against this constantly. Its first commandment is: Thou shalt conceal what passes within thee. Never betray that you are moved, that you are hungry or thirsty; every sorrow, every joy, all that is fundamental and craves utterance, must be repressed. Hence, all the notorious inhibitions—hysteria, the illness of our time, and finally that empty play-acting of which modern life is full.

We have accepted a set of commonplace, stereotyped forms of expression as part of our social armor. This armor is so rigid and narrow that it leaves hardly any room for natural impulses. We have a dozen or two cheap phrases for all occasions. We have a few ready-made expressions of sympathy, of pleasure, of dignity, and a set grimace of politeness. We ask how they feel without waiting for an answer or without paying attention if an answer is given. With a fixed intonation, which could be recorded and reproduced wholesale, we say that we are happy to see someone, though the encounter may be a matter of complete indifference to us—if it is not actually fatal. At weddings, christenings, burials, festivities, we make of handshaking and bowing, of frowning and smiling, a ghostly performance in which the absence of feeling is frightening.

The modern social code has crippled even the actor, the professional in the art of expressing emotions. When generations have been brought up to repress the emotions, in the end nothing remains to repress or to express.

Nature gives every man a face of his own. There is as little chance of finding two men who resemble each other completely as there is of finding two leaves on a tree exactly alike. Yet in the narrow channel of bourgeois existence, driven hither and thither by the currents of everyday life, human beings are in time ground down until they become like round pebbles, till one individual looks exactly like the next. The grinding process also has its effect upon their psychological makeup. The highest endowment of humanity is personality. In the arts personality is the decisive factor; it is the living nucleus we seek in every artistic work.

The nature of the actor is reflected most clearly in children. Their receptiveness is incomparable, and the urge to mold or fashion, which shows itself in their games, is irrepressible and truly creative. They want to discover the world for themselves anew and to build it themselves. Instinctively they resist taking the world from others by instruction; they do not want to be crammed with the experiences of others. Quick as a flash they change themselves into all they see, and all is changed into what they desire. The power of their imagination is compelling. The sofa?—a railway train!—already the engine rattles and steams and whistles; now someone looks with delight out of the window of the Pullman at the enchanting landscape flying past; now a severe conductor collects the tickets, and already one arrives at the destination; a porter, panting, carries pillows to the hotel; and the nearest armchair—an automobile—whisks noiselessly away; the footstool—as an airplane—soars through all the seven heavens. What is that? Theater. Ideal theater, the most exemplary dramatic art.

In the playing of children, the laws of the theater may be studied in their most fundamental form: Sets and properties are only suggested by what is actually there, transformed through the sovereign power of the imagination and yet with the clear, ever-present realization that all is only play. It is the same with the actor. It is a fairy tale in which he can ever forget the audience. Just in the moment of highest excitement it is the consciousness that thousands are watching him with breathless, trembling suspense, which pushes open the last doors to his innermost self.

With the children too, it is all play—play carried on in dead earnest, playing that requires an audience that will silently yield itself and enter reverently into the game. But what do we do? We laugh, laugh scornfully or sympathetically—at best we enthusiastically embrace the "little rascal." By our excitement and enthusiasm something is instantly brushed away. We have done what we never do in the theater, easily as we might: We have violently broken in upon the middle of the performance; a magic spell has been brutally destroyed.

The art of acting originated in the earliest childhood of the race. Man, allotted a brief existence, surrounded by the plentiful variety of individuals who were so close to him and yet so unapproachably far, had the irresistible desire to throw himself, in the play of his imagination, from one character into another, from one fate into another, from one temper into another. The possibilities inherent in him but not brought to full growth by his life thus unfolded their shadowy wings and carried him far beyond the range of his knowledge into the midst of the strangest experiences. He discovered all the delights of transformation, all the ecstasy of passion, the whole illusive world of dreams.

Made as we are in God's image, we have in us something of the godlike creative will. Therefore we create the whole world over again in the arts, with all the elements, and on the first day of creation, as the crown of our work, we make men in *our* image.

I believe in the immortality of the theater. It is the happiest loop-hole of escape for those who have secretly put their childhood in their pockets and have gone off with it to play to the end of their days. At the same time the art of the stage is a liberation from the conventional play-acting of life, because the task of the actor is not dissimulation but revelation.

We can send our voice and telegraph our image across the ocean; we can fly over it. But the way to our hearts and the human beings nearest us is still as long as the distance to the stars. The actor takes us on this way. With the light of the poet he descends into the unexplored chasms of the human soul, his own soul. And there he mysteriously transforms himself to return with his hands, eyes, and voice full of wonders.

He is at once sculptor and sculpture; he is man at the extreme borderline between reality and dreams; straddling it, he stands with his feet in both realms. The actor's power of self-suggestion is so great that he can bring about in his body not only inner and psychological but even outer and physical changes. And when one thinks of the much discussed miracles that have happened in many places through all time when simple people experienced the passion of Christ with such force of imagination that their hands and feet showed wounds and they actually wept blood, then one may judge into what mysterious fields the art of acting may lead. For it is by the same process that the actor Shakespeare describes, changes utterly his visage, stature, aspect and carriage, his whole being, to weep for Hecuba—and make others weep. Every night the actor bears the stigmata that his imagination inflict upon him, and he bleeds from a thousand wounds."

APPENDIX B
DRAMATIC APPEARANCES OF
EDWARD G. ROBINSON

STAGE

1913

Paid in Full
   Opened in April in Binghamton, New York. Played the role of Sato.

1915

Under Fire
   Opened on August 12 in the Hudson Theatre, New York City. Played the role of André Lemaire.

1916

Under Sentence
   Opened in the Harris Theatre, New York City, on October 3. Played the role of Fagan.

1917

The Pawn
   Opened on September 8 in the Fulton Theatre, New York City. Played the role of Hushmaru.

1918

The Little Teacher
   Opened on February 4 in the Playhouse Theater, New York City. Played the role of Batiste.

1919

First Is Last
   Opened September 17 in the Maxine Elliott Theater, New York City. Played the role of Steve.

Night Lodging
Opened December 22 in the Plymouth Theater, New York City. Played the role of Satan.

1920

Poldekin
Opened September 9 in the Park Theater, New York City. Played the role of Pinsky.

Samson and Delilah
Opened November 17 in the Greenwich Village Theater, New York City. Played the role of the Director.

1921

The Idle Inn
Opened December 20 in the Plymouth Theater, New York City. Played the role of Mendel.

1922

The Deluge
Opened January 27 in the Plymouth Theater, New York City. Played the role of Nordling.

Banco
Opened September 20 in the Ritz Theater, New York City. Played the role of Louis.

1923

Peer Gynt
Opened February 5 in the Garrick Theater, New York City. Played the roles of the Button Moulder and Von Eberkopf.

The Adding Machine
Opened March 19 in the Garrick Theater, New York City. Played the role of Shrdlu.

Launzi
Opened October 10 in the Plymouth Theater, New York City. Played the role of Louis.

A Royal Fandango
Opened November 12 in the Plymouth Theater, New York City. Played the role of Pascual.

1924

The Firebrand
Opened October 15 in the Morosco Theater, New York City. Played the role of Octavius.

1925

Androcles and the Lion
Opened November 23 in the Klaw Theater, New York City. Played the role of Caesar.

The Man of Destiny
Opened November 23 in the Klaw Theater, New York City. Played the role of Giuseppe.

1926

The Goat Song
Opened January 25 in the Guild Theater, New York City. Played the role of Reb Feiwell.
The Chief Thing
Opened March 22 in the Guild Theater, New York City. Played the role of the Stage Director.
Henry Behave
Opened August 23 in the Nora Bayes Theater, New York City. Played the role of Wescott P. Bennett.
Juarez and Maximilian
Opened October 11 in the Guild Theater, New York City. Played the role of Porfirio Diaz.
Ned McCobb's Daughter
Opened November 29 in the John Golden Theater, New York City. Played the role of Lawyer Grover.

1927

The Brothers Karamazov
Opened January 3 in the Guild Theater, New York City. Played the role of Smerdiakov.
Right You Are If You Think You Are
Opened March 2 in the Guild Theater, New York City. Played the role of Ponza.
The Racket
Opened November 22 in the Ambassador Theater, New York City. Played the role of Nick Scarsi.

1928

A Man with Red Hair
Opened November 8 in the Ambassador Theater, New York City. Played the role of Mr. Crispin.

1929

Kibitzer
Opened February 18 in the Royale Theater, New York City. Played the role of Lazarus.

1930

Mr. Samuel
Opened November 10 in the Little Theater, New York City. Played the role of Samuel Brisach.

1951

Darkness at Noon
Opened (on tour) at the McCarter Theater, Princeton, New Jersey, September 28. Closed at the Cox Theater, Cincinnati, Ohio, April 26, 1952. Played the role of Rubashov.

1956

Middle of the Night

Opened February 8 at the Anta Theater, New York City. On tour from October 9, 1957, at the Shubert Theater, New Haven, Connecticut, to March 29, 1958, at the Curran Theater, San Francisco, California.

FILM

1923

The Bright Shawl

First National. Directed by John J. Robertson. Based on the novel by Joseph Hergesheimer. With Richard Barthelmess, Dorothy Gish, William Powell, and Mary Astor.

1929

The Hole in the Wall

Paramount. Directed by Robert Florey. Based on the play by Fred Jackson. With Claudette Colbert, David Newell, Nelly Savage, Donald Meek.

Night Ride

Universal. Directed by John Robertson. Based on a story by Henry La Cossit. With Joseph Schildkraut and Barbara Kent.

1930

A Lady to Love

M.G.M. Directed by Victor Seastrom. Based on the play *They Knew What They Wanted* by Sidney Howard. With Vilma Banky, Robert Ames, and Lloyd Ingraham.

Outside the Law

Universal. Directed by Tod Browning. With Mary Nolan, Owen Moore, and Edwin Sturgis.

East Is West

Universal. Directed by Monta Bell. Based on the play by Samuel Shipman and John Hymer. With Lupe Velez and Lew Ayres.

1930

The Widow from Chicago

First National. Directed by Edward Cline. With Alice White, Neil Hamilton, Frank McHugh, Lee Shumway.

1931

Little Caesar

First National. Directed by Mervyn LeRoy. Based on the novel by William R. Burnett. With Douglas Fairbanks, Jr., Glenda Farrell, Sidney Blackmer, and Ralph Ince.

Smart Money
Warner Brothers. Directed by Alfred E. Green. With James Cagney, Evalyn Knapp, Margaret Livingstone, and Boris Karloff.
Five Star Final
First National. Directed by Mervyn LeRoy. Based on the play by Louis Weitzenkorn. With H. B. Warner, Marion Marsh, Anthony Bushell, Ona Munson, George E. Stone, Aline MacMahon, and Boris Karloff.

1932

The Hatchet Man
First National. Directed by William A. Wellman. Based on the play *The Honorable Mr. Wong* by Achmed Abdullah and David Belasco. With Loretta Young, Dudley Digges, Leslie Fenton, J. Carrol Naish, and Ralph Ince.
Two Seconds
First National. Directed by Mervyn LeRoy. Based on the play by Elliott Lester. With Preston Foster, Vivienne Osborne, J. Carrol Naish, and Guy Kibbee.
Tiger Shark
First National. Directed by Howard Hawks. Based on the story "Tuna" by Houston Branch. With Zita Johann, Richard Arlen, and J. Carrol Naish.
Silver Dollar
First National. Directed by Alfred E. Green. Based on the biography of H. A. W. Tabor by David Karsner. With Bebe Daniels, Aline MacMahon, Jobyna Howland, and DeWitt Jennings.

1933

The Little Giant
First National. Directed by Roy Del Ruth. With Helen Vinson and Mary Astor.
I Loved a Woman
First National. Directed by Alfred E. Green. Based on the book by David Karsner. With Kay Francis and Genevieve Tobin.

1934

Dark Hazard
First National. Based on the novel by William R. Burnett. Directed by Alfred E. Green. With Genevieve Tobin, Glenda Farrell, and Sidney Toler.
The Man with Two Faces
First National. Directed by Archie Mayo. Based on the play *The Dark Tower* by George S. Kaufman and Alexander Woollcott. With Mary Astor and Ricardo Cortez.

1935

The Whole Town's Talking
Columbia. Produced by Lester Cowan. Directed by John Ford. Based on the novel by William R. Burnett. With Jean Arthur, Arthur Hohl, Wallace Ford, Arthur Byron, and Donald Meek.

Barbary Coast
United Artists. Produced by Samuel Goldwyn. Directed by Howard Hawks. With Miriam Hopkins, Joel McCrea, Walter Brennan, Frank Craven, Brian Donlevy, Donald Meek, Harry Carey, and David Niven.

1936

Bullets or Ballots
First National. Associate producer, Louis F. Edelman. Directed by William Keighley. With Joan Blondell, Barton MacLane, Humphrey Bogart, and Frank McHugh.

1937

Thunder in the City
Columbia. Directed by Marion Gering. With Luli Deste, Nigel Bruce, and Constance Collier.
Kid Galahad
Warner Brothers. Associate producer, Samuel Bischoff. Directed by Michael Curtiz. Based on the novel by Francis Wallace. With Bette Davis, Humphrey Bogart, Wayne Morris, Jane Bryan, and Harry Carey.
The Last Gangster
M.G.M. Directed by Edward Ludwig. With James Stewart, Rose Stradner, Lionel Stander, Douglas Scott, John Carradine, and Sidney Blackmer.

1938

A Slight Case of Murder
Warner Brothers. Produced by Hal B. Wallis. Associate producer, Sam Bischoff. Directed by Lloyd Bacon. Based on the play by Damon Runyon and Howard Lindsay. With Jane Bryan, Willard Parker, Ruth Donnelly, and Allen Jenkins.
The Amazing Dr. Clitterhouse
Warner Brothers. Associate producer, Robert Lord. Directed by Anatole Litvak. Based on the play by Barre Lyndon. With Donald Crisp, Claire Trevor, Humphrey Bogart, Gale Page, Allen Jenkins, and Ward Bond.
I Am the Law
Columbia. Produced by Everett Riskin. Directed by Alexander Hall. Based on magazine articles by Fred Allhoff. With Barbara O'Neil, John Beal, Wendy Barrie, and Otto Kruger.

1939

Confessions of a Nazi Spy
Warner Brothers. Directed by Anatole Litvak. Based on the book *The Nazi Spy Conspiracy in America* by Leon G. Turrou. With Francis Lederer, George Sanders, Paul Lukas, Henry O'Neill, Lya Lys, and Grace Stafford.
Blackmail
M.G.M. Produced by John Considine, Jr. Directed by H. C. Potter. Based on the story by Endre Bohem and Dorothy Yost. With Ruth Hussey and Gene Lockhart.

1940

Dr. Ehrlich's Magic Bullet

Warner Brothers. Produced by Jack L. Warner and Hal B. Wallis. Associate producer, Wolfgang Reinhardt. Directed by William Dieterle. Story by Norman Burnside. With Ruth Gordon, Otto Kruger, Donald Crisp, Sig Rumann, and Maria Ouspenskaya.

Brother Orchid

Warner Brothers. Executive producer, Hal B. Wallis. Associate producer, Mark Hellinger. Directed by Lloyd Bacon. Story by Richard Connell. With Ann Sothern, Humphrey Bogart, Ralph Bellamy, Donald Crisp, and Allen Jenkins.

A Dispatch from Reuters

Warner Brothers. Produced by Hal B. Wallis. Associate producer, Henry Blanke. Directed by William Dieterle. Story by Valentine Williams and Wolfgang Wilhelm. With Edna Best, Eddie Albert, Albert Bassermann, Nigel Bruce, Gene Lockhart, and Otto Kruger.

1941

The Sea Wolf

Warner Brothers. Produced by Jack L. Warner and Hal B. Wallis. Associate producer, Henry Blanke. Directed by Michael Curtiz. Based on the novel by Jack London. With John Garfield, Ida Lupino, Alexander Knox, Gene Lockhart, Barry Fitzgerald, and Howard da Silva.

Manpower

Warner Brothers. Executive producer, Hal B. Wallis. Produced by Mark Hellinger. Directed by Raoul Walsh. With Marlene Dietrich, George Raft, Alan Hale, Frank McHugh, Eve Arden, Barton MacLane, Walter Catlett, Joyce Compton, and Ward Bond.

Unholy Partners

M.G.M. Produced by Samuel Marx. Directed by Mervyn LeRoy. With Laraine Day, Edward Arnold, and Marsha Hunt.

1942

Larceny, Inc.

Warner Brothers. Produced by Hal B. Wallis. Associate producers, Jack Saper and Jerry Wald. Directed by Lloyd Bacon. Based on the play *The Night Before Christmas* by Laura and S. J. Perelman. With Jane Wyman, Broderick Crawford, Jack Carson, Anthony Quinn, and Edward Brophy.

Tales of Manhattan

20th Century-Fox. Produced by Boris Morros and S. P. Eagle. Directed by Julien Duvivier. With George Sanders, James Gleason, Harry Davenport, and James Rennie.

1943

Destroyer

Columbia. Produced by Louis F. Edelman. Directed by William A. Seiter. Based on a story by Frank Wead. With Glenn Ford, Marguerite Chapman, Edgar Buchanan, Leo Gorcey, Regis Toomey, Ed Brophy, and Warren Ashe.

Flesh and Fantasy

Universal. Produced by Charles Boyer and Julien Duvivier. Directed by Duvivier. Based on the story *Lord Arthur Saville's Crime* by Oscar Wilde and stories by Laslo Vadnay and Ellis St. Joseph. With Charles Boyer, Barbara Stanwyck, Betty Field, Robert Cummings, Thomas Mitchell, Charles Winninger, Anna Lee, Dame May Whitty, C. Aubrey Smith, Robert Benchley, and Peter Lawford.

1944

Tampico

20th Century-Fox. Produced by Robert Bassler. Directed by Lothar Mendes. Original story adaptation, Ladislas Fodor. With Lynn Bari, Victor McLaglen, Robert Bailey, and Marc Lawrence.

Mr. Winkle Goes to War

Columbia. Produced by Jack Moss. Associate producer, Norman Deming. Directed by Alfred E. Green. From the novel by Theodore Pratt. With Ruth Warrick, Ted Donaldson, Bob Haymes, and Richard Lane.

Double Indemnity

Paramount. Produced by Joseph Sistrom. Directed by Billy Wilder. Based on the novel by James M. Cain. With Fred MacMurray, Barbara Stanwyck, Porter Hall, and Jean Heather.

1945

The Woman in the Window

R.K.O. Produced by Nunnally Johnson. Directed by Fritz Lang. Based on the novel *Once Off Guard by* J. H. Wallis. With Raymond Massey, Joan Bennett, Edmund Breon, and Dan Duryea.

Our Vines Have Tender Grapes

M.G.M. Produced by Robert Sisk. Directed by Roy Rowland. Based on the novel *For Our Vines Have Tender Grapes* by George Victor Martin. With Margaret O'Brien, James Craig, Agnes Moorehead, Jackie "Butch" Jenkins, and Morris Carnovsky.

1946

Scarlet Street

Universal. Executive producer, Walter Wanger. Producer-director, Fritz Lang. Based on the novel and play *La Chienne* by Georges de la Fouchardière. With Joan Bennett, Dan Duryea, Jess Barker, and Margaret Lindsay.

Journey Together

English Films. Produced by Royal Air Force Film Unit. Directed by John Boulting. With Sergeant Richard Attenborough and Aircraftsman Jack Watling.

The Stranger

R.K.O. Produced by S. P. Eagle. Directed by Orson Welles. Based on the story by Victor Trivas and Decia Dunning. With Loretta Young, Orson Welles, Philip Merivale, Richard Long, and Brian Keith.

1947

The Red House

United Artists. Produced by Sol Lesser. Directed by Delmer Daves. Based on the novel by George Agnew Chamberlain. With Lou McCallister, Judith Anderson, Allene Roberts, Julie London, Rory Calhoun, and Ona Munson.

1948

All My Sons

Universal. Produced by Chester Erskine. Directed by Irving Reis. From the play by Arthur Miller. With Burt Lancaster, Mady Christians, Louisa Horton, Howard Duff, Frank Conroy, Arlene Francis, and Henry Morgan.

Key Largo

Warner Brothers. Produced by Jerry Wald. Directed by John Huston. Based on the play by Maxwell Anderson. With Humphrey Bogart, Lauren Bacall, Lionel Barrymore, Claire Trevor, and Monte Blue.

Night Has a Thousand Eyes

Paramount. Produced by Endre Bohem. Directed by John Farrow. Based on the novel by Cornell Woolrich. With Gail Russell, John Lund, Virginia Bruce, William Demarest, Richard Webb, and Jerome Cowan.

1949

House of Strangers

20th Century-Fox. Produced by Sol C. Siegel. Directed by Joseph L. Mankiewicz. From the novel by Jerome Weidman. With Susan Hayward, Richard Conte, Luther Adler, Paul Valentine, Efrem Zimbalist, Jr., and Debra Paget.

It's a Great Feeling

Warner Brothers. Produced by Alex Gottlieb. Directed by David Butler. Story by I. A. L. Diamond. With Doris Day and Jack Carson.

1950

My Daughter Joy

Columbia. Producer-director, Gregory Ratoff. Associate producer, Phil Brandon. Based on the novel *David Golder* by Irene Nemirowsky. With Nora Swinburne, Peggy Cummins, Richard Greene, and Gregory Ratoff.

1952

Actors and Sin

United Artists. Produced and directed by Ben Hecht. With Marsha Hunt and Dan O'Herlihy.

1953

Vice Squad

United Artists. Produced by Jules Levy and Arthur Gardner. Directed by Arnold Laven. Based on the novel *Harness Bull* by Leslie T. White. With Paulette Goddard, K. T. Stevens, and Porter Hall.

Big Leaguer
M.G.M. Produced by Matthew Rapf. Directed by Robert Aldrich. Story by John McNulty and Louis Morheim. With Vera-Ellen and Jeff Richards.
The Glass Web
Universal. Produced by Albert J. Cohen. Directed by Jack Arnold. Based on the novel by Max S. Ehrlich. With John Forsythe, Marcia Henderson, and Kathleen Hughes.

1954

Black Tuesday
United Artists. Produced by Robert Goldstein. Directed by Hugo Fregonese. With Peter Graves and Jean Parker.

1955

The Violent Men
Columbia. Produced by Lewis J. Rackmil. Directed by Rudolph Mate. Based on the novel by Donald Hamilton. With Glenn Ford, Barbara Stanwyck, Dianne Foster, and Brian Keith.
Tight Spot
Columbia. Produced by Lewis J. Rackmil. Directed by Phil Karlson. Based on the novel *Dead Pigeon* by Lenard Kantor. With Ginger Rogers, Brian Keith, Lucy Marlow, Lorne Greene, Katherine Anderson, anl Allen Nourse.
A Bullet for Joey
United Artists. Produced by Samuel Bischoff and David Diamond. Directed by Lewis Allen. Story by James Benson. With George Raft and Audrey Totter.
Illegal
Warner Brothers. Produced by Frank P. Rosenberg. Directed by Lewis Allen. Based on the play *The Mouthpiece* by Frank J. Collins. With Nina Foch, Hugh Marlowe, Robert Ellenstein, Jay Adler, Albert Dekker, and Jayne Mansfield.

1956

Hell on Frisco Bay
Warner Brothers. Associate producer, George Bertholon. Directed by Frank Tuttle. Based on a novel by William P. McGivern. With Alan Ladd, Joanne Dru, William Demarest, Paul Stewart, Fay Wray, and Jayne Mansfield.
Nightmare
United Artists. Produced by William Thomas and Howard Pine. Directed by Maxwell Shane. Based on the novel by Cornell Woolrich. With Kevin McCarthy, Connie Russell, Virginia Christine, and Rhys Williams.
The Ten Commandments
Paramount. Produced and directed by Cecil B. DeMille. Based on the novels *Prince of Egypt* by Dorothy Clarke Wilson, *Pillar of Fire* by Reverend J. H. Ingraham, *On Eagle's Wings* by Reverend G. E. Southon, in accordance with The Holy Scripture. With Charlton Heston, Yul Brynner, Anne Baxter, Yvonne De Carlo, Debra Paget, John Derek, Sir Cedric Hardwicke, Nina Foch, Martha Scott, Judith Anderson, Vincent Price, John Carradine, H. B. Warner, Henry Wilcoxon, and Clint Walker.

1959

A Hole in the Head

United Artists. Produced and directed by Frank Capra. Coproducer, Frank Sinatra. Based on the play by Arnold Schulman. With Frank Sinatra, Eddie Hodges, Eleanor Parker, Carolyn Jones, Thelma Parker, Keenan Wynn, Joi Lansing.

1960

Pepe

Columbia. Produced and directed by George Sidney. Associate producer, Jacques Gelman. Based on a play by Ladislas Besh-Fekete. Story by Leonard Spigelgass and Sonya Levien. With Cantinflas, Dan Dailey, Shirley Jones, Carlos Montalban, Ernie Kovacs, and William Demarest.

1961

My Geisha

Paramount. Produced by Steve Parker. Directed by Jack Cardiff. With Shirley MacLaine, Yves Montand, Bob Cummings, Yoko Tani, Tatsuo Saito.

1962

Two Weeks in Another Town

M.G.M. Produced by John Houseman. Associate producer, Ethel Winant. Directed by Vincente Minnelli. Based on the novel by Irwin Shaw. With Kirk Douglas, Cyd Charisse, George Hamilton, Dahlia Lavi, Claire Trevor, Erich von Stroheim, Jr., and Leslie Uggams.

1964

The Prize

M.G.M. Produced by Pandro S. Berman. Associate producer, Kathryn Hereford. Directed by Mark Robson. Based on the novel by Irving Wallace. With Paul Newman, Elke Sommer, Diane Baker, and Kevin McCarthy.

Good Neighbor Sam

Columbia. Produced and directed by David Swift. Associate producer, Marvin Miller. Based on the novel by Jack Finney. With Jack Lemmon, Romy Schneider, Dorothy Provine, Michael Connors, and Neil Hamilton.

Robin and the Seven Hoods

Warner Brothers. Executive producer, Howard W. Koch. Produced by Frank Sinatra. Directed by Gordon Douglas. With Frank Sinatra, Dean Martin, Sammy Davis, Jr., Bing Crosby, Peter Falk, Barbara Rush, and Victor Buono.

The Outrage

M.G.M. Produced by A. Ronald Lubin. Associate producer, Michael Kanin. Directed by Martin Ritt. Based on the Japanese film *Rashomon*. From stories by Ryunosuke, Akutagawa, and the play *Rashomon* by Fay and Michael Kanin. With Paul Newman, Laurence Harvey, Claire Bloom, William Shatner, and Howard da Silva.

Cheyenne Autumn
Warner Brothers. Produced by Bernard Smith. Directed by John Ford. Suggested by the novel *Cheyenne Autumn* by Mari Sandoz. With Richard Widmark, Carroll Baker, Karl Malden, James Stewart, Sal Mineo, Dolores Del Rio, Ricardo Montalban, Gilbert Roland, Arthur Kennedy, Patrick Wayne, John Carradine, and Victor Jory.

1965

A Boy Ten Feet Tall
Paramount. Produced by Hal Mason. Directed by Alexander Mackendrick. Based on the novel *Sammy Going South* by W. H. Canaway. With Fergus McClelland, Constance Cummings, and Harry H. Corbett.

The Cincinnati Kid
M.G.M. Produced by Martin Ransohoff. Associate producer, John Calley. Directed by Norman Jewison. Based on the novel by Richard Jessup. With Steve McQueen, Ann-Margret, Karl Malden, Tuesday Weld, Joan Blondell, Rip Torn, Jack Weston, and Cab Calloway.

1968

La Blonde de Pekin (*"The Blonde from Peking"*)
Paramount. Directed by Nicolas Gessner. Based on the novel by James Hadley Chase. With Mireille Darc, Claudio Brook, Pascale Roberts, Françoise Brion, and Joe Warfield.

The Biggest Bundle of Them All
M.G.M. Produced by Joseph Shaftel. Associate producer, Sy Stewart. Directed by Ken Annakin. Story by Shaftel. With Robert Wagner, Raquel Welch, Godfrey Cambridge, and Vittorio da Sica.

Ad Ogni Costo
Paramount. Produced by Harry Colombo and George Papi. Directed by Giuliano Montaldo. With Janet Leigh, Adolph Celi, and Klaus Kinski.

Uno Scacco Tutto Matto (*"Mad Checkmate"*)
Produced by Franco Porro. Directed by Robert Fiz. With Terry-Thomas and Maria Grazia Buccella.

Operation St. Peter's
Paramount. Produced by Turi Vasile. Directed by Lucio Fulci. With Lando Buzzanca, Heinz Ruhmann, Jean-Claude Brialy.

Never a Dull Moment
Buena Vista. Produced by Ron Miller. Directed by Jerry Paris. Based on the novel by John Godey. With Dick Van Dyke, Dorothy Provine, Henry Silva, Joanna Moore, Tony Bill, and Slim Pickens.

1969

Mackenna's Gold
Columbia. Produced by Carl Foreman and Dimitri Tiomkin. Directed by J. Lee Thompson. Based on the novel by Will Henry. With Gregory Peck, Omar Sharif, Telly Savalas, Camilla Sparv, Keenan Wynn, Julie Newmar, Lee J. Cobb, Raymond Massey, Burgess Meredith, Anthony Quayle, Eli Wallach, and Eduardo Ciannelli.

1970

Song of Norway

Cinerama. Produced by Andrew L. and Virginia Stone. Directed by Andrew L. Stone. Suggested by the stage play. With Toralv Maurstad, Florence Henderson, Christina Schollin, Robert Morley, and Oscar Homolka.

1973

Soylent Green

M.G.M. Produced by Walter Seltzer and Russell Sathacher. Directed by Richard Fleischer. Based on the novel *Make Room, Make Room* by Harry Harrison. With Charlton Heston, Leigh Taylor-Young, Joseph Cotton, Chuck Connors, and Paula Kelly.

TELEVISION

1954

For the Defense

"The Case of Kenny Jason." With Glenn Vernon, Ann Doran, John Hoyt.

Climax

December 9. CBS. "Epitaph for a Spy." With Melville Cooper, Robert F. Simon, Ivan Tressault, Nicholas Joy.

1955

Ford Theater

January 13. NBC. ". . . And Son." With John Baer, Erin O'Brien-Moore, Willis Bouchey, and J. P. O'Donnell.

Ford Theater

December 29. NBC. "A Set of Values." With Ann Doran, Tommy Cook, Paul Fix, and Joseph Downing.

1956

The $64,000 Challenge

September 30 to October 28. CBS. With Vincent Price.

1958

Playhouse 90

October 23. CBS. "Shadows Tremble." With Ray Walston, Beatrice Straight, and Frank Conroy.

1959

Goodyear Theater

March 2. NBC. "A Good Name." With Lee Philips, Parley Baer, Jacqueline Scott, and Carleton G. Young.

Zane Grey Theater

April 2. CBS. "Loyalty." With Edward G. Robinson, Jr., and John Hackett.

1960

The Right Man
   October 24. CBS.
NBC-TV Special
   February 17. NBC. "The Devil and Daniel Webster." With David Wayne, Tim O'Connor, Betty Lou Holland, and Royal Beal.

1961

General Electric Theater
   January 29. CBS. "The Drop-Out." With Billy Gray, Carmen Matthews, and Ray Montgomery.
The Detectives
   October 6. NBC. "The Legend of Jim Riva." With Rudy Solari, Butch Patrick, Robert Taylor, Tige Andrews, Mark Goddard, Adam West.

1962

Project Twenty
   March 18. NBC. "Cops and Robbers."

1963

The World's Greatest Showman
   December 1. NBC. Hosted by E.G.R., Betty Hutton, Cornel Wilde, and Barbara Stanwyck.

1965

Hollywood Palace
   January 9. ABC. Dramatic reading of patriotic essay, "This Is It."
Xerox Special
   February 19. ABC. "Who Has Seen the Wind." With Stanley Baker, Maria Schell, Veronica Cartwright, Gypsy Rose Lee, and Victor Jory.

1967

Eye on Art
   June 17 and June 24. CBS. E.G.R. as narrator of two of six parts of this series and tour guide of galleries, museums, and art studios in Chicago on first show and Los Angeles on second.

1969

CBS Movie World Premiere: "U.M.C."
   April 17. CBS. With Richard Bradford, James Daley, Kim Stanley, Maurice Evans, Kevin McCarthy, J. D. Cannon, William Windom, Don Quine, Shelley Fabares, and James Shigeta.

1970

The ABC Movie of the Week
   October 13. ABC. "The Old Man Who Cried Wolf." With Martin Balsam, Diane Baker, Ruth Roman, Paul Picerni, Naomi Stevens, Virginia Christine, J. C. Flippen.

Bracken's World

October 23. NBC. "The Mary Tree." With Diana Hyland, Leslie Nielsen, Peter Haskell, and Edward G. Robinson, Jr.

This Is Tom Jones

October 23. ABC. Dramatic reading of "I Will Not Go Back" and Kipling's poem "The Betrothed."

1971

Hollywood Television Theatre

May 4. John Dos Passos's "U.S.A." E.G.R. delivered the prologue and epilogue.

Rod Serling's Night Gallery: "The Messiah on Mott Street"

December 15. NBC. E.G.R. was an impoverished old man who refused to die until the coming of the Messiah.

INDEX